ORGANIZATION THEORY

THE STRUCTURE AND DESIGN OF ORGANIZATIONS

STEPHEN P. ROBBINS
San Diego State University

Prentice-Hall, Inc., Englewood Cliffs, New Jersey 07632

Library of Congress Cataloging in Publication Data

ROBBINS, STEPHEN P., (date)
Organization theory.

Includes bibliographical references and index.
1. Organization. I. Title.
HD31.R565 658 82-7501
ISBN 0-13-641910-0 AACR2

Editorial/production supervision and interior design by Kim Gueterman
Cover design by Judy Matz
Cover photograph by Photo Researchers, Inc.
Manufacturing buyer: Ed O'Dougherty

Printed in the United States of America

10 9 8 7 6 5 4 3 2 1

ISBN 0-13-641910-0

PRENTICE-HALL INTERNATIONAL, INC., *London*
PRENTICE-HALL OF AUSTRALIA PTY. LIMITED, *Sydney*
PRENTICE-HALL CANADA INC., *Toronto*
PRENTICE-HALL OF INDIA PRIVATE LIMITED, *New Delhi*
PRENTICE-HALL OF JAPAN, INC., *Tokyo*
PRENTICE-HALL OF SOUTHEAST ASIA PTE. LTD., *Singapore*
WHITEHALL BOOKS LIMITED, *Wellington, New Zealand*

For My Sister, Judi Gabriel

CONTENTS

PREFACE xv

Part I INTRODUCTION: WHAT'S IT ALL ABOUT?

1 AN OVERVIEW 3

Some Basic Definitions 5

What Is an "Organization"?/ What Is "Organization Structure"?/ What Is "Organization Design"?/ What Is "Organization Theory"?

Why Study Organization Theory? 8

Organizations Are Systems 9

Definition of a System/ Types of Systems/ Characteristics of an Open System/ Importance of the Systems Point of View

The Objectives of This Book 15

Summary 16

For Review and Discussion 17

2 ORGANIZATIONAL EFFECTIVENESS 19

In Search of a Definition 20

The Goal-Attainment Approach 24

Assumptions/ Making Goals Operative/ Problems/ Value to Managers

The Systems Approach 27

Assumptions/ Making Systems Operative/ Problems/ Value to Managers

The Strategic-Constituencies Approach 31

Assumptions/ Making Strategic Constituencies Operative/ Problems/ Value to Managers

The Competing-Values Approach 33

Assumptions/ Making Competing Values Operative/ Problems/ Value to Managers

Summary 39

For Review and Discussion 40

Part II ORGANIZATIONAL STRUCTURE: DEFINING THE KEY COMPONENTS

3 COMPLEXITY 45

Defining Complexity 47

Horizontal Differentiation/ Vertical Differentiation/ Spatial Dispersion/ Do the Three Come as a Package?

Why Is Complexity Important? 54

Measuring Complexity 55

Horizontal Differentiation Measures/ Vertical Differentiation Measures/ Spatial Dispersion Measures/ An Application

Summary 59

For Review and Discussion 59

4 FORMALIZATION 61

Defining Formalization 61

Does It Have to Be in Writing?/ Range of Formalization

Why Is Formalization Important? 64

The "Make or Buy" Decision 64

Formalization Techniques 66

Selection/ Role Requirements/ Rules, Procedures, and Policies/ Training/ Rituals

Theory X, Theory Y, and Formalization 70

Relationship Between Formalization and Complexity 72

Measuring Formalization 72

Summary 74

For Review and Discussion 75

5 CENTRALIZATION 76

Defining Centralization 76

Authority and the Chain of Command 79

Authority/ Chain of Command

Decision Making and Centralization 82

Why Is Centralization Important? 84

Relationship of Centralization, Complexity, and Formalization 85

Centralization and Complexity/ Centralization and Formalization

Measuring Centralization 87

Summary 88

For Review and Discussion 89

Part III THE DETERMINANTS: WHAT CAUSES STRUCTURE?

6 STRATEGY 93

What Is Strategy? 94

Chandler's "Structure Follows Strategy" Thesis 96

Child's Strategic Choice 97

Limitations to the Strategy Imperative 99

Where Are We Today? 101

Strategy-Structure Typology/ The Research

Summary 104

For Review and Discussion 105

7 ORGANIZATIONAL SIZE 106

Defining Organization Size 107

Advocates of the Size Imperative 108

Critics of the Size Imperative 109

Conclusions on the Size-Structure Relationship 111

Size and Complexity/ Size and Formalization/ Size and Centralization

Special Issues Relating to Organizational Size 114

The Administrative Component Debate/ Organization Theory and Small Businesses

Summary 120

For Review and Discussion 120

8 TECHNOLOGY 122

Defining Technology 123

The Initial Thrust: Woodward's Research 124

Background/ Conclusions/ Evaluation

Knowledge-Based Technology: Perrow's Contribution 127

Background/ Conclusions/ Evaluation

Technological Uncertainty: Thompson's Contribution 130

Background/ Conclusions/ Evaluation

Tying It Together: What Does It All Mean? 134

Imperative versus Influence/ The Common Denominator: Routineness/ Impact of Size/ Job Level versus Organizational Level/ Conclusions

Technology and Structure 138

Technology and Complexity/ Technology and Formalization/ Technology and Centralization

Summary 140

For Review and Discussion 140

9 ENVIRONMENT 142

Defining Environment 142

General versus Specific Environment/ Actual versus Perceived Environment/ Environmental Uncertainty

Landmark Contributions 145

Burns and Stalker/ Emery and Trist/ Lawrence and Lorsch

A Synthesis 152

Four Core Environments/ The Cases "for" and "Against" the Environmental Imperative

The Environment-Structure Relationship 156

Environment and Complexity/ Environment and Formalization/ Environment and Centralization

Managing the Environment 158

Boundary Roles/ Intraorganizational Strategies/ Interorganizational Strategies/ Domain-Choice Strategies

Summary 164

For Review and Discussion 165

10 POWER-CONTROL 166

Muddying the Decision-Making Waters 167

Human Limitations/ Organizational Limitations/ Divergent Interests

Goals and Rational Behavior 170

Coalitions Fight for Power 171

Strategic Choice versus Power-Control 173

Who Makes up the Dominant Coalition?/ Authority versus Power

The Roads to Power 176

Control of Resources/ Reduce Uncertainties

Power-Control and Structure 181

Technology and Environment/ Stability and Mechanistic Structures/ Complexity/ Formalization/ Centralization

Summary 184

For Review and Discussion 185

Part IV ORGANIZATIONAL DESIGN: CHOOSING THE RIGHT FORM

11 BUREAUCRACY 189

Weber's Definition of Bureaucracy 189

Positive Qualities in Weber's "Ideal Type"/ Why Bureaucracies Work: An Example/ Summarizing Weber's Contribution

Machine versus Professional Bureaucracies 194

The Machine Bureaucracy/ The Professional Bureaucracy

Dysfunctional Consequences of Bureaucracy 196

Goal Displacement/ Inappropriate Application of Rules and Regulations/ Employee Alienation/ Concentration of Power/ Nonmember Frustration

Is Bureaucracy a Structural Dinosaur? 200

The Coming Death of Bureaucracy/ The Greatly Exaggerated Death of Bureaucracy

When Is Bureaucracy the Preferred Structure? 203

You Cannot Ignore the Obvious: Bureaucracies Are Everywhere! 205

Summary 206

For Review and Discussion 207

12 ADHOCRACY 209

Defining Adhocracy 210

Adhocracy: Its Strengths and Weaknesses 211

Strengths/ Weaknesses

The Matrix: Adhocracy in Action 212

What Is Unique About the Matrix?/ Two Types of Matrix Structures/ Advantages and Disadvantages/ Applications of the Matrix

Other Examples of Adhocracies 219

The Task Force/ The Committee Structure/ The Collegial Structure

When Is Adhocracy the Preferred Structure? 222

"It's Nice in Theory, but . . ." 222

Summary 224

For Review and Discussion 224

13 OTHER STRUCTURAL FORMS 226

The Simple Structure 226

Strengths and Weaknesses/ When Should You Use It?

The Functional Structure 229

Strengths and Weaknesses/ When Should You Use It?

The Divisional Structure 232

Strengths and Weaknesses/ When Should You Use It?

The Sector Structure 236

Strengths and Weaknesses/ When Should You Use It?

The Conglomerate Structure 239

Strengths and Weaknesses/ When Should You Use It?

Summary 242

For Review and Discussion 243

Part V APPLICATIONS: CURRENT ISSUES IN ORGANIZATION THEORY

14 MANAGING JOB DESIGN 247

The QWL Movement 248

Are Today's Employees Dissatisfied with Their Jobs? 248

The Job Characteristics Model 250

Viable Redesign Options 252

Job Rotation/ Work Modules/ Job Enlargement/ Job Enrichment/ Integrated Work Teams/ Autonomous Work Teams/ Quality Circles/ Summary

Don't Forget Individual Differences! 260

The Future of Job Redesign 261

Summary 262

For Review and Discussion 263

15 MANAGING CHANGE 264

What Do We Mean by "Managing Change"? 265

Planned Change/ Structural Change/ Organizations Are Conservative and Resist Change

A Model for Planned Organizational Change 268

Determinants of Change/ The Change Agent/ Intervention Strategies/ Implementation/ Results

Predicting Change from Structural Dimensions 280

Complexity/ Formalization/ Centralization

In the Battle Between Change and Stability, Bet on Stability! 283

Summary 285

For Review and Discussion 285

16 MANAGING CONFLICT 287

Defining Conflict 288

Transitions in Conflict Thought 289

The Traditional View/ The Behavioral View/ The Interactionist View

Anticonflict Values Permeate Our Society 292

Sources of Organizational Conflict 294

Mutual Task Dependence/ One-Way Task Dependence/ High Horizontal Differentiation/ Low Formalization/ Dependence on Common Scarce Resources/ Differences in Evaluation Criteria and Reward Systems/ Participative Decision Making/ Heterogeneity of Members/ Status Incongruence/ Role Dissatisfaction/ Communication Distortions

Resolution Techniques 300

Superordinate Goals/ Reducing Interdependence Between Units/ Expanding Resources/ Mutual Problem Solving/ Appeals Systems/ Formal Authority/ Increasing Interaction/ Organizationwide Evaluation Criteria and Reward System/ Merging Conflicting Units

Stimulation Techniques 306

Communications/ Heterogeneity/ Competition

Summary 308

For Review and Discussion 308

17 MANAGING GROWTH AND DECLINE 309

American Values Favor Growth 309

Bigger Is Better/ Growth Increases the Likelihood of Survival/ Growth Becomes Synonymous with Effectiveness/ Growth Is Power

Decline Is Alien to American Values 313

Why the Recent Concern with Management of Decline? 314

Is Managing Decline the Reverse of Managing Growth? 315

The Administrative Component Revisited/ An Enhanced Case for Power-Control/ Declines Follow Stages

A Case Study in Decline: Chrysler Corporation 318

Potential Managerial Problems When Organizations Decline 320

Increased Conflict/ Increased Politicking/ Increased Resistance to Change/ Increased Turnover/ Decaying Organizational Climate

Summary 323

For Review and Discussion 323

18 MANAGING JAPANESE STYLE: THE THEORY Z ORGANIZATION 325

Explaining the Success of Japanese Organizations 326

The Japanese Management System 327

Focus/ Strategies/ Techniques/ Summary

Theory A and Theory Z Organizations 333

Implementing the Theory Z Organization 335

Theory Z in Practice 338

Kyocera/ Hewlett-Packard

Summary 340

For Review and Discussion 341

Part VI APPLICATIONS: CASES IN ORGANIZATION THEORY

1 The Larger Company (A) 345

2 Will a Shake-up Revive Burroughs? 348

3 The Park Towers Homeowners Association 350

4 Supra Oil Company 352

5 Winthrop Hospital 358

6 What Makes Tandem Run? 360

7 Behind the Exodus at National Semiconductor 364

8 What Undid Jarman: Paperwork Paralysis 368

9 A Short Shorter-Workweek Program 372

10 How Sears Became a High-Cost Operator 375

11 Finding a Place for Product Planning 382

12 The Air Force A-7D Brake Problem 384

13 The Politics of Organizational Decision Making 397

14 Line and Staff at ITT 408

GLOSSARY 417

NAME INDEX 425

SUBJECT INDEX 429

PREFACE

When I decided to undertake the writing of this book, it was very clear what I wanted to achieve. My goal was to write a book on organization theory that would cover the contemporary material in a rigorous fashion but that would be interesting and relevant to the reader. It was the last part of my goal—to create interest and relevance—that I saw as the greatest challenge. A number of books have been published recently that cover the macro aspects of organizations successfully. These books fully meet the test of academic legitimacy and rigor. But it is my impression, and that of a number of my colleagues, that these books were written for other academicians and people interested in doing research in organization theory, not for students and practitioners of management. I perceived a major need for a textbook on organization theory written for students and practitioners. This is the group of readers I had in mind as I wrote this book.

What did I do to try to make this book interesting and relevant to the reader? Basically, four things. First, I tried to separate the wheat from the chaff in organization theory and sought to identify the essential issues and avoid dwelling on the esoteric. Second, wherever possible, I avoided fancy jargon and substituted clear and simple English. Third, I relied heavily on examples to clarify the more difficult and complex ideas. Fourth, I gave attention to the political factors influencing structural decisions. The power-control perspective, introduced in Chapter 10, is used throughout the latter part of the book to explain why, for example, bureaucracies, simple structures, and the functional form are so prevalent; why adhocracies are far more popular in theory than in practice; and why, despite all the attention given by academicians to planned organizational change, organizations are extremely stable over time and the little change that does take place is rarely of the planned variety.

In summary, this book takes the reader along the same road and makes the same stops that most researchers and teachers expect of a textbook on organization theory. However, the trip has fewer detours, and your "tour guide" spends considerably more time identifying points of interest along the road.

Acknowledgments

I would like to acknowledge some of the people who contributed to this book's completion. The comments of my reviewers were extremely helpful. My thanks to Professors John Anstey (University of Nebraska at Omaha), Richard H. Hall (State University of New York at Albany), Arlyn J. Melcher (Kent State University), and Cynthia Pavett (University of San Diego).

At Prentice-Hall, I want to single out and thank my local representative, Gerry Johnson; acquisition editor, Jayne L. Maerker; Jayne's "all seeing, all knowing" assistant, Linda Albelli; production editor, Kim Gueterman; and marketing manager, Paul Misselwitz.

Finally, I want to acknowledge and thank my daughter, Dana, for another excellent typing job.

Stephen P. Robbins
Baltimore, Maryland

PART I

INTRODUCTION: WHAT'S IT ALL ABOUT?

CHAPTER

1

AN OVERVIEW

In 1966, Bob Anderson was a 17-year-old high school senior in Overland Park, Kansas. A runner on both the school's track and cross country teams, Bob had a voracious appetite for any reading material on running. But at that time, very little was available. So with $100 he had saved, he decided to create a journal for others who wanted more information on training and other running-related topics. The first issue of *Distance Running News* sold for 75 cents, had one advertisement (for a shoe company), was made up of twenty-eight pages of typed material, and was concocted in Bob's "editorial office" in his bedroom. A thousand copies of this primitive "magazine" were printed and sold. Bob did most of the work to turn out that first issue. He did the editing and the production work, handled the subscription orders, and did the leg work to find prospective advertisers. He did, however, ask some well-known coaches and runners to contribute articles for the journal.

Interest in *Distance Running News* spread. In 1967, Bob expanded publication to four times a year and ran the magazine while at the same time putting in his freshman year at Kansas State. But the increasing demands of the magazine forced Bob to give up college in the fall of 1967 to devote full time to his business.

By 1969, Bob's magazine was coming out every other month. He had established an international correspondent network of part-time reporters and hired his first full-time employee, who was given the title of managing editor.

In early 1970, Bob made several major decisions. First, he moved to the more favorable climate of California. Second, he changed the name of his magazine to *Runner's World*. Third, he hired an assistant to help handle the increasing work load. But there still was little specialization. In 1971, for instance, Bob's assistant worked with subscription correspondence, distributed mail, helped with shipping, and did most of the accounting—virtually everything but the editorial and artwork assignments.

During the next ten years, *Runner's World* experienced exponential growth in sales and staff. In 1982, the magazine's monthly circulation reached 500,000, and Bob employed more than 100 full-time people. Bob is still the top dog, carrying the title of editor and publisher. But now a large number of individuals are performing specialized functions. There is an executive editor, a managing editor, and a photo editor. Each of these, in turn, has a staff to help them carry out their assignments. There is also a features editor, a columns editor, and a copy editor. In addition, there are directors of production, creative arts, advertising, sales, circulation, and personnel, each of whom has a supporting staff.

In fifteen years, *Runner's World* has moved to fifth place in total revenues among all sport monthlies. However, it ranks fourth in subscription sales and first in newsstand sales. Not bad for a venture that started off a decade and a half earlier as a one-man show in a high schooler's bedroom! Yet these achievements could never have been made by Bob Anderson alone. The original idea was his, but the magazine's current success is obviously due largely to the help of his employees.

Bob became aware, as circulation grew, that his time and abilities were limited. He was unable to do everything himself. He had to hire others to help. And these "others" didn't necessarily all do the same activities. Rather, Bob divided up the work to be done and allocated specific activities to each employee. He broke down jobs into smaller and more specialized pieces. People doing similar activities were grouped together, and he called these groups "departments." To supervise these departments, he created a hierarchy of directors responsible for supervising people in their respective areas, and he held them responsible for completing their department's work within the assigned time and budget constraints.

Additionally, as the number of employees grew, as employee tasks became more specialized, and as new departments were created, it became necessary to establish formal written policies, regulations, and rules. Why? For several reasons. Bob had to ensure that all employees were treated consistently and fairly. He needed to ensure further that the activities of the various departments were coordinated and directed toward the company's goals, and this required formal guidelines and directives. Finally, since the size of the company now precluded Bob from knowing everything about everyone's job, written job descriptions were needed to guide the selection, supervision, and appraisal of employees.

How are decisions made at *Runner's World* magazine? Not at the top by Bob alone. The major decisions are made participatively by the seven senior executives, a group that includes Bob Anderson. The more minor and routine decisions are made by managers in the departments, who are most knowledgable about the issues.

In summary, we find that Bob has created an organization. To produce and sell a half a million copies of his magazine each month, he has had to develop a coordinated structure of people doing specific work tasks. The success of *Runner's World* depends not only on producing an attractive and informative magazine but also on obtaining advertisers and subscribers, collecting bills, ensuring that magazines are shipped to subscribers and newsstands on time, and many other activities. And these could not be achieved without planned and coordinated effort. This, as we'll see, is what organization theory is all about.

SOME BASIC DEFINITIONS

The Bob Anderson story illustrates the formation and growth of an organization. But what precisely do we mean by the term "organization"? Perhaps not as obvious, Bob Anderson was also involved with "organization structure," "organization design," and "organization theory." Since all four terms are important and often confused, let us clarify them.

What Is an "Organization"?

An organization is the planned coordination of the collective activities of two or more people who, functioning on a relatively continuous basis and through division of labor and a hierarchy of authority, seek to achieve a common goal or set of goals. That's a mouthful of words, so let us break it down into its most relevant parts.

Planned coordination implies management. The activities that go on do not just emerge; rather, they are premeditated. Because organizations are composed of more than one person, activities must be balanced and harmonized to minimize redundancy yet ensure that critical tasks are being completed. Our definition, therefore, assumes explicitly the need for coordination.

People in an organization have some ongoing bond. This, of course, does not mean lifelong membership. On the contrary, organizations face constant change in their memberships, although while they are members, the people in an organization participate with some degree of regularity. For a salesperson at Sears, Roebuck, that may require being at work eight hours a day, five days a week. At the other extreme, someone functioning on a relatively continuous basis as a member of the National Organization for Women may only attend a few meetings a year or merely pay the annual dues.

Two identifying characteristics of an organization are a division of labor and a hierarchy of authority. Jobs are broken down into sets of tasks that are allocated among employees. Additionally, there exists a multilevel formal structure, with a hierarchy of positions, each lower position under the supervision and control of a higher one. These two characteristics are major determinants of the organization's formal structure.

Finally, organizations exist to achieve something. These "somethings" are goals, and they usually are either unattainable by individuals working alone or, if attainable individually, are achieved more efficiently through group effort. While it is not necessary for all members to endorse the organization's goals fully, our definition implies general agreement with the mission of the organization.

Notice how all the parts of our definition align with the organization that Bob Anderson built to publish *Runner's World.* Bob's goal was to produce and sell for profit a magazine for individuals interested in running. He hired people, gave them specialized tasks to perform, and developed a hierarchy of superior-subordinate positions that he coordinated through both formally written documents and direct supervision. Certainly there is a lot more to making Bob Anderson's organization, or any organization, successful than these several sentences imply, but they give you a brief introduction to what we mean when we use the term organization.

What Is "Organization Structure"?

Our definition of "organization" includes division of labor and a hierarchy of authority. These are actually subcomponents of what we call "organization structure."

We define an organization's structure as having three components: complexity, formalization, and centralization. The importance of each is exemplified by the fact that they represent the subjects of Chapters 3, 4 and 5 of this book.

Complexity considers the extent of differentiation within the organization. This includes the degree of specialization or division of labor, the number of levels in the organization's hierarchy, and the extent to which the organization's units are dispersed geographically. As tasks at the *Runner's World* Magazine Company became increasingly specialized and more levels were added in the hierarchy, the organization became increasingly complex. Complexity, of course, is a relative term. *Runner's World,* for instance, has a long way to go to approach the complexity of a General Electric or an IBM, where there are hundreds of occupational specialities and nearly a dozen levels between production workers and the chief executive officer.

The degree to which an organization relies on rules and procedures to direct the behavior of employees is *formalization.* Some organizations operate with a minimum of such standardized guidelines; others, some of which are even quite small in size, have all kinds of regulations instructing employees as to what they can and cannot do.

Centralization considers where the locus of decision-making authority lies. In some organizations, decision making is highly centralized. Problems flow upward and the senior executives choose the appropriate action. In other cases, such as at *Runner's World,* decision making is decentralized. Authority is dispersed downward in the hierarchy. It is important to recognize that, as with complexity and formalization, an organization is not *either* centralized or not. Centralization and decentralization represent two extremes on a continuum. Organizations *tend* to be centralized or *tend* to be decentralized. The placement of the organization on this continuum, however, is one of the major factors in determining the type of structure that exists.

What Is "Organization Design"?

Our third term—organization design—emphasizes the management side of organization theory. Organization design is concerned with constructing and changing an organization's structure to achieve the organization's goals.

As you proceed through this text, you will see a consistent concern with offering prescriptions of how organizations can be *designed* to facilitate the attainment of the organization's goals. This should not be surprising, as this book is intended for business students and managers. You are probably more interested in learning how to design organizations than merely knowing how organizations function. You have a managerial perspective, consistently looking for the application potential in concepts. As such, when organization theory is studied from the perspective of the needs of managers and future managers, it is oriented heavily toward organization design.

What Is "Organization Theory"?

From our previous definitions, it is not too difficult to deduce what we mean by the term "organization theory." It is the discipline that studies the structure and design of organizations. Organization theory refers to both the descriptive and prescriptive aspects of the discipline. It describes how organizations are actually structured and offers suggestions on how they can be constructed to improve their effectiveness. At the end of this chapter, we introduce a model that identifies explicitly the major subparts that make up this discipline we call organization theory.

WHY STUDY ORGANIZATION THEORY?

To this point, we have merely assumed that you are aware of the value of studying organization theory (OT). This may be an incorrect assumption. Therefore, before we introduce the idea that organizations are systems, review the objectives of OT, and consider how those objectives have influenced the content of this book, let us address the question directly: Why study OT?

Organizations are the dominant form of institutions in our society. You were probably born in a hospital and you will probably be put to rest by a mortuary. Both are organizations. The schools that educate us are organizations, as are the stores where we buy our food, the companies that make our automobiles, and the people who take our income tax, collect our garbage, provide for our military defense, and print our daily newspapers.

Organizations pervade all aspects of contemporary life—society as a whole, the economy, as well as our personal lives. It is not unreasonable, then, to expect us to want to understand this phenomenon that is so intertwined in our lives. Even though you may have no desire to apply your knowledge, you may simply seek an answer to why organizations with which you interact (and by which you will probably be employed) are structured the way they are.

At a more sophisticated level, you may want to replace your intuitive theories of organization with ones that have been derived scientifically and systematically. Whether or not you study organizations formally, you carry around with you a set of theories about how organizations operate. You go to the State Department of Motor Vehicles to get your driver's license renewed; you make a reservation with an airline; you talk to the loan officer at your bank about arranging a student loan; you order it "your way" at the local fast-food hamburger outlet. You undertake all these activities by using some "theory" about how each of these organizations operates and why its members behave as they do. So the issue is not whether you should use theories for dealing with organizations—reality tells us that we use such theories every day. Doesn't it make sense to use theories that have undergone systematic study?

When we use the phrase "systematic study," we mean looking at relationships, attempting to attribute causes and effects, and basing our conclusions on scientific evidence; that is, data gathered under controlled conditions and measured and interpreted in a reasonably rigorous manner. The objective is to replace intuition or that "gut feel" one has as to "why organizations are designed as they are" or "what works best when" with scientifically based theories.

Probably the most popular reason for studying OT is that you are interested in pursuing a career in management. You want to know how organizations operate, have that knowledge based on some scientific evidence, and then use this knowledge for constructing and changing an organization's structure to achieve the organization's goals. In other words, you expect to practice organization design as a manager, administrator, personnel analyst, organizational specialist, or the like.

The final reason for studying OT may not be very exciting, but it is pragmatic—it may be a requirement for a particular degree or certificate you are seeking. You may perceive yourself as a captive in a required course, believing that studying OT may offer no obvious end that has value to you. If this is the case, then the studying of OT is only a means toward that end. It is hoped that one of the earlier reasons holds more relevance for you.

ORGANIZATIONS ARE SYSTEMS

There is high agreement among organizational theorists that a systems perspective offers important insights into the workings of an organization. The following pages introduce the idea of systems and demonstrates how an open-systems approach can help you to conceptualize better just what it is that organizations do.

Definition of a System

A system is a set of interrelated and interdependent parts arranged in a manner that produces a unified whole. Societies are systems, and so too are automobiles, plants, and human bodies. They take inputs, transform these inputs, and produce some output.

The unique characteristic of the systems viewpoint is the interrelationship of parts within the system. It dramatizes that organizations are made up of parts or subsystems and that organizations themselves are subsystems within larger systems. Just as the human heart is a subsystem within the body's physiological system, the Graduate School of Management is a subsystem within the UCLA system. If we focus our attention on UCLA as the system, then we also recognize that it functions as part of the larger suprasystem called the University of California campuses. So, not only are there systems, but there are subsystems and suprasystems. The classification of these three depends on the unit of analysis. If we focus our attention on the Graduate School of Management and make it the system, then UCLA becomes the suprasystem and departments within the graduate school become the subsystems.

Types of Systems

Systems are classified typically as either closed or open. Closed-system thinking stems primarily from the physical sciences. It views the system as self-contained. Its dominant characteristic is that it ignores the environment. More idealistic than practical, the closed-system perspective has little applicability to the study of organizations.

The open system recognizes the dynamic interaction of the system with its environment. A simplistic graphic representation of the open system appears in Figure 1–1.

No student of organizations could build much of a defense for viewing organizations as closed systems. Organizations obtain their raw materials and human resources from the environment. They further depend on clients and customers in the environment to absorb their output. Banks take in deposits, convert these deposits into loans and other investments, and use the resulting profits to maintain themselves and grow and export the remainder in the form of dividends and taxes. The bank system, therefore, interacts actively with its environment made up of people with savings to invest, other people in need of loans, potential employees looking for work, regulatory agencies, and the like.

Figure 1–2 provides a more complex picture of an open system as it would apply to an industrial organization. We see inputs of materials, labor, and capital. We see a technological process created for transforming raw materials into finished product. The finished product, in turn, is sold

FIGURE 1–1 Basic open system

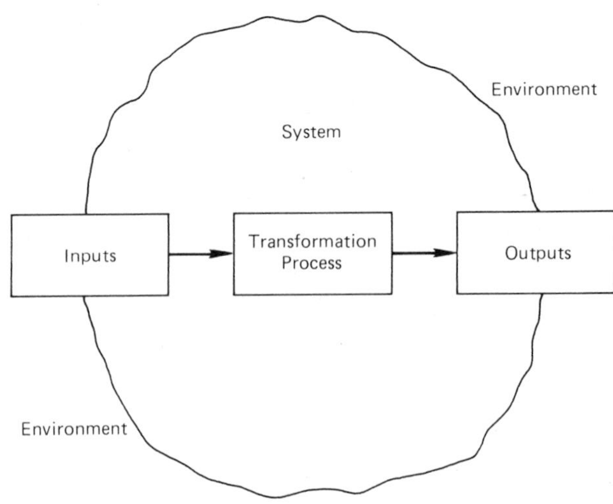

FIGURE 1–2 An industrial organization as an open system

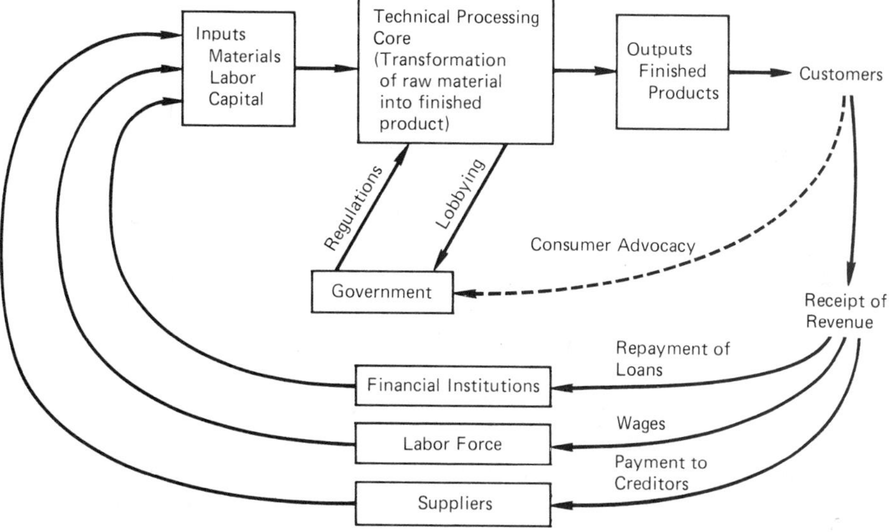

to a customer. Financial institutions, the labor force, suppliers, and customers are all part of the environment, as is government.

If you stop to think about it for a moment, it is difficult to conceive of any system as being fully closed. All systems must have some interaction with their environments if they are to survive. Probably the most relevant way in which to look at the closed-open dichotomy is to consider it as a range rather than as two clearly separate classifications. In this way, we can explain that the degree of openness or closedness varies within systems. An open system, for instance, may become more closed if contact with the environment is reduced over time. The reverse would also be true. General Motors, from its inception through the early 1960s, operated as if it were basically a closed system. Management decided on the products it wanted to sell, produced those products, and offered them to customers. GM assumed that whatever it made would sell, and for decades it was right. Government was generally benign, and consumer advocate groups were nonexistent or had little influence. GM virtually ignored its environment, for the most part, because its executives saw the environment as having almost no impact on the company's performance. While some critics of GM still attack the firm for being too insulated from its environment, GM has certainly become more open. The actions of consumer groups, stockholders, government regulators, and foreign competition have forced GM to interact with, and be more responsive to, its environment. So, while it may not be the model for an open system, GM is more open today than it was twenty years ago.

Characteristics of an Open System

All systems have *inputs, transformation processes,* and *outputs.* They take things such as raw materials, energy, information, and human resources and convert them into goods and services, profits, waste materials, and the like. Open systems, however, have some additional characteristics that have relevance to those of us studying organizations.[1]

Environment awareness. One of the most obvious characteristics of an open system is its recognition of the interdependency between the system and its environment. There is a boundary that separates it from its environment: changes in the environment affect one or more attributes of the system, and, conversely, changes in the system affect its environment.

Without a boundary there is no system, and the boundary or boundaries determine where systems and subsystems start and stop. Boundaries can be physical, as the clear lines that separate the United States from its neighbors to the north and south. They also can be maintained psychologically through symbols such as titles, uniforms, and indoctrination rituals. At this point, it is sufficient to acknowledge that the concept of boundaries is required for an understanding of systems and that their demarcation for the study of organizations is problematic.

The interdependency of a system and its environment was highly visible in 1981 as Chrysler Corp. tried valiantly to avoid bankruptcy. Chrysler certainly was affected by its environment—the most obvious being foreign competition, OPEC nations' increasing the prices of gasoline, and a federal government determined to fight inflation by keeping interest rates at record highs. Both GM and Ford were confronted with the same dilemmas, but they had a larger volume of sales over which to spread the investment of billions of dollars necessary to retool and produce smaller and more efficient cars. GM and Ford also had substantially stronger financial positions. But the relationship between Chrysler and its environment was two way. Suppliers, the State of Michigan, the United Automobile Workers, and the federal government (by way of loan guarantees) were all influenced visibly by what happened to Chrysler. While few organizations have the impact on their environment of a Chrysler, the fact still remains that all open systems affect their environment to some degree.

[1]This section adapted from Daniel Katz and Robert L. Kahn, *The Social Psychology of Organizations,* 2nd ed. (New York: John Wiley, 1978), pp. 23–30.

Cyclical character. Open systems are cycles of events. The system's outputs furnish the means for new inputs that allow for the repetition of the cycle. This was demonstrated in Figure 1–2: the revenue received by the customers of the industrial firm must be adequate enough to pay creditors and the wages of employees and to repay loans if the cycle is to be perpetuated and the survival of the organization maintained.

Negative entropy. The term "entropy" refers to the propensity of a system to run down or disintegrate. A closed system, because it does not import energy or new inputs from its environment, will run down over time. In contrast, an open system is characterized by negative entropy—it can repair itself, maintain its structure, avoid death, and even grow because it has the ability to import more energy than it outputs.

Steady state. The input of energy to arrest entropy maintains some constancy in energy exchange resulting in a relatively steady state. Even though there is a constant inflow of new inputs into the system and a steady outflow, on balance the character of the system remains the same. Your body will replace most of its dying cells in any given year, but your physical appearance alters very little. So, while an open system is active in processing inputs to outputs, the system tends to maintain itself over time.

Movement toward growth and expansion. The steady-state characteristic is descriptive of simple or primitive open systems. As the system becomes more complex and moves to counteract entropy, open systems move toward growth and expansion. This is not a contradiction of the steady-state thesis.

To ensure their survival, large and complex systems operate to acquire some margin of safety beyond the immediate level of existence. The many subsystems within the system, to avoid entropy, tend to import more energy than is required for its output. The result is that the steady state is applicable to simple systems but, at more complex levels, becomes one of preserving the character of the system through growth and expansion. We see this in our bodies as they attempt to store fat. We see it too among large corporations and government bureaucracies that, not satisfied with the status quo, attempt to increase their chances of survival by actively seeking growth and expansion.

A final point on this characteristic needs to be made: the basic system does not change directly as a result of expansion. The most common growth pattern is one in which there is merely a multiplication of the same type of cycles or subsystems. The quantity of the system changes while the quality remains the same. Most colleges and universities, for instance, expand by doing more of the same thing rather than by pursuing new or innovative activities.

Balance of maintenance and adaptive activities. Open systems seek to reconcile two, often conflicting, activities. Maintenance activities ensure that the various sybsystems are in balance and that the total system is in accord with its environment. This, in effect, prevents rapid changes that may unbalance the system. In contrast, adaptive activities are necessary so that the system can adjust over time to variations in internal and external demands. So, whereas one seeks stability and preservation of the status quo through the purchase, maintenance, and overhaul of machinery, the recruitment and training of employees, and mechanisms such as the provision and enforcement of rules and procedures, the other focuses on change through planning, market research, new product development, and the like.

Both maintenance and adaptive activities are required if a system is to survive. Stable and well-maintained organizations that do not adapt as conditions change will not endure long. Similarly, the adaptive but unstable organization will be inefficient and unlikely to survive for long.

Equifinality. The concept of equifinality argues that there are a number of ways to skin a cat. More exactly, it states that a system can reach the same final state from differing initial conditions and by a variety of paths. This means that an organizational system can accomplish its objectives with varied inputs and transformation processes. As we discuss the managerial implications of organization theory, it will be valuable for you to keep the idea of equifinality in mind. It will encourage you to consider a variety of solutions to a given problem rather than to seek some rigid optimal solution.

Importance of the Systems Point of View

The systems point of view is a useful framework for students of management to conceptualize organizations. For managers and future managers, the systems perspective permits seeing the organization as a whole with interdependent parts—a system composed of subsystems. It prevents, or at least deters, lower-level managers from viewing their jobs as managing static, isolated elements of the organization. It encourages all managers to identify and understand the environment in which their system operates. It helps managers to see the organization as stable patterns and actions within boundaries and to give insights into why organizations are resistant to change. Finally, it directs managers' attention to alternative inputs and processes for reaching their goals.

As a counterpoint, systems should not be viewed as a panacea. The system's framework has its limitations, the most telling being its abstractness. It is one thing to argue that everything depends on everything else. It is a much different thing to offer suggestions to managers on what precisely will change, and to what degree, if a certain action is taken. Its value, therefore, lies more in its conceptual framework than in its direct applicability to solving managers' organizational problems.

THE OBJECTIVES OF THIS BOOK

Almost every issue within the field of OT can be cataloged as an answer to one of five questions:

1. How do we know if an organization is successful?
2. What are the components of an organization?
3. What determines the structure of an organization?
4. What options do managers have for designing their organization and when should each be used?
5. How do you apply a knowledge of organization theory to the resolution of current management problems?

Because these five questions are the critical ones in OT, it is only logical that answers to them be the framework or objectives for a text on OT. This logic has not been lost on your author. Let us preview the content of this book and demonstrate how it leads to answering the five questions.

The issue of organizational success is subsumed under the topic of *effectiveness.* That is *the* dependent variable. It is the primary object of our attention. Chapter 2 covers this topic. It considers what organizations are trying to do, how various constituencies may define and appraise the same organization's effectiveness differently, and provides guidelines to help you evaluate an organization's effectiveness.

Organization structure has a definite and complex meaning. Much research leads us to conclude that the three primary components or characteristics of an organization are *complexity, formalization,* and *centralization.* They are reviewed in Chapters 3 through 5.

The most vocal debate in OT surrounds the question of what determines structure. *Strategy, size, technology, environment,* and *power-control* each have their supporters. In Chapters 6 through 10, we review the meaning of each, determine how they are measured, discuss the research findings on their relation to structure, and draw conclusions based on the evidence.

If we want to manage an organization's design, we need to know what structural alternatives are at our disposal. And given the various structural types, what are each of their strengths and weaknesses? Under what conditions is each preferable? In Chapters 11 through 13, we introduce the major structural forms that comprise the tools of the organizational designer. These chapters also offer suggestions on when to use each and their likely consequences.

A limited number of issues are receiving the bulk of attention by organization theorists as they attempt to offer solutions to organizational problems currently plaguing managers. *Job design, change, conflict, growth and decline* (particularly decline), and *the Japanese-style organization* have been five of the most attended. Chapters 14 through 18 look at each of these issues and demonstrate how OT concepts can assist in their management.

The book concludes with a set of cases. They provide the reader with additional opportunities to apply OT concepts to the solution of management problems.

Figure 1–3 summarizes the objectives of this book. We want to know what determines or causes structure, and we want to know the impact of structure on effectiveness. Effectiveness is treated first. Then we define structure's components. This is followed by an assessment of the major variables that researchers have argued determine structure. The section on typologies develops out of the chapters on components. The final chapters apply OT concepts to five current managerial issues.

SUMMARY

An organization is the planned coordination of the collective activities of two or more people who, functioning on a relatively continuous basis and through division of labor and a hierarchy of authority, seek to achieve a

FIGURE 1–3 Organization theory model

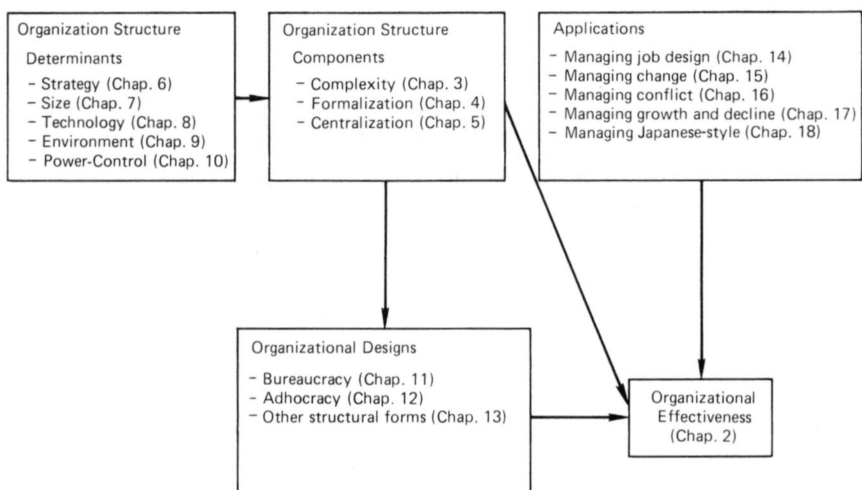

common goal or set of goals. Organization structure is made up of three components: complexity, formalization, and centralization. Organization design is the constructing and changing of structure to achieve the organization's goals. Organization theory is the discipline that studies the structure and design of organizations.

There is no singular reason for studying organization theory. It may be merely to understand organization structure. It may be to develop systematic theories of organizations. For many, OT is studied because they expect to be making choices about how organizations will be designed. Realistically, it must also be noted that some study OT not for any direct personal end but rather as a means for fulfilling a degree or certificate's requirements.

Organizations are depicted as open systems—made up of interrelated and interdependent parts that produce a unified whole that interacts with its environment. The systems point of view provides a useful framework whereby managers can understand the interdependent parts of an organization and the organization's relationship to its environment.

This book's content can be condensed into five areas: organizational effectiveness, organizational components, determinants of structure, organizational design, and applications.

FOR REVIEW AND DISCUSSION

1. Are all groups organizations? Discuss.
2. Is a small business, with only two or three employees, an organization? Discuss.
3. Is OT a prescriptive or a descriptive discipline?
4. How can the systems perspective help you better understand organizations?
5. Compare *open* with *closed* systems.
6. Which one of the following is the more closed system?
   a. General Motors
   b. AT&T
   c. the Ford Foundation
7. Give an example of (a) negative entropy and (b) equifinality.
8. How can a system be stable yet directed toward growth?
9. Why study organization theory?
10. For each of the following organizations, identify their inputs, transformation processes, outputs, relevant subsystems, and environment. Be as specific as possible.

a. U.S. Steel Corporation
b. the Roman Catholic Church
c. Toronto Maple Leafs hockey team
d. American Heart Association
e. Attica (N.Y.) State Prison
f. U.S. Air Force
g. St. Joseph's Hospital in Philadelphia
h. a local drugstore
i. a local franchised steak house

CHAPTER

2

ORGANIZATIONAL EFFECTIVENESS

In 1982, the Pentagon's budget was $183 billion. Factoring out inflation, that was still 20 percent more than had been allocated to the Pentagon five years earlier. Was the Pentagon 20 percent more effective in 1982 than in 1977?

In 1980, IBM made a profit of $3.6 billion on sales of $26 billion. On the other hand, General Motors lost $760 million on sales of $58 billion. If you wanted to determine which company was more effective, do you use profits, sales, or some other criterion?

How do you determine if a college is doing a good job or not? If all its students get jobs upon graduation, does that tell us the college is effective? Or should we be looking at the percentage increase or decrease in freshmen applications, a statistical report of the number of books checked out from the library by students during the past academic year, a survey asking seniors what they thought of their college experience, the number of publications by faculty members, awards won by graduates, or the average salary of former students twenty years after graduation?

These examples are meant to introduce the problems inherent in defining and measuring organizational effectiveness (OE). As you will see, academicians have historically had considerable difficulty in trying to agree on what the term means. Yet almost all these same academicians are quick to acknowledge that this term—organizational effectiveness—is the central theme in organization theory. In fact, it is difficult to conceive of a theory of organizations that does *not* include the concept of effectiveness.[1]

[1]Paul S. Goodman and Johannes M. Pennings, "Perspectives and Issues: An Introduction," in P. S. Goodman, J. M. Pennings, and Associates, eds., *New Perspectives on Organizational Effectiveness* (San Francisco: Jossey-Bass, 1977), p. 2.

IN SEARCH OF A DEFINITION

The early approach to OE—which probably lasted up to and through the 1950s—was innocently simple. Effectiveness could be defined as the degree to which an organization realizes its goals.[2] Hidden in this definition, however, were many ambiguities that severely curtailed both research on the subject and practicing managers' ability to grasp and use the concept. For example: Whose goals? Short-term goals or long-term goals? The organization's official goals or actual goals?

Our point may be clearer when we take a goal that most researchers and practitioners agree is a necessary condition for an organization's success. That is *survival*.[3] If there is anything that an organization seeks to do, it is to survive. But the use of survival as a criterion presumes the ability to identify the death of an organization. Survival is an "alive or dead" evaluation. Unfortunately, organizations don't die neatly. When is an organization "dead"? Aren't there organizations that survive yet are ineffective? Of course there are. For some organizations—and favorite targets include government agencies and large corporations—death practically never occurs.[4] So even a goal that almost everyone agrees is important bogs down under more careful scrutiny.

The 1960s and early 1970s saw a proliferation of OE studies. A review of these studies (see Table 2–1) found thirty different criteria—all purporting to measure "organizational effectiveness."[5] The fact that few studies used multiple criteria and that the criteria themselves ranged from general measures such as quality and morale to more specific factors such as accident rates and absenteeism certainly leads to the conclusion that organizational effectiveness means different things to different people. No doubt part of the length of Table 2–1 is due to the diversity of organizations being evaluated. Additionally, it also reflects the different interests of the evaluators. As we argue later in this chapter, when we consider more specifically how values impact organizational effectiveness, the criteria chosen to define OE may tell more about the person doing the evaluation than about the organization being evaluated. But all thirty criteria cannot be relevant to every organization, and certainly some must be more important than others. The researcher who tabulated these thirty criteria concluded that, since an organization can be effective or ineffective on a number of

[2]Amitai Etzioni, *Modern Organizations* (Englewood Cliffs, N.J.: Prentice-Hall, 1964), p. 8.

[3]John R. Kimberly, "Issues in the Creation of Organizations: Initiation, Innovation, and Institutionalization," *Academy of Management Journal*, September 1979, p. 438.

[4]Jeffrey Pfeffer, "Usefulness of the Concept," in P. S. Goodman, J. M. Pennings, and Associates, eds., *New Perspectives on Organizational Effectiveness*, p. 139; and H. Kaufman, *Are Government Organizations Immortal?* (Washington, D.C.: Brookings Institution, 1976).

[5]John P. Campbell, "On the Nature of Organizational Effectiveness," in P. S. Goodman, J. M. Pennings, and Associates, eds., *New Perspectives on Organizational Effectiveness*, pp. 36–41.

different facets that may be relatively independent of one another, organizational effectiveness has no "operational definition."[6]

This belief that OE defies definition has been widely accepted. From a research perspective, this may be true. On the other hand, a close look at the recent OE literature does see movement toward agreement. Even more important, from a practical standpoint, all of us have and use some operational definition of OE on a regular basis. This is so in spite of a supposed problem by academicians to define it. Let us elaborate on each of these points.

It may have been correct ten years ago to argue that defining OE was equivalent to trying to nail Jello to the wall. A close look at the recent OE literature, however, indicates that scholars may have been focusing for so long on differences that commonalities have been overlooked. As will become evident by the time you finish reading this chapter, there is almost unanimous agreement today that OE requires multiple criteria, that different organizational functions have to be evaluated using different characteristics, and that OE must consider both means (process) and ends (outcomes). If the search was to find a single and universal criterion of OE, then disappointment is understandable. But because organizations do many things and their success depends on adequate performance in a number of areas, OE's definition must reflect this complexity. The result is that we have to hold our statement of a formal definition to the end of this chapter, after a number of OE concepts have been discussed.

It is occasionally lost on researchers that, regardless of whether they can define and label a phenomenon, that phenomenon is still real and continues to function. Gravitation existed for a long time before Newton "discovered" it. While researchers may debate about whether or not OE can be defined, the fact is that all of us have a working definition of the term. You and I make OE judgments regularly, whenever we buy stock, choose a college, select a bank or car repair shop, decide which organization will get our donations, and make other similar decisions. Managers and administrators, of course, also make regular OE determinations when they appraise and compare units or allocate budgets to these units. The point is that evaluating the effectiveness of an organization is a widespread and ongoing activity. From a managerial perspective alone, judgments of OE are going to be made with or without agreement on a formal definition. When managers seek answers to whether things are going well or not, what needs change, or attempt to compare their organization with others, they are making OE judgments.

The remainder of this chapter is devoted to presenting the diverse approaches that the study of OE has taken. It concludes with an integrative framework that acknowledges the earlier approaches, deals overtly with

[6]Ibid., p. 15.

TABLE 2–1 Criteria and measures of organizational effectiveness

1. *Overall effectiveness.* The general evaluation that takes into account as many criteria facets as possible. It is measured usually by combining archival performance records or by obtaining overall ratings or judgments from persons thought to be knowledgable about the organization.
2. *Productivity.* Usually defined as the quantity or volume of the major product or service that the organization provides. It can be measured at three levels: individual, group, and total organization via archival records or ratings or both.
3. *Efficiency.* A ratio that reflects a comparison of some aspect of unit performance to the costs incurred for that performance.
4. *Profit.* The amount of revenue from sales left after all costs and obligations are met. Percentage return on investment or percentage return on total sales are sometimes used as alternative definitions.
5. *Quality.* The quality of the primary service or product provided by the organization that may take many operational forms, which are determined largely by the kind of product or service provided by the organization.
6. *Accidents.* The frequency of on-the-job accidents resulting in lost time.
7. *Growth.* Represented by an increase in such variables as total work force, plant capacity, assets, sales, profits, market share, and number of innovations. It implies a comparison of an organization's present state with its own past state.
8. *Absenteeism.* The usual definition stipulates unexcused absences, but even within this constraint there are a number of alternative definitions (e.g., total time absence versus frequency of occurrence).
9. *Turnover.* Some measure of the relative number of voluntary terminations, which is almost always assessed via archival records.
10. *Job satisfaction.* Has been conceptualized in many ways but the modal view might define it as the individual's satisfaction with the amount of various job outcomes that he or she is receiving.
11. *Motivation.* In general, the strength of the predisposition of an individual to engage in goal-directed action or activity on the job. It is not a feeling of relative satisfaction with various job outcomes but is more akin to a readiness or willingness to work at accomplishing the job's goals. As an organizational index, it must be summed across people.
12. *Morale.* The model definition seems to view morale as a group phenomenon involving extra effort, goal communality, commitment, and feelings of belonging. Groups have some degree of morale, whereas individuals have some degree of motivation (and satisfaction).
13. *Control.* The degree, and distribution, of management control that exists within an organization for influencing and directing the behavior of organization members.
14. *Conflict/cohesion.* Defined at the cohesion end by an organization in which the members like one another, work well together, communicate fully and openly, and coordinate their work efforts. At the other end lies the organization with verbal and physical clashes, poor coordination, and ineffective communication.
15. *Flexibility/adaptation.* Refers to the ability of an organization to change its standard operating procedures in response to environmental changes.
16. *Planning and goal setting.* The degree to which an organization systematically plans its future steps and engages in explicit goal-setting behavior.

TABLE 2–1 (cont.)

17. *Goal consensus.* Distinct from actual commitment to the organization's goals, consensus refers to the degree to which all individuals perceive the same goals for the organization.
18. *Internalization of organizational goals.* Refers to the acceptance of the organization's goals. It includes their belief that the organization's goals are right and proper.
19. *Role and norm congruence.* The degree to which the members of an organization are in agreement on such things as desirable supervisory attitudes, performance expectations, morale, role requirements, and so on.
20. *Managerial interpersonal skills.* The level of skill with which managers deal with supervisors, subordinates, and peers in terms of giving support, facilitating constructive interaction, and generating enthusiasm for meeting goals and achieving excellent performance.
21. *Managerial task skills.* The overall level of skills with which the organization's managers, commanding officers, or group leaders perform work-centered tasks and tasks centered on work to be done and not the skills employed when interacting with other organizational members.
22. *Information management and communication.* Completeness, efficiency, and accuracy in analysis and distribution of information critical to organizational effectiveness.
23. *Readiness.* An overall judgment concerning the probability that the organization could successfully perform some specified task if asked to do so.
24. *Utilization of environment.* The extent to which the organization interacts successfully with its environment and acquires scarce and valued resources necessary to its effective operation.
25. *Evaluations by external entities.* Evaluations of the organization, or unit, by the individuals and organizations in its environment with which it interacts. Loyalty to, confidence in, and support given the organization by such groups as suppliers, customers, stockholders, enforcement agencies, and the general public would fall under this label.
26. *Stability.* The maintenance of structure, function, and resources through time and, more particularly, through periods of stress.
27. *Value of human resources.* A composite criterion that refers to the total value or total worth of the individual members, in an accounting or balance sheet sense, to the organization.
28. *Participation and shared influence.* The degree to which individuals in the organization participate in making the decisions that affect them directly.
29. *Training and development emphasis.* The amount of effort that the organization devotes to developing its human resources.
30. *Achievement emphasis.* An analog to the individual need for achievement referring to the degree to which the organization appears to place a high value on achieving major new goals.

Source: Adapted from John P. Campbell, "On the Nature of Organizational Effectiveness,' in P. S. Goodman, J. M. Pennings, and Associates, eds., *New Perspectives on Organizational Effectiveness* (San Francisco: Jossey-Bass, 1977), pp. 36–41. With permission.

their differences, and provides a clear but complex definition of organizational effectiveness.

THE GOAL-ATTAINMENT APPROACH

An organization is, by definition, created deliberately to achieve one or more specified goals. It should come as no surprise then to find that goal attainment is probably the most widely used criterion of effectiveness.

The goal-attainment approach states that an organization's effectiveness must be appraised in terms of the accomplishment of *ends* rather than means. It is the bottom line that counts. Popular goal-attainment criteria include profit maximization, bringing the enemy to surrender, winning the basketball game, restoring patients to good health, and the like. Their common denominator is that they consider the ends to which the organization was created to achieve.

Assumptions

Underlying goal attainment is a set of assumptions that must be valid for the approach to be usable. First, organizations must have ultimate goals. Second, these goals must be identified and defined well enough to be understood. Third, these goals must be few enough to be manageable. Fourth, there must be general consensus or agreement on these goals. Finally, progress toward these goals must be measurable.

Making Goals Operative

Given that the assumptions cited are valid, how would managers operationalize the goal-attainment approach? The key decision makers would be the group from which the goals would be obtained. This group would be asked to state the organization's specific goals. Once identified, it would be necessary to develop some measurement device to see how well the goals are being met. If, for instance, the consensus goal were profit maximization, measures such as return on investment, return on sales, or some similar computation would be selected.

The goal-attainment approach is probably most explicit in management by objectives (MBO). MBO is a well-known philosophy of management that assesses an organization and its members by how well they achieve the specific goals that superiors and subordinates have jointly established. Tangible, verifiable, and measurable goals are developed. The conditions under which they are to be accomplished is specified. The degree to which each goal must be satisfied is also specified. Actual performance is then measured and compared with the goals. Because either an organization accomplishes the specific tasks that it is supposed to or it does not, it represents the ultimate in a goal-oriented approach to effectiveness.[7]

Problems

The goal-attainment approach is fraught with a number of problems that makes its exclusive use highly questionable. Many of these problems relate directly back to the assumptions that we noted earlier.

It is one thing to talk about goals in general, but when you operationalize the goal-attainment approach you have to ask: Whose goals? Top management's? If so, who is included and who is excluded? In some large corporations, just surveying vice presidents and above can include dozens of respondents. It's also possible that some of the decision makers with real power and influence in the organization are not members of senior management. There are cases in which individuals with a number of years of experience or particular expertise in an important area have a significant impact on determining their organization's goals (they are part of the dominant coalition), even though they are not among the senior executive cadre.

What an organization states officially as its goals does not always reflect the organization's actual goals. Official goals tend to be influenced strongly by standards of social desirability. Representative statements such as "to produce quality products at competitive prices," "to be a responsible member of the community," "to ensure that our productive efforts do nothing to damage the environment," "to maintain our reputation for integrity," and "to hire the handicapped and members of minorities" were gleaned from several corporate brochures. These vague "apple pie and flag" official statements may sound good, but rarely do they make any contribution to understanding what the organization is actually trying to accomplish. Given the likelihood that official and actual goals will be different, an assessment of an organization's goals should probably include the statements made by the dominant coalition plus an additional listing derived from observations of what members in the organization are actually doing.

An organization's short-term goals are frequently different from its long-term goals. For instance, one firm's primary short-term goal was directed financially—to raise $20 million of working capital within the next twelve months. Its five-year goal, however, was to increase its product market share from 4 to 10 percent. In applying the goal-attainment approach, which goals—short or long term—should be used?

The fact that organizations have multiple goals, too, creates difficulties. They can compete with each other and are, sometimes, even incompatible. The achievement of "high product quality" and "low unit cost,"

[7] Ibid., p. 26.

for example, may be directly at odds with each other. The goal-attainment approach assumes consensus on goals. Given that there are multiple goals and diverse interests within the organization, consensus may not be possible unless goals are stated in such ambiguous and vague terms as to allow the varying interest groups to interpret them in a way favorable to their self-interests. This, in fact, may explain why most official goals in large organizations are traditionally broad and intangible. They act to placate the many different interest groups within the organization.

Multiple goals must be ordered according to importance if they are to have meaning to members. But how do you allocate relative importance to goals that may be incompatible and represent diverse interests? Add to this the fact that, as personnel change and power relationships within the organization change, so will the importance attributed to various goals, and you begin to realize the difficulty that operationalizing the goal-attainment approach poses.

A last insight should be made before we conclude this section on problems. It just may be that, for many organizations, goals do not direct behavior. "The common assertion that goal consensus must occur prior to action obscures the fact that consensus is impossible unless there is something tangible around which it can occur. And this 'something tangible' may well turn out to be actions *already completed*."[8] In some cases, official goals may merely be rationalizations to explain actions that have happened in the past rather than as guides to future actions. If this were true, measuring organizational effectiveness by surveying the dominant coalition should not result in benchmarks against which actual performance can be compared but, rather, formal descriptions of the dominant coalition's perceptions of prior performance.

What does all this mean? It would appear that only the naïve would accept the formal statements made by senior management to represent the organization's goals. As one author concluded after finding that corporations issue one set of goals to stockholders, another to customers, a third set to employees, a fourth to the public, and still a fifth set for management itself, formal statements of goals should be treated "as fiction produced by an organization to account for, explain, or rationalize its existence to particular audiences rather than as valid and reliable indications of purpose."[9]

Value to Managers

These problems, while certainly damning, should not be construed as a blanket indictment of goals. Organizations exist to achieve goals—the problems lie in their identification and measurement. The validity of those goals

[8]Karl Weick, *The Social Psychology of Organizing* (Reading, Mass.: Addision-Wesley, 1969), p. 8. (Author's Emphasis).

[9]Charles K. Warriner, "The Problem of Organizational Purpose," *The Sociological Quarterly*, Spring 1965, p. 140.

identified can probably be increased significantly by (1) ensuring that input is received from all those having a major influence on formulating the official goals, even if they are not part of senior management; (2) including actual goals obtained by observing the behavior of organization members; (3) recognizing that organizations pursue both short- and long-term goals; (4) insisting on tangible, verifiable, and measurable goals rather than relying on vague statements that merely mirror societal expectations; and (5) viewing goals as dynamic entities that change over time rather than as rigid or fixed statements of purpose.

If managers are willing to confront the complexities inherent in the goal-attainment approach, they *can* obtain reasonably valid information for assessing an organization's effectiveness. But there is more to OE than identifying and measuring specific ends.

THE SYSTEMS APPROACH

In Chapter 1, we described organizations in a systems framework. Organizations acquire inputs, engage in transformation processes, and generate outputs. It has been argued that defining OE solely in terms of goal-attainment results in only a partial measure of effectiveness. Goals focus on outputs. But an organization should also be judged on its ability to acquire inputs, process these inputs, channel the outputs, and maintain stability and balance. Another way to look at OE, therefore, is through a systems approach.[10]

The systems approach has developed more as a counterpoint to goal attainment than as an extension. Thus, it has emphasized inputs, acquisition of resources, and processes. In other words, the systems approach has focused not so much on specific ends as on the means needed for the achievement of those ends. Its time frame is also longer term since it is oriented toward assessing the organization's ability to survive and considering all those factors that can and do impact on survival.

Assumptions

The assumptions underlying a systems approach to OE are the same that applied in our discussion of systems in the previous chapter. A few of the more evident ones can be elaborated upon.

A systems approach to OE implies that organizations are made up of interrelated subparts. If any one of these subparts performs poorly, it will impact on the performance of the whole system.

Effectiveness requires awareness and successful interactions with en-

[10]Ephraim Yuchtman and Stanley E. Seashore, "A Systems Resource Approach to Organizational Effectiveness," *American Sociological Review*, December 1967, pp. 891–903.

vironmental constituencies. Management cannot fail to maintain good relations with customers, suppliers, government agencies, unions and other similar constituencies that have the power to disrupt the stable operation of the organization.

Survival requires a steady replenishment of those resources consumed. Raw materials must be secured, vacancies created by employee resignations and retirements must be filled, declining product lines must be replaced, changes in the economy and the tastes of customers or clients need to be anticipated and reacted to, and so on. Failure to replenish will result in the organization's decline and, possibly, death.

Making Systems Operative

Let us turn now to the issue of how managers can apply the systems approach. First, we look at a sampling of criteria that systems advocates consider relevant; then we consider the various ways in which managers measure these criteria.

The systems view looks at factors such as relations with the environment to assure continued receipt of inputs and favorable acceptance of outputs, flexibility of response to environmental changes, the efficiency with which the organization transforms inputs to outputs, the clarity of internal communications, the level of conflict among groups, and the degree of employee job satisfaction. In contrast to the goal-attainment approach, the system approach focuses on the means necessary to assure the organization's continued survival. And it should be noted that systems advocates do not negate the importance of specific end goals as a determinant of organizational effectiveness. Rather, they question the validity of the goals selected and the measures used for assessing the progress toward these goals.

It has been suggested that the critical systems interrelationships can be converted into OE variables or ratios.[11] These could include output/input *(O/I)*, transformations/input *(T/I)*, transformations/output *(T/O)*, changes in input/input ($\Delta I/I$), and so on. Table 2–2 gives some examples of measurement criteria that could be used along with these variables in a business firm, a hospital, and a college.

Another systems approach was used by researchers at the University of Michigan for studying the performance of seventy-five insurance agencies.[12] They used archival records of sales and personnel data to look at ten effectiveness dimensions:

[11]William M. Evan, "Organizational Theory and Organizational Effectiveness: An Exploratory Analysis," in S. Lee Spray, ed., *Organizational Effectiveness: Theory, Research, Utilization* (Kent, Ohio: Kent State University Press, 1976), pp. 21–24.

[12]Stanley E. Seashore and Ephraim Yuchtman, "Factorial Analysis of Organizational Performance," *Administrative Science Quarterly*, December 1967, pp. 377–395.

TABLE 2–2 Examples of effectiveness measures for different types of organizations

SYSTEM VARIABLES	BUSINESS FIRM	HOSPITAL	COLLEGE
O/I	Return on investment	Total number of patients treated	Number of faculty publications
T/I	Inventory turnover	Capital investment in medical technology	Cost of information systems
T/O	Sales volume	Total number of patients treated	Number of students graduated
ΔI/I	Change in working capital	Change in number of patients treated	Change in student enrollment

Source: Adapted from William M. Evan, "Organization Theory and Organizational Effectiveness: An Exploratory Analysis," in S. Lee Spray, ed., *Organizational Effectiveness: Theory, Research, Utilization* (Kent, Ohio: Kent State University Press, 1976), pp. 22–23. With permission.

Business volume. Number and value of policies sold related to size of agency.

Production cost. Cost per unit of sales volume.

New member productivity. Productivity of agents having less than five years' tenure.

Youthfulness of members. Productivity of members under 35 years of age.

Business mix. A combination of three conceptually unrelated performance indices, interpreted as reflecting the ability of agencies to achieve high overall performance through any of several strategies.

Work force growth. Relative and absolute change in work force levels.

Devotion to management. Sales commissions earned by agency managers.

Maintenance cost. Cost to maintain accounts.

Member productivity. Average new business volume per agent.

Market penetration. Proportion of potential market being exploited.

This study considered the key outputs (business volume, member productivity, market penetration). But it is a systems approach because it also considered important means that must be satisfied if the organization is to survive over the long haul. For instance, the inclusion of "new member productivity" and "youthfulness of members" variables recognizes that successful future sales depend on investing in and developing young talent.

Still another systems application to OE is the management audit.[13]

[13]Jackson Martindell, *The Scientific Appraisal of Management* (New York: Harper & Row, 1962).

Developed by Jackson Martindell and his American Institute of Management, it analyzes the key activities in a business firm, past, present, and future, to ensure that the organization is getting the maximum effort out of its resources. Using a 10,000-point analysis sheet, Martindell appraises performance in ten areas: economic function, organization structure, health of earnings, service to stockholders, research and development, board of directors, fiscal policies, production efficiency, sales vigor, and executive evaluation. Although a number of the criteria are relevant to profit-making organizations alone, the concept could be modified for use in the nonprofit sector. The ten areas carry various weights, reflecting the importance that Martindell has assigned to each variable in terms of its contribution to the organization's overall performance. Again, it is a systems approach because it recognizes that no organization can reach its performance potential if one or more of its subsystems is performing inadequately.

Problems

The two most telling shortcomings of the systems approach relate to measurement and the issue of whether means really matter.

Measuring specific end goals may be easy compared with trying to measure process variables such as "flexibility of response to environmental changes" or "clarity of internal communications." The problem is that, while the terms may carry a layperson's meaning, the development of valid and reliable measures for tapping their quantity or intensity may not be possible. Whatever measures are used, therefore, may be constantly open to question.

In sports, it is frequently said that "It's *whether* you win or lose that counts, *not* how you play the game!" It can be argued that the same holds true for organizations. If ends are achieved, are means important? The objective is to win, not to get out there and look good losing! The problem with the systems approach, at least according to its critics, is that its focus is on the means necessary to achieve effectiveness rather than on organizational effectiveness itself.

This criticism may take on more substance if we conceptualize both goal-attainment and systems approaches as goal oriented. The first uses *end* goals; the latter uses *means* goals. Looked at from this perspective, it may be arguable that, since both use goals, you might as well use ones that are more meaningful and that (despite their own measurement problems) are easier to quantify; that is, the goal-attainment approach!

Value to Managers

Managers who use a systems approach to OE are less prone to look for immediate results. They are less likely to make decisions that trade off the organization's long-term health and survival for ones that will make them look good in the near term. Additionally, the systems approach increases the managers' awareness of the interdependency of organizational activities.

For instance, if management fails to have raw materials on hand when they are needed or if the quality of those raw materials is poor, it will restrict the organization's ability to achieve its end goals.

A final plus for the systems approach is its applicability where end goals are either very vague or defy measurement. Managers of public organizations frequently use "ability to acquire budget increases" as a measure of effectiveness—substituting an input criterion for an output criterion.

THE STRATEGIC-CONSTITUENCIES APPROACH

A more recent perspective on OE proposes that an effective organization is one that satisfies the demands of those constituencies in its environment from whom it requires support for its continued existence.[14] This strategic-constituencies approach is similar to the systems view, yet it has a different emphasis. Both consider interdependencies, but the strategic-constituencies view is not concerned with all of the organization's environment. It seeks to appease only those in the environment who can threaten the organization's survival. In this context, most public universities must consider effectiveness in terms of acquiring *students,* but need not be concerned with potential *employers* of their graduates. Why? Because these universities' survival is not influenced by whether its graduates get jobs or not. On the other hand, private universities, which charge considerably more than their public counterparts, do spend a great deal of time and money in attempting to place their graduates. When parents spend $40,000 or more to get their son or daughter a bachelor's degree, they expect it to lead to a job or acceptance in a good graduate school. If this does not occur, it will be increasingly difficult for the private school to acquire freshmen applications. The converse of this example is the university's relations with the legislature in the state within which it operates. Public institutions devote considerable effort to wooing state legislators. Failure to have their cooperation is sure to have adverse budget effects on the public university. The private university's effectiveness, in contrast, is little affected by whether or not it has a favorable relationship with the key people in the state capitol.

Assumptions

The strategic-constituencies approach assumes that an organization is faced with frequent and competing demands from a variety of interest groups. Not all these interest groups are of equal importance, so effectiveness is

[14]Jeffrey Pfeffer and Gerald Salancik, *The External Control of Organizations* (New York: Harper & Row, 1978).

determined by the organization's ability to identify its critical or strategic constituencies and to satisfy the demands they place upon the organization. Further, this approach assumes that managers pursue a number of goals and that the goals selected represent a response to those interest groups who control the resources necessary for the organization to survive.

Making Strategic Constituencies Operative

The manager wishing to apply this perspective might begin by asking members of the dominant coalition to identify the constituencies that they consider to be critical to the organization's survival. This input can be combed and synthesized to arrive at a list of strategic constituencies.

As an example, a large tire company such as B. F. Goodrich might have strategic constituencies that include suppliers of critical petroleum products used in the tire manufacturing process; officers of the United Rubber Workers' union; officials at banks where the company has sizable short-term loans; government regulatory agencies such as those that grade tires and inspect facilities for safety violations; security analysts at major brokerage firms who specialize in the tire and rubber industry; regional tire jobbers and distributors; and purchasing agents responsible for the acquisition of tires at General Motors, Mack Truck, Caterpillar, and other vehicle manufacturers.

This list could then be evaluated to determine the relative power of each. Basically, this means looking at each constituency in terms of how dependent on it our organization is. Do they have considerable power over us? Are there alternatives for what this constituency provides? How do these constituencies compare in the impact that they have on the organization's operations?

The third step requires identifying the expectations that these constituencies hold for the organization. What do they want of it? Given that each constituency has its own set of special interests, what goals does each seek to impose on the organization? Stockholders' goals may be in terms of profit or appreciation in the stock's price; the union's may be in acquiring job security and high wages for its members; whereas the Environmental Protection Agency will want the firm's manufacturing plants to meet all minimum air, water, and noise pollution requirements.

The strategic-constituencies approach would conclude by comparing the various expectations, determining common expectations and those that are incompatible, assigning relative weights to the various constituencies, and formulating a preference ordering of these various goals for the organization as a whole. This preference order, in effect, represents the relative power of the various strategic constituencies. The organization's effectiveness then would be assessed in terms of its ability to satisfy these goals.

Problems

As with the previous approaches, this one too is not without problems. The task of separating the strategic constituencies from the larger environment is easy to say but difficult to do in practice. Because the environment changes rapidly, what was critical to the organization yesterday may not be so today. Even if the constituencies in the environment can be identified and are assumed to be relatively stable, what separates the strategic constituencies from the "almost" strategic constituencies? Where do you cut the set? And won't the interests of each member in the dominant coalition strongly impact on what he or she perceives as strategic? An executive in the accounting function is unlikely to see the world—or the organization's strategic constituencies—in the same way as an executive in the purchasing function. Finally, identifying the expectations that the strategic constituencies hold of the organization presents a problem. How do you tap that information accurately?

Value to Managers

If survival is important for an organization, then it is incumbent upon managers to understand upon just whom (in terms of constituencies) that survival is contingent. By operationalizing the strategic-constituencies approach, managers decrease the chance that they might ignore or severely upset a group whose power could significantly hinder the organization's operations. If management knows whose support it needs if the organization is to maintain its health, it can modify its preference ordering of goals as necessary to reflect the changing power relationships with its strategic constituencies.

THE COMPETING-VALUES APPROACH

Our final view offers an integrative framework for assessing organizational effectiveness. It has been labeled the competing-values approach.[15]

What you value—return on investment, market share, new product innovation, job security—depends on who you are and the interests you represent. It is not surprising that stockholders, unions, suppliers, management, or internal specialists in marketing, personnel, production, or accounting may look at the same organization but evaluate its effectiveness entirely differently. You can relate to this fact by thinking about how you evaluate your course instructor. In any class with thirty or more students, you can expect evaluations of the instructor to differ markedly. Probably

[15]Robert E. Quinn and John Rohrbaugh, "A Competing Values Approach to Organizational Effectiveness." Working paper, SUNY–Albany, 1979.

some students saw the instructor as one of the best they have had. Others will appraise the instructor as one of the worst. The instructor's behavior is a constant; it is the evaluators who bring their own standard of what a "good teacher" is that creates the different ratings. The rating, therefore, probably tells us more about the values of the evaluator (what they prefer in terms of an instructor) than it tells us about the teacher's effectiveness.

An additional illustration from the political arena may be instructive. You would think that effectiveness in a presidential primary would be fairly easy to define. The winner of the primary is, by definition, most effective. Apparently presidential candidates do not see it that way. The day after the Democratic presidential primary in Maine in early 1980, the results showed the incumbent, Jimmy Carter, with 43 percent; Massachusett's senator Ted Kennedy with 40 percent; and California's governor, Jerry Brown, with 13 percent. Carter presented himself as the winner—"I got the most votes." Kennedy proclaimed himself the winner based on the reasoning that, after losing 2 to 1 to Carter the prior month in Iowa, "I nearly beat the incumbent president." Finally, Brown was not to be outdone. He concocted his victory on the following logic: "Carter couldn't get a majority. Kennedy couldn't win in his own backyard. No one expected anything from me and I got 13 percent. I won!" Notice how the criteria changed to reflect the interests of the evaluator. Both beauty and effectiveness is in the eye of the beholder!

Assumptions

Before we present the competing values approach explicitly, the assumptions upon which it was conceived need to be identified. It begins with the assumption that there are competing values that create conflicting goals. There is no single goal in an organization. There is also no consensus around the goals that can be identified.

What is the source of these different goals? The values and interests of those doing the defining! If you take an organization such as Xerox, you might find financial analysts defining OE in terms of high profitability; production executives focusing on the amount and quality of equipment manufactured; marketing people and competitors looking at the percentage of market that Xerox's various products hold; personnel specialists viewing OE in terms of ability to hire competent workers and an absence of strikes; research and development scientists keying in on the number of new inventions and products that the company generates; and the Stamford, Connecticut city council (where Xerox is headquartered) defining OE as a steadily expanding work force.

The competing-values approach, in summary, views the assessment of OE as an exercise founded on values. It assumes that what an evaluator values will go a long way in determining what that evaluator chooses to assess.

Making Competing Values Operative

To apply this approach, it's necessary to go into more detail of how it evolved. It began by looking for common themes among the thirty characteristics presented in Table 2–1. What was found were three basic sets of competing values.

The first set relates to organizational structure, from an emphasis on *flexibility* to an emphasis on *control.* This flexibility-control dimension reflects a basic dilemma of organizational life: the debate over the value of innovation, adaptability, and change versus authority, order, and control. It is very similar to the adaptation-maintenance dichotomy presented in Chapter 1.

The second set relates to organization focus, from an emphasis on the well-being and development of the *people* in the organization to an emphasis on the well-being and development of the *organization* itself. Here, too, is another basic dilemma of organizational life: the concern for the feelings and needs of people versus the concern for productivity and task accomplishment.

The third set of values relates to organizational *means* and *ends,* from an emphasis on processes to an emphasis on final outcomes. The competing values of whether the organization should be evaluated on long-term criteria (means) or short-term criteria (ends) are reflected in this final dimension.

Figure 2–1 depicts these values in a three-dimensional perspective. It also shows how the three dimensions can be combined to create eight cells or OE criteria. These cells, in turn, can be arranged so as to define four effectiveness models. Figure 2–2 illustrates this idea. The result is four diverse models or definitions of organizational effectiveness, no one of which is right for assessing all organizations. They are labeled human relations, open systems, rational goal, and internal process.

> The human relations model emphasizes people and flexibility and stresses the effectiveness criteria shown in the upper left section of Figure 2–2: cohesion and morale (as means) and human resource development (as an end). The open systems model emphasizes organization and flexibility and stresses the effectiveness criteria shown in the upper right section of Figure 2–2: flexibility and readiness (as means) and growth, resource acquisition, and external support (as ends). The rational goal model emphasizes organization and control and stresses the effectiveness criteria shown in the lower right section of Figure 2–2: planning and goal setting (as means) and productivity and efficiency (as ends).

FIGURE 2–1 A three-dimensional model of organizational effectiveness

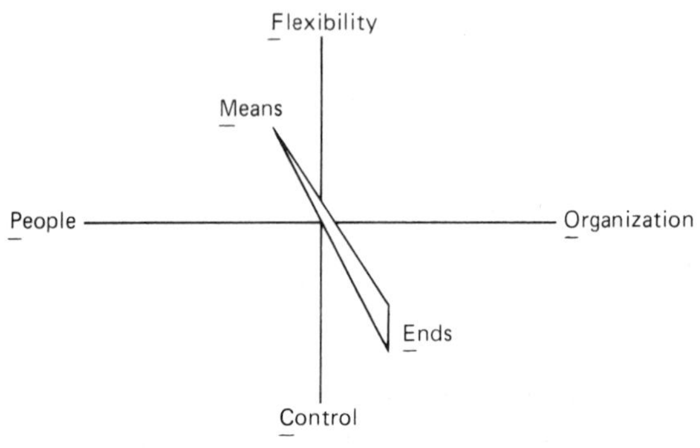

THE EIGHT CELLS	*DEFINITIONS OF THE EIGHT CRITERIA*
OEC	*Productivity/efficiency.* Volume of output, the ratio of output over input.
OCM	*Planning and goal setting.* The amount of emphasis on the planning, objective setting, and evaluation process.
OFE	*Resource acquisition.* The capacity to capture assets and develop external support.
OFM	*Flexibility-readiness.* The ability to adapt to shifts in external conditions and demands.
PCE	*Stability-control.* Smoothness of internal conditions, continuity, equilibrium.
PCM	*Information management-communication.* Sufficiency of information flows, adequacy of internal orchestration.
PFE	*Value of human resources training.* The enhancement and maintenance of overall staff capacity.
PFM	*Cohesion-morale.* The level of communality and commitment among the staff members.

Source: Robert E. Quinn and Kim Cameron, "Organizational Life Cycles and the Criteria of Effectiveness." Working paper: SUNY-Albany, 1979. Reprinted with permission.

> The internal process model is represented in the lower left section of Figure 2–2. It emphasizes people and control and stresses the role of information management and communication (as means) and stability and control (as ends) in the assessment of effectiveness.[16]

Note how each model represents a particular set of values and has a polar opposite with contrasting emphases. "The human relations model with its effectiveness criteria reflecting people and flexibility stands in stark

[16]Ibid., p. 19.

FIGURE 2–2 Four models of effectiveness values

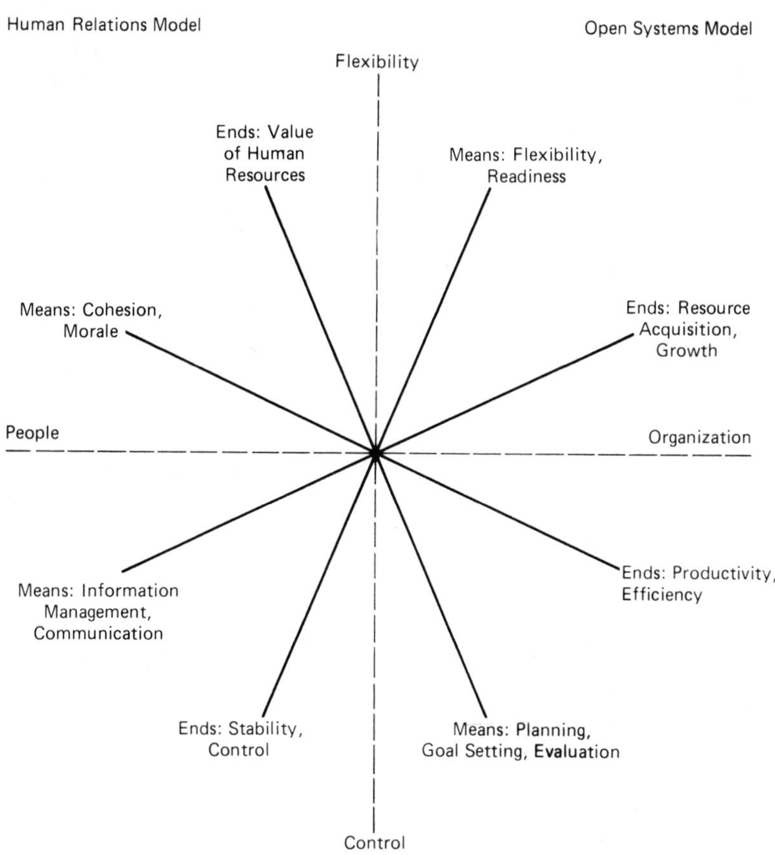

Source: Robert E. Quinn and Kim Cameron, "Organizational Life Cycles and the Criteria of Effectiveness." Working paper: SUNY-Albany, 1979. Reprinted with permission.

contrast to the rational goal model's value-based stress on organization and stability. The open system model, defined by values upon the organization and flexibility, runs counter to the internal process model, the effectiveness criteria of which reflect a focus on people and stable structures."[17]

The competing-values approach has been carried further. It has been used as the framework within which to ask the question: When is each model of effectiveness preferred? A tentative answer has been postulated: it depends on which stage the organization is in its life cycle.[18]

[17]Ibid., pp. 19–20.

[18]Robert E. Quinn and Kim Cameron, "Organizational Life Cycles and the Criteria of Effectiveness." Working paper: SUNY–Albany, 1979.

Conceptualize, if you will, organizations as proceeding through a life cycle. First is birth or the *entrepreneurial stage,* typified by innovation, creativity, and the marshalling of resources. Second is the *collectivity stage,* where the dominant activities are informal communication and structure, creating a sense of "family" and cooperativeness among members, and developing high member commitment. This is followed by the *formalization stage,* typified by stability, efficiency of operations, rules and procedures, and conservative trends. Finally, an organization reaches the *elaboration of structure stage,* where emphasis is on monitoring the external environment so that the organization can renew itself and grow. These stages can occur in rapid sequence or develop very slowly. But they do represent a general pattern that organizations follow.

Each of these stages emphasizes different activities. Evaluation of effectiveness, therefore, should be predicated on assessing those activities that should be dominant during the particular stage at which the organization is currently operating. So, during the entrepreneurial stage, the strongest emphasis appears to be on the open-system criteria of effectiveness. Similarly, the human relations model is most associated with the collectivity stage, the internal process and rational goal models appear most dominant in the formalization stage, and the open-systems model receives the most emphasis in the elaboration of structure stage.

With this said, how would a manager attempt to apply the competing-values approach? He or she would first need to identify the life-cycle stage of the organization in question. This will suggest the dominant effectiveness criteria. The specific criteria—both means and ends—could then be selected from Table 2–3. Of course, the life-cycle consideration does not mean that criteria other than those stipulated might not be important. It merely suggests that certain ones appear to *dominate* in defining OE at particular stages.

Problems

The major problem with the competing-values approach is its lack of research-based support. We cannot say that it is valid or invalid. Only research can determine this. While there has been some promising results,[19] more research is necessary to confirm that (1) there exists, in fact, four distinct models and (2) when the models are linked with life stages, the effectiveness criteria identified are the dominant ones.

A secondary, but certainly relevant problem for practitioners, is as-

[19]See, for example, John Rohrbaugh, "The Monitoring of Organizational Effectiveness: Application of a Competing-Values Methodology in the Employment Service," paper presented at the Fortieth Annual Meeting of the Academy of Management, Detroit, 1980.

TABLE 2–3 Models, values, and effectiveness criteria

		EFFECTIVENESS CRITERIA	
MODEL	*VALUES*	*MEANS*	*ENDS*
Human relations	People and flexibility	Maintaining cohesion and morale	Value and development of human resources
Open systems	Flexibility and organization	Maintaining flexibility and readiness	Growth, resource acquisition, and external support
Rational goal	Organization and control	Planning, objective setting, and evaluation	Productivity and efficiency
Internal process	Control and people	Information management and coordination	Stability and equilibrium

sessing life-stage cycles. How does a manager accurately determine just where in the life cycle his or her organization is?

Value to Managers

Competing values acknowledges that multiple criteria and conflicting interests underlie any effort at defining and assessing OE. Additionally, by reducing a large number of effectiveness criteria into four conceptually clear organizational models, the competing-values approach can guide the manager in identifying the appropriateness of different criteria to different situations—specifically the changing activities and characteristics of the organization over its life cycle.

SUMMARY

Organizational effectiveness has proven difficult, some even say impossible, to define. Yet, as the central theme in organization theory, its meaning and measurement must be confronted. Four approaches have been offered as guides out of the organizational effectiveness "jungle."

The two dominant positions, and frequent antagonists, are the goal-attainment and systems approaches. The former defines OE as the accomplishment of ends. The latter focuses on means—defining OE as the ability to acquire inputs, process these inputs, channel the outputs, and maintain stability and balance in the system.

A more recent offering is the strategic-constituencies approach. It defines OE as satisfying the demands of those constituencies in the environment from which the organization requires support for its continued existence. Success, then, is the ability to placate those individuals, groups, and institutions upon which the organization depends for its continued operation.

The final perspective is one based on competing values. It has sought to synthesize the large number of OE criteria into four models, each of which is based on a given set of values, and each of which additionally is preferred depending on where an organization is in its life cycle.

To those who desire a simple definition of organizational effectiveness, this chapter will have proved a disappointment. OE is conceptually complex and, therefore, so must its definition. OE can be defined as *the degree to which an organization attains its short- (ends) and long-term (means) goals, the selection of which reflects strategic constituencies, the self-interest of the evaluator, and the life stage of the organization.*

FOR REVIEW AND DISCUSSION

1. On what factors do almost all definitions of OE agree?
2. Describe briefly the main contention of the
   a. goal-attainment approach.
   b. systems approach.
   c. strategic-constituencies approach.
   d. competing-values approach.
3. "The final test of an organization's effectiveness is survival." Build an argument to support this statement. Then build an argument to refute this statement.
4. "For a business firm, the bottom line is profit. You don't need any other measures of effectiveness." Build an argument to support this statement. Then build an argument to refute this statement.
5. MBO was presented as a goal-attainment approach. Could it also be part of the systems approach? Explain.
6. Contrast the value to managers of the four OE approaches presented in this chapter.
7. Select three or four organizations familiar to you and members of your class. How have you, *historically*, evaluated their effectiveness? How would you now assess their effectiveness using the goal-attainment, systems, and strategic-constituencies approaches?
8. Discuss this statement: "The Concorde SST is effective. In spite of being noisier, less fuel efficient, having less passenger seating, being less comfortable, and having higher initial cost and higher operating cost than the 747, DC-10, or L-1011, it flies three times faster."

9. "Goals are a viable standard against which OE can be measured." Build an argument to support this statement. Then build an argument to refute this statement.
10. Why might the administrator of a public agency use "ability to acquire budget increases" as a measure of OE? Could such a measure be dysfunctional?

PART II

ORGANIZATIONAL STRUCTURE: DEFINING THE KEY COMPONENTS

CHAPTER

3

COMPLEXITY

This chapter is the first of three concerned with identifying and describing the major components or dimensions comprising organizational structure. These three chapters constitute the foundation upon which most of the book sets. After we define what organization structure is, Chapters 6 through 10 analyze its causes, whereas Chapters 11 through 13 consider how the three structural components can be mixed and matched to create different organizational designs.

The three components we use for making up organization structure are complexity, formalization, and centralization. Acceptance of these components as the core dimensions of organizational structure, while generally widespread today, is not universal. Before we begin to discuss the first of these—complexity—it is worthwhile to list a dozen or so of the more popular variables used to define structural dimensions. Notice, if you will, how several of these variables have been defined differently by various theorists:

Administrative component. The number of line supervisors, managers, and staff personnel relative to the total number of employees.[1]

Autonomy. The extent to which top management has to refer certain typical decisions to a higher level of authority.[2]

[1]Bernard C. Reimann, "Dimensions of Structure in Effective Organizations: Some Empirical Evidence," *Academy of Management Journal*, December 1974, pp. 693–708.

[2]Ibid.

Centralization. The proportion of jobs whose occupants participate in decision making and the number of areas in which they participate;[3] or concentration of power arrangements;[4] or an index reflecting the locus of decision making with respect to major and specific policies, the degree of information sharing between levels, and the degree of participation in long-range planning.[5]

Complexity. The number of occupational specialties, the professional activity, and the professional training of employees.[6]

Delegation of authority. The ratio of the number of specific management decisions the chief executive delegated to the number he has the authority to make.[7]

Differentiation. The number of specialty functions represented in a firm[8] or the difference in cognitive and emotional orientation among managers in different departments.[9]

Formalization. The extent to which an employee's role is defined by formal documentation.[10]

Integration. The quality of the state of collaboration that exists among departments that are required to achieve unity of effort[11] or plans or feedback used for coordination between organizational units.[12]

Professionalization. The degree to which employees use a professional organization as a major reference, belief in service to the public, belief in self-regulation, dedication to one's field, and autonomy.[13]

Span of control. The number of subordinates that an individual manager can and should supervise.[14]

Specialization. The number of occupational specialties and the length of training required by each[15] or the degree to which highly specialized requirements are spelled out in formal job descriptions for various functions.[16]

[3]Jerald Hage, "An Axiomatic Theory of Organizations," *Administrative Science Quarterly,* December 1965, pp. 289–320.

[4]James D. Thompson, *Organizations in Action* (New York: McGraw-Hill, 1967).

[5]Reimann, "Dimensions of Structure."

[6]Jerald Hage and Michael Aiken, "Relationship of Centralization to Other Structural Properties," *Administrative Science Quarterly,* June 1967, pp. 79–80.

[7]Reimann, "Dimensions of Structure."

[8]Max Weber, *The Theory of Social and Economic Organizations,* ed., Talcott Parsons, and trans., A. M. Henderson and Talcott Parsons (New York: Free Press, 1947).

[9]Paul R. Lawrence and Jay W. Lorsch, *Organization and Environment* (Boston: Division of Research, Graduate School of Business Administration, Harvard University, 1967).

[10]Reimann, "Dimensions of Structure."

[11]Lawrence and Lorsch, *Organization and Environment.*

[12]Charles Perrow, *Organizational Analysis: A Sociological View* (Belmont, Calif.: Wadsworth, 1970).

[13]Richard H. Hall, "Professionalization and Bureaucratization," *American Sociological Review,* February 1968, pp. 92–104.

[14]William G. Ouchi and John B. Dowling, "Defining the Span of Control," *Administrative Science Quarterly,* September 1974, pp. 357–365.

[15]Hage, "An Axiomatic Theory of Organizations."

[16]Reimann, "Dimensions of Structure."

Standardization. The range of variation that is tolerated within the rules defining the jobs.[17]

Vertical span. The number of levels in the authority hierarchy from the bottom to the top.[18]

This listing is meant to indicate that there is, by no means, complete agreement among theorists as to what makes up the term organizational structure. As you proceed through this and the following two chapters, you will find that almost all the dimensions cited are considered directly or indirectly. So a more accurate conclusion may be that theorists *generally* agree on the dimensions of organization structure but disagree on operational definitions and whether a dimension is primary or subsumed under some larger dimension.

With acknowledgment made to the divergent labels and definitions given to structure, let us proceed to construct an in-depth understanding of the term by looking at the first of our dimensions—complexity.

DEFINING COMPLEXITY

Complexity refers to the degree of differentiation that exists within an organization. *Horizontal differentiation* considers the degree of horizontal separation between units. *Vertical differentiation* refers to the depth of the organizational hierarchy. *Spatial dispersion* encompasses the degree to which the location of an organization's facilities and personnel are dispersed geographically. An increase in any one of these three factors will increase an organization's complexity.

Horizontal Differentiation

Horizontal differentiation refers to the degree of differentiation between units based on the orientation of members, the nature of the tasks they perform, and their education and training. We can state that the larger the number of different occupations within an organization that require specialized knowledge and skills, the more complex that organization is. Why? Because diverse orientations make it more difficult for organizational members to communicate and more difficult for management to coordinate their activities. For instance, when organizations create specialized groups or expand departmental designations, they differentiate groups from each other, making interactions between those groups more complex. If the organization is staffed by people who have similar backgrounds, skills, and training, they are likely to see the world in more similar terms. Conversely, diversity increases the likelihood that they will have different goal em-

[17]Hage, "An Axiomatic Theory of Organizations."

[18]Reimann, "Dimensions of Structure."

phases, time orientations, and even a different work vocabulary. Job specialization reinforces differences—the chemical engineer's job is clearly different from that of the personnel recruitment interviewer. Their training is different. The language that they use on their respective jobs is different. They are typically assigned to different departments, which further reinforces their divergent orientations.

The most visible evidence in organizations of horizontal differentiation is job specialization and departmentation. As we will show, the two are interrelated. But let us begin by looking at job specialization. Our position will be that, all other things being equal, the more specialized the jobs in an organization, the more complex that organization becomes. Why does increased specialization lead to greater complexity? The answer, as we show later in this chapter, is that it requires more sophisticated and expensive methods for coordination and control. Yet most organizations rely heavily on specialization. This is because there are inherent efficiencies in the division of labor.

Over two hundred years ago, Adam Smith in his *Wealth of Nations,* discussed how specialization worked in the manufacturing of straight pins.[19] Smith noted that ten men, each doing particular tasks, could produce about 48,000 pins a day among them. However, if each worked separately and independently, those ten workers combined would be lucky to make 200, or even 10, pins in one day. If each had to draw the wire, straighten it, cut it, pound the head for the pin, sharpen the point, and solder the head and pin shaft, it would be quite a feat to produce 10 pins a day!

Why does division of labor work? First, in highly sophisticated and complex jobs, no one person can perform all the tasks due to physical limitations. If one person had to build a complete Chevrolet alone, even possessing the hundreds of skills necessary, it would take months of full-time effort. Second, limitations of knowledge act as a constraint. Some tasks require highly developed skills; others can be performed by the untrained. If many of the tasks require a large amount of skill, it may be impossible to find people capable of performing all the tasks involved. Further, if all employees are engaged in each step of, say, an organization's manufacturing process, all must have the skills necessary to perform both the most demanding and the least demanding tasks. The result would be that, except when performing the most skilled or highly sophisticated task, employees would be working below their skill level. Since skilled workers are paid more than unskilled, and their wages should reflect their highest level of skill, it represents poor usage of resources to pay individuals for their ability to do complex and difficult tasks while requiring them to do easy ones.

[19]Adam Smith, *An Inquiry into the Nature and Causes of the Wealth of Nations,* ed., Edward Cannan, 4th ed. (London: Methuen, 1925). Published originally in 1776.

Another element in favor of division of labor is efficiency. One's skill at performing a task increases through repetition. Efficiency is also exhibited in reducing time spent in changing tasks; the time spent in putting away one's tools and equipment from a prior step in the work process and getting ready for another are eliminated through specialization. Additionally, training for specialization is more efficient from the organization's perspective. It is easier and less costly to train workers to do a specific and repetitive task than to train them for difficult and complex activities. Finally, division of labor increases efficiency and productivity by encouraging the creation of special inventions and machinery.

Division of labor creates groups of specialists. The way in which we group these specialists is called departmentation. Departmentation is, therefore, the way in which organizations typically coordinate activities that have been horizontally differentiated. Departments can be created on the basis of simple numbers, function, product or service, client, geography, or process. Most large corporations will use all six. For instance, the basic segmentation may be by function (e.g., finance, manufacturing, sales, personnel). Sales, in turn, may be segmented by geography, manufacturing by product, individual production plants by process, and so forth. On the other hand, in a very small organization, simple numbers represent an informal and highly effective method by which people can be grouped.

One of the easiest ways in which to group activities is through allocating people on the basis of *simple numbers.* For example, if we have three supervisors and forty-five operative employees, we could divide the forty-five employees into three groups of fifteen and provide a supervisor for each. Although not sophisticated, the method is fast and easy and provides superficial equity. In small organizations, or at the lower levels of more complex organizations, it may be justified.

One of the most popular ways in which to group activities is by *function.* A hospital might have departments devoted to research, patient care, accounting, and so forth. A professional football organization would have units entitled Player Personnel, Ticket Sales, and Travel and Accommodations. Functional departmentation is most appropriate where highly specialized expertise must be consolidated.

Product or service departmentation is used at General Motors when activities are allocated to various divisions: Chevrolet, Pontiac, Oldsmobile, Buick, and Cadillac. Each of these divisions operates with considerable autonomy, supported by its own manufacturing, sales, and research and development groups. Wherever there are diverse and rapidly changing product or service lines, this form of departmentation is advantageous.

The particular type of *client* or customer that the organization seeks to reach can be the primary way in which it is departmentalized. For example, we may have sales units that handle only retailers, wholesalers, jobbers, or distributors. Similarly, a large law office may be segmented on the basis of corporate and individual clients, or a college along the lines of credit and noncredit courses. This method is appropriate where the differentiated needs of a clientele require consolidation for more rapid or comprehensive service.

Still another way in which to departmentalize can be on the basis of *geography* or territory. A sales organization may have western, midwestern, and eastern sales divisions. A large school district may have six high schools to provide for each of the major geographic territories within the district. This method of departmentation takes advantage of localized knowledge for more rapid decision making with comprehensive information.

When a customer or product must go through a series of units because of specialized equipment or personnel needs, the *process* form of departmentation may be best suited. Since each process requires different skills, this method offers a basis for the homogeneous categorizing of activities. The issuance of motor vehicle licenses in one state office provides an example. The process is made up of three steps, each representing a separate department: (1) validation, by Motor Vehicles; (2) processing, by Licensing; and (3) payment collection, by Treasury.

Vertical Differentiation

Vertical differentiation refers to the depth in the structure. Differentiation increases, and hence complexity, as the number of hierarchical levels in the organization increases. The more levels that exist between top management and operatives, the greater the potential of communication distortion, the more difficult it is to coordinate the decisions of managerial personnel, and the more difficult it is for top management to oversee the actions of operatives.

Vertical and horizontal differentiation should not be construed as independent of each other. Vertical differentiation may be understood best as a response to an increase in horizontal differentiation. As work is divided into smaller parts, it becomes increasingly necessary to coordinate tasks. Since high horizontal differentiation means that members will have diverse training and background, it may be difficult for the individual units to see how their tasks fit into the greater whole. A company specializing in road construction will employ surveyors, grading architects, bridge designers, clerical personnel, asphalt tenders, cement masons, truck drivers, and heavy-duty equipment operators. But someone must supervise each of these occupational groups to ensure that the work is done according to plan and on time. The result is a need for increased coordination, which shows itself in the development of vertical differentiation.

Organizations with the same number of employees need not have the same degrees of vertical differentiation. Organizations can be tall, with many layers of hierarchy, or flat, with few levels. The determining factor is the span of control.

The *span of control* defines the number of subordinates that a manager can direct effectively. If this span is wide, managers will have a number of subordinates reporting to them. If it is narrow, managers will have few underlings. All things being equal, the smaller the span, the taller the organization. This point is important and requires elaboration.

> Simple arithmetic will show that the difference between an average management span of, say, four, and one of eight in a company of 4,000 nonmanagerial employees can make a difference of two entire levels of management and of nearly 800 managers![20]

This statement is illustrated in Figure 3–1. You will note that each of the operative (lowest) levels contain 4,096 employees. All the other levels represent management positions: 1,365 managers (levels 1–6) with a span of 4; 585 managers (levels 1–4) with a span of 8. The narrower span (4) creates high vertical differentiation and a tall organization. The wider span creates a flatter organization.

The evidence is clouded on whether the tall or flat organization is more effective. Tall structures provide closer supervision and tighter "boss-

FIGURE 3–1 Contrasting spans of control

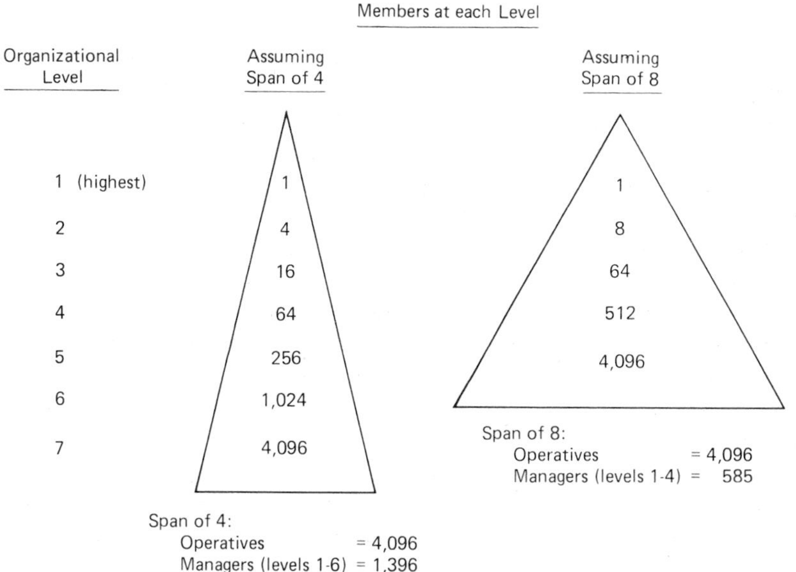

[20]Harold Koontz, "Making Theory Operational: The Span of Management," *Journal of Management Studies*, October 1966, p. 229.

oriented" controls, and coordination and communication become complicated because of the increased number of layers through which directives must go. Flat structures have a shorter and more simple communication chain, less opportunity for supervision since each manager has more people reporting to him, and reduced promotion opportunities as a result of fewer levels of management.

An early study at Sears, Roebuck lent support for the flat organization or low vertical differentiation case.[21] Two groups of Sears's stores, having between 150 and 175 employees, were the subject of the investigation. One group had only two levels of management: the store manager and approximately 30 department managers. The second group, in contrast, had three levels: a store manager, group managers, and merchandise managers. The conclusions drawn from this investigation were that, among the stores studied, the two-level organizations outperformed the three-level stores on sales volume, profit, and morale criteria.

It would be simplistic to conclude that wider spans lead to higher organizational performance. A more recent study, for instance, found no support for the general thesis that flat organizations are preferable.[22] The evidence suggested that the larger the organization, the less effective the flat organizations. Increased size brings with it complexity and more demands on every manager's time. Tall structures, with their narrow spans, reduce the manager's day-to-day supervisory responsibilities and give more time for involvement with the manager's own boss. Further evidence indicates that, in addition to the size of the organization, type of job and the individual characteristics of the jobholder will moderate the span-organizational effectiveness relationship.[23] Certain jobs require more direction, whereas others require less, and individuals, because of their education, skills, and personal characteristics, prefer varying degrees of freedom or control.

Spatial Dispersion

An organization can perform the same activities with the same degree of horizontal differentiation and hierarchical arrangement in multiple locations. Yet this existence of multiple locations increases complexity. Therefore, the third element in complexity is spatial dispersion, which refers to the degree to which the location of an organization's offices, plants, and personnel are dispersed geographically.

[21]James C. Worthy, "Organization Structure and Employee Morale," *American Sociological Review*, April 1950, pp. 169–179.

[22]Lyman W. Porter and E. E. Lawler, III, "Properties of Organization Structure in Relation to Job Attitudes and Job Behavior," *Psychological Bulletin*, July 1965, pp. 23–51.

[23]John M. Ivancevich and James H. Donnelly, Jr., "Relation of Organization and Structure to Job Satisfaction, Anxiety-Stress, and Performance," *Administrative Science Quarterly*, June 1975, pp. 272–280.

Spatial dispersion can be thought of as an extended dimension to horizontal and vertical differentiation. That is, it is possible to separate tasks and power centers geographically. This separation includes dispersion by both number and distance. Several examples may make this clearer.

A manufacturing company differentiates horizontally when it separates marketing functions from production. Yet, if essentially identical marketing activities are carried on in six geographically dispersed sales offices—Seattle, Los Angeles, Atlanta, New York, Toronto, and Brussels—while all production is done in a large factory in Cleveland, this organization is more complex than if both the marketing and production activities were performed at the same facility in Cleveland. Similarly, consider two banks. Both have assets of $300 million. But one operates in a branch-banking state—for example, California—while the other is in a unit-banking state—for example, Illinois—that legally forbids branch offices. The California bank might have a dozen branch offices in a dozen different cities to do the same amount of volume that the Illinois bank does under one roof. It's only logical that communication, coordination, and control are made easier for management in the Illinois bank where spatial dispersion is low.

The spatial concept also applies with vertical differentiation. While tall structures are more complex than flat ones, a tall organization in which different levels of authority are dispersed geographically is more complex than is its counterpart whose management is physically concentrated. If senior executives reside in one city, middle managers in half a dozen cities, and lower-level managers in a hundred different company offices around the world, complexity is increased. Even though computer technology has dramatically improved the ability for these separated decision makers to retrieve information and communicate with each other, complexity has still increased.

Finally, the spatial dispersion element considers distance as well as numbers. If the State of Delaware has two regional welfare offices—one in Dover and another in Wilmington—they will be approximately 45 miles apart. Even though the State of Alaska also has only two comparably sized offices—in Anchorage and Fairbanks, which are separated by 350 miles—the Delaware welfare organization is less complex.

In summary, spatial dispersion is the third element in defining complexity. It tells us that, even if horizontal and vertical differentiation were to remain the same across spatially separated units, the physical separation itself would increase complexity.

Do the Three Come as a Package?

What, if any, relationship is there among the three elements—horizontal differentiation, vertical differentiation, and spatial dispersion? At the extreme ranges of organization size, you would expect a high intercorrelation. Exxon, Polaroid, the Catholic Church, the U.S. Postal System, and most of the diversified industrial or government organizations with which you are familiar rate high on all three elements. Moe's Dry Cleaning, a small shop made up of only Moe and his wife, is low on all three. Can we generalize, however, beyond the extreme cases?

The answer is "No!" The three elements do not have to come as a package. It's been noted, for instance, that colleges usually have a low degree of vertical differentiation and little or no spatial dispersion, but a high degree of horizontal differentiation.[24] On the other hand, an army battalion is characterized by high vertical differentiation and little horizontal differentiation.[25]

A closer look at organizations tells us that the various elements may differ significantly within a given organization. This is particularly evident with horizontal differentiation. The work that employees have to do is most repetitive at the lowest levels in the organization, particularly at the operating core. This would include production and clerical activities. We would expect these types of jobs to have high horizontal differentiation. The manager's job, because of its varied activities, is not likely to be heavily horizontally differentiated.

WHY IS COMPLEXITY IMPORTANT?

We have identified the key elements in complexity. It would not be inappropriate now to inquire: So what? What does it mean for managers if their organization is high in complexity or low?

Organizations contain subsystems that require communication, coordination, and control if they are to be effective. The more complex an organization, the greater the need for effective communication, coordination, and control devices. In other words, as complexity increases, so do the demands on management to ensure that differentiated and dispersed activities are working smoothly and together toward achieving the organization's goals. The need for devices such as committees, computerized information systems, and formal policy manuals are reduced for organizations that are low in complexity. It is when there is a number of employees each doing a very small part of the activities that the organization needs to have done (most of these employees having little idea of what exactly others in the organization do every day), an elaborate hierarchy of management positions, and facilities and personnel spread over a large geographical area that it becomes clear that these communication and coordinating devices are absolutely necessary. So one way of answering the "what does complexity mean to managers?" question is to say

[24]Richard H. Hall, *Organizations: Structure and Process*, 2nd ed. (Englewood Cliffs, N.J.: Prentice-Hall, 1977), p. 139.

[25]Ibid.

that it creates different demands and requirements on the managers' time. The higher the complexity, the greater amount of attention they must pay to dealing with problems of communication, coordination, and control.

This has been described as a paradox in the analysis of organizations.[26] Management's decision to increase differentiation and dispersion is made typically in the interests of economy and efficiency. But these decisions create cross-pressures to add managerial personnel to facilitate control, coordination, and conflict reduction. So the economies that complexity creates may be counterbalanced by the increased burden of keeping the organization together. In fact, there may be a built-in automatic process in organizations that fosters increased complexity. Placed in a systems perspective, we know that organizations have a natural propensity to grow to survive. Over time, therefore, those organizations that survive will tend to become more complex as their own activities and the environment around them become more complex. We can add, then, that an understanding of complexity is important for it is a characteristic that managers should look for and expect if their organization is healthy.

MEASURING COMPLEXITY

Developing valid measures of complexity is an important methodological issue for the OT researcher. The issue is also of extreme value to practicing managers. The manager's interest is not in having elaborate measures to tap the elements of complexity but, rather, to answer the question: How can I determine whether an organization is high, moderate, or low in complexity? In the following pages, we try to answer this question by identifying measures of complexity. Consistent with our managerial focus, we avoid the precision that the researcher would demand and settle for measures that will provide reasonable estimates.

Horizontal Differentiation Measures

A number of measures can be used to determine the degree of horizontal differentiation. These include the number of departments, number of different job titles, level of training, extent of professional activity, degrees held, routineness of tasks, number of occupational specialties, and amount of professional activity.[27]

The two most critical factors appear to be the number of occupational specialties and level of training.[28] The greater the number of occupations

[26]Ibid., p. 147.

[27]See, for example, Hage and Aiken, "Relationship of Centralization"; and Robert Dewar and Jerald Hage, "Size, Technology, Complexity, and Structural Differentiation: Toward a Theoretical Synthesis," *Administrative Science Quarterly*, March 1978, pp. 111–136.

[28]Hage, "An Axiomatic Theory of Organizations."

and the longer the period of training required, the more complex the organization. We propose that managers can use the number of different job titles as an appropriate measure of occupational specialties. If this is unduly burdensome, the number of discrete subunits or departments in the organization may be substituted. The level of training can be calculated by computing the average length of training required by each occupational specialty.

Vertical Differentiation Measures

The measurement of vertical differentiation is quite simple. Since we want to know the depth of the structure, we need only to count the number of levels separating the chief executive from the employees working on the output. However, since this may vary within various divisions of the organization, we should consider both the extreme case and the average. This can be done by determining the number of levels in the deepest single division and the mean number of levels for the organization as a whole.[29]

Spatial Dispersion Measures

Spatial dispersion is a concept that actually embraces the number of geographically discrete facilities, the distance between these facilities, and the allocation of personnel among the discrete locations. So our measure of spatial dispersion must include more than merely a count of the number of geographic locations in the organization. It must also measure the average distance of the separated places from the organization's headquarters and the number of people in these separated locations in relation to the number at headquarters.[30] These latter measures acknowledge that complexity increases with the distance separating a unit from headquarters and the proportion of personnel located at these separated units.

An Application

This last section proposes a few simple (some may say "simplistic") questions to guide the practicing manager in assessing complexity, presents a scoring table for calculating an overall complexity score, and then compares a university with a major public transit district.

Table 3–1 presents seven questions, the answers to which can provide you with a reasonably accurate estimate of an organization's degree of complexity. The higher the score an organization receives on these questions, the greater the complexity.

[29]Richard H. Hall, J. Eugene Haas, and Norman J. Johnson, "Organizational Size, Complexity, and Formalization," *American Sociological Review*, December 1967, pp. 905–912.

[30]Ibid.

TABLE 3–1 Complexity questionnaire

Circle your response to each of the following items as they apply to the organization in question.

1. How many different job titles are there?
   a. very few
   b. small number
   c. moderate number
   d. large number
   e. great number
2. What proportion of employees hold advanced degrees or have many years of specialized training?
   a. 0–10%
   b. 11–20%
   c. 21–50%
   d. 51– 75%
   e. 76–100%
3. How many vertical levels separate the chief executive from those employees working on output in the deepest single division?
   a. 1 or 2
   b. 3 to 5
   c. 6 to 8
   d. 9 to 12
   e. more than 12
4. What is the mean number of levels for the organization as a whole?
   a. 1 or 2
   b. 3 to 5
   c. 6 to 8
   d. 9 to 12
   e. more than 12
5. What is the number of separate geographic locations where organization members are employed?
   a. 1 or 2
   b. 3 to 5
   c. 6 to 15
   d. 16 to 30
   e. more than 30
6. What is the average distance of these separate units from the organization's headquarters?
   a. less than 10 miles
   b. 11 to 100 miles
   c. 101 to 500 miles
   d. 501 to 3500 miles
   e. more than 3500 miles
7. What proportion of the organization's total work force are located at these separate units?
   a. less than 10%
   b. 11 to 25%
   c. 26 to 60%
   d. 61 to 90%
   e. more than 90%

Scoring: For all items, a = 1, b = 2, c = 3, d = 4, e = 5. Add up the score for all seven items. The sum of the item scores is the degree of complexity (out of a possible 35).

Two points are important to note. First, the result is an estimate. It is not a precise measuring tool. It is meant only to give you a rough measure of the three elements making up complexity. Second, your result means little in absolute terms. It is a relative measure. Texas Instruments may receive a higher complexity score than Walt Disney Productions, but remember that Exxon or ITT would probably outpoint Texas Instruments;

and Walt Disney Productions is immensely more complex than Moe's Dry Cleaning.

Now let us try applying the questions in Table 3–1 to two real-life organizations: San Diego State University (SDSU) and the San Francisco Bay Area Rapid Transit District (BART). SDSU has an enrollment of 35,000 students and employs 3,600 faculty and staff. There is an average of five levels from the president to the individual faculty member. The deepest division—in the area of Business and Financial Affairs—is seven. SDSU has eight colleges and sixty-seven separate departments or programs. It operates on two campuses—the main one in San Diego and a small satellite facility, with thirty faculty, about a hundred miles to the east.

BART employs 2,100 people to provide rapid transit service for the San Francisco–Oakland area. Approximately 30 percent of these employees hold advanced degrees or highly specialized training. The average number of levels in the organization is five; the longest is seven. BART has forty-eight separate locations where employees work, but 80 percent of its personnel are stationed at the headquarter's site.

In calculating SDSU's complexity score, we got the following: 1 = d, 2 = e, 3 = c, 4 = b, 5 = a, 6 = b, 7 = a, for a total of 18 points. BART's score is 1 = e, 2 = c, 3 = c, 4 = b, 5 = e, 6 = a, 7 = d, or 23 total points. What do these numbers tell us about these two organizations?

From a comparative viewpoint, BART is more complex, but not significantly so. On some items (numbers 2 and 6), SDSU is more complex. On others (1, 5, and 7), BART scores highest. There is some canceling out that occurs as a result of the two organizations' scoring differently on the seven items. So, while the organizations may differ significantly on some individual items, their total complexity scores are not dramatically different.

What do these scores mean to management? To answer this, we have to leave the relative security of making comparisons between absolute numbers and venture into the much more treacherous area of attaching labels to scores. It is dangerous to establish cutoff points for low, moderate, and high complexity scores, but nevertheless it has to be done. If we say that managers face increased coordination problems where complexity is high, we cannot avoid defining what is "high." With the caveat that any cutoff point is going to be somewhat arbitrary, we suggest the following interpretations: scores under 15 represent relatively low complexity, scores above 22 indicate relatively high complexity, and scores of 15 to 22 make up the moderate range. Using these definitions, SDSU would be labeled moderate and BART high in complexity.

A final comment before we move on to Chapter 4. The direct relationship we have proposed between high complexity scores and increased need for coordination has to be qualified to reflect the degree of formalization and centralization. As the next two chapters demonstrate, standardized rules and regulations and the determination of where decisions will be made can increase or decrease the need for coordination. Formalization and centralization may even be used as substitutes for managers performing direct coordinating activities.

SUMMARY

This chapter has described *complexity,* one of the three main components that defines organization structure. The term refers to the degree of differentiation that exists within an organization. It is composed of three elements: horizontal differentiation, vertical differentiation, and spatial dispersion.

Horizontal differentiation considers the degree of horizontal separation between units. It is measured by calculating the number of occupational specialties and the average length of training required by each. Vertical differentiation refers to the depth of the organization and is measured by counting the number of hierarchical levels separating the chief executive from the employees working on the organization's output. Spatial dispersion encompasses the degree to which jobs are dispersed geographically. It is measured by the number of separate locations, the average distance of these sites from headquarters, and the proportion of the organization's personnel located at these separate units.

The greater the horizontal differentiation, holding the span of control constant, the taller the hierarchy; the more geographically dispersed the organizational units, the more complex the organization. And the more complex the organization, the greater the difficulties of communication, coordination, and control.

FOR REVIEW AND DISCUSSION

1. Define complexity.
2. What are the advantages and disadvantages to division of labor?
3. What do we mean when we say that activities are "grouped by function?" Give several examples.
4. From a management perspective, is a tall or flat structure preferred? Explain.
5. What relationship is there between spatial dispersion and the two differentiation measures?
6. Are the three complexity measures intercorrelated? Discuss.
7. To assess the degree of complexity in an organization, describe the minimum information you would need.

8. Table 3–1 offers a short and quick measure of complexity. From a researcher's perspective, what criticisms could you lodge against this measure?
9. "An organization's revenues or budget and its complexity score are highly correlated." Do you agree or disagree? Discuss.
10. How might a manager's job differ in an organization low in complexity compared with his or her counterpart managing a highly complex organization?

CHAPTER

4

FORMALIZATION

The second component of organization structure is formalization. In this chapter, we define the term, explain its importance, introduce the two general ways in which management can achieve it, demonstrate the more popular formalization techniques, compare formalization with complexity, and conclude with a short list of questions, the answers to which can give you a good estimate of how formalized an organization is.

DEFINING FORMALIZATION

Formalization refers to the degree to which jobs within the organization are standardized. If a job is highly formalized, the job incumbent has a minimum amount of discretion over what is to be done, when it is to be done, and how he or she should do it. Employees can be expected to always handle the same input in exactly the same way, resulting in a consistent and uniform output. There are explicit job descriptions, lots of organizational rules, and clearly defined procedures covering work processes in organizations where there is high formalization. Where formalization is low, employees' behavior would be relatively nonprogrammed. Such jobs would offer employees a great deal of freedom to exercise discretion in their work. So formalization is a measure of standardization. Since an individual's discretion on the job is inversely related to the amount of behavior that is preprogrammed by the organization, the greater the standardization, the less input the employee has into how his or her work is to be done. This standardization not only eliminates employees' engaging in alternative behaviors, but also removes the need for employees to consider alternatives.

Does It Have to Be in Writing?

There is some debate as to whether the rules and procedures of formalization have to be in writing or whether the standardization of behavior created by tradition and unwritten regulations should also be included in the definition.

For instance, formalization has been defined as "the extent to which rules, procedures, instructions, and communications are written."[1] Following this definition, formalization would be measured by determining if the organization has a "policies and procedures manual," assessing the number and specificity of its regulations, reviewing job descriptions to determine the extent of elaborateness and detail, and looking at other similar official documents of the organization.

An alternative approach argues that formalization applies to both written and unwritten regulations.[2] Perceptions, then, are as important as reality. For measurement purposes, formalization would be calculated by considering, in addition to official documents of the organization, *attitudes* of employees as to the degree to which job procedures were spelled out and rules were enforced.

Of this debate, you might ask: Who cares? While the differences between these two positions might appear minor, this is not the case. When both approaches have been used, they obtain different results.[3] Although originally thought to merely be two separate ways of measuring the same construct—one measuring hard data and the other hard data and attitudes—research indicates otherwise. So the issue of whether formalization considers only the organization's written documents is critical to its definition.

Our position is that formalization should be construed in the larger context—including both written records and employee perceptions. This stand merely reflects the reality of organizational life. An employee's behavior is certainly influenced by the *informal* rules, procedures, and customs of the organization. If all sales representatives at Control Data Corporation "know" that they are expected to wear suits when calling on clients, does

[1]D. S. Pugh, D. J. Hickson, C. R. Hinings, and C. Turner, "Dimensions of Organization Structure," *Administrative Science Quarterly*, June 1968, p. 75.

[2]Jerald Hage and Michael Aiken, "Relationship of Centralization to Other Structural Properties," *Administrative Science Quarterly*, June 1967, p. 79.

[3]Johannes Pennings, "Measures of Organization Structure: A Methodological Note," *American Journal of Sociology*, November 1973, pp. 686–704; and Eric J. Walton, "The Comparison of Measures of Organization Structure," *Academy of Management Review*, January 1981, pp. 155–160.

it really have to be prescribed officially in writing to be effective? The answer is "No!" Its effect on behavior can be equally compelling.

Range of Formalization

It's important to recognize that the degree of formalization can vary widely among and within organizations. Certain jobs are well known to have little formalization. College book travelers—the people from various publishers who call on professors to discuss their companies' new publications—have a great deal of freedom in their jobs. They have no standard sales pitch, and the extent of rules and procedures governing their behavior may be little more than requiring the submission of a weekly sales report and some suggestions on what to emphasize for the various new titles. At the other extreme, on other jobs (for example, the clerical and editorial positions in the same publishing houses for which the college book travelers work), employees are required to "clock in" at their work station by 8 A.M. or be docked a half hour's pay and, once at that work station, are required to follow a set of precise procedures dictated by management.

It is generally true that the narrowest of unskilled jobs—those that are simplest and most repetitive—are most amenable to high degrees of formalization. The greater the professionalization of a job, the less likely it is to be highly formalized. Yet there are obvious exceptions. Public accountants and consultants, for instance, are required to keep detailed records of their hour-by-hour activities so that their companies can bill clients appropriately for their services. In general, however, the relationship holds. The jobs of lawyers, engineers, social workers, librarians, and like professionals tend to rate low on formalization.

Formalization differs not only with whether the jobs are unskilled or professional but also by level in the organization and by functional department. Employees higher in the organization are increasingly involved in activities that are less repetitive and require unique solutions. The discretion that managers have increases as they move up the hierarchy. So formalization tends to be inversely related to level in the organization. Additionally, the kind of work in which people are engaged influences the degree of formalization. Jobs in production are typically more formalized than are those in sales or research. Why? Because production tends to be concerned with stable and repetitive activities. Such jobs lend themselves to standardization. In contrast, the sales department must be flexible to respond to changing needs of customers, while research must be flexible if it is to be innovative.[4]

[4]Henry Mintzberg, *The Structuring of Organizations* (Englewood Cliffs, N.J.: Prentice-Hall, 1979), pp. 91–92.

WHY IS FORMALIZATION IMPORTANT?

Organizations use formalization because of the benefits that accrue from regulating employees' behavior. Standardizing behavior reduces variability. McDonald's, for example, can be confident that a "Big Mac" will look and taste the same whether it is made at an outlet in Portland, Maine; Biloxi, Mississippi; Fairbanks, Alaska; or Paris, France. The reason is that McDonald's relies on high formalization.

Standardization also promotes coordination. Football coaches spend dozens of hours introducing a complex set of procedures for their players. When the quarterback calls "Wing-Right-44-on-3," each team member knows exactly what task he is to perform. Formalization allows automobiles to flow smoothly down the assembly line, as each worker on the line performs a highly standardized set of repetitive activities. It also prevents members of a paramedic unit from standing around at the scene of an accident and arguing about who is to do what. If you watch the behaviors of the medical staff in the operating room on an episode of the TV series, "M.A.S.H.," you will observe a highly coordinated group of organizational members performing a precise set of standardized procedures.

The economics of formalization should also not be overlooked. The greater the formalization, the less discretion required from a job incumbent. This is relevant because discretion costs money. Jobs that are low on formalization demand greater judgment. Given that sound judgment is a scarce quality, organizations have to pay more (in terms of wages, salaries, and benefits) to acquire the services of individuals who possess this ability. To secure the services of a plant purchasing agent who can perform purchasing duties effectively and efficiently *with no formal directives* might cost an organization $40,000 a year. However, if the purchasing agent's job is highly formalized to the point that a comprehensive manual is available to resolve nearly any question or problem that might occur, this job may be done just as competently by someone with far less experience and education—for $15,000 a year!

This explains, incidentally, why many large organizations have accounting manuals, personnel manuals, and purchasing manuals, occasionally running to several thousand pages in length. These organizations have chosen to formalize jobs wherever possible so as to get the most effective performance from employees at the lowest cost.

THE "MAKE OR BUY" DECISION

We noted earlier the difference between unskilled and professional employees and indicated a relationship between each classification and the propensity to formalize jobs. In this section we propose that formalization can take place on the job or off. When it's done on the job, we use the term *externalized* behavior. This means that the formalization is external to the employee; that is, the rules, procedures, and regulations governing the individual's work activity are specifically defined, codified, and enforced through direct management supervision. This characterizes the formalization of unskilled employees. It is also what is typically meant by the term "formalization." Professionalization is another alternative—it creates *internalized* behavior. Professionals are socialized before entering the organization. So, while formalization can take place in the organization, we will show how others are hired preprogrammed with their rules already built in. When it comes to formalization, therefore, organizations can choose to "make or buy" the behaviors they desire.[5]

Socialization refers to an adaptation process by which individuals learn the values, norms, and expected behavior patterns for the job and organization in which they will be a part. We discuss this term in detail later in this chapter. However, it is important, at this time, to recognize that all organizations socialize their members. All employees will receive at least some molding and shaping on the job, but for certain members, the socialization process will be substantially accomplished *before* they join the organization. This is specifically true of professionals.

Professionals undergo many years of education and training before they practice their craft. Engineers, for instance, must spend four or more years studying before they can be certified. This education process gives the engineer a common body of knowledge that can be called upon in performing the job. It is often overlooked, however, that this training also includes molding the person to think and act like an engineer. In a similar vein, it can be argued that one of the main tasks of a business school is to socialize students to the attitudes and behaviors that business firms want. If business executives believe that successful employees value the profit ethic, are loyal, will work hard, desire to achieve, and willingly accept directives from their superiors, they can hire individuals out of business schools who have been premolded in this pattern.

So management has two decisions. First, what degree of standardization of behavior is desired? Second, will the standardization desired be "made" in house or "bought" outside. The in-house variety is emphasized with unskilled employees, although all members will get some of this if only to fine tune the member to the unique culture of the particular organization. For the most part, unskilled jobs are highly differentiated—both horizontally and vertically—and formalization by way of rules, work flow procedures, and training is used to coordinate and control the behavior of people performing these jobs. In contrast, when management hires

[5]Charles Perrow, *Complex Organizations: A Critical Essay* (Glenview, Ill.: Scott, Foresman, 1972), p. 27.

professionals, it is "buying" individuals whose prior training has included internalizing their job descriptions, procedures, and rules.

Direct on-the-job formalization and professionalization are basically substitutes for each other. "The organization can either control [employee behavior] directly through its own procedures and rules, or else it can achieve indirect control by hiring duly trained professionals."[6] We can expect to find that, as the level of professionalization increases in an organization, the level of formalization decreases.

FORMALIZATION TECHNIQUES

Managers have at their disposal a number of techniques by which they can bring about the standardization of employee behavior. In this section, we review the most popular of these techniques.

Selection

Organizations do not choose employees at random. Job applicants are processed through a series of hurdles designed to differentiate individuals likely to be successful job performers from those likely to be unsuccessful. These hurdles typically include completion of application blanks, employment tests, interviews, and background investigations. Applicants can and do get rejected at each of these steps.

An effective selection process will be designed to determine if job candidates "fit" into the organization. A "good" employee is defined as one who will not only perform his or her job in a satisfactory manner, but whose personality, work habits, and attitudes align with what the organization desires. If the selection process does anything, it tries to prevent the employment of misfits; that is, individuals who do not accept the norms of the organization. A recruiter for an executive search firm once confided that he believed that the secret to the successful placement of middle- and top-level managers was attaining a reading of the organization's personality or climate and then screening applicants for compatibility. He noted that it was rarely difficult to find candidates with the experience and abilities to fill a vacancy. The problem was finding the right chemistry between a candidate and the people who were doing the hiring. The recruiter said he spent considerable time just talking with executives in the client company. This was done in the belief that certain "types" of people are more likely than others to fit into the company.

Selection should be recognized as one of the most widely used techniques by which organizations control employee discretion. Whether the

[6]Ibid., p. 101.

hiring covers unskilled or professional employees, organizations use the selection process to screen in the right people and screen out those who think and act in ways that management considers undesirable. The selection of professionals may be done with greater latitude than the selection of unskilled employees—the former's prior professionalization reducing the need for the organization to identify misfits. Part of this task was assumed by the universities and associations that confer the professional's certification. However, all new members must meet the organization's minimum requirements of an acceptable employee, and the selection process provides one of the most popular mechanisms for achieving this end.

Role Requirements

Individuals in organizations fulfill roles. Every job carries with it expectations on how the role incumbent is supposed to behave. Job analysis, for instance, defines the jobs that need to be done in the organization and what employee behaviors are necessary to perform the jobs. This analysis develops the information from which job descriptions are created. The fact that organizations identify jobs to be done and the desirable role behaviors that go with those jobs means that role expectations play a major part in regulating employee behavior.

Role expectations may be explicit and defined narrowly. In such cases, the degree of formalization is high. Of course, the role expectations attributed to a given job by management and members of a role set can traverse the spectrum from explicit and narrow to very loose. The latter, for instance, allows employees freedom to react to situations in unique ways. It puts minimum constraints on the role incumbent. So organizations that develop exacting and complicated job descriptions go a long way toward defining the expectations of how a particular role is to be played. By loosening or tightening role expectations, organizations are actually loosening or tightening the degree of formalization.

Rules, Procedures, and Policies

Rules are explicit statements that tell an employee what he or she ought or ought not to do. Procedures are a series of interrelated sequential steps that employees follow in the accomplishment of their job tasks. Policies are guidelines that set constraints on decisions that employees make. Each of these represents techniques that organizations use to regulate the behavior of members.

Sales clerks are told that no checks can be accepted unless the customer has three pieces of identification. All level 3 managers are instructed that expenditures over $500 require approval by a superior. Employees are required to submit expense reimbursement reports, typed, on form B-446, in duplicate, within thirty days of the outlay. Each of these examples represents the imposition of rules on employees. Their identifying characteristic is that they tell employees explicitly what they can do, how they are to do it, and when they are to do it. Rules leave no room for employee judgment or discretion. They state a particular and specific required behavior pattern.

Procedures are established to ensure standardization of work processes. The same input is processed in the same way and the output is the same each day. If one were to ask an accounts payable clerk what his or her job involved, the answer would probably correspond closely with the procedurized description of his or her activities. Rather than have the clerk, through trial and error, develop an individualized way of handling the accounts payable (which might include some critical deviations from the pattern that management wants the clerk to follow), the organization has provided a procedure. For example, when invoices are received daily, they are stamped in, alphabetized, and merged with purchase orders; then tabulations are checked and vouchers are prepared. Vouchers are to be completed as follows: use preprinted voucher tags, place voucher number in top right corner, place date in top left corner, write in appropriate accounts to be charged, check to ensure total of accounts equals invoice amount, initial in bottom right corner. These steps follow a specific standardized sequence that results in a uniform output.

Policies provide greater leeway than do rules. Rather than specifying a particular and specific behavior, policies allow employees to use discretion but within limited boundaries. The discretion is created by including judgmental terms (such as "best," "satisfied," "competitive"), which the employee is left to interpret. The statement from the personnel manual at a major midwestern hospital that it will "pay competitive wages" illustrates a policy. This policy does not tell the wage and salary administrator what should be paid, but it does provide parameters for wage decisions to be made. The term "competitive" requires interpretation, yet it sets discretionary limits. If other local hospitals pay between \$4.75 and \$5.40 an hour for an inexperienced orderly, hourly rates of \$4.20 or \$6.25 would clearly not be within the guidelines set by the policy.

Policies need not be written to control discretion. Employees pick up on an organization's implied policies merely by observing the actions of members around them. An employment interviewer in the personnel department of the hospital just described may never find in writing a policy that the hospital gives hiring preference to relatives of current employees, but nepotism may be an observable practice. The interviewer can be expected to be socialized to this implied policy, and its impact on the interviewer's behavior will be just as strong as if it were printed in boldface type in the personnel policy manual.

Training

Many organizations provide training to employees. This includes the on-the-job variety where understudy assignments, coaching, and apprenticeship methods are used to teach employees preferred job skills, knowledge, and attitudes. It also includes off-the-job training such as classroom lectures, films, demonstrations, simulation exercises, and programmed instruction. Again, the intent is to instill in employees preferred work behaviors and attitudes.

New employees are often required to undergo a brief orientation program where they are familiarized with the organization's objectives, history, philosophy, and rules as well as relevant personnel policies such as hours of work, pay procedures, overtime requirements, and benefit programs. In many cases, this is followed by specific job training. For instance, new computer programmers at one bank undergo several days of training to learn the organization's system. Counter help at McDonalds are required to read the company's policy manual, after which they undergo several weeks of on-the-job training where their job behaviors receive close scrutiny by the operating managers. The recent liberal arts graduate who is hired by a New York book publisher to be a production editor may understudy a seasoned veteran for three to six months before being set free on his or her own.

Rituals

Rituals are used as a formalization technique with members who will have a strong and enduring impact on the organization. This certainly includes individuals who aspire to senior-level management positions, but also pledges seeking active status in a fraternity or faculty members vying for tenure. The common thread underlying rituals is that members must prove that they can be trusted and are loyal to the organization before they can be "knighted." The "proving process" is the ritual.

Business firms that promote from within do not put new employees into top management positions. The typical reason cited would be that they lack relevant experience. Given the fact that many promotions place an employee in situations very unlike their previous jobs, it is probably correct to conclude that experience is only part of the explanation. Another part is that top management positions are held out as rewards to those in the company that prove by their abilities, length of service, and loyalty that they are committed to the goals and norms of the firm. Managers are, after all, "the guardians of the organization's ideology."[7] Senior managers are the *primary* gatekeepers. As such, the organization has a heavy stake in

[7]Ibid., p. 100.

ensuring that managers have proven themselves before they are promoted to influential senior positions. Even among firms that may fill their senior positions from outside the organization, great care is taken to assure that the candidate has paid his or her "dues" on earlier jobs and, based on personality tests and extensive interviews with top executives, appears likely to fit in.

College faculty members go through a similar ritual in their quest for permanent employment—tenure. Typically, the faculty member is on probation for six years. At the end of that period, the member's colleagues must make one of two choices: extend a tenured appointment or issue a one-year terminal contract. What does it take to receive tenure? It usually requires satisfactory teaching performance, service to the department and university, and scholarly activity. But, of course, what satisfies the requirements for tenure at one university may be appraised as inadequate at another. The key is that the tenure decision, in essence, asks those who are tenured to assess whether the candidate has demonstrated, based on six years of performance, whether he or she fits in. Colleagues who have been socialized properly will have proved themselves worthy of being granted tenure. Every year, some good faculty members at colleges and universities throughout North America are denied tenure. In some cases, this action is a result of poor performance across the board. More often, however, the decision can be traced to the faculty member's not doing well in those areas that the tenured faculty believe are important. The instructor who spends dozens of hours of each week preparing for class, achieves outstanding evaluations by students, but neglects his or her research and publication activities may be passed over for tenure. What has happened, simply, is that the instructor has failed to adapt to the norms set by the organization. The astute faculty member will assess early on in the probationary period what attitudes and behaviors his or her colleagues want and will then proceed to give it to them. And, of course, by doing so the tenured faculty have made significant strides toward standardizing tenure candidates.

THEORY X, THEORY Y, AND FORMALIZATION

How much formalization is desirable? More than twenty years ago, psychologist Douglas McGregor proposed two views on the nature of man that can be useful to management in resolving the degree of formalization that is appropriate.[8]

McGregor's two views—labeled Theory X and Theory Y—have re-

[8]Douglas McGregor, *The Human Side of Enterprise* (New York: McGraw-Hill, 1960).

ceived considerable attention by students of management. After viewing the way in which managers dealt with employees, McGregor concluded that a manager's view of human nature is based on a certain grouping of assumptions and that people tend to mold their behavior toward subordinates according to these assumptions.

Under Theory X, the four assumptions held by managers are:

1. Employees inherently dislike work and, whenever possible, will attempt to avoid it.
2. Since employees dislike work, they must be coerced, controlled, or threatened with punishment to achieve desired goals.
3. Employees will shirk responsibilities and seek formal direction whenever possible.
4. Most workers place security above all other factors associated with work and will display little ambition.

In contrast to these negative views toward human nature, McGregor listed four other assumptions that he called Theory Y:

1. Employees can view work as being as natural as rest or play.
2. People will exercise self-direction and self-control if they are committed to the objectives.
3. The average person can learn to accept, even seek, responsibility.
4. Creativity—that is, the ability to make good decisions—is widely dispersed throughout the population and is not necessarily the sole province of those in managerial positions.

We will not address the issue of whether people can be pegged into one of two "theories." But, given that managers' behavior does reflect general acceptance of one set of assumptions over the other, it seems reasonable to postulate that the sets of assumptions that managers hold about other people, especially as they relate to subordinates, will be a major influence on the degree of formalization they think is desirable.

If managers hold Theory Y assumptions—employees are seen as being responsible and having good judgment and self-control—formalization should be low. If employees are perceived as being incapable of making their own decisions, then management will probably want to develop a large body of rules and regulations to guide their behavior. The result is that formalization can be expected to be high. Other contingencies influencing the degree of formalization are discussed in Chapters 6 through 10, but management assumptions about employees is probably an important factor in determining the degree of formalization they select.

RELATIONSHIP BETWEEN FORMALIZATION AND COMPLEXITY

There is no simple relationship between formalization and complexity. From one perspective, both result in increased control. Specialization, standardization through rules and regulations, and professionalization all improve management's ability to predict employee behavior. One argument, therefore, is that the greater the degree of complexity, the lower the formalization.[9] For instance, the highly trained specialist or professional would not require a great number of rules and regulations. High formalization would only be redundant. Another argument, however, is that, if employees are highly specialized by tasks, their routines will be standardized and an increased number of rules and regulations will govern their behavior.[10] Assembly-line workers have highly specialized jobs with standardized routines and a wealth of formal rules and procedures to follow.

What is the answer? Both positions are correct. The critical determinant is whether complexity is achieved by increasing vertical differentiation or horizontal differentiation.

High vertical differentiation means that the organization will have an increased number of managers, technical specialists, and professionals. In contrast to operatives, these personnel do nonroutine tasks. Their previous socialization will have instilled internal standards of control, so that organizationally imposed formalization will tend to be low. High horizontal differentiation, on the other hand, is achieved typically by hiring unskilled personnel to perform routine and repetitive tasks. Division of labor will result in a high degree of formalization to facilitate coordination and control. The direction of the differentiation, then, determines the relationship between formalization and complexity.

MEASURING FORMALIZATION

Table 4–1 presents a brief test, the answers to which can give you a reasonable estimate of the degree of formalization in a unit or organization. It taps the major elements in formalization: the degree to which job descriptions and regulations are specified, the degree of supervision, the amount of freedom given to subordinates and managers, the degree of work standardization, and the degree to which regulations exist and are enforced.

The questionnaire differentiates levels in the hierarchy. For definitional purposes, operative employees are all nonsupervisory and nonman-

[9]Jerald Hage, "An Axiomatic Theory of Organizations," *Administrative Science Quarterly*, December 1965, p. 303.

[10]Pugh et al., "Dimensions of Organization Structure," pp. 65–105.

TABLE 4–1 Formalization questionnaire

Circle your response to each of the following items as they apply to the organization in question.

1. Written job descriptions are available for
   a. operative employees only.
   b. operative employees and first-line supervisors only.
   c. operative, first-line supervisory, and middle management personnel.
   d. operative, first-line supervisory, middle and upper-middle management personnel.
   e. all employees, including senior management.

2. Where written job descriptions exist, how closely are employees supervised to ensure compliance with standards set in the job description?
   a. very loose
   b. loose
   c. moderately close
   d. close
   e. very close

3. How much latitude are employees allowed from the standards?
   a. a great deal
   b. a large amount
   c. a moderate amount
   d. very little
   e. none

4. What percentage of nonmanagerial employees are given written operating instructions or procedures for their jobs?
   a. 0–20%
   b. 21–40%
   c. 41–60%
   d. 61– 80%
   e. 81–100%

5. Of those nonmanagerial employees given written instructions or procedures, to what extent are they followed?
   a. none
   b. little
   c. some
   d. a great deal
   e. a very great deal

6. To what extent are supervisors and middle managers free from rules, procedures, and policies when they make decisions?
   a. a very great deal
   b. a great deal
   c. some
   d. little
   e. none

7. What percentage of all the rules and procedures that exist within the organization are in writing?
   a. 1–20%
   b. 21–40%
   c. 41–60%
   d. 61– 80%
   e. 81–100%

Scoring: For all items, a = 1, b = 2, c = 3, d = 4, e = 5. Add up the score for all seven items. The sum of the item scores is the degree of formalization (out of a possible 35).

agerial personnel, and first-line supervisors are the people who directly oversee operatives.

As in Chapter 3, let us establish some categories from which interpretations can be made and then work through an application. Our experiments with Table 4–1 indicate that scores under 18 represent relatively low formalization, scores above 25 indicate relatively high formalization, and scores of 18 to 25 show moderate formalization. Of course, our measurement questionnaire is not a precise tool. It would be reasonable to expect deviations based on differences in interpretation, but these should amount to no more than several points either way. So, while scores of 17 and 19 may suggest the difference between low and moderate formalization, common sense suggests caution in such labeling. Scores with large differences, though, are important. A score of 15 is low, whereas one of 30 is high. The latter organization is considerably more formalized than is the former.

We used our seven-item questionnaire with two units in the same organization to demonstrate not only how the instrument works but also that different parts of an organization may have significantly different degrees of structure. The organization is Western Electric (WE), the manufacturing arm of the Bell System. WE's production facilities were found to be highly regulated. In the unit, for instance, that assembles relay equipment, all employees have formal job descriptions and are supervised closely, procedure manuals exist for all jobs, and managers follow closely the corporate policy manual in the making of day-to-day decisions. This unit scored 29 points on the formalization questionnaire. Evaluation of WE's research and development labs told a completely different story. Staffed by professionals, many with Ph.D.s and years of scientific training, you would expect less formalization. Our score of 16 suggests this to be the case, but not to the degree that one might have predicted. The research scientists had a great deal of freedom, but supervisors and managers had to follow corporate policies and file many of the same reports that those in the more routine divisions did. Additionally, the jobs of clerical employees in the lab were as programmed as their counterparts in production.

SUMMARY

Formalization refers to the degree to which jobs within the organization are standardized. The higher the formalization, the more regulated the behavior of the employee.

Formalization can be achieved on the job. In such cases, the organization would make use of rules and procedures to regulate what employees do. But a pseudoformalization process can occur off the job in the training the employee received prior to joining the organization. This characterizes professional employees. The professionalization they have undergone has socialized them to think and behave in accordance with the norms of their profession.

The most popular formalization techniques are the selection process (for identifying individuals who will fit in to the organization); role requirements; rules, procedures, and policies; training; and having employees undergo rituals to prove their loyalty and commitment to the organization.

FOR REVIEW AND DISCUSSION

1. Define formalization.
2. "Management would probably prefer high formalization." Do you agree or disagree? Discuss.
3. "Employees would probably prefer high formalization." Do you agree or disagree? Discuss.
4. Compare the formalization of unskilled workers with that of professionals.
5. What can management do to increase formalization?
6. What are Theories X and Y? How do they relate to formalization?
7. "An organization that is high in complexity will be high in formalization." Do you agree or disagree? Discuss.
8. What factors would you want to look at if you were trying to measure formalization?
9. How would you derive an overall measure of an organization's formalization if units of the organization differ greatly on their individual scores?
10. How might the systems framework better help you to understand the concept of formalization?

CHAPTER

5

CENTRALIZATION

Where are decisions made in the organization: up on top by senior management or down low where the decision makers are closest to the action? This question introduces the last of the components that make up organization structure. The subject of this chapter is centralization and, its counterpart, decentralization.

DEFINING CENTRALIZATION

Centralization is the most problematic of the three components. Most theorists concur that the term refers to the degree to which decision making is concentrated at a single point in the organization. A high concentration implies high centralization, whereas a low concentration indicates low centralization or what may be called decentralization. There is also agreement that it is distinctly different from spatial dispersion. Centralization is concerned with the dispersion of authority to make decisions within the organization, not geographic dispersion. However, beyond these points, the water quickly becomes muddy. The following questions suggest the breadth of the problem.

1. *Do we look only at formal authority?* There is no doubt that the term should encompass those individuals in the organization who are authorized formally to make decisions. But what about those people who have informal influence over decisions? Jim Miller is a $6.80-an-hour metal handler at a large steel company, but his fiancée's father is vice president for manu-

facturing at the firm. The future father-in-law frequently asks for and follows the advice provided by Jim. At a major television network, Barbara Harris is a staff research specialist in the programming department. Her job is to identify characteristics that differentiate successful from unsuccessful prime-time programs. She prepares reports on her findings, but she has no formal authority. Yet the director of programming has her attend meetings informally where decisions for future programming are made. Additionally, he rarely makes a major programming decision without checking out Barbara's opinion. Jim and Barbara have no formal authority in their positions, but they do affect decisions. Is this consistent with high centralization or low?

2. *Can policies override decentralization?* Many organizations push the making of decisions down to lower levels, but then the decision makers are bound by policies. Because decision choices are constrained by policies, do these low-level decision makers actually have discretion or is it artificial? In other words, has decentralization really occurred if policies force the decisions to conform with what they would be if top management made them themselves? One could argue that, even though employees low in the organization are making many decisions but those decisions are programmed by organizational policies, a high degree of centralization exists.

3. *What does "concentration at a single point" mean?* There may be agreement that centralization refers to concentration at a single point, but exactly what that means is not clear. Does a "single point" mean an individual, a unit, or a level in the organization? Most people think of centralized decisions as being made high in the organization, but this may not be true if the single point is a low-level manager. Does it matter to operative employees whether decisions are made one level above them or six? Either way, they are allowed little input into their work. If operative employees are not permitted to participate in decisions about their work, isn't decision making centralized regardless of whether it is concentrated at the next level up or at the very top of the organization?

4. *Does an information processing system that closely monitors decentralized decisions maintain centralized control?* Advanced information technology, via computers, facilitates decentralization. But that same technology allows top managers to learn of the consequences of any decision rapidly and to take corrective action if the decision is not to top management's liking. While discretion is apparently delegated downward, is it real decentralization? There is no real sharing of control in the organization. One could agree that there is only the appearance of decentralization, and top management maintains effective centralized control.

5. *Does the control of information by lower-level members result in the decentralization of what appears to be centralized decisions?* Managers rely on those beneath them to provide the information from which decisions are made. Information is passed upward but, of course, it is filtered. If it were not screened and filtered, top management would be inundated with information. But this filtering requires subordinates to make judgments and interpretations of what information should be transmitted. Thus, the filtering process gives subordinates power to pass onto top management only that information that they want top management to have. Further, they can structure that information in such a way so as to get the decisions made that the lower-level members want. As such, even though it may appear that decision making is centralized with top management, is it not really decentralized, since the decision inputs, and hence eventually the decisions, are controlled by lower-level personnel?

These questions were not introduced to confuse you. They are meant to dramatize our position that centralization is a tough concept to nail down. Yet our pragmatic approach demands that we develop a definition that can resolve these issues. Toward that end, centralization can be described more specifically as *the degree to which the formal authority to make discretionary choices is concentrated in an individual, unit, or level (usually high in the organization), thus permitting employees (usually low in the organization) minimum input into their work.*

This more elaborate definition answers the questions posed earlier. (1) Centralization is concerned only with the formal structure, not the informal organization. It applies only to formal authority. (2) Centralization looks at decision discretion. Where decisions are delegated downward but extensive policies exist to constrain the discretion of lower-level members, there is increased centralization. Policies can, therefore, act to override decentralization. (3) Concentration at a single point can refer to an individual, unit, or level, but the single point *implies* concentration at a high level. (4) Information processing can improve top management control, but the decision choice is still with the low-level member. Thus, an information processing system that closely monitors decentralized decisions does not maintain centralized control. (5) The transference of all information requires interpretation. The filtering that occurs as information passes through vertical levels is a fact of life. The top managers are free to verify the information they receive and to hold subordinates accountable in their choices of what they filter out, but control of information input is a form of de facto decentralization. Management decisions are centralized if concentrated at the top, but the more the information input to those decisions is filtered through others, the less concentrated and controlled the decision is.

AUTHORITY AND THE CHAIN OF COMMAND

The concept of centralization meshes with the concepts of authority and the chain of command. Authority is what is centralized or decentralized, and the chain of command defines the path that decentralization follows. The importance of these two concepts requires a clear understanding of what they mean.

Authority

Authority is the right to act, or command others to act, toward the attainment of organizational goals. The most important term in this definition is the word *right*. It is this term that specifies legitimacy in our organizational context.

Authority, therefore, is related to one's position within the organization. Each managerial position has specific inherent rights that incumbents acquire from the position's rank or title. It has nothing to do directly with the person. Authority lies in the position. The expression "The King is dead; long live the King" illustrates the concept of authority. Since the rights are inherent in the job, as soon as you accept a position, you assume the authority that goes with it. Of course, when you vacate that position, your rights are lost.

The two types of authority referenced most widely are line and staff. Line authority is a superior's authority over all the activities of his or her subordinates. Staff authority, on the other hand, is restricted. Those who hold staff authority can give advice and service to the line, but they have no authority to put their recommendations into action. So all superior-subordinate relationships are characterized by line authority. But when legal personnel provide advice to the line or the assistant to the President helps the boss by analyzing a report, both are acting through staff authority. Those with staff authority can study a problem and make decisions and recommendations, but they have no authority to put their recommendations into action. If you saw a letter signed, "John Billings *for* William R. Stanton," John Billings would be staff and William R. Stanton would be line. Billings's position is without the authority to act, so he must act through the authority inherent in Stanton's position. In a typical industrial firm, departments such as personnel, accounting, and marketing are staff units that support the line manufacturing function.

Chain of Command

Figure 5–1 is the organization chart of a metropolitan hospital. As with all organization charts, it shows authority relationships. More specifically, however, it identifies the chains of command. These are the superior-sub-

FIGURE 5—1 Hospital organization chart

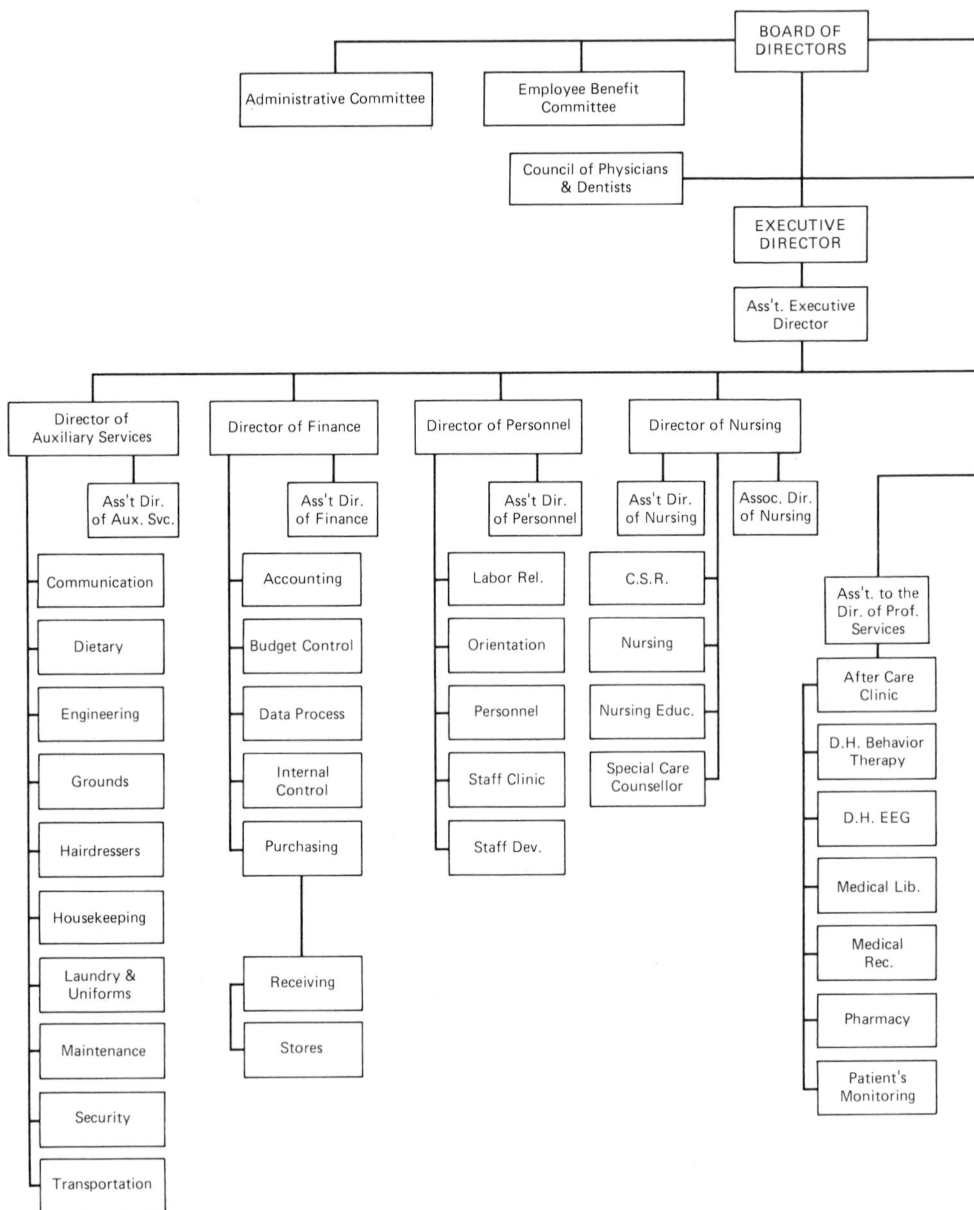

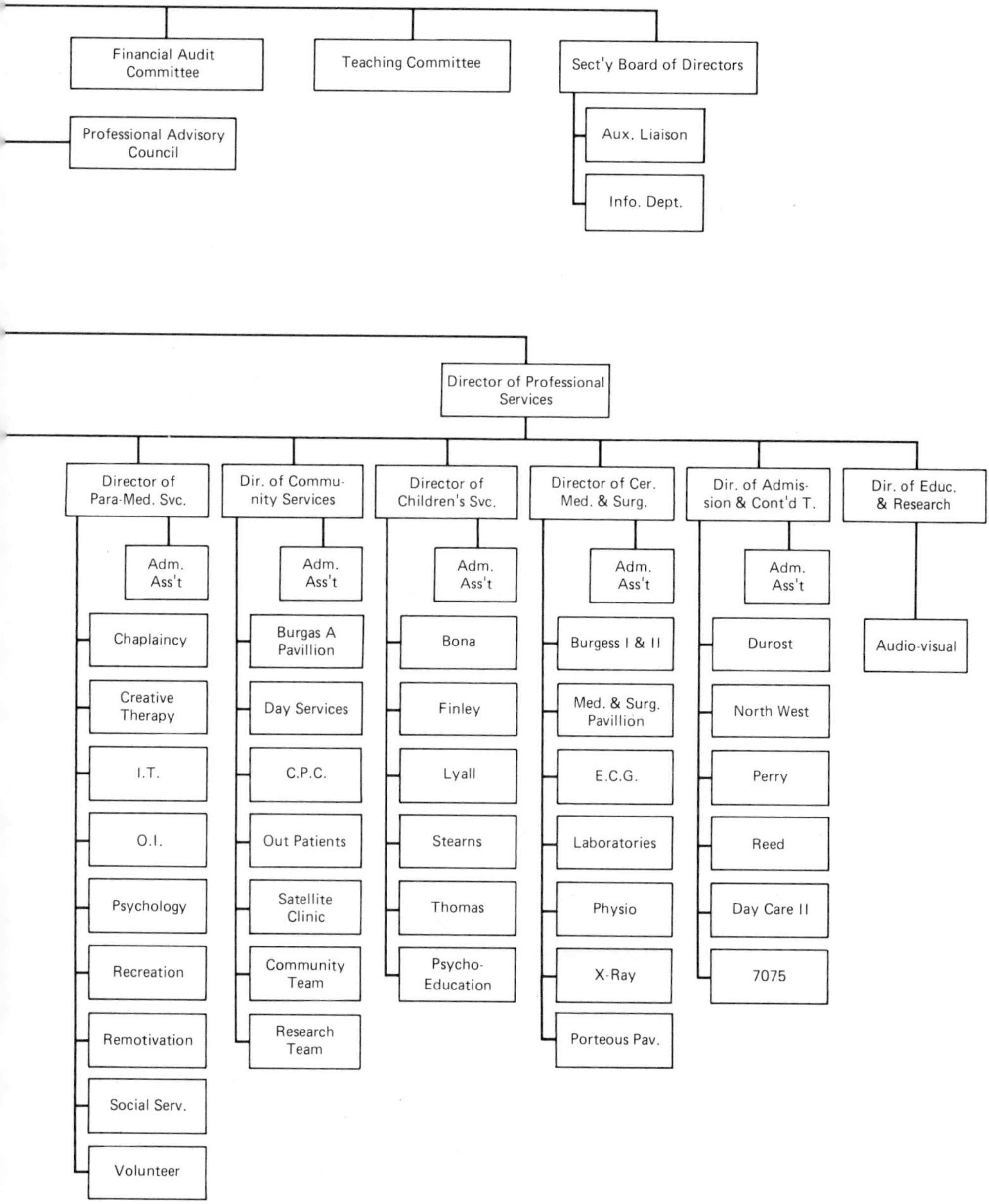

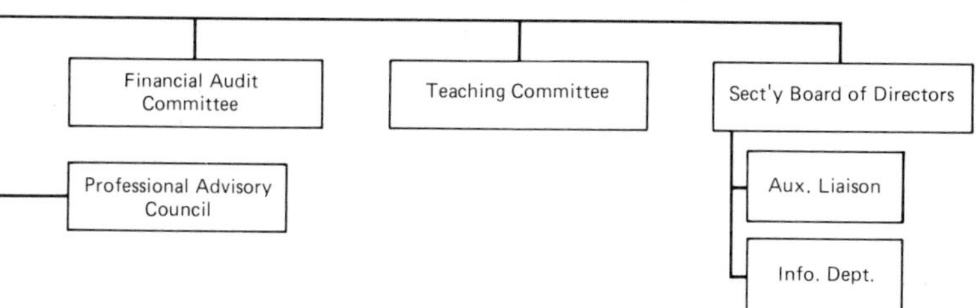

- Director of Professional Services
  - Director of Para-Med. Svc.
    - Adm. Ass't
    - Chaplaincy
    - Creative Therapy
    - I.T.
    - O.I.
    - Psychology
    - Recreation
    - Remotivation
    - Social Serv.
    - Volunteer
  - Dir. of Community Services
    - Adm. Ass't
    - Burgas A Pavillion
    - Day Services
    - C.P.C.
    - Out Patients
    - Satellite Clinic
    - Community Team
    - Research Team
  - Director of Children's Svc.
    - Adm. Ass't
    - Bona
    - Finley
    - Lyall
    - Stearns
    - Thomas
    - Psycho-Education
  - Director of Cer. Med. & Surg.
    - Adm. Ass't
    - Burgess I & II
    - Med. & Surg. Pavillion
    - E.C.G.
    - Laboratories
    - Physio
    - X-Ray
    - Porteous Pav.
  - Dir. of Admission & Cont'd T.
    - Adm. Ass't
    - Durost
    - North West
    - Perry
    - Reed
    - Day Care II
    - 7075
  - Dir. of Educ. & Research
    - Audio-visual

ordinate connections, and they begin at the top of the organization and fan out in an increasing number at the lower levels of the organization.

For example, one chain in Figure 5–1 is board of directors → executive director → assistant executive director → director of finance → purchasing → receiving. Another chain is board of directors → executive director → assistant executive director → director of professional services → director of community services → outpatients. When decisions are decentralized, authority flows downward along the chains. If purchasing decisions are decentralized, the first chain described provides the path that the delegated authority will follow.

When you combine the individual chains, you form the organization's overall chain of command. This sets up the organization's official authority hierarchy. All formal communications are to take place along this chain or line of authority. Notice how every position fits into the organization's overall chain of command at some point. This cohesive linking ensures that every individual reports, either directly or indirectly, to the chief executive or governing board. Conversely, it provides a map outlining the path that management can take when it determines that certain types of decisions can be made more effectively at a lower level in the organization.

DECISION MAKING AND CENTRALIZATION

Managers—regardless of where they are in the organization—make decisions. The typical manager must make choices about goals, budget allocations, personnel, the ways in which work is to be done, and ways to improve his or her unit's effectiveness. As critical as a knowledge of authority and the chain of command are to the understanding of centralization, of equal importance is the awareness of the decision-making process. The degree of control one holds over the full decision-making process is, itself, a measure of centralization.

Decision making is presented traditionally as the making of choices. After developing and evaluating at least two alternatives, the decision maker chooses a preferred alternative. From the perspective of individual decision making, this is an adequate presentation. But from an organizational perspective, the making of a choice is only one step in a larger process.[1]

Figure 5–2 depicts this larger process. Information must be gathered. This input establishes the parameters of what can be done. The information gathered goes a long way toward controlling what should and will be done. As noted earlier, the fact that top-level managers rely on information fed

[1]T. T. Paterson, *Management Theory* (London: Business Publications, 1969), p. 150.

FIGURE 5–2 Organization decision-making process

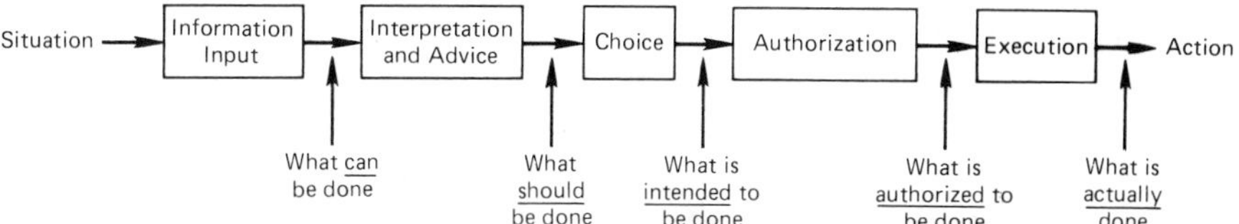

Source: Adapted from T. T. Paterson, *Management Theory* (London: Business Publications, 1969), p. 150.

to them from individuals lower in the vertical hierarchy gives those subordinates the opportunity to communicate the information they want. Once the information is gathered, it must be interpreted. The interpretations are then transmitted as advice to the decision maker as to what should be done. The third step is acting on the advice to make the choice. Much of the choosing, of course, has been done previously when that information was selectively screened and interpreted. The decision choice establishes what the decision maker desires or intends to have done. Wishes, unfortunately, do not always become actions. The decision must be authorized and conveyed before it can be executed. Where there are many layers in the vertical hierarchy, the final execution may differ from the intention. Breakdowns in communication can result in a divergence between intentions and actions. So, too, can the interests of those who initiate action. President John Kennedy found this out in 1962 when he ordered, on several occasions, that his Secretary of State see that U.S. missiles in Turkey be removed because he thought that they may precipitate war with Russia.[2] Despite his formal orders and impassioned personal pleas, State Department officials in Turkey saw such action as having harmful effects on Turkish public opinion, so they did nothing.

Referring to Figure 5–2, it can be said that decision making is most centralized when the decision maker controls all the steps: "he collects his own information, analyzes it himself, makes the choice, needs seek no authorization of it, and executes it himself."[3] As others gain control over these steps, the process becomes decentralized. Therefore, decentralization will be greatest when the decision maker controls only the making of the choice; this is the least that one can do in the process and still be a decision maker. So viewing the organizational decision process as more than merely choosing between alternatives gives us insight into the intricacies involved in defining and assessing the degree of centralization in an organization.

[2]Graham T. Allison, *Essence of Decision: Explaining the Cuban Missile Crisis* (Boston: Little, Brown, 1971), pp. 141–142.

[3]Henry Mintzberg, *The Structuring of Organizations* (Englewood Cliffs, N.J.: Prentice-Hall, 1979), p. 187.

WHY IS CENTRALIZATION IMPORTANT?

The heading for this section may mislead you. That it implies centralization, in contrast to decentralization, is important. The term "centralization," in this context, is meant to be viewed as were complexity and formalization. It represents a range—from high to low. It may be clearer, therefore, if we ask: Why is the centralization-decentralization issue important?

As described, in addition to being collections of people, organizations are decision-making and information-processing systems. Organizations facilitate the achievement of goals through coordinating group effort; decision making and information processing are central for coordination to take place. Yet—and this point is often overlooked by students of decision-making and organization theory—information itself is not the scarce resource in organizations. Advanced information technology provides managers with bundles of data to assist in the making decisions. We live in a world that drenches us with information. The scarce resource is the processing capacity to attend to information.[4]

Managers are limited in their ability to give attention to data they receive. Every manager has some limit to the amount of information that he or she can process. After that limit is reached, further input results in information overload. To avoid reaching the point where a manager's capacity is exceeded, some of the decisions can be given to others. The concentration of decision making at a single point can be dispersed. This dispersion or transfer is decentralization.

There are other reasons as to why organizations might decentralize. Organizations need to respond rapidly to changing conditions at the point at which the change is taking place. Decentralization facilitates speedy action because it avoids the need to process the information through the vertical hierarchy. It can be acted upon by those closest to the issue. This explains why marketing activities tend to be decentralized. This function must be able to react quickly to the needs of customers and actions of competitors. Similarly, the American Broadcasting Company believed that speed and accuracy could be achieved best in the gathering of news by dispensing with the centralized anchorperson on its "ABC's World News Tonight" program and going with three anchors—one each in London, Washington, and Chicago.

In addition to speed, decentralization can provide more detailed input into the decision. If those most familiar with an issue make a decision, more of the specific facts relevant to that issue will be available. The sales people at a company's facilities in Rio de Janiero are much more likely to

[4]Herbert A. Simon, *Administrative Behavior*, 3rd ed. (New York: Free Press, 1976), p. 294.

know the relevant facts for making pricing decisions on the company's products in Brazil than would a sales executive 5,000 miles north in New York.

Decentralizing decision making can provide motivation to employees by allowing them to participate in the decision-making process. Professionals and skilled employees are particularly sensitive to having a say in those decisions that will affect how they will do their jobs. If management holds Theory Y assumptions, the firm will favor decentralization. If certain groups are likely to hold Theory Y values, they are the professionals and the skilled. Because these people desire to share in the decision-making process, the opportunity to do so should be motivating. On the other hand, if management holds Theory X assumptions and centralizes authority, employee motivation can be predicted to be low.

A final plus for decentralization is the training opportunity that it creates for low-level managers. By delegating authority, top management permits less experienced managers to learn by doing. By making decisions in areas where impact is less critical, low-level managers get decision-making practice with the potential for minimum damage. This prepares them for assuming greater authority as they rise in the organization.

Of course, the goal of decentralization is not always desirable. There are conditions under which centralization is preferred. When a comprehensive perspective is needed in a decision or where concentration provides significant economies, centralization offers distinct advantages. Top-level managers are obviously in a better position to see the big picture. This provides them with advantages in choosing actions that will be consistent with the best interests of the whole organization rather than merely benefiting some special-interest group. Further, certain activities are clearly done more efficiently when centralized. This explains, for instance, why financial and legal decisions tend to be centralized. Both functions permeate activities throughout the organization and there are distinct economies to centralizing this expertise.

This discussion leads to the conclusion that either high or low centralization may be desirable. Situational factors will determine the "right" amount. But *all* organizations process information so that managers can make decisions. As such, attention must be given to identifying the most effective way in which to organize where those decisions should be made.

RELATIONSHIP OF CENTRALIZATION, COMPLEXITY, AND FORMALIZATION

As we bring to a close our three chapters on structural components, it is important to attempt to identify what relationships there are, if any, between centralization and complexity and centralization and formalization.

Centralization and Complexity

The evidence strongly supports an inverse relationship between centralization and complexity.[5] Decentralization is associated with high complexity. For example, an increase in the number of occupational specialties means an increase in the expertise and ability necessary to make decisions. Similarly, the more that employees have undergone professional training, the more likely they are to participate in decision making. Conversely, the evidence finds that the greater the centralization of work decisions, the less professional training is likely to be exhibited by employees. We expect, therefore, to find high complexity associated with decentralization when we examine the structure of organizations.

Centralization and Formalization

The centralization-formalization relationship is as ambiguous as the centralization-complexity relationship is clear. A review of the evidence is marked by inconsistent results.

The early work found no strong relationships between centralization and formalization.[6] Later research reported a strong negative relationship between the two components; that is, organizations were both highly formalized and decentralized.[7] One follow-up effort, attempting to reconcile the controversy, yielded inconclusive results.[8] The most recent efforts support the high formalization-decentralization hypothesis.[9] Obviously, the relationship is complex. Given this caveat, however, we can suggest a tentative analysis.

High formalization can be found coupled with either a centralized or decentralized structure. Where employees in the organization are predominantly unskilled, you can expect lots of rules and regulations to guide these people. Theory X assumptions also tend to dominate, so management keeps authority centralized. Control is exercised through both formalization and concentration of decision making in top management.

With professional employees, on the other hand, you might predict

[5]See, for example, Jerald Hage and Michael Aiken, "Relationship of Centralization to Other Structural Properties," *Administrative Science Quarterly*, June 1967, pp. 72–91; and John Child, "Organization Structure and Strategies of Control: A Replication of the Aston Study," *Administrative Science Quarterly*, June 1972, pp. 163–177.

[6]D. S. Pugh, D. J. Hickson, C. R. Hinings, and C. Turner, "Dimensions of Organization Structure," *Administrative Science Quarterly*, June 1968, pp. 65–105.

[7]John Child, "Organization Structure and Strategies of Control: A Replication of the Aston Study."

[8]Lex Donaldson, John Child, and Howard Aldrich, "The Aston Findings on Centralization: Further Discussion," *Adminstrative Science Quarterly*, September 1975, pp. 453–460.

[9]Peter H. Grinyer and Masoud Yasai-Ardekani, "Dimensions of Organizational Structure: A Critical Replication," *Academy of Management Journal*, September 1980, pp. 405–421.

both low formalization and decentralization. Research confirms this alignment.[10] Yet the type of decision moderates this relationship. Professionals expect decentralization of decisions that affect their work directly, but this does not necessarily apply to personnel issues (i.e., salary and performance appraisal procedures) or strategic organization decisions. Professionals want the predictability that comes with standardization of personnel matters, so you might expect to find decentralization paired with extensive rules and regulations. Additionally, professionals' interest is in their technical work, not in strategic decision making. This can result in low formalization and centralization. Centralization, however, is confined to strategic rather than to operative decisions, the former having little impact on the work activities of the professional.

MEASURING CENTRALIZATION

As with the prior two chapters, a short questionnaire is provided to assist you in making a rough appraisal of an organization's degree of centralization. This questionnaire is depicted in Table 5–1.

The questionnaire taps the degree of influence that top management has over key parts of the decision-making process and the amount of discretion that the typical first-line supervisor has over the critical elements in his or her job. The scoring of the questionnaire is along the lines of the previous ones. Approximate guides for translating scores into categories are 40 points and above represents high centralization, 21 to 39 is moderate, and 20 or less indicates low centralization (or decentralization).

To illustrate how this questionnaire might be used, let us compare a prestigous research-oriented university with a state penitentiary. The university should be decentralized. Decisions about hiring, firing, promotions, performance, and goals originate at the department levels by faculty members themselves. Departments in a research university are highly autonomous. A test of our questionnaire at several such campuses substantially confirmed this notion. As a professional organization, matters relating to teaching and research were controlled almost entirely by the faculty members. Even the department chairmen had little input above the one vote they carried in departmental meetings. But that was far more than the dean, vice chancellor, or president had. Scores of 12 to 15 are fairly typical in such organizations. Some decisions—those of a more strategic nature—were centralized. Issues such as campus construction, future campus enrollment projections, and the like were made by senior administrators.

Analysis of a state penitentiary presents an entirely different picture of decision making. The warden and his close associates were in almost total control. Regardless of the type of decision, authority to make it was

[10]Hage and Aiken, "Relationship of Centralization to Other Structural Properties."

TABLE 5–1 Centralization questionnaire

Circle your response to each of the following items as they apply to the organization in question.

1. How much direct involvement does top management have in gathering the information input that they will use in making decisions?
   - a. none
   - b. little
   - c. some
   - d. a great deal
   - e. a very great deal

2. To what degree does top management participate in the interpretation of the information input?
   - a. 0–20%
   - b. 21–40%
   - c. 41–60%
   - d. 61– 80%
   - e. 81–100%

3. To what degree does top management directly control the execution of the decision?
   - a. 0–20%
   - b. 21–40%
   - c. 41–60%
   - d. 61– 80%
   - e. 81–100%

For Questions 4 through 10, use the following responses:

- a. very great
- b. great
- c. some
- d. little
- e. none

4–10. How much discretion does the typical first-line supervisor have over

4. establishing his or her unit's budget?
5. determining how his or her unit's performance will be evaluated?
6. hiring and firing personnel?
7. personnel rewards (i.e., salary increases, promotions)?
8. purchasing of equipment and supplies?
9. establishing a new project or program?
10. how work exceptions are to be handled?

Scoring: For all items, a = 1, b = 2, c = 3, d = 4, e = 5. Add up the score for all ten items. The sum of the item scores is the degree of centralization (out of a possible 50).

at the top. Guards, for instance, had almost no say in decisions, even those that directly affected them. Using the questionnaire in Table 5–1, the particular penal institution we evaluated scored 44 points, clearly well into the high centralization range.

SUMMARY

Centralization is the most problematic of the three components. It is defined as the degree to which the formal authority to make discretionary choices is concentrated in an individual, unit, or level (usually high in the organization), thus permitting employees (usually low in the organization) minimum input into their work.

The degree of control that an individual holds over the full decision-making process can be used as a measure of centralization. The five steps in this process are (1) collecting information to pass onto the decision maker about what can be done, (2) processing and interpreting that information to present advice to the decision maker about what should be done, (3) making the choice as to what is intended to be done, (4) authorizing elsewhere what is intended to be done, and (5) executing or doing it. Decision making is most centralized when the decision maker controls all these steps.

Decentralization reduces the probability of information overload, facilitates rapid response to new information, provides more detailed input into a decision, instills motivation, and represents a potential vehicle for training managers in developing good judgment. On the other hand, centralization adds a comprehensive perspective to decisions and can provide significant efficiencies.

The evidence strongly supports an inverse relationship between centralization and complexity. The centralization-formalization correlation, however, is not nearly so clear. It appears that the type of employees and the type of decision influence the relationship. Unskilled employees are associated with both high formalization and centralization. Professional employees, however, tend to be associated with low formalization (except with personnel decisions) and low centralization (except with strategic organization decisions).

FOR REVIEW AND DISCUSSION

1. Define the concepts of centralization and decentralization.
2. "Decentralization is a relative concept." Do you agree or disagree? Discuss.
3. Reconcile the following two statements: (a) Where decisions are delegated downward but extensive policies exist to constrain the discretion of lower-level members, there is increased centralization. (b) An information-processing system that monitors decentralized decisions does not maintain centralized control.
4. What is authority? How is it related to centralization?
5. What is the chain of command? How is it related to vertical differentiation?
6. Describe the organizational decision-making process? Is it different from the individual decision-making process? Discuss.
7. Discuss the advantages and disadvantages to centralization.

8. What is the relationship between centralization and complexity?
9. What is the relationship between centralization and formalization?
10. You are evaluating an organization's degree of centralization. You find that legal decisons are highly centralized, whereas marketing decisions are decentralized. How do you arrive at an *organizationwide* measure of centralization?

PART III

THE DETERMINANTS: WHAT CAUSES STRUCTURE?

CHAPTER

6

STRATEGY

If you had studied organization theory thirty years ago, the subject of this chapter (but certainly not its current content) would have been the only variable considered as *causing* structure. That is, in those days there was a single answer to the question: What determines structure? That answer was "the organization's goals and strategies."

A lot has happened in the last three decades. Researchers have identified a number of variables as determinants, some looking a great deal more promising than others. Strategy is now just one in that set of variables. In this chapter, we review the current state of the strategy imperative (an imperative *dictates* structure). Chapters 7 through 10 consider four alternative variables.

The early acceptance of goals and strategy as determinants of an organization's structure was founded on assumptions inherent in classical economic theory. These included

1. The organization has a goal or goals toward which it drives.
2. It moves toward its goals in a "rational" manner.
3. The organization exists to transform economic inputs to outputs.
4. The environment within which the organization operates is a given.[1]

If these assumptions are valid, an organization's structure can be interpreted as the outcome of a rational process. "Structure is a means for

[1]Joseph McGuire, *Theories of Business Behavior* (Englewood Cliffs, N.J.: Prentice-Hall, Inc., 1964), p. 47.

attaining the objectives and goals of an institution. Any work on structure must therefore start with objectives and strategy."[2]

Notice that this approach takes a closed-systems perspective. The environment is given. "Once the goals of the organization have been determined, or specified, then the development of structure, the flow of authority, and the other relationships clearly follow in a logical manner."[3] Structure is seen as just a rational means by which inputs are translated to outputs.

WHAT IS STRATEGY?

The previous paragraphs used the terms *goals* and *strategy* as if they meant the same thing. As we point out, they are interrelated but they are not the same.

Goals refer to ends. Strategy refers to both means and ends. As such, goals are part of an organization's strategy. We discussed goals in Chapter 2, so let us clarify the concept of strategy:

> *Strategy* can be defined as the determination of the basic long-term goals and objectives of an enterprise, and the adoption of courses of action and the allocation of resources necessary for carrying out these goals. Decisions to expand the volume of activities, to set up distant plants and offices, to move into new economic functions, or to become diversified along many lines of business involve the defining of new basic goals. New courses of action must be devised and resources allocated and reallocated in order to achieve these goals and to maintain and expand the firm's activities in the new areas in response to shifting demands, changing sources of supply, fluctuating economic conditions, new technological developments, and the actions of competitors.[4]

This definition does not tell us whether strategy has to be premeditated or whether it can just emerge. These, in fact, represent two views on strategy and deserve expanded attention.[5]

One view can be called a *planning mode.* This view describes strategy as a plan or explicit set of guidelines developed in advance. Managers

[2]Peter F. Drucker, *Management: Tasks, Responsibilities, Practices* (New York: Harper & Row, 1974), pp. 523–524.

[3]Henry L. Tosi, *Theories of Organization* (Chicago: St. Clair Press, 1975), p. 30.

[4]Alfred D. Chandler, Jr., *Strategy and Structure: Chapters in the History of the Industrial Enterprise* (Cambridge, Mass.: M.I.T. Press, 1962), p. 13.

[5]Henry Mintzberg, "Research in Strategy-Making," *Proceedings of the Academy of Management,* thirty-second meeting (Minneapolis, Minn., 1972), pp. 90–94.

identify where they want to go; then they develop a systematic and structured plan to get there. Until recently, this viewpoint dominated the OT literature.

A more current perspective is what we can call an *evolutionary mode.* Strategy is not necessarily a well-thought-out and systematic plan. Rather, it evolves over time as a pattern in a stream of significant decisions. President Richard Nixon, for example, made a number of decisions during his first term that appeared to enhance Republican voting support in the South.[6] While Nixon never announced a "Southern strategy," it evolved as if it had been planned ahead of time.

Just as goals can be seen as something that are preestablished and that guide subsequent behavior or as explanations developed after the behavior to justify or rationalize it, strategy can be viewed as premeditated or as something that can only become clear over time. The early writers looking at the strategy-structure relationship assumed the planning mode to be the proper way in which to view strategy. As we have noted, the broader evoluntary perspective has been gaining acceptance in recent years. Its major advantage lies in being able to cope with both static and dynamic strategies. If there is a strategy imperative, then strategy should predict structure. Also, as strategy changes—whether explicitly planned or implicitly evolving—structure should follow.

In summary, strategy considers both means and ends. The goals and decisions making up an organization's strategy may be planned ahead of time or may just evolve as some consistent pattern. Either way, those advocates of the "strategy determines structure" position perceive decision makers as *choosing* the structure they have. It may be true, as we shall see in later chapters, that the organization's transformation processes, environment, and other factors are major determinants of structure, but these are one step removed from the actual change process. This is shown in Figure 6–1. The case can and will be made in this book that even if an organization's transformation processes and environment determine structure, they are not givens. They are chosen by the organization's dominant decision makers.

FIGURE 6–1 The strategy imperative

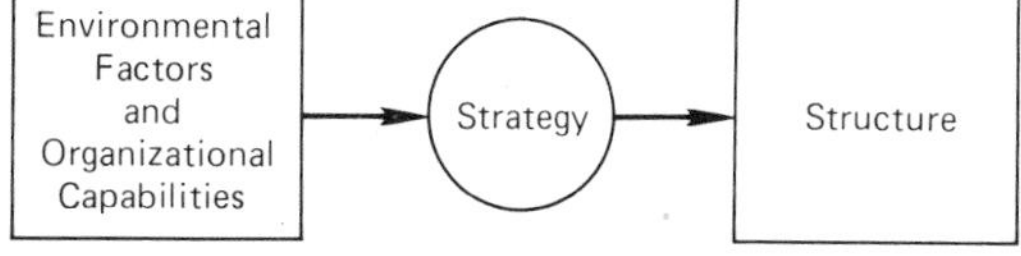

[6]Ibid.

CHANDLER'S "STRUCTURE FOLLOWS STRATEGY" THESIS

The classic work on the relationship between organizational strategy and structure was done by Harvard historian Alfred Chandler in his study of close to a hundred of America's largest industrial firms.[7] Tracing the pattern of development of these organizations from 1909 to 1959, which included extensive case histories of such companies as DuPont, General Motors, Standard Oil of New Jersey, and Sears, Roebuck, Chandler concluded that changes in corporate strategy precede and lead to changes in an organization's structure.

Chandler found that the companies began as centralized structures. This reflected the limited product they offered. As demand for their products grew, the companies expanded. They increased their product lines and had to develop different structures to cope with their changing strategies. For instance, they integrated vertically by purchasing many of their own sources of supply. This reduced their dependency on suppliers. To produce a greater variety of products more efficiently, they created separate product groups within the organization. The result were structures that were fundamentally different. Growth and diversification gave rise to the need for an autonomous multidivisional structure. The highly centralized structure became inefficient and impractical for dealing with the significantly greater complexity. As Chandler summarized,

> growth without structural adjustment can lead only to economic inefficiency. Unless new structures are developed to meet new administrative needs which result from an expansion of a firm's activities into new areas, functions, or product lines, the technological, financial, and personnel economies of growth and size cannot be realized.[8]

Chandler's study, while rich in historical data and analysis, must be put in perspective. His findings were certainly important. They confirmed general patterns and clearly shaped the "structure follows strategy" thesis. But to generalize from his sample is certainly dangerous. His companies were not a cross section of organizations in general. He looked only at very large and powerful business firms. Whether his findings would be applicable to small- and medium-sized organizations or to those in the public sector could not be answered from his sample. In addition, Chandler did not ignore other factors. He acknowledged, for instance, that external conditions played a very important role in explaining why and how organization structures changed.

[7]Chandler, *Strategy and Structure.*

[8]Ibid., p. 16.

CHILD'S STRATEGIC CHOICE

In the early 1970s, the term *strategic choice* was introduced by John Child to emphasize that decision makers have available a range of options.[9] Building on the work of Chandler, Child developed a comprehensive argument in support of the strategy imperative.

Child argued that, while there are constraints on managerial decision discretion, managers still have significant latitude for making choices. Just as they choose objectives, personnel, or control techniques, managers also choose the structural design. External factors such as competitors, unions, and government agencies are part of the constraints, but rather than impinging directly on an organization's structure, these factors are mediated by managerial choice. This is consistent with Figure 6–1. Child's argument can be condensed basically into three points.[10]

First, *decision makers have more autonomy than that inferred by those arguing for the dominance of environmental, technological, or other forces.* Managers can select from among a wide range of viable alternatives compatible with the niche they occupy, or they can choose to enter a new niche. Businesses enter and leave markets regularly, whereas schools make decisions as to what curricula to offer, hospitals choose what type of patients to serve, and so forth. Organizations are *not* constrained to do what they have done in the past. Given the fact that environmental niches are fairly broad, there may be a variety of organizational forms that are viable, rather than a single one.

Of course, just because decision makers have autonomy does not mean that they will exercise it. They have to believe that there is a relationship between structural arrangements and levels of effectiveness, for otherwise their choices would be irrelevant. They further have to believe that the source of problems is an inadequate organizational structure rather than personnel who were poorly selected, trained, or are lacking in motivation. In other words, they have to attribute problems to the structure. Finally, if we accept that decision makers "satisfice" rather than optimize, we can assume a wider range of choices. Managers do not optimize. They seek outcomes that are satisfactory and sufficient; that is, they make choices that are good enough.[11] This means that decision makers may be content with varying levels of performance, so long as they all meet or exceed the minimally satisfactory level. The range between maximizing and "good enough" creates an area in which managers can utilize their discretion.

Child's second point was that *organizations occasionally have the power*

[9]John Child, "Organization Structure, Environment, and Performance—The Role of Strategic Choice," *Sociology*, January 1972, pp. 1–22.

[10]Ibid.

[11]Herbert A. Simon, *Administrative Behavior*, 3rd ed. (New York: Free Press 1976).

to manipulate and control their environments. Organizations are not always pawns, being acted upon by their environments. Managers of large companies are able to create demand for their products and control their competitive environments.[12] Large and small organizations alike can enter into informal relationships with competitors to limit the severity, scope, and danger posed by the competition. Other actions can include mergers, joint ventures, vertical integration, or even lobbying for government regulation. The merger of Shearson and American Express in 1981 produced a new organization more powerful in controlling its environment. The Kinney Shoe Co. expanded its control when it integrated vertically—from the manufacturing of shoes to both the manufacturing and retailing of its shoes. An extensive study of the pharmaceutical industry demonstrates a successful case of organizations' manipulating and controlling environmental forces.[13]

The pharmaceutical industry has been extremely effective in shaping its environment, particularly in the areas of pricing and distribution of products, patent and copyright law, and the cooptation of external opinion leaders. After World War II, the pharmaceutical industry turned to government legislation to protect itself against the growing number of companies producing chemically equivalent products to their own. The large manufacturers formed the National Pharmaceutical Council, which lobbied before state boards of pharmacy to make it illegal for a pharmacist to substitute a chemically equivalent generic drug for a brand name. This council was enormously successful. Within eight years, thirty-eight state boards of pharmacy had enacted the council's antigeneric position. The result, of course, was to bolster the profits of the brand names and substantially increase the costs of entry into the industry for new firms.

Until the pharmaceutical firms brought pressure on the U.S. Patent Office to relax its traditional interpretation of the law, no "naturally occurring" substances were patentable, including antibiotics. Competition was fierce as new firms sought to produce standard antibiotics. The price of penicillin in 1955, for instance, was only 6 percent of what it had been in 1945. Industry representatives lobbied for patent protection under the guise that it was necessary if firms were to be economically motivated to develop new drugs. The lobbying effort was successful, allowing firms to patent nearly 2,000 variations of antibiotics between 1950 and 1958. The results on profits were sizable: the patented antibiotics generated a gross profit 75 percent above that from the unpatented antibiotics.

[12]John Kenneth Galbraith, *The New Industrial State* (Boston: Houghton Mifflin, 1967).

[13]Paul Hirsch, "Organizational Effectiveness and the Institutional Environment," *Administrative Science Quarterly*, September 1975, pp. 327–344.

The pharmaceutical firms were also very successful in coopting institutional gatekeepers, particularly the American Medical Association (AMA). Pharmaceutical firms and the AMA moved from an adversarial relationship in the 1940s to the complete cooptation of the AMA by the drug companies in the 1960s. During the 1950s, the AMA dropped its strict stand on drug advertising in its journals and permitted any drug approved by the Federal Drug Administration to be listed by brand name. The AMA's Council on Drugs was replaced by a committee with more lenient standards. The result was that, between 1953 and 1960, the income of the AMA from journal advertisements tripled. During this same period, revenues from membership dues and subscriptions increased only 20 percent.

The third point made by Child was that *perceptions and evaluations of events are an important intervening link between environments and organizations' actions.* There is a difference between objective characteristics of the environment and the perception and evaluation of these characteristics by organization members. People do not always perceive environmental characteristics accurately. Their interpretations will show themselves in the decisions they choose. Their strategic choices, in other words, are likely to exert a significant influence on structural design, regardless of the actual characteristics of the environment. Decision makers evaluate the organization's environment, make interpretations based on their experience, and use this to influence the design of the internal structure.

LIMITATIONS TO THE STRATEGY IMPERATIVE

Chandler and Child have argued the positive case for strategy determining structure. Of course, there is another side in the debate.

No one argues that strategy *cannot* determine structure. That possibility does exist. Attacks on the strategy imperative lie basically in questioning the degree of discretionary latitude that managers actually have. For instance, it seems logical that the impact of strategy would be greater in the early development period of an organization. Once personnel are hired, equipment purchased, and procedures and policies established, they are a whole lot tougher to change. When the organization is in its infancy, vested interests have yet to be solidified. But once the die is cast, managers may be severely restricted in their discretion. Similarly, it is logical that the capital-to-labor ratio in an organization will affect the impact of strategy on structure. If the ratio is low (i.e., labor intensive), then managers have much more flexibility, and hence discretion, to exercise change and influence structure.

One author has developed counterpoints to each of Child's propositions.[14] There are constraints on the capacity of decision makers to make optimal choices of new environmental niches. These constraints are barriers to entry that prevent potential entrants from gaining a position in a market already served by existing organizations. These include (1) the economies of scale that favor those who are already in the market and command a substantial market share, (2) the absolute costs to enter a new market that may be lower for existing firms because of knowledge or technology not available to new entrants, and (3) product differentiation that favors existing firms who have achieved high visibility and whose brands have gained wide recognition.

There are limits on the power of organizations to influence their environments. Ability to significantly affect one's environment is almost totally the province of large organizations or those that are well connected politically. But our society is made up predominantly of small and uninfluential organizations. Only slightly more than 3 percent of all businesses employ more than fifty people. In 1972, about two-thirds of all businesses took in less than $25,000 in receipts. It's unlikely that these small organizations could have much power to affect their environments. While it's true that the 11 percent of corporations with sales of over $1 million account for almost 90 percent of all corporate sales, it is questionable whether a theory of structural determinants should be built on exceptional organizations. Since the great majority of organizations are neither large nor powerful, few organizations can influence their environments to any significant degree.

There are limits to choice implied by a logical extension of Child's distinction between actual environments and perceptions of environments. Participants' perceptions play some role in their actions, but a variety of social forces limit the possibility for really "strategic" choices. It is particularly important to note that there are collective socialization processes in organizations that reinforce strong commitments to existing, socially approved perceptions. These include recruitment and selection procedures, training, and informal organizational norms. This socialization reduces pressures for change and instills routine, rather than strategic, choice-making processes.

These points attempt to counter the strategic-choice argument. Decision makers may have some autonomy in selecting strategies, but there are severe restrictions on their ability to select new environments, manipulate and control their environments, or institute organizational change. Strategy, therefore, may be more important in organizations that are large, are early in their development period, are labor intensive, have developed

[14]Howard E. Aldrich, *Organizations and Environments* (Englewood Cliffs, N.J.: Prentice-Hall, 1979), pp. 149–159.

strong political connections, or have few barriers to enter new markets (i.e., retail and service industries in contrast to manufacturing).

WHERE ARE WE TODAY?

Where strategy *is* related to structure, can we define types of strategies and use this to predict specific structural variations? A review of the literature has resulted in a framework that can help us toward this end.[15]

Strategy-Structure Typology

Organizations can be classified into one of four strategic types: defenders, prospectors, analyzers, and reactors. While the following discussion centers on business firms, the categories probably have their counterparts in nonprofit organizations.

Defenders seek stability by producing only a limited set of products directed at a narrow segment of the total potential market. Within this limited niche or domain, defenders strive aggressively to prevent competitors from entering their "turf." Organizations do this through standard economic actions such as competitive pricing or producing high-quality products. But defenders tend to ignore developments and trends outside their domains, choosing instead to grow through market penetration and perhaps some limited product development. There is little or no scanning of the environment to find new areas of opportunity, but there is intensive planning oriented toward cost and other efficiency issues. The result is a structure made up of high horizontal differentiation, centralized control, and an elaborate formal hierarchy for communications. Over time, true defenders are able to carve out and maintain small niches within their industries that are difficult for competitors to penetrate. An example of a defender strategy is the manufacturer of Soft-Soap. The company has chosen a narrow domain—the liquid hand and body soap market—and hopes to compete against firms such as Procter & Gamble by promoting aggressively and developing a narrow range of similar products.

Prospectors are almost the opposite of defenders. Their strength is finding and exploiting new product and market opportunities. Innovation may be more important than high profitability. This describes, for instance, several magazine publishers that introduce new magazine titles almost monthly, constantly attempting to identify new market segments. The prospectors' success depends on developing and maintaining the capacity

[15]The following discussion is based on Raymond E. Miles, Charles C. Snow, Alan D. Meyer, and Henry J. Coleman, Jr., "Organizational Strategy, Structure, and Process," *Academy of Management Review*, July 1978, pp. 546–562.

to survey a wide range of environmental conditions, trends, and events. Therefore, prospectors invest heavily in personnel who scan the environment for potential opportunities. Since flexibility is critical to prospectors, the structure will also be flexible. It will rely on multiple technologies that have a low degree of routinization and mechanization. There will be numerous decentralized units. The structure will be low in formalization, have decentralized control, with lateral as well as vertical communications. "In short, the prospector is effective—it can respond to the demands of tomorrow's world. To the extent that the world of tomorrow is similar to that of today, the prospector cannot maximize profitability because of its inherent inefficiency."[16]

Analyzers try to capitalize on the best of both the previous two types. They seek to minimize risk and maximize the opportunity for profit. Their strategy is to move into new products or new markets only after viability has been proved by prospectors. Analyzers live by imitation. They take the successful ideas of prospectors and copy them. Manufacturers of mass-marketed fashion goods, which are rip-offs of designer styles, follow the analyzer strategy. Analyzers, therefore, must have the ability to respond to the lead of key prospectors, yet at the same time maintain operating efficiency in their stable product and market areas. Analyzers will tend to have smaller profit margins in the products and services that they sell than will prospectors, but they are more efficient. Prospectors have to have high margins to justify the risks that they take and their productive inefficiencies.

Analyzers seek both flexibility and stability. They respond to these goals by developing a structure made up of dual components. Parts of these organizations have high levels of standardization, routinization, and mechanization for efficiency. Other parts are adaptive, to enhance flexibility. In this way, they seek structures that can accommodate both stable and dynamic areas of operation. But in this compromise, there can be costs. If situations change rapidly, demanding that organizations move fully in either direction, their ability to take such action is severely limited.

Reactors represent a residual strategy. The label is meant to describe the inconsistent and unstable patterns that arise when one of the other three strategies is pursued improperly. In general, reactors respond inappropriately, perform poorly, and as a result are reluctant to commit themselves aggressively to a specific strategy for the future. What can cause this? Top management may have failed to make the organization's strategy clear. Management may not have fully shaped the organization's structure to fit the chosen strategy. Management may have maintained its current strategy-structure relationship despite overwhelming changes in environmental conditions. Whatever the reason, however, the outcome is the

[16]Ibid., p. 553.

TABLE 6–1 Strategy-structure typologies

STRATEGY	*GOAL*	*STRUCTURAL CHARACTERISTICS*
Defender	Stability and efficiency	Tendency toward functional structure with extensive division of labor and high degree of formalization
		Centralized control and complex vertical information systems
		Simple coordination mechanisms and conflict resolved through hierarchical channels
Prospector	Flexibility	Tendency toward product structure with low division of labor and low degree of formalization
		Decentralized control and simple horizontal information systems
		Complex coordination mechanisms and conflict resolved through integrators
Analyzer	Stability and flexibility	Tendency toward a loose structure combining both functional and product structures
		Moderately centralized control
		Extremely complex and expensive coordination mechanisms; some conflict resolution through product managers, some through normal hierarchical channels

Source: Adapted from Raymond E. Miles, Charles C. Snow, Alan D. Meyer, and Henry J. Coleman, Jr., "Organizational Strategy, Structure, and Process," *Academy of Management Review,* July 1978, pp. 552, 554, 556.

same. The organization lacks a set of response mechanisms with which to face a changing environment.

Table 6–1 summarizes the primary strategy-structure typologies. It shows the goal(s) of each and the structural mechanisms that management would choose to help achieve the goal(s).

The Research

There is far more speculation on the strategy-structure relationship than there are hard research findings. Chandler's work lends support, but, as we noted, it was limited to only very large and powerful companies. Chandler also recognized that the environment played an important role in explaining structure. Child's position, while interesting, offered no new empirical research to support his argument. In our discussion of the limits to the strategy imperative, we postulated a number of factors that might increase the strategy-structure causation, but these were substantially based on conjecture. Research is needed to validate that which appears intuitively logical.

So where does the strategy-structure relationship stand? Are there empirical data to support that managerial choice is a major determinant of structure? At best, strategy appears to only impact certain structural dimensions. It was found, for instance, that managerial discretion was the dominant determinant of specialization, formalization, and autonomy.[17] Other factors better explained dimensions such as vertical differentiation, centralization, and hierarchical control. Yet the strategy-structure relationship may be attacked at a more fundamental level. A search of the empirical literature led one reviewer to conclude that the two are related, but suggested that the real issue is: Which is cause and which is effect?[18] A study of fifty-four firms listed among the top half of *Fortune*'s 500 found that structure influences and constrains strategy, rather than the other way around.[19] If further research were to support this conclusion, we could state that, as a structural determinant, strategy is of little importance.

SUMMARY

The early position on "what determines structure" was the organization's goals and strategies. Structure was seen as just a rational means to facilitate the attainment of goals. More recently, strategy has been offered as but one of a number of variables vying for the crown of "major determinant of structure."

Strategy was defined as including both the long-term goals of an organization plus a course of action that will provide the means toward their attainment. To some, it is seen as planned in advance; to others, it is viewed as evolving over time as a pattern in a stream of significant decisions.

Chandler studied nearly one hundred of America's largest business firms and concluded that "structure follows strategy." Child supported Chandler's findings, arguing that managers have considerable autonomy, that organizations occasionally can control their environments, and that

[17]John R. Montanari, "An Expanded Theory of Structural Determination: An Empirical Investigation of the Impact of Managerial Discretion on Organization Structure." Unpublished doctoral dissertation, University of Colorado, Boulder, Colorado, 1976.

[18]Robert A. Pitts, "The Strategy-Structure Relationship: An Exploration into Causality." Working paper, Pennsylvania State University, 1979.

[19]Ibid.

perceptions are an important link between environments and organizations' actions. On the other hand, strong arguments can be made against the validity of Chandler and Child's positions.

A four-category strategy-structure typology was offered to clarify popular strategies and their impact on structure. The empirical research, unfortunately, fails to lend substantial support to strategy as a major influence on an organization's structure. Other variables appear more fruitful in their explanatory powers. The next chapter looks at one such variable—organization size.

FOR REVIEW AND DISCUSSION

1. What is an "imperative"?
2. Contrast (a) goals, (b) strategy, and (c) managerial choice.
3. "The strategy imperative is based on classical economic assumptions." Build an argument to support this statement.
4. Contrast planning and evolutionary modes. Which dominates the management theory literature?
5. What patterns did Chandler find in his historical analysis?
6. What criticisms can you direct at Chandler's research?
7. Give several examples of organizations that could be classified in each of the following strategic categories: (a) defender, (b) prospector, (c) analyzer, (d) reactor. Are your examples structured along the lines suggested by the strategy-structure typology?
8. Under what conditions might you expect strategy to exert a significant influence on structure?
9. "Strategy follows structure, rather than vice versa." Build an argument to support this statement. Then build an argument to refute this statement.
10. Relate the "structure follows strategy" thesis to the systems framework.

CHAPTER

7

ORGANIZATION SIZE

A quick glance at the organizations with which we deal regularly in our lives would lead most of us to conclude that size would have some bearing on an organization's structure. The 900,000 employees of the Bell System, for example, do not neatly fit into one building or into several departments supervised by a couple of managers. It is hard to envision 900,000 people being organized in any manner other than one that would be labeled as high in complexity. On the other hand, a local telephone answering service that employs ten people and generates less than $300,000 a year in service fees is not likely to need decentralized decision making or formalized procedures and regulations.

A little more thought suggests that the same conclusion—size influences structure—can be arrived at through a more sophisticated reasoning process. As an organization hires more operative employees, it will attempt to take advantage of the economic benefits from specialization. The result will be increased horizontal differentiation. Grouping like functions together will facilitate intragroup efficiencies, but at the expense of intergroup relations suffering as each performs its different activities. Management, therefore, will need to increase vertical differentiation to coordinate the horizontally differentiated units. This expansion in size is also likely to result in spacial dispersion. All this increase in complexity will reduce top management's ability to supervise directly the activities within the organization. The control achieved through direct surveillance, therefore, will be replaced by the implementation of formal rules and regulations. This increase in formalization may also be accompanied by still greater vertical differentiation as management creates new units to coordinate the expanding and diverse activities of organizational members. Finally, with top management further removed from the operating level, it becomes difficult for senior executives to make rapid and informative decisions. The solution is to substitute decentralized decision making for centralization. Following this reasoning, we see changes in size leading to major structural changes.

While the preceding description is logical enough, does it actually happen in practice? This chapter, after addressing the issue of defining size, reviews the evidence on the size-structure relationship and attempts to test the validity of our logical scenario.

DEFINING ORGANIZATION SIZE

There is wide agreement by OT researchers on how an organization's size is determined. Over 80 percent of studies using size as a variable define it as the total number of employees.[1] High agreement, of course, does not necessarily mean correctness. For example, the total number of employees may be an adequate measure for organizations composed solely of full-time employees.

But what if the organization has a large number of part-time workers. How are they to be counted? Or what if the business is seasonal? It's not unusual for retail stores to increase their sales staff by 50 percent during the Christmas season. How should these seasonal workers be assessed? It's also been noted that using a count of the total number of employees as the measure of organizational size inherently mixes size with efficiency.[2] If one organization requires one hundred people to carry out the same activities performed by fifty people in another organization, is the first twice as large or merely half as efficient? The answers to these questions are not easy.

Although it can be argued that different measures of size are not interchangeable,[3] most of the evidence suggests that counting the total number of employees is as good as many other measures, the reason being that it is highly related to them. For instance, one study found the correlation between number of employees and the organization's net assets to be .78.[4] Number of employees also appears valid in hospitals and colleges. The correlation between total hospital labor force and average daily patient

[1]J. R. Kimberly, "Organizational Size and the Structuralist Perspective: A Review, Critique, and Proposal," *Administrative Science Quarterly*, December 1976, pp. 571–597.

[2]Nina Gupta, "Some Alternative Definitions of Size," *Academy of Management Journal*, December 1980, p. 761.

[3]Ibid., pp. 759–766.

[4]D. S. Pugh, D. J. Hickson, C. R. Hinings, and C. Turner, "The Context of Organization Structures," *Administrative Science Quarterly*, March 1969, pp. 91–114.

load was found to exceed .96,[5] whereas size of full-time and part-time faculty correlates with student enrollment at above .94.[6] One can conclude from these studies that the total number of employees appears to be highly related to other popular gauges of size. As such, it should be a fairly accurate measure across organizations.

ADVOCATES OF THE SIZE IMPERATIVE

One of the strongest arguments for the importance of size as a determinant of structure has been made by Peter Blau and Richard Schoenherr.[7] Based on studies of government agencies, universities, and department stores, they concluded that "size is the most important condition affecting the structure of organizations."[8] For instance, in one of Blau's most cited studies, he looked at fifty-three autonomous state and territorial employment security agencies whose responsibilities included administering unemployment insurance and providing employment services. In addition, his analysis included the structure of over 1,200 local agency branches and 350 headquarters divisions.[9] What Blau found was that increasing size promotes structural differentiation, but at a decreasing rate. Increases in organization size are accompanied by initially rapid and subsequently more gradual increases in the number of local branches into which the agency is spatially dispersed, the number of official occupational positions expressing division of labor, the number of vertical levels in the hierarchy, the number of functional divisions at the headquarters, and the number of sections per division. So, while size and differentiation are related, the rate of differentiation decreases with increasing size.

Research at the University of Aston in Great Britain also found size to be the major determinant of structure.[10] For example, the Aston group looked at forty-six organizations and found that increased size was associated with greater specialization and formalization.[11] They concluded that

[5]Theodore Anderson and Seymour Warkov, "Organization Size and Functional Complexity: A Study of Administration in Hospitals," *American Sociological Review*, February 1961, p. 25.

[6]Amos Hawley, Walter Boland, and Margaret Boland, "Population Size and Administration in Institutions of Higher Education." *American Sociological Review*, April 1965, p. 253.

[7]Peter M. Blau and Richard A. Schoenherr, *The Structure of Organizations* (New York: Basic Books, 1971).

[8]Ibid.

[9]Peter M. Blau, "A Formal Theory of Differentiation in Organizations," *American Sociological Review*, April 1970, pp. 201–218.

[10]See, for example, Pugh et al., "The Context of Organization Structures"; and D. J. Hickson, D. S. Pugh, and D. C. Pheysey, "Operations Technology and Organization Structure: An Empirical Reappraisal," *Administrative Science Quarterly*, September 1969, pp. 378–397.

[11]Pugh et al., "The Context of Organization Structures."

"an increased scale of operation increases the frequency of recurrent events and the repetition of decisions," which makes standardization preferable.[12]

One researcher's efforts to replicate the Aston findings resulted in supportive evidence.[13] He found that organizational size was related positively to specialization, formalization, and vertical span and negatively to centralization. In further comparing his results with Blau, he concluded that "larger organizations are more specialized, have more rules, more documentation, more extended hierarchies, and a greater decentralization of decision making further down such hierarchies."[14] He also agreed with Blau that the impact of size on these dimensions expanded at a decreasing rate as size increased. That is, as size increased, specialization, formalization, and vertical span also increased but at a declining rate, whereas centralization decreased but at a declining rate as size increased.

One of the strongest cases for the size imperative has been made by Meyer.[15] Acknowledging that a relationship between size and structural dimensions does not imply causation, he designed a research project that allowed for causal inferences. He created a longitudinal study of 194 city, county, and state departments of finance in the United States. He compared them in 1966 and again in 1971. He argued that only by comparing organizations over time would it be possible to determine the time ordering of variables. That is, even if size and structure were found to be related among a set of organizations at a specific point in time, only a longitudinal analysis would permit the elimination of the counterhypothesis that structure causes size. Meyer's findings led him to conclude that "one cannot underestimate the impact of size on other characteristics of organizations."[16] Specifically, he found that the effects of size showed itself everywhere; that the relationship was unidirectional (that is, size caused structure but not the reverse); and the impact of other variables that appeared to affect structure disappeared when size was controlled.

CRITICS OF THE SIZE IMPERATIVE

There has been no shortage of critics of the size imperative. Attacks have been launched specifically against Blau's and the Aston group's research. In addition, independent studies have demonstrated no or minimal impact of size upon structure.

[12]Ibid., p. 112.

[13]John Child and Roger Mansfield, "Technology, Size, and Organization Structure," *Sociology*, September 1972, pp. 369–393.

[14]John Child, "Predicting and Understanding Organization Structure," *Administrative Science Quarterly*, June 1973, p. 171.

[15]Marshall W. Meyer, "Size and the Structure of Organizations: A Causal Analysis," *American Sociological Review*, August 1972, pp. 434–441.

[16]Ibid., p. 440.

Chris Argyris analyzed Blau's data, questioned his measures, and argued that civil service organizations are unique.[17] On this last point, he noted that civil service organizations have budget limitations, distinct geographical boundaries, predetermined staff sizes, and are influenced primarily by regulations. He also acknowledged the role of managerial discretion. Managers in government bureaus follow traditional management theories regarding task specialization, unity of command, span of control, and so forth. As such, you would expect to find that an increase in the number of employees was accompanied by an increase in differentiation because managers believe in the appropriateness of management theories and are able to act on their beliefs. Size may be related to structure, concluded Argyris, but you cannot say that it causes it.

Blau's size imperative was also challenged by Mayhew and his associates.[18] Using a computer program that determined the degrees of differentiation possible for each level of size, they concluded that Blau's findings of a relationship between size and complexity were a mathematical certainty when equal probabilities were assigned to all possible structural combinations.

The Aston group's research has had its share of critics, too. Aldrich reanalyzed the Aston data and proposed several alternative and equally plausible interpretations.[19] For example, size is the *result* not the cause: technology determines structure, which in turn determines size. Aldrich said that the firms that were high in complexity and formalization simply needed to employ a larger work force than did less structured firms.

Even some of the Aston researchers have questioned the group's original position after an abbreviated replication.[20] They used fourteen of the organizations that had been included previously. Since some time had transpired between the original study and the replication, there was an opportunity to do a partial longitudinal test of Aston's original findings. The data, however, showed that, although size generally decreased over the time period, the measure of structure dimension increased. This was counter to the original findings.

A general attack on the size imperative has come from Hall and his associates.[21] They studied seventy-five highly diverse organizations. They

[17]Chris Argyris, *The Applicability of Organizational Sociology* (London: Cambridge University Press, 1972), pp. 1–19.

[18]B. H. Mayhew, R. L. Levinger, J. M. McPherson, and T. F. James, "System Size and Structural Differentiation in Formal Organizations: A Baseline Generator for Two Major Theoretical Propositions," *American Sociological Review*, October 1972, pp. 629–633.

[19]Howard E. Aldrich, "Technology and Organization Structure: A Reexamination of the Findings of the Aston Group," *Administrative Science Quarterly*, March 1972, pp. 26–43.

[20]J. H. K. Inkson, D. S. Pugh, and D. J. Hickson, "Organizational Context and Structure: An Abbreviated Replication," *Administrative Science Quarterly*, September 1970, pp. 318–329.

[21]Richard H. Hall, J. Eugene Haas, and Norman J. Johnson, "Organizational Size, Complexity, and Formalization," *American Sociological Review*, December 1967, pp. 903–912.

ranged in size from 6 to over 9,000 employees and included business, governmental, religious, educational, and penal organizations. Hall believed that, if size and the structural dimensions of complexity and formalization were related, this diverse set of organizations would allow that relationship to surface. Their results were mixed. The researchers concluded that "neither complexity nor formalization can be implied from organizational size."[22] Even though some relationships were statistically significant, enough deviant cases existed to seriously question the assumption that large organizations are necessarily more complex than small ones. Hall sided with Aldrich's structure-causes-size thesis when he concluded, "If a decision is made to enlarge the number of functions or activities carried out in an organization, it then becomes necessary to add more members to staff the new functional areas."[23] However, in terms of objectivity, it must be noted that the evidence was more inconsistent than damning. Hall and his associates, therefore, may question the size-structure relationship, but their research has certainly not demonstrated that the two are unrelated.

CONCLUSIONS ON THE SIZE-STRUCTURE RELATIONSHIP

The previous review of the size-structure data does not allow for easy assimilation. Certainly, in overview terms, the relationship between size and structure is not clear.[24] Although some have found a strong relationship and argue for its causal nature, others have challenged these findings on methodological grounds or have argued for size being a consequence rather than a cause of structure. But when we look at the research in more specific terms, a clearer pattern seems to evolve. We will demonstrate that size certainly does not dictate all of an organization's structure but that it is important in predicting some dimensions of structure.

Size and Complexity

Blau found that the impact of size on complexity was at a decreasing rate. As noted by Argyris, this conclusion may apply only to government-type agencies that had the unique characteristics of the unemployment offices studied. Meyer's findings certainly cannot be ignored. Although also restricted to government offices, he demonstrated strong evidence in favor of the size imperative. We might conclude tentatively that size affects

[22]Ibid., p. 911.

[23]Ibid., p. 912.

[24]Jeffrey D. Ford and John W. Slocum, Jr., "Size, Technology, Environment and the Structure of Organizations," *Academy of Management Review*, October 1977, p. 566.

complexity, but at a decreasing rate, in government organizations. Whether this also holds in business firms is problematic. It may well be that in business organizations, where managers have greater discretion, structure causes size. Consistent with the strategy imperative, if managers have discretion, they may choose to make their structures more complex (consistent with management theory) as more activities and personnel are added. It cannot be ruled out, too, that the size-structure relationship is circular. There is evidence indicating that size generates differentiation and that increasing differentiation also generates increasing size.[25]

The strongest case can be made for the effect of size on vertical differentiation.[26] In fact, one study found that size alone was the dominant predictor of vertical differentiation, explaining between 50 and 59 percent of the variance.[27] A less strong but certainly solid case can be made for the size-horizontal differentiation relationship. That is, the larger the organization, the more pronounced (at declining rates) the division of labor within it, the same being true for the functional differentiation of the organization into divisions.[28]

The size-spatial dispersion relationship is problematic. Blau's high correlations are almost certainly attributable to the kind of organizations he studied. Other efforts to assess this relationship have failed to generate Blau's strong positive relationship; however, still other investigations support Blau.[29] Further research covering diverse types of organizations is needed before conclusions of any substance can be drawn.

What about the criticism of the Aston group's work and Hall's research? Our position is that they have not demonstrated the impotence of size. More longitudinal studies are needed to clarify the size-structure causation. But in the interim, we propose that the critics have pointed out methodological problems with several of the important studies confirming the impact of size on complexity and suggested potential alternative hypotheses, although they certainly have not demonstrated size to be irrelevant. Even Hall noted that six of his eleven measures of complexity were significantly related to size.[30]

[25]N. P. Hummon, P. Doriean, and K. Teuter, "A Structural Control Model of Organizational Change," *American Sociological Review,* December 1975, pp. 813–824.

[26]Dennis S. Mileti, David F. Gillespie, and J. Eugene Haas, "Size and Structure in Complex Organizations," *Social Forces,* September 1977, pp. 208–217.

[27]John R. Montanari, *An Expanded Theory of Structural Determination: An Empirical Investigation of the Impact of Managerial Discretion on Organization Structure.* Unpublished doctoral dissertation, University of Colorado, Boulder, 1976.

[28]See, for example, Mileti, Gillespie, and Haas, "Size and Structure in Complex Organizations," pp. 213–214; and George A. Miller and Joseph Conaty, "Differentiation in Organizations: Replication and Cumulation," *Social Forces,* September 1980, pp. 265–274.

[29]Mileti, Gillespie, and Haas, "Size and Structure of Complex Organizations," p. 214.

[30]Hall, Haas, and Johnson, "Organizational Size," pp. 903–912.

Size and Formalization

The Aston findings supported the view that size affects formalization. Hall's conclusion was that formalization could not be implied from knowledge of organization size, but he also acknowledged that it could not be ignored either. "Relatively strong relationships exist between size and the formalization of the authority structure, the stipulation of penalties for rule violation in writing, and the orientation and in-service training procedures. A general association does exist to the extent that larger organizations tend to be more formalized on the other indicators, even though the relationship is quite weak."[31]

There would appear to be a logical connection between an increase in size and an increase in formalization. Management seeks to control the behavior of employees. Two popular methods are direct surveillance and the use of formalized regulations. While not perfect substitutes for each other, as one increases, the need for the other should decrease. Because surveillance costs should increase very rapidly as organizations expand in size, it seems reasonable to propose that there would be economies for management to substitute formalization for direct surveillance as size increases. The evidence supports this contention.[32] Rules and surveillance are both aspects of control. The former is impersonal; the latter requires such activities as supervising work closely and inspecting the quantity and quality of work. In small organizations, control through surveillance may be achieved relatively easily through informal face-to-face relationships. But as the organization grows, there are more subordinates to supervise, so that it becomes increasingly efficient to rely more on rules and regulations for exerting control. An analysis of U.S. manufacturing firms found support for the size-formalization relationship.[33] We can expect, therefore, to find an increase in formal rules and regulations within an organization as that organization increases in size.

After reviewing the size-formalization literature, one author proposed boldly that "the larger the organization, the more formalized its behavior."[34] His explanation, however, emphasized that larger organizations formalize those activities that have a propensity to reoccur often. The larger the organization, the more that behaviors repeat themselves, and, hence, man-

[31]Ibid., p. 911.

[32]William A. Rushing, "Organizational Size, Rules, and Surveillance," in Joseph A. Litterer, ed., *Organizations: Structure and Behavior*, 3rd ed. (New York: John Wiley, 1980), pp. 396–405; and Y. Samuel and B. F. Mannheim, "A Multidimensional Approach Toward a Typology of Bureaucracy," *Administrative Science Quarterly*, June 1970, pp. 216–228.

[33]Rushing, "Organizational Size."

[34]Henry Mintzberg, *The Structuring of Organizations* (Englewood Cliffs, N.J.: Prentice-Hall, 1979), p. 233.

agement is motivated to handle them more efficiently through standardization. With increased size comes greater internal confusion. Given managements' general desires to minimize this confusion, they seek means to make behavior at lower levels in the hierarchy more predictable. Management turns to rules, procedures, job descriptions, and other formalization techniques to bring about this predictability.

Size and Centralization

"It is only common sense that it is impossible to control large organizations from the top: because much more is happening than an individual or set of individuals can comprehend, there is inevitable delegation."[35] But is that the way the evidence stacks? As we concluded, formalization increases with size. These rules and regulations *allow* top management to delegate decision making while at the same time ensure that the decisions are made in accordance with the desires of top management. The research supports that increases in size also lead to decentralization.[36] In small organizations, it's possible for management to exercise control by keeping decisions centralized. As size increases and management is physically unable to maintain control in this manner, it is forced to decentralize. But decentralization is accompanied by increased formalization.

SPECIAL ISSUES RELATING TO ORGANIZATION SIZE

In this section we address two issues related to size. First, as the number of operative personnel increases, what impact does it have on the number of administrators and supporting staff? Second, is organization theory applicable to small organizations?

The Administrative Component Debate

Most of us have heard of Parkinson's law. Written partly in jest and partly in truth, Parkinson declared that "work expands so as to fill the time available for its completion."[37] He argued that, in government at least, "there need be little or no relationship between the work to be done and the size of the staff to which it may be assigned."[38] According to Parkinson,

[35]Richard H. Hall, *Organizations: Structure and Process*, 2nd ed. (Englewood Cliffs, N.J.: Prentice-Hall, 1977), p. 184.

[36]Blau and Schoenherr, *The Structure of Organizations*, Child and Mansfield, "Technology, Size and Organization Structure"; and Pradip N. Khandwalla, "Mass Output Orientation of Operations Technology and Organization Structure," *Administrative Science Quarterly*, March 1974, pp. 74–97.

[37]C. Northcote Parkinson, *Parkinson's Law* (Boston: Houghton Mifflin, 1957), p. 33.

[38]Ibid.

the number of officials in an organization and the quantity of work to be done are not related to each other at all. To "prove" his law, he trotted out figures on the British Royal Navy. As shown in Table 7-1, between 1914 and 1928, the number of warships commissioned declined by nearly 68 percent. Total personnel in the Navy declined by approximately 32 percent. But that apparently had no bearing on the administrative staff whose purpose it was to manage the ships and personnel. The number of on-shore officials and clerks rose by 40 percent over the fourteen-year period, and the officer corp increased a startling 78 percent!

Parkinson's insight initiated a wealth of research into what is now referred to as the "administrative component." It has been stated, in fact, that more studies have probably been conducted on the relationship between organizational size and the administrative component than on any other aspect of organization structure.[39] But what exactly does this term "administrative component" mean?

As with so many concepts to which you have been introduced in this book, the administrative component has no universally agreed-upon definition. Some examples include the ratio between managers and employees; the proportion of line managers and their support staff to operating or production personnel; staff versus line, with the staff composing the administrative component; and all the personnel in an organization who engage in "support" activities.[40] Although there is no general agreement on one of these definitions, we will use the last one. It can be used in various types of organizations and attempts to identify administrative overhead. "Thus, custodial workers, some drivers, cafeteria employees, clerical help, and so on, are included in the administrative component,

TABLE 7–1 Comparative data on the British Royal Navy, 1914 versus 1928

CATEGORY	*1914*	*1928*	*% INCREASE OR DECREASE*
Ships in commission	62	20	−67.74%
Total Navy personnel	146,000	100,000	−31.50
Dockyard workers	57,000	62,439	+9.54
Dockyard officials and clerks	3,249	4,558	+40.28
Admiralty officers	2,000	3,569	+78.45

Source: C. Northcote Parkinson *Parkinson's Law* (Boston: Houghton Mifflin, 1957).

[39]John Child, "Parkinson's Progress: Accounting for the Number of Specialists in Organizations," *Administrative Science Quarterly*, September 1973, pp. 328–346.

[40]Ibid., p. 329.

regardless of whether they are directly employed in 'staff' or 'general administrative' divisions."[41] Those persons who contribute indirectly to the attainment of the organization's goals, whether operatives or managers, become part of the administrative component. This, then, is our working definition. However, keep in mind that researchers have used various definitions and that this may explain some of the diversity in the findings that we will report.

The positive correlation argument. Parkinson's thesis says basically that there would be a positive relationship between organizational size and the administrative component. As organizations increased in size, the relative size of the administrative component would increase disproportionately. Can this relationship be defended intuitively? The basic explanation would be that administrators and staff are responsible for providing coordination, and because coordination becomes increasingly difficult as more employees who contribute directly to the organization's goals are added, the administrative component can be expected to increase out of proportion to increases in size. Some studies support this positive relationship. For instance, a study of over four hundred California school districts found that the administrative component—superintendent, assistants, principals, business managers, and other support staff—increased as the size of the school district increased.[42] But there are far more studies showing the size-administrative component relationship to be either negative or curvilinear.

The negative correlation argument. Exclusive of any empirical data, it seems more reasonable to expect the administrative component to decline as size increases. We are not arguing that the absolute number of supportive personnel would decline, but rather that it should decline as a *proportion* as size increases. This conclusion is based on the assumption of efficiencies from economies of scale. As organizations expand they, of course, require more managers and staff to facilitate coordination. But not in the same proportion as size increases. A manufacturing firm that does $5 million a year in sales and employs sixty people may require the services of a full-time purchasing agent. If sales doubled, it's unlikely that the firm would need two purchasing agents. Similarly, a typical hospital can increase its patient load by 10 percent with little or no addition in accounting personnel, dietitians, and the like. Both examples illustrate economies of scale that suggest that as an organization grows there should be a decrease in the proportion of personnel allocated to indirect activities. The logic of this argument has received substantial empirical support.

[41]Hall, *Organizations: Structure and Process*, p. 110.

[42]Frederic W. Terrien and Donald L. Mills, "The Effect of Changing Size upon the Internal Structure of Organizations," *American Sociological Review*, February 1955, pp. 11–14.

A study of Veterans Administration hospitals found the administrative component to decrease as the organizations increased in size.[43] An investigation of five sets of organizations—including package delivery services, automobile dealerships, volunteer fire companies, labor union locals, and political associations—also found a negative relationship.[44] In each of the sets of organizations, as the size of the organizations increased, the administrative component declined. Census information by industry was used by another investigator to test the size-administrative component relationship.[45] While a negative relationship was found, it was concluded that this could be explained better as due to the loss of control across hierarchial levels than to economies of scale with large size. Moreover owner-managed organizations and partnerships were found to be less likely to add administrators than were incorporated firms because to do so would result in dilution of the owners' personal power. So, while this research confirms the negative correlation, it suggests that maintenance of control may be a primary motivator for owners of firms to keep the number of administrators and support staff in check as the size of the organization increases.

The curvilinear argument. There is also evidence to suggest that the size-administrative component relationship is not linear.[46] Rather, it is curvilinear—the administrative component is greater for smaller and larger organizations than for those of moderate size. As organizations move out of the small category, defined in one study as 700 or fewer employees,[47] they enjoy the benefits from economies of scale. But as they become large (defined in this same study as over 1,400 employees), they lose these benefits and become so complex as to require significant increases in the administrative component to facilitate coordination and control.

Conclusions. Trying to draw practical conclusions from the research on the administrative component may be impossible. No consistent patterns emerge. Whether this is due to the fact that *any* relationship found

[43]Theodore Anderson and Seymour Warkov, "Organizational Size and Functional Complexity: A Study of Administration in Hospitals," *American Sociological Review*, February 1961, pp. 23–28.

[44]Bernard P. Indik, "The Relationship Between Organization Size and Supervision Ratio," *Administrative Science Quarterly*, December 1964, pp. 301–312.

[45]Louis R. Pondy, "Effects of Size, Complexity, and Ownership on Administrative Intensity," *Administrative Science Quarterly*, March 1969, pp. 47–60.

[46]See, for example, John E. Tsouderos, "Organizational Change in Terms of a Series of Selected Variables," *American Sociological Review*, April 1955, pp. 206–210; J. Eugene Haas, Richard H. Hall, and Norman Johnson, "The Size of the Supportive Component in Organizations: A Multi-Organizational Analysis," *Social Forces*, October 1963, pp. 9–17; and Hawley, Boland, and Boland, "Population Size and Administration."

[47]Haas, Hall, and Johnson, "The Size of the Supportive Components," p. 14.

between size and the administrative component is purely spurious or due to inconsistencies in the way that the administrative component is measured can only be answered through more research. It's possible, for example, that the dominant determinant of the administrative component is not size at all. Arguments have been made that better predictors include complexity,[48] technology and environment,[49] or whether the organization is declining or growing.[50] On this last determinant, for instance, several investigations have found that the process of decline in organizations does not have the opposite effect on the administrative component as does growth. The administrative component tends to increase on the upswings but decreases less on the downswings, suggesting that management may be reluctant to let members of the administrative component go during periods of decline. We will discuss the different problems associated with growth versus decline at length in Chapter 17.

So where does all this leave us? First, there are economies of scale operating to reduce the relative size of the administrative component as the organization's size increases. But these economies do not exist *regardless* of the increase in size. At some point, the diseconomies of size offset the economies, and more support staff is required to coordinate the organization's activities. Just where this "point" is, however, is unclear. It undoubtedly varies by industry or type of organization, reflecting different technologies and environments.

Second, size is not the only factor that influences the administrative component. Other factors undoubtedly include the type of organization, environment and technology, complexity, and whether the organization is undergoing growth or decline.

Finally, maybe Parkinson was right given the "animal" he chose to observe—the British Royal Navy. The Navy was probably operating in the diseconomy zone, where increases in size were accompanied by comparable or large increases in the administrative component. Also, government employees have little motivation to keep the administrative component in check as we might expect in the owner-dominated business firm. Maybe what Parkinson discovered is that "in the absence of direct performance measures, managers build empires."[51] However, Parkinson's observation

[48]William A. Rushing, "The Effects of Industry Size and Division of Labor on Administration," *Administrative Science Quarterly*, September 1967, pp. 273–295; and Sheila R. Klatzky, "Relationship of Organizational Size to Complexity and Coordination," *Administrative Science Quarterly*, December 1970, pp. 428–438.

[49]John H. Freeman, "Environment, Technology, and the Administrative Intensity of Manufacturing Organizations," *American Sociological Review*, December 1973, pp. 750–763.

[50]Gerry E. Hendershot and Thomas F. James, "Size and Growth as Determinants of Administrative-Production Ratios in Organizations," *American Sociological Review*, April 1972, pp. 149–153; John H. Freeman and Michael T. Hannan, "Growth and Decline Processes in Organizations," *American Sociological Review*, April 1975, pp. 215–228.

[51]Mintzberg, *The Structuring of Organizations*, p. 240.

is undoubtedly not a "law"; rather, he has given us an accurate description of what occurs under certain specific conditions.

Organization Theory and Small Businesses

We live in a society dominated by large organizations. It is true that more than 30 percent of all U.S. organizations have three or fewer employees, but they employ less than one-half of 1 percent of the work force.[52] In contrast, organizations with a thousand or more employees may not be many in number—only about 8,000 of the 4 million organizations in the United States fall in this category—but they employ nearly 25 percent of the entire work force! While there may be a great number of small organizations, large organizations have the greatest impact on our society.

These considerations have not been lost on those who study organization theory. Studies are made up almost exclusively of medium-sized and large organizations, those with hundreds of employees or more. Even textbook authors fall prey to this bias—you'll find lots of references to large school districts and government agencies, or General Motors, Exxon, and IBM-sized firms in this book, but rarely a mention of the small business, particularly the owner-managed firm. As such, it may be appropriate to ask: Does the organization theory being described in this book have any application to those who manage or expect to manage a small business?[53]

Because small organizations have been substantially overlooked by organization theorists, there is an inherent assumption that their findings are universally appropriate. Yet the few studies that have looked at small organizations indicate the inapplicability of parts of large-organization theory. The small-business owner is often willing to settle for lesser monetary reward in return for personal control and accountability. Certainly this can and does affect the type of structure that he or she will design. Also, such issues as vertical differentiation, decentralization, or information control take on a lesser, or at least a different, role in small organizations than they do in large ones.

Just the large number of small organizations is enough to make them significant. The additional fact that small organizations have less tolerance for inefficiency than do established larger organizations is certainly cause for attention. Organization theory may be more important to the small firm because it does not have the slack resources so often prevalent in its larger counterpart to absorb its mistakes.

Some of the OT concepts presented in this book undoubtedly are

[52]U.S. Department of Labor, Bureau of Labor Statistics, *Employment and Wages, First Quarter 1976* (Springfield, Va.: National Technical Information Service, 1979), pp. 548–549.

[53]This section is substantially adapted from Thomas C. Dandrige, "Children Are Not 'Little Grown-ups': Small Business Needs Its Own Organization Theory," *Journal of Small Business Management*, April 1979, pp. 53–57.

applicable to any size of organization. But many are not. Unfortunately, we do not know which apply and which do not. So we must conclude that, at least at this point in time, OT is a special theory. It *may* apply to small businesses, but we cannot say this with certainty. A great deal more research is needed, specifically covering small businesses, so that we can expand OT into a field applicable to all organizations. Currently, its findings come from minority-type organizations. As such, these findings must be qualified to reflect their limitations.

SUMMARY

Organizational size is defined as the total number of employees. Strong arguments have been proposed indicating that size is the major determinant of structure, but there has been no shortage of critics to this position.

A review of the evidence indicates that size has a significant influence on vertical differentiation. The effect of size on spatial dispersion is unclear. Increases in formalization appear to be related closely to increases in organizational size. Finally, increases in size and decentralization tend to be found together.

More studies have probably been conducted on the relationship between organization size and the administrative component than any other aspect of organization structure. We defined the administrative component as all the personnel in an organization who engage in supportive activities. Our literature review led us to conclude that the relationship between size and the administrative component is curvilinear and that other factors—the type of organization, environment and technology, complexity, and whether the organization is growing or declining—in addition to size, influence the administrative component.

This chapter closed by noting that OT is based on studies made up almost exclusively of medium-sized and large organizations. As a result, any conclusions as to OT's applicability to small businesses must be guarded.

FOR REVIEW AND DISCUSSION

1. American College has 100 full-time faculty, 10 part-time faculty, and 1,500 full-time students. National College has 30 full-time faculty, 150 part-time faculty, and 2,000 full-time students. Continental College has 50 full-time faculty, 30 part-time faculty, and 2,500 students. Assuming that each has a support staff of 75 and no part-time students, which organization is the largest in size? Explain.
2. "One of the strongest cases for the size imperative has been made by Meyer." What is the support for this statement?

3. "Size is the major determinant of structure." Build an argument to support this statement. Then build an argument to refute this statement.
4. What is the relationship between size and complexity?
5. What is the relationship between size and formalization?
6. What is the relationship between size and centralization?
7. What is the "administrative component"? Why is it an important issue in OT?
8. "Size and the administrative component should be correlated positively." Build an argument to support this statement. Then build an argument to refute this statement.
9. Relate (a) the administrative component, (b) economies of scale, and (c) coordination.
10. What specific concepts in the first seven chapters of this book do you think have limited applicability to small business? Why?

CHAPTER

8

TECHNOLOGY

The Ford Motor Company and the Avanti Motor Company both produce automobiles. You know about Ford. It builds about 3 million cars a year, worldwide, on an assembly-line basis. A typical Ford production line turns out forty to fifty cars per hour. In contrast, you may not have ever heard of Avanti Motors. Operating out of a plant in South Bend, Indiana, it makes custom luxury sedans based on a twenty-year-old Studebaker design. Avanti builds each car to order, one at a time, and it turns out about twenty cars a month. While both are in the automobile manufacturing industry, they use dramatically different technologies to build their vehicles. Forgetting for a moment that Ford's size overwhelms Avanti, the former making more cars in ten minutes worldwide than the latter produces in a year, you would expect these differences to impact the structures of their respective organizations. For instance, the tasks that employees do—highly routine and specialized at Ford and quite loose, flexible, and interchanging at Avanti—should have a significant influence on each one's structure. And, of course, it does.

This example illustrates that the way in which an organization converts its inputs to outputs has some bearing on structure. Is it *the* dominant determinant of a structure or is it merely *a* determinant? By the time you finish reading this chapter, you will find that it can be both. As usual, however, let us begin by clarifying what we mean by the term. As with so many concepts in OT, the way in which it is defined and measured has a great deal to do with the consistency of the research surrounding it and the confidence we have in generalizing from this research. There is probably no construct in OT where diversity of measurement has produced more incompatible findings and confusion than the research on technology.

DEFINING TECHNOLOGY

As long as we stay at a relatively abstract level, there is general agreement among OT researchers that technology refers to the processes or methods that transform inputs into outputs in the organization. That is, technology looks at *how* the inputs are transferred to outputs. There is also agreement that the concept of technology, despite its mechanical or manufacturing connotation, is applicable to all types and kinds of organizations. As discussed in Chapter 1, all organizations turn inputs into outputs. Regardless of whether the organization is a manufacturing firm, a bank, a hospital, a social service agency, a research laboratory, a newspaper, or a military squadron, it will use a technology of some sort to produce its product or service. This even includes colleges, which can use a number of instruction technologies to teach their students. There is the ever-popular formal lecture method, but there are other ways in which to transform the uninformed into the enlightened; for instance, there is the case analysis method, the group discussion method, the experiential exercise method, and the programmed learning method.

The problems begin when we move from the abstract to the specific. At issue is basically the question: How does one measure technology? Researchers have used a number of technology classifications. A partial list would include operations techniques used in work flow activities; characteristics of the materials used in the work flow; varying complexities in the knowledge system used in the work flow; the degree of continuous, fixed-sequence operations; the extent of automation; and the degree of interdependence between work systems. Each of these measures of technology is a bit different, and you would expect them to obtain different results even if they were applied to the same organization.

But this introduces several additional problems: varying types and sizes of organizations and different levels of analysis. Some studies have been limited to manufacturing firms. Others have included only very large organizations. Still others have been directed at the organizational level, yet the researchers attempt to compare their findings with studies conducted at the job level. Not surprisingly, these efforts to compare apples with oranges, under the guise of fruit, or generalizing to all organizations from samples that are highly limited, might be expected to end up producing conflicting results. And that is exactly what has happened.

Where does this leave us? To minimize confusion, we will restrict our discussion to only the landmark contributions to the technology-structure debate. We present the three paradigms cited most frequently and evaluate the research undertaken to test their validity. The three take very different perspectives on technology, but they will give you the basics for understanding what we know about how technology affects structure. After reviewing these three positions, we tie them together, ascertain where we stand today on the technological imperative, and determine what specific statements we can make accurately as to the impact of technology on structure.

THE INITIAL THRUST: WOODWARD'S RESEARCH

The initial interest in technology as a determinant of structure can be traced to the mid-1960s and the work of Joan Woodward.[1] Her research, which focused on production technology, was the first major attempt to view organization structure from a technological perspective.

Background

Woodward chose approximately one hundred manufacturing firms in the south of England. These firms ranged in size from fewer than 250 employees to over 1,000. She gathered data that allowed her to compute various measures of structure: the number of hierarchial levels, the span of control, the administrative component, the extent of formalization, and the like. She also gathered financial data on each firm (profitability, sales, market share, etc.) that allowed her to classify the companies as above average, average, or below average in terms of success or organizational effectiveness. Her objective was straightforward: Is there a correlation between structural form and effectiveness? Her hypothesis, derived from the classical prescriptions of management theorists, was that there is one optimum form of organizational structure that leads to organizational effectiveness.

Her efforts to link common structures with effectiveness were a dismal failure. The structural diversity among the firms in each of her effectiveness categories was so great that it was impossible to establish any relationship or draw any meaningful conclusions between what was regarded as sound organizational structure and effectiveness. It was only after Woodward grouped the firms according to their typical mode of production technology that relationships between structure and effectiveness became apparent.

Woodward categorized the firms into one of three types of technologies: unit, mass, or process production. She treated these categories as a scale with increasing degrees of technological complexity, with unit being the least complex and process being the most complex. Unit producers

[1]Joan Woodward, *Industrial Organization: Theory and Practice* (London: Oxford University Press, 1965).

would manufacture custom-made products such as tailor-made suits, turbines for hydroelectric dams, battle ships, or Avanti cars. Mass producers would make large-batch or mass-produced products such as refrigerators or Ford automobiles. The third category, process production, included heavily automated continuous-process producers such as oil and chemical refiners.

Conclusions

Woodward found that there were (1) distinct relationships between these technology classifications and the subsequent structure of the firms and (2) the effectiveness of the organizations were related to the "fit" between technology and structure.

For example, the degree of vertical differentiation increased with technical complexity. The median levels for firms in the unit, mass, and process categories were three, four, and six. More important, from an effectiveness standpoint, the above-average firms in each category tended to cluster around the median for their production group.

Woodward also found that the administrative component varied directly with type of technology; that is, as technological complexity increased, so did the proportion of administrative and supportive staff personnel. But not all the relationships were linear. For instance, the mass-production firms had the smallest proportion of skilled workers, and the mass-production firms scored high in terms of overall complexity and formalization, whereas the unit and process firms tended to rate low on these structural dimensions.

A careful analysis of her findings led Woodward to conclude that, for each category on the technology scale (unit-mass-process) and for each structural component, there was an optimal range around the median point that encompassed the positions of the more effective firms. That is, within each technological category, the firms that conformed most nearly to the median figures for each structural component were the most effective. The mass-production technology firms were highly differentiated, relied on extensive formalization, and did relatively little to delegate authority. Both the unit and process technologies, in contrast, were structured more loosely. Flexibility was achieved through less vertical differentiation, less division of labor and more group activities, more widely defined role responsibilities, and decentralized decision making. High formalization and centralized control apparently was not feasible with unit production's custom-made, nonroutine technology and not necessary in the heavily automated, inherently tightly controlled, continuous-process technology.

Woodward's investigation demonstrated a link among technology, structure, and effectiveness. There was, she argued, no one best way in which to organize manufacturing firms. The key to understanding the relationship between structure and effectiveness was to consider technology. Organizations that had developed structures that conformed to their technologies were more successful than were those that did not.

Evaluation

Several follow-up studies have supported Woodward's findings, but she has also had her share of criticism. Let us review what others have had to say about Woodward's research.

Edward Harvey was an early advocate of Woodward.[2] He believed that the underlying foundation of Woodward's scale was technical specificity. That is, he assumed that more specific technologies present fewer problems that require new or innovative solutions than do more diffuse or complex technologies. So he took forty-three different industrial organizations and rated them as technically diffuse (which closely paralleled Woodward's unit production), technically intermediate (akin to mass production), and technically specific (similar to Woodward's process production). These categories were based on the number of major product changes that the sample firms had experienced in the ten years prior to the study. Harvey found, consistent with Woodward's technological imperative, a relationship between technical specificity and structure. Basically, organizations with specific technologies had more specialized subunits, more authority levels, and higher ratios of managers to total personnel than did those with diffuse technologies.

Woodward's findings were also supported in another study of manufacturing firms.[3] The researcher found, as did Woodward, no evidence that there was such a thing as a universally optimum structural form. His data constituted strong evidence to confirm Woodward's claim that unit, mass, and process production result in different structural forms and that proper fit within categories increased the likelihood that the organization would be successful.

Woodward's research and analysis by no means developed a tightly sealed argument for the technological imperative. Attacks have been made at a number of levels.[4] Her measure of technology has been criticized as unreliable. Her methodology, since it relied primarily on subjective observations and interviews, is open to interpretational bias. Woodward implies causation, yet her methodology can only allow her to claim association.

[2]Edward Harvey, "Technology and the Structure of Organizations," *American Sociological Review*, April 1968, pp. 247–259.

[3]William L. Zwerman, *New Perspectives on Organization Theory* (Westport, Conn.: Greenwood Publishing, 1970).

[4]See, for example, Lex Donaldson, "Woodward Technology, Organizational Structure, and Performance—A Critique of the Universal Generalization," *Journal of Management Studies*, October 1976, pp. 255–273.

Her measures of organizational success are open to attack as lacking rigor. Finally, since her firms were all British companies engaged almost exclusively in manufacturing, any generalizations to all organizations, or even to manufacturing firms outside Great Britain, must be guarded.

KNOWLEDGE-BASED TECHNOLOGY: PERROW'S CONTRIBUTION

One of the major limitations of Woodward's perspective on technology was its manufacturing base. Since manufacturing firms represent less than half of all organizations, technology needs to be operationalized in a more general way if the concept is to have meaning across all organizations. Charles Perrow has proposed such an alternative.[5]

Background

Perrow looked at knowledge technology rather than at production technology. He defined technology as "the action that an individual performs upon an object, with or without the aid of tools or mechanical devices, in order to make some change in that object."[6] Perrow then proceeded to identify what he believed to be the two underlying dimensions of knowledge technology.

The first dimension considered the number of exceptions encountered in one's work. Labeled *task variability,* these exceptions would be few in number if the job is high in routineness. Jobs that normally have few exceptions in their day-to-day practice would include those on an automobile assembly line or being a fry cook at McDonald's. At the other end of the spectrum, if a job has a great deal of variety, a large number of exceptions can be expected. Typically, this would characterize top management positions, consulting jobs, or the work of those who make a living by putting out fires on off-shore oil platforms. So task variability appraises work by evaluating it along a variety-routineness continuum.

The second dimension assesses the type of search procedures followed to find successful methods for responding adequately to task exceptions. The search can, at one extreme, be described as well defined. An individual can use logical and analytical reasoning in search for a solution. If you are basically a high "B" student and you suddenly fail the first exam given in a course, you logically analyze the problem and find a solution. Did you spend enough time studying for the exam? Did you study the right material? Was the exam fair? How did other good students do? Using this kind of logic, you can find the source of the problem and rectify it.

[5]Charles Perrow, "A Framework for the Comparative Analysis of Organizations," *American Sociological Review,* April 1967, pp. 194–208.

[6]Ibid.

In contrast, the other extreme would be ill-defined problems. If you are an architect assigned to design a building to conform to standards and constraints that you have never read about or encountered before, you will not have any formal search technique to use. You will have to rely on your prior experience, judgment, and intuition to find a solution. Through guess work and trial and error you might find an acceptable choice. Perrow called this second dimension *problem analyzability,* ranging from well defined to ill defined.

These two dimensions—task variability and problem analyzability—can be used to construct a two-by-two matrix. This is shown in Figure 8–1. The four cells in this matrix represent four types of technology: routine, engineering, craft, and nonroutine.

Routine technologies (cell 1) have few exceptions and easy-to-analyze problems. The mass-production processes used to make steel or automobiles or to refine petroleum belong in this category.Engineering technologies (cell 2) have a large number of exceptions, but they can be handled in a rational and systematized manner. The construction of office buildings would fall in this cell. Craft technologies (cell 3) deal with relatively difficult problems, but with a limited set of exceptions. This would include shoemaking or furniture restoring. Finally, nonroutine technologies (cell 4) are characterized by many exceptions and difficult-to-analyze problems. Basically, this describes many aerospace operations or, more specifically, the kind of work that NASA personnel confronted in the late 1960s as they prepared to launch a manned spacecraft that would land on and return from the moon.

In summary, Perrow argued that, if problems can be studied systematically, using logical and rational analysis, cells 1 or 2 would be appropriate. Problems that can be handled only by intuition, guesswork, or unanalyzed experience require the technology of cells 3 or 4. Similarly, if

FIGURE 8–1 Perrow's technology classification

Problem Analyzability / Task Variability	Routine with few exceptions	High variety with many exceptions
Well defined and analyzable	Routine 1	Engineering 2
Ill defined and unanalyzable	Craft 3	Nonroutine 4

new, unusual, or unfamiliar problems appear regularly, they would be in either cells 2 or 4. If problems are familiar, then cells 1 or 3 are appropriate.

Conclusions

Perrow argued that control and coordination methods should vary with technology type. The more routine the technology, the more highly structured the organization should be. Conversely, nonroutine technologies require greater structural flexibility. Perrow then identified the key aspects of structure that could be modified to the technology: (1) the amount of *discretion* that can be exercised for completing tasks, (2) the *power* of groups to control the unit's goals and basic strategies, (3) the extent of *interdependence* between these two groups, and (4) the extent to which these groups engage in *coordination* of their work using either feedback or the planning of others.

What does all this mean? Simply that the most routine technology (cell 1) can be accomplished best through standardized coordination and control. These technologies should be aligned with structures that are high in both formalization and centralization. At the other extreme, nonroutine technologies (cell 4) demand flexibility. Basically, they would be decentralized, have high interaction among all members, and be characterized as having a minimum degree of formalization. In between, craft technology (cell 3) requires that problem solving be done by those with the greatest knowledge and experience. That means decentralization. And engineering technology (cell 2), because it has many exceptions but analyzable search processes, should have decisions centralized but maintain flexibility through low formalization.

Evaluation

The two-by-two matrix of technologies, and the predictions of what structural dimensions are most compatible with these technologies, was not examined empirically by Perrow. But others have tested the theory.

One study of fourteen medium-sized manufacturing firms that looked only at the two extreme cells—routine and nonroutine technologies—found support for Perrow's predictions.[7] Another, covering sixteen health and welfare agencies, confirmed (1) that organizations do have diverse technologies and (2) that the more routine the work, the more likely decision making will be centralized.[8]

[7]Karl Magnusen, *Technology and Organizational Differentiation: A Field Study of Manufacturing Corporations.* Unpublished doctoral dissertation, University of Wisconsin, Madison, 1970.

[8]Jerald Hage and Michael Aiken, "Routine Technology, Social Structure, and Organizational Goals," *Administrative Science Quarterly*, September 1969, pp. 366–377.

State employment service agencies were the set of organizations analyzed in yet another test of Perrow's theory.[9] In this study, technology was operationalized at the unit rather than organizational level, in the belief that, if routineness of technology actually affects structure, this effect should be greatest at the unit level. Again, the results proved consistent with Perrow's predictions: work that was high in routineness was associated with high formalization.

In summary, there appears to be considerable support for Perrow's conclusions. Organizations and organizational subunits with routine technologies tend to have greater formalization and centralization than do their counterparts with nonroutine technologies.

One note of caution before we move on. Perrow's original theory went somewhat beyond what we have presented here. He predicted, for instance, relationships between the type of technology and structural aspects such as hierarchial discretion levels and types of coordination. These other relationships have found limited support by way of empirical studies.[10] We point this out to acknowledge that Perrow has his critics and that there is ammunition available for attacking his matrix theory. But at the general level—and by that we mean the issues of whether technologies can be differentiated on the basis of routineness and whether more routine technologies are associated with higher degrees of formalization and centralization—the evidence is largely supportive.

TECHNOLOGICAL UNCERTAINTY: THOMPSON'S CONTRIBUTION

The third major contribution to the technology-structure literature has been made by James Thompson.[11] In contrast to Woodward and Perrow, Thompson is not a member of the technological imperative school. Rather, as will be shown, Thompson's contribution lies in demonstrating that technology determines the selection of a strategy for reducing uncertainty and that specific structural arrangements can facilitate uncertainty reduction.

Background

Thompson sought to create a classification scheme that was general enough to deal with the range of technologies found in complex organizations. He proposed three types that are differentiated by the tasks that an organizational unit performs.

[9]Andrew H. Van de Ven and André L. Delbecq, "A Task Contingent Model of Work-Unit Structure," *Administrative Science Quarterly,* June 1974, pp. 183–197.

[10]See, for example, Lawrence Mohr, "Operations Technology and Organizational Structure," *Administrative Science Quarterly,* December 1971, pp. 444–459.

[11]James D. Thompson, *Organizations in Action* (New York: McGraw-Hill, 1967).

Long-linked technology. If tasks or operations are sequentially interdependent, Thompson called them long-linked. This technology is characterized by a fixed sequence of repetitive steps, as shown in Figure 8–2A. That is, act A must be performed before act B, act B before act C, and so forth. Examples of long-linked technology include mass-production assembly lines and most school cafeterias.

Because long-linked technologies require efficiency and coordination among activities, due to sequential interdependencies, the major uncertainties facing management lie on the input and output sides of the organization. Acquiring raw materials, for instance, and disposing of finished goods become major areas of concern. As a result, management tends to respond to this uncertainty by controlling inputs and outputs. One of the best means for achieving this end is to integrate vertically—forward, backward, or both. This allows them to encompass important sources of uncertainty within their boundaries. Reynolds Metals has large plants for manufacturing aluminum foil. It integrates backward by controlling its input, operating aluminum mines and reduction mills that provide the raw materials to the foil plants. It integrates forward by controlling its output,

FIGURE 8-2 Thompson's technology classification

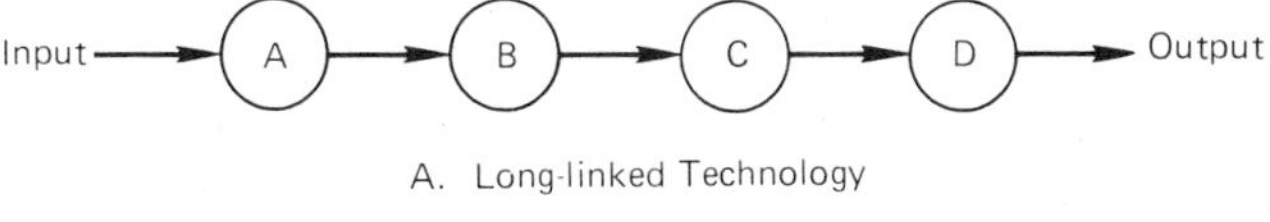

A. Long-linked Technology

B. Mediating Technology

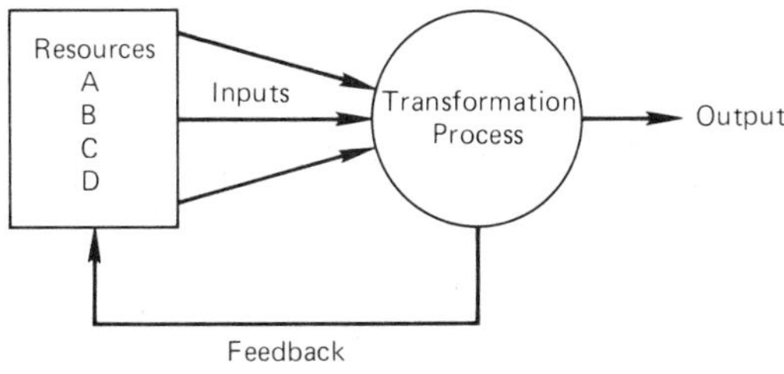

C. Intensive Technology

marketing much of its foil through supermarkets under the name of Reynolds Wrap.

Mediating technology. Thompson identified mediating technology as one that links clients on both the input and output side of the organization. Banks, telephone utilities, employment and welfare agencies, and post offices are examples. As shown in Figure 8–2B, mediators perform an interchange function linking units that are otherwise independent. The linking unit responds with standardizing the organization's transactions and establishing conformity in client's behavior. Banks, for instance, bring together those who want to save (depositors) with those who want to borrow. Neither know each other, but the bank's success depends on attracting both. A bank with money and no borrowers cannot succeed. Failure can also occur when borrowers are plentiful but no one wants to leave his or her money with the bank. As a result, the managers of mediating technologies face uncertainty as a result of the organization's potential dependency on clients and the risks inherent in client transactions.

How does one deal with this uncertainty? By increasing the populations served. The more clients one has, the less dependent one is upon any single client. So banks seek many depositors and attempt to develop a diversified loan portfolio. Similarly, employment agencies seek to fill jobs for many employers so that the loss of one or two major accounts will not jeopardize the organization's survival.

Intensive technology. Thompson's third category—intensive technology—represents a customized response to a diverse set of contingencies. The exact response depends on the nature of the problem and the variety of problems, which cannot be predicted accurately. This includes technologies dominant in hospitals, universities, research labs, or military combat teams.

> The intensive technology is most dramatically illustrated by the general hospital. At any moment an emergency admission may require some combination of dietary, x-ray, laboratory, and housekeeping or hotel services, together with the various medical specialties, pharmaceutical services, occupational therapies, social work services, and spiritual or religious services. Which of these, and when, can be determined only from evidence about the state of the patient.[12]

Figure 8–2C demonstrates that intensive technology achieves coordination through mutual adjustment. A number of multiple resources are

[12]Ibid., p. 17.

available to the organization, but only a limited combination is used at a given time depending on the situation. The selection, combination, and ordering of these resources are determined by feedback from the object itself. Because of this need for flexibility of response, the major uncertainty that managers confront is the problem itself. So managers respond by ensuring the availability of a variety of resources to prepare for any contingency. As in our hospital example, the organization has a wealth of specialized services and skills available with which it can respond to a variety of situations.

Conclusions

The structural implications from Thompson's framework are less straightforward than are those derived from the work of Woodward and Perrow. Basically, each technology creates a type of interdependence. Long-linked technology is accompanied by *sequential* interdependence—the procedures are highly standardized and must be performed in a specified serial order. Mediating technology has *pooled* interdependence—two or more units each contribute separately to a larger unit. Intensive technology creates *reciprocal* interdependence—the outputs of each unit become inputs for the others. Each of these interdependencies, in turn, demands a certain type of coordination that will facilitate organizational effectiveness yet minimize costs.

In general terms, we can translate Thompson's insights into structural terminology. He argued that the demands placed on decision making and communication as a result of technology increased from mediating (low) to long-linked (medium) to intensive (high). Mediating technology is coordinated most effectively through rules and procedures. Long-linked should be accompanied by planning and scheduling. Intensive technology requires mutual adjustment. This suggests that:

Mediating technology = low complexity and high formalization

Long-linked technology = moderate complexity and formalization

Intensive technology = high complexity and low formalization

Let us look at the research to evaluate empirically the validity of Thompson's predictions.

Evaluation

There is, unfortunately, a shortage of data against which Thompson's predictions can be judged. The only study of consequence using Thompson's dimensions did not measure structure, but rather the technology-organizational effectiveness relationship.[13] Analyzing 297 subunits from seventeen business and industrial firms, investigators were able to support part of Thompson's model. Long-linked and mediating technologies were associated closely with the use of standardization, rules, and advanced planning, whereas intensive technologies were characterized by mutual adjustments to other units. They concluded that the criteria of effectiveness varies with the type of technology used by the organizational unit.

The lack of data makes it impossible to conclude whether Thompson's framework is valid or invalid. It is interesting and it allows for comparing a wide range of varying organizations. Its value, however, may lie far more in offering a rich and descriptive technology classification than in providing insights into the relationship between technology and structure.

TYING IT TOGETHER: WHAT DOES IT ALL MEAN?

In this section, we integrate what we know about technology and draw some meaningful generalizations from what is clearly a highly heterogeneous body of research. We can begin by contrasting the "technological imperative" position to the "technological influence" position.

Imperative versus Influence

As with strategy and size, there are those who view technology as *the* determinant of structure. This technological imperative group includes Woodward and Perrow. However, keep in mind that technology can have an important effect on structure without being imperative. Technology and structure are both multidimensional concepts, and we should not expect them to be related in any simple manner.

A more reasonable position may be that technology constrains managers. If managers have a considerable degree of choice over their organization's technology, there is little basis for the imperative argument. Technology would only control structure to the degree that managers chose a technology that demanded certain structural dimensions. For instance, it has been argued that organizations choose their domain and, hence, the activities in which they will engage.[14] If an organization decides to offer consulting advice tailored to the needs of its clients, it is not likely to use long-linked technology. Similarly, the fact that Volkswagen of America chose to build a manufacturing facility in Pennsylvania that could produce

[13]Thomas A. Mahoney and Peter J. Frost, "The Role of Technology in Models of Organizational Effectiveness," *Organizational Behavior and Human Performance*, February 1974, pp. 122–138.

[14]Jeffrey Pfeffer, *Organizational Design* (Arlington Heights, Ill.: AHM Publishing, 1978), p. 99.

at least 600 cars a day, which could, in turn, retail in the $7,000 to $9,000 range, pretty well eliminated any technology other than mass production. Had VW of America decided to produce only six cars a day at that plant and to charge $100,000 or more for each car (which describes more accurately the production facility at Rolls Royce), then mass production might not at all be appropriate. The point is that "choice of a domain, and a set of activities and tasks, tends to constrain the organization's technology, but the domain is still chosen."[15]

The Common Denominator: Routineness

The common theme throughout this chapter, sometimes more explicitly evident than others, is that the processes or methods that transform inputs into outputs differ by their degree of routineness.[16]

Woodward identified three types of technology—unit, mass, and process—each representing, respectively, an increased degree of technological complexity. At the extremes, unit technology deals with custom or nonroutine activities; process technology describes automated and standardized activities. Her mass technology is basically routine in nature. Perrow, too, presented two extremes—routine and nonroutine technologies. His "in-between" technologies—engineering and craft—also differ on routineness, the former more standardized than the latter. Finally, Thompson's categories include two technologies that are relatively routine (long-linked and mediating) and one that is nonroutine (intensive). Table 8–1 summarizes these observations.

The research on technology has gone a number of different ways, yet there is a common underlying theme. Of course, Woodward, Perrow,

TABLE 8–1 Cataloging technologies as routine or nonroutine

	TECHNOLOGY	
CONTRIBUTOR	*ROUTINE*	*NONROUTINE*
Woodward	Mass, Process	Unit
Perrow	Routine, Engineering	Craft, Nonroutine
Thompson	Long-linked, Mediating	Intensive

[15]Ibid.

[16]Donald Gerwin, "Relationships Between Structure and Technology at the Organizational and Job Levels," *Journal of Management Studies*, February 1979, p. 71.

Thompson, and others' technology paradigms are not substitutable for each other. But this is not a book for researchers. Our intention is to provide some meaningful insights into organization theory for use by managers. Given this less demanding objective, conceptualizing technology as differing by degrees of routineness should be adequate for our analysis, included at the end of this chapter, which evaluates technology's impact on our three structural components.

Impact of Size

The strongest attacks against the technological imperative has come from those who argue that organizational size is the critical determinant of structure.[17] For instance, several of the Aston group studies failed to find an association between technology and organization structure.[18] Rather, size was found to have a more dominant influence on structure.

In one case, the Aston group was able to support Woodward's conclusions between technology and structure, but again the explanation for the association was based on size.[19] If technology has an influence on structure, the Aston group reasoned, it is most likely to affect those activities closest to the technology itself. Therefore, the larger the size of the organization, the smaller the role technology is likely to play. Conversely, the smaller the organization, the more likely it is that the whole organization will be impinged upon by the production work flow or operating core. They then noted that the firms Woodward sampled were basically small in size and thus more likely to be influenced by their technology. Their conclusion: in smaller organizations the structure of operations is likely to be dominated by the primary transformation process, but in large organizations the impact of technology is not likely to be so powerful. And where is technology's influence the greatest? On those organizational units immediately impinged upon by the operating core.

Job Level versus Organizational Level

The size argument makes an excellent introduction to our next topic: the difference between job-level studies and organizational-level studies. A very strong argument has been built on the fact that (1) research studies

[17]See, for example, David J. Hickson, D. S. Pugh, and Diana C. Pheysey, "Operations Technology and Organization Structure: An Empirical Reappraisal," *Administrative Science Quarterly*, September 1979, pp. 378–397.

[18]Ibid., and D. S. Pugh, D. J. Hickson, C. R. Hinings, and C. Turner, "The Context of Organization Structures," *Administrative Science Quarterly*, March 1969, pp. 91–114.

[19]Hickson, Pugh, and Pheysey, "Operations Technology and Organization Structure."

on technology have been undertaken at two diverse levels; (2) the findings from these studies have been treated as comparable, although they are not; and (3) when the studies are separated by level, a very solid case for the technological imperative can be made.[20] We present the evidence on each of these points and then demonstrate how the conclusions we reach are fully consistent with our previous discussion on size.

Technology research has been undertaken at the organizational and job levels. Both view technology as the means by which tasks are accomplished, but one considers the organization as the unit of analysis and the other considers the job as the primary unit. Organizational-level analysis starts with the major product or service offered, which leads it to focus on the dominant conversion technology. Job-level analysis starts with the tasks performed by individual employees, which leads it to consider the methods by which they are accomplished.

When these two types of studies are combined, it is difficult if not impossible to draw meaningful conclusions. However, when they are separated, a clear pattern emerges. The organizational-level studies still are mixed, with few consistent relationships appearing between technology and structure. But the job-level studies provide a completely different picture. In evaluating the relationship between technology and a set of structural variables in eight job-level studies, at least half the correlations were found to be significant and all were in the same direction.[21]

Why do job-level studies support the technological imperative, whereas those at the organizational level do not? Several explanations have been offered.[22] First, job-level studies have far fewer conceptual and methodological problems. They hold a unified concept of technology. There is high agreement among their measurement scales. They represent a homogeneous collection of sample units; job-level studies have been conducted primarily in U.S. health-related institutions. The other reason for the high technology-structure correlation at the job level is undoubtedly related to size. Job-level studies are looking at technology at the operating core. If there is a technological imperative, this is where it should be most evident because technology's impact should be greatest closest to the core. The fact that organizational-level studies are conceptually and methodologically heterogeneous, plus the realization that technology at this level should have a lesser effect on structure, suggests that a reasonable doubt must remain concerning the demise of the technological imperative. And, if there is such an imperative, it may only exist with small organizations.

[20]Gerwin, "Relationships Between Structures and Technology at the Organizational and Job Levels."

[21]Ibid.

[22]Ibid.

Conclusions

The technology-structure relationship is not at all clear. Technology has, in most studies, been presented in a narrow and singular view. That is, firm X uses technology Y and has a structure described as Z. In reality, firm X undoubtedly employs several technologies. Since organizations do diverse things, most use different methods with different activities. Even accepting the simplified single technology perspective, technology's impact on structure is not *all pervasive.* It is more likely applicable to structural dimensions at or near the organization's operating core and to smaller more than larger organizations. Consistent with selectivity, it also affects some structural dimensions more than others. Its varying impact on these structural dimensions is the subject of our next section.

TECHNOLOGY AND STRUCTURE

As we have done with strategy and size, we now want to review the literature to determine the relationship of technology to the three structural dimensions of complexity, formalization, and centralization. Despite all the qualifications stated in the previous section, there are some important findings.

Technology and Complexity

The evidence, while not overwhelming, indicates that routine technology is positively associated with low complexity. The greater the routineness, the fewer the number of occupational groups and the less the training possessed by professionals.[23] This relationship is more likely to hold for the structural activities in or near the operating core—such as the proportion of maintenance employees and the span of control of first-line supervisors.

The reverse also holds; that is, nonroutine technology is likely to lead to high complexity. As the work becomes more sophisticated and customized, the span of control narrows and vertical differentiation increases.[24] This, of course, is intuitively logical. Customized responses require a greater use of specialists, and managers require a smaller span of control

[23]Hage and Aiken, "Routine Technology, Social Structure, and Organizational Goals," pp. 366–377.

[24]See, for example, Stanley H. Udy, Jr., *Organization of Work* (New Haven, Conn: HRAF Press, 1959); Hickson, Pugh, and Pheysey, "Operations Technology and Organization Structure"; and Raymond G. Hunt, "Technology and Organization," *Academy of Management Journal,* September 1970, pp. 235–252.

because the problems that they confront are mostly of the nonprogrammed variety.

Technology and Formalization

A review of five major technology studies found routine technology to be positively related with formalization. While only one of the simple correlations was statistically significant, all were positive, which has a 1 in a 1,000 occurrence due to chance.[25] However, when size was controlled for, the relationship vanished. Another study also supported the routineness-formalization relationship.[26] Routineness was significantly associated with the presence of a rules manual, presence of job descriptions, and the degree to which job descriptions were specified.

These studies suggest that care must be taken in generalizing about technology's impact on formalization. That they are related is undoubtedly true. But when controlled for size, most of this association disappears. We propose, therefore, that the relationship holds for small organizations and activities at or near the operating core. As the operating core becomes more routine, the operating work becomes more predictable. In such situations, high formalization is an efficient coordination device.

Technology and Centralization

The technology-centralization relationship generates inconsistent results. The logical argument would be that routine technologies would be associated with a centralized structure, whereas the nonroutine technology, which would rely more heavily on the knowledge of the specialist, would be characterized by delegated decision authority. This position has met with some support.[27]

A more generalizable conclusion is that the technology-centralization relationship is moderated by the degree of formalization.[28] Both formal regulations and centralized decision making are control mechanisms, and management can substitute them for one another. Routine technologies should be associated with centralized control if there is a minimum of rules

[25]Gerwin, "Relationships Between Structure and Technology at the Organizational and Job Levels."

[26]Hage and Aiken, "Routine Technology, Social Structure, and Organizational Goals."

[27]Andrew Van de Ven, André Delbecq, and Richard Koenig, Jr., "Determinants of Coordination Modes Within Organizations," *American Sociological Review,* April 1976, pp. 322–338.

[28]Jerald Hage and Michael Aiken, "Relationship of Centralization to Other Structural Properties," *Administrative Science Quarterly,* June 1967, pp. 72–92.

and regulations. However, if formalization is high, routine technology can be accompanied by decentralization. So we would predict routine technology to lead to centralization, but only if formalization is low.

SUMMARY

Technology refers to the processes or methods that transform inputs into outputs in the organization. The three landmark contributions to understanding technology were presented by Joan Woodward, Charles Perrow, and James Thompson.

Woodward proposed three types of production technology: unit, mass, and process. Her major contribution lay in identifying distinct relationships among these technology classes and the subsequent structure of the firms and in indicating that the effectiveness of the firms was related to the "fit" between technology and structure.

Perrow proposed a broader view of technology by looking at knowledge. He identified two underlying dimensions of knowledge technology: task variability and problem analyzability. These combine to create four types of technology: routine, engineering, craft, and nonroutine. Perrow concluded that the more routine the technology, the more highly structured the organization should be.

Thompson demonstrated that the interdependency created by a technology is important in determining an organization's structure. Specifically, he identified long-linked, mediating, and intensive technologies; noted the unique interdependency of each; determined how each dealt with the uncertainty it faced; and predicted the structural coordination devices that were most economical for each.

We concluded that the technological imperative, if it exists, is supported best by job-level research, is most likely to apply only to small organizations and to those structural arrangements at or near the operating core, and that "routineness" is the common denominator underlying most of the research on technology.

Finally, evidence indicates that routine technology is positively associated with low complexity and high formalization. Routine technology is positively correlated with centralization, but only if formalization is low.

FOR REVIEW AND DISCUSSION

1. What does the term "technology" mean?
2. What are the main contributions to OT made by Joan Woodward?
3. What are the main contributions to OT made by Charles Perrow?
4. What are the main contributions to OT made by James Thompson?

5. Describe the various technologies that might be used in
   a. a grocery store.
   b. a stock brokerage firm.
   c. a firm that manufactures wristwatches.
6. Clarify how "routineness" reconciles the more specific technology classifications.
7. How are "technology" and "interdependence" related, if at all?
8. Differentiate between job-level and organizational-level analyses of technology. Which has proven to be more valuable in explaining organization structures? Why?
9. "Technology is really part of strategy." What does this mean?
10. Under what conditions is technology likely to be a major determinant of structure?

CHAPTER

9

ENVIRONMENT

In Chapter 1, we discussed organizations in an open-systems framework. The key to understanding organizations as open systems, we said, was the recognition that organizations interact with their environment. But since that introduction, we have said little about the environment and its impact on the organization. In this chapter, that omission will be rectified.

A common theme in organization theory is that organizations must adapt to their environments if they are to maintain or increase their effectiveness. In open-system terms, we can think of organizations as developing monitoring and feedback mechanisms to identify and follow their environments, sense changes in those environments, and make appropriate adjustments as necessary. This chapter clarifies what we mean by the term "environment," assesses the relationship between environment and structure, and describes ways in which organizations adjust or manage their environments. A central point throughout this chapter is that different organizations face different degrees of environmental uncertainty. Since managers do not like uncertainty, they try to eliminate it or, at least, minimize its impact on their organization. We demonstrate that structural design is a major tool that managers have for controlling environmental uncertainty.

DEFINING ENVIRONMENT

There is no shortage of definitions for environment. Their common thread is consideration of factors outside the organization itself. For instance, one popular definition identifies the environment as composed of those institutions or forces that affect the performance of the organization, but over which the organization has little or no direct control.[1] Another author has proposed that ascertaining an organization's environment appears simple enough. "Just take the universe, subtract from it the subset that represents the organization, and the remainder is environment."[2] We agree with this writer when he adds that, unfortunately, it really isn't that simple. First, let us differentiate between an organization's general and its specific environment.

General versus Specific Environment

The general environment aligns with the second definition offered. It includes everything, such as economic factors, political conditions, the social milieu, the legal structure, the ecological situation, and cultural conditions. The general environment encompasses conditions that may impact the organization *potentially*, but their relevance is not overtly clear. The political uncertainty in Quebec—in respect to whether the province will separate from Canada and become an independent country—has little or no immediate effect on the operations of Bell Canada. If Quebec were to actually separate, Bell Canada would certainly be directly affected. Or consider genetic engineering, which is in the general environment for drug firms. Though there is little current applicability of genetic engineering to products offered by drug companies, it is very likely that breakthroughs in this area will totally reshape the products that drug manufacturers will be marketing in the 21st century. The management at Merck, Schering, and Bristol-Myers must recognize that advances in genetic engineering will undoubtedly have a far-reaching impact on their organizations' future growth and profitability. But the impact of genetic engineering on drug firms, like Quebec's possible separation on Bell Canada, is only potentially relevant. As a result, organizations give the bulk of their attention to their specific environment.

The specific environment is that part of the environment that is directly relevant to the organization in achieving its goals. At any given moment, it is the part of the environment with which management will be concerned because it is made up of those critical constituencies that can positively or negatively influence the organization's effectiveness. It is unique to each organization and it changes with conditions. Typically, it will include clients or customers, suppliers of inputs, competitors, government regulatory agencies, labor unions, trade associations, and public pressure groups. For instance, a number of companies that had done business with

[1]C. W. Churchman, *The Systems Approach* (New York: Dell, 1968), p. 36.

[2]Robert H. Miles, *Macro Organizational Behavior* (Santa Monica, Calif.: Goodyear Publishing, 1980), p. 195.

the Iranian government through 1978 were trying in 1981 to collect money due them from Iran. Their specific environment included the U.S. State Department and the current Iranian government. An appliance manufacturer, who had never sold to Sears, Roebuck, recently signed a three-year contract to sell 40 percent of its output of washing machines to Sears to be sold under the retailer's Kenmore brand. This action moved Sears from the manufacturer's general environment to its specific environment.

An organization's specific environment will vary depending on the domain it has chosen. *Domain* refers to the claim that the organization stakes out for itself with respect to the range of products or services offered and markets served. It identifies the organization's niche. Volkswagen and Mercedes are both German firms that manufacture automobiles, but they operate in distinctly different domains. Similarly, Miami-Dade Junior College and the University of Michigan are both public institutions of higher education, but they do substantially different things and appeal to different segments of the higher-education market. These two colleges have identified different domains.

Why is the concept of domain important? It is because the domain of an organization determines the points at which it is dependent upon its specific environment.[3] Change the domain and you will change the specific environment. We discuss later in this chapter how the choice of domain is a distinct strategy by which management can attempt to control its organization's environment.

Actual versus Perceived Environment

Any attempt to define environment requires making a distinction between the objective or actual environment and the one that managers perceive. Evidence indicates that measures of the actual environment's characteristics and measures of perceived characteristics are not highly correlated.[4] What you see depends on where you sit! Further, it is perceptions—not reality—that lead to the decisions that managers make regarding organization design.

Unfortunately, an organization's environment is not like a 1,000-pound gorilla. You cannot miss the latter, but environments are not readily spotted and clearly demarcated. The same environment that one organization perceives as unpredictable and complex may be seen as static and easily understood by another organization.[5] People low in an organization may select

[3]James D. Thompson, *Organizations in Action* (New York: McGraw-Hill, 1967), p. 27.

[4]H. Kirk Downey, Don Hellriegel, and John W. Slocum, Jr., "Environmental Uncertainty: The Construct and Its Application," *Administrative Science Quarterly,* December 1975, pp. 613–629.

[5]William H. Starbuck, "Organizations and Their Environments," in Marvin D. Dunnette, ed., *Handbook of Industrial and Organizational Psychology* (Chicago: Rand McNally, 1976), p. 1080.

parts of that something "out there" and call it the specific environment whereas people higher up in that same organization see something else to be the firm's specific environment. You can also expect differences based on background, education, and functional area within which individuals work. Even senior managers in the same firm are likely to see the environment dissimilarly. This suggests that organizations construct or invent their environments and that the environment created depends on perception.

It should not be lost that it is the perceived environment that counts. Managers respond to what they see. As we proceed in our discussion, keep in mind that the structural decisions that managers make to better align their organization with the degree of uncertainty in their specific environment depends on the managers' perception of what makes up the specific environment and their assessment of uncertainty.

Environmental Uncertainty

From our perspective, the environment is important because not all environments are the same. They differ by what we call "environmental uncertainty." Some organizations face relatively static environments: few forces in their specific environment are changing. There are no new competitors, no new technological breakthroughs by current competitors, little activity by public pressure groups to influence the organizations, and so forth. Other organizations face very dynamic environments: rapidly changing government regulations affecting their business, new competitors, difficulties in acquiring raw materials, continually changing product preferences by customers, and so on. Static environments create significantly less uncertainty for managers than do dynamic ones. And since uncertainty is a threat to an organization's effectiveness, management will try to minimize it.[6] In this chapter, we show that management's concern is with reducing environmental uncertainty and that this can be accomplished through manipulation of the organization's structure.

LANDMARK CONTRIBUTIONS

You are undoubtedly not interested in reviewing the dozens of studies that contribute to the body of literature on organizational environments. But several are so important in influencing the current way in which we look at the environment that we would be derelict in not reviewing them briefly. In the following pages, we have summarized the landmark work of Burns and Stalker, Emery and Trist, and Lawrence and Lorsch.

[6]William R. Dill, "Environment as an Influence on Managerial Autonomy," *Administrative Science Quarterly*, March 1958, pp. 409–443.

Burns and Stalker

Tom Burns and G. M. Stalker studied twenty English and Scottish industrial firms to determine how their organizational structure and managerial practice might differ based on different environmental conditions.[7] Using interviews with managers and their own observations, they evaluated the firms' environmental conditions in terms of the rate of change in their scientific technology and their relevant product markets. What they found was that the type of structure that existed in rapidly changing and dynamic environments was significantly different from that in organizations with stable environments. Burns and Stalker labeled the two structures as organic and mechanistic, respectively.

Mechanistic structures were characterized by high complexity, formalization, and centralization. They performed routine tasks, relied heavily on programmed behaviors, and were relatively slow in responding to the unfamiliar. *Organic structures* were relatively flexible and adaptive, with emphasis on lateral rather than on vertical communication, influence based on expertise and knowledge rather than authority of position, loosely defined responsibilities, and emphasis on exchanging information rather than giving directions.

Burns and Stalker believed that the most effective structure is one that adjusts to the requirements of the environment, which means using a mechanistic design in a stable, certain environment, and an organic form in a turbulent environment. However, they recognized that the mechanistic and organic forms were ideal types defining two ends of a continuum. No organization is purely mechanistic or purely organic but, rather, moves toward one or the other. Moreover, they emphasized that one was not preferred over the other. The nature of the organization's environment determined which structure is superior.

Efforts to test Burns and Stalker's conclusions have met with general support.[8] For instance, NASA must deal with an endless series of unpredictable problems.[9] It requires a structure that can allow the organization to respond and adapt to continual change. It should not be surprising, therefore, to find that NASA's structure closely follows the characteristics of an organic form.

Emery and Trist

Fred Emery and Eric Trist proposed a more sophisticated view by offering a model that identified four kinds of environment that an organization might confront: (1) *placid-randomized*, (2) *placid-clustered*, (3) *disturbed-reactive*,

[7]Tom Burns and G. M. Stalker, *The Management of Innovation* (London: Tavistock, 1961).

[8]See Henry Mintzberg, *The Structuring of Organizations* (Englewood Cliffs, N.J.: Prentice-Hall, 1979), pp. 270–272.

[9]Margaret K. Chandler and Leonard R. Sayles, *Managing Large Systems* (New York: Harper & Row, 1971), p. 180.

and (4) *turbulent field.*[10] Emery and Trist described each as increasingly more complex than the previous one.

1. *The placid-randomized environment* is relatively unchanging, therefore posing the least threat to an organization. Demands are distributed randomly, and changes take place slowly over time. It has been described as analogous to the economist's state of pure competition in which there are enough buyers to absorb the organization's product and nothing the organization does affects the market. As such, uncertainty is low. While not many organizations are fortunate enough to find themselves in a placid-randomized environment, a state worker's compensation agency in many respects enjoys this type of environment. Its environment is relatively stable, and no single client can have any significant impact on the agency's operation.

2. *The placid-clustered environment* also changes slowly, but threats to the organization are clustered rather than random. So it is more important for the organization to know its environment than when threats were random. For instance, input suppliers or output distributors may join forces to form a powerful coalition. The placid-clustered environment would characterize the Bell System. If Bell attempts to deal with an element in its environment unilaterally, without adequate regard for the potential impacts on other organized environmental elements, it opens the potential for a unified reaction. So organizations in a placid-clustered environment are motivated to enage in long-range, strategic planning and their structures will tend to be centralized.

3. *The disturbed-reactive environment* is much more complex than the previous two. There are many competitors seeking similar ends. One or more organizations in the environment may be large enough to exert influence over their own environment and over other organizations. Two or three large companies in an industry can dominate it. A couple of large firms, for instance, can exert price leadership in such industries as steel, aluminum, automobiles, and tobacco. Bethlehem or Armco Steel cannot afford to ignore the future plans and current actions of U.S. Steel. Organizations facing a disturbed-reactive environment develop planned series of tactical initiatives, calculate reactions by others, and evolve counteractions. This competition requires flexibility to survive, and the structure of these organizations tends toward decentralization.

4. *The turbulent-field environment* is the most dynamic and has the highest uncertainty. Change is ever present and elements in the environment are increasingly interrelated. Many experts arguing along the lines

[10]Fred E. Emery and Eric L. Trist, "The Causal Texture of Organizational Environments," *Human Relations,* February 1965, pp. 21–32.

of *Future Shock* believe that this environment became more and more evident in the 1970s and that it may be the dominant one of the 1980s. In a turbulent-field environment, the organization may be required to develop new products or services on an ongoing basis to survive. Also, it may have to reevaluate its relationship to government agencies, customers, and suppliers continually. This environment characterized word processing computer manufacturers in the early 1980s.

Before we relate Emery and Trist's classifications to preferred structural arrangements, we should spend a moment to elaborate on our statement that many experts believe that the turbulent-field environment "may be the dominant one of the 1980s." This position results from assessing the rapid changes that we have undergone in North America in the past several decades. A few of these changes are listed in Table 9-1.

The argument can be made that organizations today face far more dynamic and turbulent environments than in previous times. Certainly the environment is more turbulent for some organizations than for others, but we may have entered an era in which the turbulent field is the rule rather than the exception.

Although Emery and Trist offered no specific suggestions as to the type of structure suited best to each environment, their classifications are not difficult to reconcile with Burns and Stalker's terminology. Emery and Trist's first two environments will be responded to with more mechanistic structures, whereas the dynamic environments will require a structure that offers the advantages of the organic form. Regardless of the terms used, the theme underlying Emery and Trist's four-environments model is also compatible with the research findings on technology; that is, the less rou-

TABLE 9–1 Major environment changes in recent years

Technological
- Introduction of microcomputers
- Telecommunication satellites
- Worldwide telephone direct dialing

Social
- Women's movement
- Unprecedented growth in higher education enrollments
- Resurgence of urban centers for commercial and residential development

Economic
- Unprecedented escalation of oil prices
- Skyrocketing rise in interest rates
- Demise of long-term fixed-rate mortgage

Political
- End of the military draft
- Election of conservative candidates
- Shift of government powers from the federal to state levels

tine the technology, the greater the uncertainty, the less effective the mechanistic qualities, and the more important it is to use flexible structural forms. Routine technology is associated with stability, and it is handled best by structures that have well-coordinated and highly structured forms. Uncertainty means instability and the potential for major and rapid changes. Only a flexible structure can respond promptly to such changes.

Lawrence and Lorsch

Paul Lawrence and Jay Lorsch, both of the Harvard Business School, went beyond the works of Burns and Stalker and Emery and Trist in search of learning more about the relationship between environmental differences and effective organization structures.[11] They chose ten firms in three industries—plastics, food, and containers—in which to carry out their research.

The industries were chosen because they operated in what the researchers believed were diverse environments. The plastics industry is highly competitive. The life cycle of any product is historically short, and firms are characterized by considerable new product and process development. The container industry, on the other hand, is quite different. There have been no significant new products in two decades. Sales growth has kept pace with population growth, but nothing more. Lawrence and Lorsch described the container firms as operating in a relatively certain environment, with no real threats to consider. The food industry is midway between the two. There has been heavy innovation, but new product generation and sales growth have been less than plastics and more than containers.

Lawrence and Lorsch sought to match up the internal environments of these firms with their respective external environments. They hypothesized that the more successful firms within each industry would have better matches than would the less successful firms. Their measure of the *external* environment sought to tap the degree of uncertainty. This included the rate of change in the environment over time, the clarity of information that management held about the environment, and the length of time it took for management to get feedback from the environment on actions taken by the organization. But what constituted an organization's *internal* environment? Lawrence and Lorsch looked at two separate dimensions: *differentiation* and *integration.*

The term "differentiation" as used by Lawrence and Lorsch closely parallels our definition of horizontal differentiation. But, in addition to task segmentation, Lawrence and Lorsch argued that managers in various departments can be expected to hold different attitudes and behave differently

[11]Paul Lawrence and Jay W. Lorsch, *Organization and Environment: Managing Differentiation and Integration* (Boston: Division of Research, Harvard Business School, 1967).

in terms of their goal perspective, time frame, and interpersonal orientation. Different interests and differing points of view mean that members in each department often find it difficult to see things the same way or to agree on integrated plans of action. Therefore, the degree of differentiation becomes a measure of complexity and indicates greater complications and more rapid changes. The other dimension that interested Lawrence and Lorsch was "integration," the quality of collaboration that exists among interdependent units or departments that are required to achieve unity of effort.

The unique, and probably the most important, part of Lawrence and Lorsch's study was that they did not assume the organization or the environment to be uniform and singular. In contrast to previous researchers, they perceived both the organization and the environment as having subsets; that is, that *parts* of the organization deal with *parts* of the environment. They were proposing what was patently obvious, except that no one had said it before: that an organization's internal structure could be expected to differ, from department to department, reflecting the characteristics of the subenvironment with which it interacts. They postulated that a basic reason for differentiating into departments or subsystems was to deal more effectively with subenvironments. For example, in each of the ten organizations that Lawrence and Lorsch studied, the researchers were able to identify market, technical-economic, and scientific subenvironments. These three subenvironments corresponded to the sales, production, and research and development functions within the organizations.

Lawrence and Lorsch postulated that the more turbulent, complex, and diverse the external environment facing an organization, the greater the degree of differentiation among its subparts. If the external environment were very diverse and the internal environment were highly differentiated, they reasoned further that there would be a need for an elaborate internal integration mechanism to avoid having units going in different directions. The need for increased integration to accommodate increases in differentiation related to the different goals of departmental managers. In all three industries, the researchers found manufacturing people to be most concerned with cost efficiency and production matters. Research and engineering people emphasized scientific matters. Marketing people's orientation was toward the marketplace.

In reference to their three industries, Lawrence and Lorsch hypothesized that the plastics firms would be the most differentiated, followed by food and container firms, in that order. And this is precisely what they found. When they divided the firms within each industry into high, moderate, and low performers, they found that the high-performing firms had a structure that best fit their environmental demands. In diverse environments, subunits were more differentiated than in homogeneous environments. In the turbulent plastics industry, this meant high differentiation.

The production units had relatively routine activities, in contrast to sales and research and engineering. Where the greatest standardization existed, in the container industry, there was the least differentiation. Departments within the container firms generally had similar structures. The food firms, as postulated, were in the middle ground. Additionally, the most successful firms in all three industries had a higher degree of integration than their low-performing counterparts.

What does all this mean? First, there are multiple specific environments with different degrees of uncertainty. Second, successful organizations' subunits meet the demands of their subenvironments. Since differentiation and integration represent opposing forces, the key is to match the two appropriately, creating differentiation between departments to deal with specific problems and tasks facing the organization and getting people to integrate and work as a cohesive team toward the organization's goals. Successful organizations have more nearly solved the dilemma of providing both differentiation and integration by matching their internal subunits to the demands of the subenvironment. Finally, Lawrence and Lorsch present evidence to confirm that the environment in which an organization functions—specifically in terms of the level of uncertainty present—is of foremost importance in selecting the structure appropriate for achieving organizational effectiveness.

Before we leave Lawrence and Lorsch, it should be mentioned that they have been criticized sharply for their use of perceptual measures of environmental uncertainty.[12] As noted earlier, actual and perceived degrees of uncertainty are likely to differ. Attempts to replicate Lawrence and Lorsch's work using objective measures of uncertainty have failed most often, suggesting that their results may be a function of their measure.[13] From a research standpoint, this criticism is valid. However, from the practicing manager's perspective, it is his or her perceptions that count. So, while you should recognize that Lawrence and Lorsch have used perceptual measures and that defining the environment in terms of certainty-uncertainty criteria is by no means simple, you should also recognize that the findings of Lawrence and Lorsch represent an important contribution to our understanding of the environment's impact on organization structure.

[12]See, for example, Henry L. Tosi, Ramon J. Aldag, and Ronald G. Storey, "On the Measurement of the Environment: An Assessment of the Lawrence and Lorsch Environmental Subscale," *Administrative Science Quarterly*, March 1973, pp. 27–36; and H. Kirk Downey and John W. Slocum, Jr., "Uncertainty: Measures, Research, and Sources of Variation," *Academy of Management Journal*, September 1975, pp. 562–578.

[13]Ramon J. Aldag and Ronald G. Storey, "Environmental Uncertainty: Comments on Objective and Perceptual Indices," in Arthur G. Bederian, A. A. Armenakis, W. H. Holley, Jr., and H. S. Feild, Jr. eds., *Proceedings of the Annual Meeting of the Academy of Management* (Auburn, Alabama: Academy of Management, 1975), pp. 203–205.

A SYNTHESIS

In this section we look for common threads in the studies presented earlier. Since our goal is integration and clarity rather than merely presenting "lots of diverse research findings," we think it is important to seek some common ground in the environmental literature. We also use this synthesis section to consider the cases "for" and "against" the environmental imperative.

Four Core Environments

Environmental uncertainty is relevant because it impacts managerial decision making. Therefore, it has been proposed that environmental uncertainty can be broken down into two dimensions.[14] The first considers the number of factors in decision making and their degree of similarity. This is the *simple-complex* dimension. The second considers the degree to which factors change. This is the *static-dynamic* dimension. These combine, as shown in Table 9-2, to create four core dimensions.

The table's four environment cells translate into four specific types of structure. Organizations operating in *static-simple* environments (cell 1) experience the least amount of perceived uncertainty in decision making, whereas organizations in *dynamic-complex* environments (cell 4) experience the greatest amount of perceived uncertainty. Research to test Table 9-2 suggests that the two dimensions do not have an equal impact on uncertainty.[15] The data, based on twenty-two decision-making groups in six organizations, revealed that the static-dynamic dimension makes the largest contribution to perceived uncertainty. Specifically, "decision units with dynamic environments always experience significantly more uncertainty in decision making regardless of whether their environment is simple or complex."[16]

Regardless of the terminology used, several conclusions appear evident. There is evidence that relates the degree of environmental uncertainty to different structural arrangements. This, in fact, is compatible with our discussion in Chapter 8 of the research on technology. Routine technologies operate in relative certainty, whereas nonroutine technologies imply relative uncertainty. High environmental uncertainty or technology of a nonroutine nature both require organic-type structures. Similarly, low environmental uncertainty or routine technology can be managed more effectively in mechanistic structures. In addition, the evidence in this chapter demonstrates that neither organizations nor their environments are

[14]Robert B. Duncan, "Characteristics of Organizational Environments and Perceived Environmental Uncertainty," *Administrative Science Quarterly,* September 1972, pp. 313–327.

[15]Ibid.

[16]Ibid., p. 325.

TABLE 9–2 Four core environments and their structures

	SIMPLE	*COMPLEX*
STATIC	1. Low perceived uncertainty Environment: Small number of factors and components in the environment; these factors and components are somewhat similar to one another, remain basically the same, and are not changing. Structure: High complexity, high formalization, and centralization. Examples: Lawrence and Lorsch's container firms and Woodward's mass-production manufacturing firms.	2. Moderately low perceived uncertainty Environment: Large number of factors and components in the environment; these factors and components are not similar to one another but remain basically the same. Structure: High complexity, high formalization, and decentralization. Examples: Hospitals, universities.
DYNAMIC	3. Moderately high perceived uncertainty Environment: Small number of factors and components in the environment; these factors are somewhat similar to one another, and they are in a continual process of change. Structure: Low complexity, low formalization, and centralization. Examples: Entrepreneurial firms, where the chief executive maintains tight, personal control.	4. High perceived uncertainty Environment: Large number of factors and components in the environment; these factors and components are not similar to one another and they are in a continual process of change. Structure: Low complexity, low formalization, and decentralization. Examples: Lawrence and Lorsch's plastic firms, NASA, electronic firms.

Source: Adapted from Robert Duncan, "What is the Right Organization Structure?" *Organization Dynamics,* Winter 1979, p. 63; and Henry Mintzberg, *The Structuring of Organizations* (Englewood Cliffs, N.J.: Prentice-Hall, 1979), p. 286.

homogeneous. If we want to understand the environment-structure relationship, we should direct our attention at matching up subunits with their subenvironments.

The Cases "For" and "Against" the Environmental Imperative

As a result of our synthesis, you should now have a reasonable understanding of what environment is and what some scholars have found in their efforts to better understand the environment-structure relationship. You now have the background to interpret more fully the cases "for" and "against" the environmental imperative.

The case "for." The case for environment determining structure has been made by Burns and Stalker, Emery and Trist, and Lawrence and Lorsch. Basically, they believe that environmental pressures generate task demands that are met by appropriate technical structures. A more elaborate defense can be built using the systems perspective.

Organizations are dependent on acquiring inputs and disposing of outputs if they are to operate and survive. These flow from and to the environment. In a closed system, the most effective organization would be one that was technologically efficient. Since you assume no interactions or problems with the environment in a closed system, success depends on internal efficiencies. The structural design, therefore, would be one that handled the transformation process most efficiently. But organizations cannot ignore their environments. Its true that some organizations need to pay much closer attention than do others and that some subunits within an organization must monitor their subenvironments more closely than other subunits, but no organization is so autonomous that it can insulate itself completely from its environment.

Because all organizations are dependent, in some degree, on their environments, that dependency creates uncertainty for managers. Those things that management cannot control directly create uncertainties. But managers do not like making decisions under conditions of high uncertainty. Since they cannot eliminate uncertainties, they look to options within their control that can reduce it. One of those options is designing the organization so as to be able to respond best to the uncertainty. If uncertainty is high, therefore, the organization will be designed along flexible lines to adapt to rapid changes. If uncertainty is low, management will opt for a structure that is most efficient and offers the highest degree of managerial control, which is the mechanistic form.

The case "against." If there is an environmental imperative, it may be limited only to those subunits at the boundary of the organization—those that interact directly with the environment. For instance, the structure of purchasing and marketing functions may be a direct response to their dependency on the environment. Yet it may have little or no impact on production, R&D, accounting, and similarly insulated activities. It may also be, since environments are perceived, that environments are created to reflect the structures from which they are seen.[17] If environments are creations, then it is possible that differentiated structures will perceive a heterogeneous environment or that decentralized structures will perceive more environmental uncertainty as a consequence of their structural arrangement. This may, in fact, explain Lawrence and Lorsch's findings. A stronger case, however, may be built around the argument that the environment is relatively impotent in effecting structure.

A major contention of the environmental imperative supporters is that organizations structure themselves to minimize the impact of uncertainty; that is, events that the organization cannot forecast. As noted earlier in our discussion of the specific environment, not all uncertainty in the environment may have consequences for the organization. Uncertainty, therefore, is relevant only when it occurs along with dependence.[18] Moreover, uncertainty is *unplanned* variation. "Mere change, or rate of change, is no guarantee that the situation is uncertain. Change, variation, and a dynamic environment may all be capable of being predicted, in which case, there is no uncertainty."[19] For instance, the twentieth century can be characterized as a period of constant and unrelenting change. The issue, presented earlier, that we have entered an era when most organizations face dynamic and turbulent environments, can be looked at from a different perspective. Instead of reflecting increasing change, they may only represent management's reduced ability to forecast. The past is no longer a prologue to the future. There may be no more dynamic changes going on in the 1970s and 1980s than occurred in the 1940s, 1950s, or 1960s. Only back in those days, the direction and degree of change were easier to predict. We have entered an age of discontinuity, which makes our forecasts of the future highly prone to error. So change may be a constant; it is only our reduced ability to predict it that may have *created* turbulent environments.

To take an even more extreme position, it can be argued that the claim that today's organizations face far more dynamic and turbulent environments than in previous times is just completely erroneous. As Nobel prizewinner Herbert Simon has noted, the years of real environmental uncertainty took place between the Civil War and World War I.[20] The world

[17]Karl E. Weick, *The Social Psychology of Organizing* (Reading, Mass.: Addison-Wesley, 1969).

[18]Jeffrey Pfeffer, *Organizational Design* (Arlington Heights, Ill.: AHM Publishing, 1978), p. 133.

[19]Ibid.

[20]Herbert A. Simon, *The New Science of Management Decision*, rev. ed. (Englewood Cliffs, N.J.: Prentice-Hall, 1977), pp. 100–101.

changed from a rural, agricultural, horse-powered society to an urban, industrialized world with railroads, telegraphs, steamships, electric lights, automobiles, and airplanes. Dramatic technological breakthroughs were coming from all directions. Simon argues that nothing in the past sixty years, "with the possible exception of The Bomb, has so changed the basic terms of human existence as those new technologies did."[21] In relative terms, today's managers may be facing a far less dynamic environment than were their counterparts of three generations ago.

Finally, it has been said that the environmental imperative is just not in agreement with observed reality.[22] Not only do organizations that operate in ostensibly similar environments have different structures, they often show no significant difference in effectiveness. Further, many organizations have similar structures and very diverse environments. This latter point is consistent with your author's observation that the mechanistic form of structure is dominant in America today. Look around you. Schools, businesses, governmental agencies, hospitals, athletic teams, and even social clubs essentially fit the mechanistic model. If the environment is actually turbulent, shouldn't organic structures be in the majority?

THE ENVIRONMENT-STRUCTURE RELATIONSHIP

It is time to attempt some specific formulations on the environment-structure relationship. As in the previous chapters, we look at the effect on complexity, formalization, and centralization. However, before we make these formulations, several general predictions about the environment-structure relationship are offered.

Every organization depends on its environment to some degree, but we cannot ignore the obvious, namely, that some organizations are much more dependent on the environment and on certain subenvironments than are others. The environment's effect on an organization, therefore, is a function of its vulnerability, which in turn is a function of dependence.[23] In the early 1980s, General Motors was less vulnerable to economic fluctuations than was Chrysler. Firms such as Safeway Stores and Revlon are more vulnerable to consumer advocate groups than, say, manufacturers of cement. Organizations whose employees are unionized are more vulnerable to union activity and their effectiveness is more dependent on maintaining good relations with the union's leadership than are nonunionized organizations.

The evidence demonstrates that a dynamic environment has more

[21]Ibid.

[22]John Child, "Organizational Structure, Environment, and Performance: The Role of Strategic Choice," *Sociology*, January 1972, pp. 1–22.

[23]David Jacobs, "Dependency and Vulnerability: An Exchange Approach to the Control of Organizations," *Administrative Science Quarterly*, March 1974, pp. 45–59.

influence on structure than does a static environment.[24] A dynamic environment will push an organization toward an organic form, even if large size or routine technology suggests a mechanistic structure. However, a static environment will not override the influence of size and technology. This evidence, when linked with our observation on the dearth of organic structures, implies that (1) dynamic environments are not, in actuality, that prevalent; (2) managers may not recognize dynamic environments when they see them; or (3) organizations have devised ways in which to reduce their dependencies when facing dynamic environments.

Environment and Complexity

The studies we have reviewed in this chapter allow us to state that complexity and environmental uncertainty are inversely related. But, given the findings of Lawrence and Lorsch, this should be moderated to reflect a subunit's activities. Those departments within the organization that are most dependent on the environment should be relatively lowest in complexity. For instance, it has been found that organizations with a greater concern for specific environment agents had fewer hierarchical levels.[25] In addition, those activities at the boundary of the organization, which have the greatest interaction with the environment, can be predicted to be lowest in complexity.

Environment and Formalization

Our predictions for formalization parallel those for complexity. Stable environments should lead to high formalization. Why? Because stable environments create a minimal need for rapid response and economies exist for organizations that standardize their activities. But, again, we caution against assuming that a dynamic environment must lead to low formalization throughout the organization. Management's preference will undoubtedly be toward insulting operating activities from uncertainty. If successful, a dynamic environment is likely to lead to low formalization of boundary activities, while maintaining relatively high formalization within other functions.

Environment and Centralization

The more complex the environment, the more decentralized the structure.[26] Regardless of the static-dynamic dimension, if a large number of dissimilar factors and components exist in the environment, the organization can best

[24]Mintzberg, *The Structuring of Organizations*, p. 272.

[25]Anant R. Negandhi and Bernard C. Reimann, "Task Environment, Decentralization, and Organizational Effectiveness," *Human Relations*, April 1973, pp. 203–224.

[26]Mintzberg, *The Structuring of Organizations*, pp. 273–276.

meet the uncertainties that this causes through decentralization. It is difficult for management to comprehend a highly complex *environment* (note that this is different from a complex *structure*). Management information-processing capacity becomes overloaded, so decisions are carved up into subsets and are delegated to others.

Disparities in the environment are responded to through decentralization.[27] When different responses are needed to different subenvironments, the organization creates decentralized subunits to deal with them. So we can expect organizations to decentralize selectively. This can explain why, even in organizations that are generally highly centralized, marketing activities are typically decentralized. This is a response to a disparity in the environment; that is, even though the environment is generally static, the market subenvironment tends toward being dynamic.

Finally, the evidence supports that extreme hostility in the environment drives organizations to, at least temporarily, centralize their structures.[28] A wildcat strike by the union, an antitrust suit by the government, or the sudden loss of a major customer all represent severe threats to the organization and top management responds by centralizing control. When survival is in question, top management wants to oversee decision making directly. Of course, you may note that this appears to contradict an earlier prediction. You would expect this dynamic environment to be met with decentralization. What appears to happen is that two opposing forces are at work, with centralization the winner. The need for innovation and responsiveness (via decentralization) is overpowered by top management's fear that the wrong decisions may be made.

In contrast to our other "imperatives," a large body of literature has developed around the idea that the environment can be *managed*. In the following section, we consider what actions managers can take to reduce environmental uncertainty.

MANAGING THE ENVIRONMENT

Once management recognizes its dependence on one or more elements in its environment, it can develop a strategy to reduce this dependence. But just because dependence exists does not mean that management will recognize it. I meet or come into contact with many people every day, but not all of them can influence my behavior. Similarly, all the elements in an organization's environment are not part of its specific environment. How do organizations read their environments and identify those elements that can influence their success or failure? They create boundary roles.

[27]Ibid., pp. 282–285.
[28]Ibid., pp. 281–282.

Boundary Roles

Boundary roles are the linkages or mechanisms that organizations create to reduce the threats of uncertainty posed by dependence.[29] They can interface between the organization and its environment, in which case the role is external. Examples of these job titles include sales representative, marketing researcher, purchasing agent, lobbyist, public relations specialist, and personnel recruiter. Typically when the term boundary role is used, it refers to this external role. But there is also an internal boundary role to describe those that interface between subunits in the organization. Examples of these job titles include expediter, liaison officer, and product manager.

What do those who occupy boundary-spanning roles do? Quite a lot! They handle input acquisition and disposal of output transactions, filter inputs and outputs, search and collect information, represent the organization to the environment, and protect and buffer the organization.[30] "It is through the reports of boundary agents that other organization members acquire their knowledge, perceptions, and evaluations of organization environments. It is through the vigilance of boundary agents that the organization is able to monitor and screen important happenings in the environment."[31] When information obtained from boundary agents indicates dependence, management will want to choose some action that can reduce its impact. Available options fall into three categories: intraorganizational strategies, interorganizational strategies, and domain-choice strategies.

Intraorganizational Strategies

Intraorganizational strategies do not attempt to change events in the environment. They seek to shield the organization's technological core from the events themselves. Four popular intraorganizational strategies are buffering, smoothing, forecasting, and rationing.[32]

Buffering. Organizations can buffer their operating core from environmental influences at the input or output side. On the input side, buffering is evident when organizations stockpile materials and supplies, engage in preventive maintenance, or recruit and train new employees. Each of these activities is designed to protect the operating function of the

[29]J. Stacy Adams, "Interorganization Processes and Organization Boundary Activities," in Barry M. Staw and Larry L. Cummings, eds., *Research in Organizational Behavior*, vol. 2 (Greenwich, Conn.: JAI Press, 1980), pp. 328–332.

[30]Dennis W. Organ, "Linking Pins Between Organizations and Environments," *Business Horizons*, December 1971, p. 74.

[31]Ibid.

[32]Thompson, *Organizations in Action*, pp. 20–23.

organization from the unexpected. The appliance manufacturer that stockpiles a ninety-day supply of steel allows itself to continue to operate for several months in event of a strike in the steel industry. Preventive maintenance substitutes known costs for the unknown. Just as you may take your car in every few months for a checkup and precautionary service to avoid the surprise and expense of the unexpected breakdown, organizations can do the same. Buffering can also be done with human resources. Since organizations require trained personnel, their unavailability or lack of appropriate skills can mean a loss in productive efficiency. Management can meet this uncertainty through recruitment and training.

Buffering at the output level allows fewer options. The most obvious method is through the use of inventories. If an organization creates products that can be carried in inventory without damage, then maintaining warehouse inventories allows the organization to produce its goods at a constant rate regardless of fluctuations in sales demand. Toy manufacturers, for example, typically ship most of their products to retailers in the early fall for selling during the Christmas season. These manufacturers, of course, produce their toys year round and merely stockpile them for shipping during the fall.

Buffering provides benefits by reducing environmental uncertainties. We would predict management's propensity to buffer to be related directly to the degree of routinization in the organization's technology. However, the benefits must be appraised against the costs. The more obvious of these costs are the increased carrying expense of buffering activities and the risk of obsolescence inherent in stockpiling.

Smoothing. Smoothing seeks to level out the impact of fluctuations in the environment. Organizations that use this technique include telephone companies, retail stores, car rental agencies, magazines, and sports teams. The heaviest demand on telephone equipment is by business between the weekday hours of 8:00 A.M. and 5:00 P.M. Telephone companies have to have enough equipment to meet peak demand during this period. But the equipment is still there during the rest of the time. So what do they do? They smooth demand by charging the highest prices during their peak period and low rates, to encourage you to call "home," during the evenings and on weekends. Retail clothing stores know that their slowest months are January (following the Christmas "blitz") and August (prior to "back-to-school"). To reduce this "trough" in the revenue curve, retail stores typically run their semiannual sales at these times of the year. Car rental agencies make extensive use of smoothing. The same car that rents for $40 a day during the week is frequently half that price on the weekend. The reason is that business people are heavy users of rental cars and their usage is during the week. Rather than have the cars sit idle on weekends, the rental agencies smooth demand by cutting prices. Magazine publishers frequently give you a substantial discount—sometimes up to 50 percent off newsstand prices—if you become a mail subscriber. Why do they do this? It smooths demand. Finally, we suggest that sports teams usually give fans reduced prices when they buy season tickets covering all the home games. Even if the team has a very poor win-loss record, management has assured itself of a certain amount of income.

Forecasting. To the extent that management can forecast environmental fluctuations, it can reduce uncertainty. The manufacturing firm that can anticipate changes in demand for its products correctly can plan or schedule operations of its technical core ahead of time and thereby minimize the impact of these changes. Similarly, the consulting firm that can forecast accurately which contracts it will win during the next six months is better prepared in having the right number and mix of consultants available to handle these projects.

Rationing. A fourth approach available to management for dealing with environmental uncertainty—usually taken as a last resort—is to ration products or services; that is, to allocate output according to some priority system. Examples of rationing can be found in hospitals, business schools, post offices, the homebuilding industry, and clothes manufacturing. Hospitals often ration beds for nonemergency admissions. In case of disasters—earthquakes, fires, floods—beds are made available only to the most serious cases. Many business schools during the early 1980s were forced to ration the limited number of spaces they had. Demand for business programs in most colleges exceeded the supply of seats available. Many raised their entrance requirements significantly to determine who would be admitted. The post office resorts to rationing particularly during the peak Christmas rush. First-class mail takes priority, and lesser classes are handled on an "as available" basis. Even homebuilders have had occasion to ration their products. During the 1976–1977 real estate boom in Southern California, some builders actually used lotteries to select who would be able to buy newly constructed homes. Stories abounded, during that period, of people who waited in line for three days to get a number that merely allowed them a chance to be selected! Finally, apparel manufacturers have on occasion been forced to resort to rationing when demand for their products exceeded the supply. Levi Strauss, for instance, had to ration a few of its more popular designs on more than one occasion during the 1970s.

These examples represent efforts by management to minimize environmental uncertainty by controlling excess demand. It is obviously not a pleasant solution for management, for it signifies that revenues are being suboptimized. But for temporary situations, which do not justify or allow for changes in prices or expansion of output, rationing does provide stability.

Interorganizational Strategies

Another approach to managing the environment is to control those elements in the environment on which the organization depends. We call these interorganizational strategies. The more popular of these include contracting, coopting, coalescing, third-party soliciting, and advertising.

Contracting. Organizations can contract to reduce uncertainty on either the input or the output side. For instance, they may agree to a long-term fixed contract to purchase materials and supplies or to sell a certain part of the organization's output. Airlines contract with oil companies to buy fuel on a fixed-term contract, thus reducing their susceptibility to fluctuations in availability and price. A major soap manufacturer—whose products are household names—contracts to sell 10,000 cases a month of its standard detergent to a large discount chain that will be marketed under the chain's private label. This assures the soap manufacturer of a certain amount of sales and reduces its dependency on the fluctuating preferences of consumers.

Coopting. Organizations may resort to coopting their uncertainties; that is, absorbing those individuals or organizations in the environment that threaten their stability or existence. During the early 1970s, a number of companies who were under attack from consumer activist groups appointed one or more prominent members of these groups to their boards of directors. Critics are less vocal when they are required to criticize decisions in which they participated. The managers of companies in financial difficulties frequently seek to appoint bankers to their boards to assure themselves of access to the money markets.

Coalescing. When the organization combines with one or more other organizations for the purpose of joint action, it is called coalescing. It brings to life the adage that "if you can't beat them, join'em!" This approach includes, but is not limited to, tactics such as agreeing to market share splits, price fixing, geographical splits of territories, mergers, joint ventures, and the creation of interlocking directorships. Unwritten, and sometimes illegal, reciprocity agreements and referral practices can stabilize an environment, especially when concentration is high. Probably the most notorious example of this took place in the late 1950s, when executives from General Electric, Westinghouse, and several other large electrical equipment manufacturers secretly met annually and agreed to a price-fixing scheme that divided up that year's major bid contracts among the conspirators and allowed the "winner" of each extremely high profits. When discovered, the companies were fined and some senior executives in these firms were actually imprisoned.

Third-party soliciting. Organizations can use other organizations or individuals to solicit on their behalf to achieve outcomes favorable to the first. Lobbying falls in this category, as does the use of trade associations, professional associations, and government regulatory agencies. The Tobacco Institute and the American Rifle Association fight hard in Washington to reduce uncertainties that might affect tobacco and gun interests, respectively. Some organizations even use the power of the government to stabilize relationships in an industry. Doctors, chiropractors, and other professionals can use state licensing boards to restrict entry, regulate competition, and keep their professions more stable. The airlines and trucking industries historically were regulated and that regulation was supported substantially by firms within the industries. In contrast to the notion that regulation exists to protect the interests of the general public, a strong counterargument can be built that government regulation maintains monopoly power (and thus less environmental uncertainty) in the hands of the regulated.

Advertising. An obvious interorganizational strategy used extensively by organizations is advertising. The organization that succeeds in creating attitudinal differences between their product or service and that of others, in the minds of potential customers, effectively manages its environment and reduces uncertainty. The classic example is Bayer Aspirin. The content of aspirin is the same regardless of brand name. Yet the manufacturer of Bayer has convinced a significant segment of the aspirin-buying public that Bayer's "pure aspirin" is superior to its competitors and justifies a price from two to five times higher than generic brands.

Domain-Choice Strategies

Another approach for managing the environment is to shift the organization's domain to align with a more favorable environment.[33] We defined the domain of an organization earlier as the niche that the organization stakes out for itself in terms of the markets served and the range of products or services offered. It is not fixed. Management can decide to change its domain to one with less environmental uncertainty. Two of the most popular tactics are to diversify or divest. The tobacco industry is an excellent example of firms choosing new domains. In the mid-1960s, scared by the Surgeon General's report on the negative effects of smoking on health, the major tobacco companies began active diversification programs. American Tobacco added Jim Beam, Sunshine Biscuit, Andrew Jergens, and Master

[33]See, for example, James D. Thompson and William J. McEwen, "Organizational Goals and Environment: Goal-Setting as an Interaction Process," *American Sociological Review*, February 1958, pp. 23–31.

Lock and then changed its name to American Brands. Reynolds Tobacco became R. J. Reynolds Industries and purchased Del Monte, Chun King, and Hawaiian Punch. This move to diversify exemplifies organizations' changing domains to reduce the uncertainty that would have existed if they had remained entrenched in only tobacco.

In addition to diversification or divesture, an organization may move into a completely new market. Many organizations are constantly on the lookout for a domain where they can dominate and control—where there are few competitors, strong barriers to entry, little regulation, yet plenty of suppliers and customers. Unfortunately, because there are not many opportunities for organizations to become unregulated monopolies, most domain-choice decisions substitute one set of environmental uncertainties for another.

SUMMARY

The theme of this chapter has been that different organizations face different degrees of environmental uncertainty and that structural design is a major tool that managers can use to eliminate or minimize the impact of environmental uncertainty.

The environment was defined as composed of those institutions or forces that affect the performance of the organization, but over which the organization has little control. Our concern, however, is with the specific environment—that part most relevant to the organization. Management desires to reduce uncertainty created by this specific environment.

Three landmark contributions were cited. Burns and Stalker argued that an organization's structure should be mechanistic in a stable, certain environment and organic when the environment is turbulent. Emery and Trist identified four kinds of environments—placid randomized, placid clustered, disturbed reactive, and turbulent field—the inference being that different environments require different structural arrangements. Lawrence and Lorsch's major contributions included the recognition that there are multiple specific environments with different degrees of uncertainty, that successful organizations' subunits meet the demands of their subenvironments, and that the degree of environmental uncertainty is of utmost importance in the selection of the right structure. We synthesized the studies into four core environments derived by combining two key dimensions: simple-complex and static-dynamic.

The environment-structure relationship is complicated, but we concluded that (1) the environment's effect on an organization is a function of dependence, (2) a dynamic environment has more influence on structure than does a static one, (3) complexity and environmental uncertainty are inversely related, (4) formalization and environmental uncertainty are inversely related, (5) the more complex the environment, the greater the decentralization, and (6) extreme hostility in the environment leads to temporary centralization.

Organizations manage their environments by creating boundary roles. They also engage in intraorganizational, interorganizational, and domain-choice strategies to reduce environment-structure dependency.

FOR REVIEW AND DISCUSSION

1. What is the difference between an organization's general environment and its specific environment?
2. Why do managers dislike environmental uncertainty? What can they do to reduce it?
3. Describe the technology and environment that fit best with (a) mechanistic and (b) organic structures.
4. Why would an organic structure be inefficient in a stable environment?
5. "Turbulent field best describes the environment that most organizations face today." Build an argument to support this statement. Then build an argument to refute your previous position.
6. What was Lawrence and Lorsch's main contribution to OT?
7. "Differentiation and integration are opposing forces." Do you agree or disagree? Discuss.
8. Define each of the following environmental dimensions: (a) simple, (b) complex, (c) static, and (d) dynamic.
9. Under what conditions is environment likely to be a major determinant of structure?
10. Explain how the management of the following organizations might attempt to manage their environments:
    a. a radio station
    b. an automobile dealer
    c. a college bookstore
    d. a law firm
    e. a large homebuilding firm

CHAPTER

10

POWER-CONTROL

In the previous four chapters, we looked at strategy, size, technology, and environment as independent determinants of structure. We found that none of these four variables was *the* determinant of structure. Each contributed by explaining a part, but only a part. Is it possible that the problem is that the variables interrelate; that is, by combining them, could we get a whole greater than the sum of the parts? Efforts in this direction suggest that (1) there is an interaction among the variables so that by combining them we can explain more of the variance,[1] but (2) at best, these four factors explain only 50 to 60 percent of the variability in structure.[2] Obviously, a major piece of the puzzle is still missing. That piece appears to lie outside the more rational and normative confines viewed so far. In this chapter we venture into the "twilight zone" of organizational politics, power, and coalition formation.

The theme of this chapter is that an organization's structure, at any given time, is the result of a power struggle by internal constituencies that are seeking to further their interests. In contrast to the previous chapters, we now directly question the assumption that decision makers are concerned with developing a structural arrangement that will ensure the efficient transformation of inputs to outputs. "Organizational structures are

[1]Jeffrey D. Ford and John W. Slocum, Jr., "Size, Technology, Environment and the Structure of Organizations," *Academy of Management Review,* October 1977, pp. 561–575.

[2]John Child, "Organization Structure, Environment and Performance: The Role of Strategic Choice," *Sociology,* January 1972, pp. 1–22; and Derek S. Pugh, "The Management of Organization Structures: Does Context Determine Form?" *Organizational Dynamics,* Spring 1973, pp. 19–34.

emergent activities; that is, they are the result of the conscious political decisions of particular actors and interest groups."[3] Building on the notion presented in Chapter 6 that managers have the discretion to choose structure, this chapter questions the criteria that managers use when they make organizational design decisions.

The power-control explanation of organization structure says that managers will choose criteria and weight them so that the "preferred choice" will meet the minimal demands of the organization but also satisfy or enhance the interests of the decision maker. We propose that organizational effectiveness should be construed as a range instead of a point. Rather than seeking a structure that would result in *high* effectiveness, the power-control view expects decision makers to select structures that satisfy the minimal requirements of effectiveness but that emphasize the preferences and interests of the decision makers. So organizational effectiveness is neither an optimum point nor is it irrelevant. It is a range, and power-control advocates argue that decision makers have a great deal of discretion within this range. Size, technology, and environmental uncertainty account for some aspects of structure—they set the general parameters for organizational effectiveness. These variables act as constraints on how much discretion will be available. But within the parameters there is a great deal of room to maneuver, and our position is that discretionary choices within these parameters will reflect the self-interests of the decision maker.

MUDDYING THE DECISION-MAKING WATERS

We can begin our analysis by reviewing the traditional decision-making process as it is proposed in management theory and how it is modified in practice.

The decision-making process can be described as having six steps:

1. Ascertain the need for a decision.
2. Establish decision criteria.
3. Allocate weights to criteria.
4. Develop alternatives.
5. Evaluate alternatives.
6. Select the best alternative.

The decision-making process begins by determining that a problem exists; that is, that there is an unsatisfactory condition. Frequently this is expressed as a disparity between what is and what should be. Once the

[3]Samuel B. Bacharach and Edward J. Lawler, *Power and Politics in Organizations* (San Francisco: Jossey-Bass, 1980), p. 2.

need for a decision has been determined, the decision maker must identify all the decision criteria. These are the factors that are important in making the decision. They are selected based on the best interests of the organization. Then these factors must be weighted to reflect their relative importance. After the criteria have been identified and weighted, the decision maker lists all the alternatives that might solve the problem and meet the criteria requirements. Once listed, the alternatives must be evaluated against the criteria. The strengths and weaknesses of each is assessed, and, based on this evaluation, the best alternative is chosen.

The process as described is simple and clear but, unfortunately, not a very accurate telling of how real decision makers in organizations make choices. In practice, there are human and organizational constraints that act to modify this normative process.[4]

Human Limitations

Decision makers are human beings and thus have human frailities. They recognize only a limited number of decision criteria. They propose only a limited number of alternatives. Their choice of criteria and the weights they give them, and their choice of alternatives and assessment of those alternatives, will reflect the self-interests of the decision maker. The result is that a decision maker's selection of the best solution is not an optimum choice but one that "satisfices."[5] The final choice is both satisfactory and sufficient. Rather than considering *all* alternatives and listing them from most preferred to least preferred, the decision maker searches until an alternative emerges that is good enough. Decision making, therefore, is not a comprehensive process of searching for an optimum solution. It is an incremental process, whereby the decision maker assesses choices until one is found that meets the minimum acceptable level. Once this level is attained, the search stops and the choice is made. The final outcome, therefore, is satisficing rather than optimizing.

Organizational Limitations

To human limitations, we must add constraints imposed by the organization. By this we mean that the organization itself limits the decision maker. The "system" imposes constraints through such factors as its performance evaluation and reward procedures. The evaluation or appraisal system and the reward structure within an organization influence decision makers by suggesting to them what choices are preferable in terms of their

[4]For a complete discussion of these constraints, see Stephen P. Robbins, *The Administrative Process*, 2nd ed. (Englewood Cliffs, N.J.: Prentice-Hall, 1980), pp. 103–115.

[5]Herbert A. Simon, *Administrative Behavior*, 2nd ed. (New York: Macmillan, 1957).

payoff. The decision makers can be expected to be "looking over their shoulder" constantly to assess the consequences of their actions.

The implication of these organizational constraints, when coupled with the human constraints documented earlier, is that we formulate a picture of the decsion maker as a political animal. Based on these human and organizational constraints, decision makers can be expected to make choices that are consistent with their self-interests. Further, they will want to expand their influence to control those decisions that could affect their self-interests.

Divergent Interests

The realities of organizational decision making tell us that the interests of the decision maker and the interests of the organization are rarely one and the same. The traditional six-step decision process, however, assumes them to be. Figure 10–1 depicts reality. While it would be highly desirable, in terms of organizational effectiveness, for the two circles (representing the individual's interests and the organization's interests) to align perfectly, this is far more likely to be the exception rather than the rule. Given that the two circles do not align, what can we predict and what does it mean to decision making?

Since decision makers act in their self-interests, their choices will reflect only the criteria and preferences compatible with the shaded area. That is, at no time would a decision maker be likely to sublimate his or her own interests to those of the organization. Moreover, if confronted with a set of choices, all of which met the "good enough" criterion, the decision maker would obviously choose the one most beneficial personally. So, referring to Figure 10–1, the overlapping area of the circles represents the region in which the decision maker acts consistently with organizational effectiveness criteria. In this area, for instance, we can expect managers to be concerned with economic efficiencies and to prefer an organization structure that would facilitate these efficiencies. This area also represents

FIGURE 10–1 Interplay of decision maker and the organization's interests

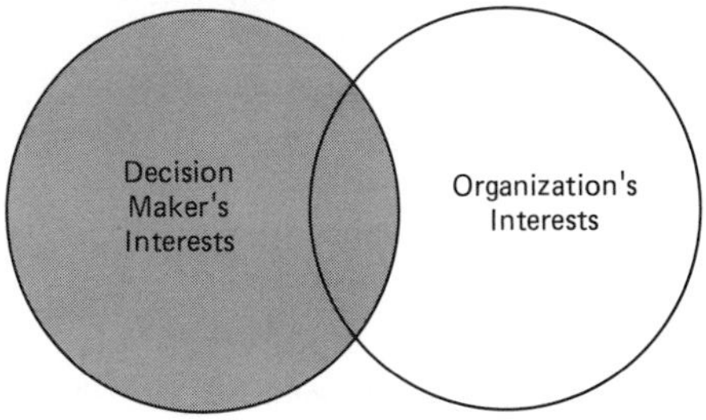

the discretionary range in which, given the constraints of size, technology, and environment, managers still have room for making choices that can be self-serving. The shaded area outside the overlap represents situations in which the decision maker has chosen criteria or preferences that are not compatible with the best interests of the organization but are beneficial to the decision maker.

For instance, phasing out one's department may be in the best interest of the organization but rarely is it in the best interest of the decision maker. As a result, do not expect managers to make that selection. But *expanding* one's department usually means greater responsibilities, status, and remuneration. Those are rewards that managers value. As a result, we can expect managers to try to increase the size and domain of their units regardless of the effect on the organization. It should be noted that the reward system can be designed to encourage managers to phase out their departments; only this is rarely the case. It should also be said that the decision to expand the department will be couched in nonpolitical terms. Overt politics is frowned upon in organizations, so self-serving decisions will always be packaged in terms of improving organizational effectiveness.

GOALS AND RATIONAL BEHAVIOR

A full understanding of the power-control position demands a review of organizational goals and consideration of the requirements necessary for decision making to be categorized as rational. Our analysis begins by reflecting back on Chapter 2 and the competing-values approach to organizational effectiveness.

The competing-values approach proposed that the evaluation of an organization's effectiveness depends on who is doing the evaluating. Different criteria are emphasized by different constituencies. Inherent in this approach is the acknowledgment that organizations have multiple goals. The reality of multiple goals is also an important part of the power-control explanation of how organizations are structured. Basically, the logic is that those who support strategy, size, technology, or environment as structural determinants assume rationality. But rationality is defined as goal-directed behavior. Since organizations have multiple goals that are almost always diverse, rationality does not apply. That is, "since rationality is defined with respect to some preference for outcomes, when there is no consensus on outcome preference it is difficult to speak of rationality."[6] Organizations do not have a singular goal or multiple goals with which everyone agrees, so the whole notion that organization structure is a rational response to such factors as the degree of technological routineness or environmental uncertainty is open to debate.

[6]Jeffrey Pfeffer, *Organizational Design* (Arlington Heights, Ill.: AHM Publishing, 1978), p. 8.

Once we accept the existence of multiple and diverse goals, at least the possibility for nonrational decision-making behavior, and the notion that decision makers act in their self-interests, the power-control position begins to take on increasing credibility. We can begin to think of an organization's structure as the result of a power struggle between special-interest groups or coalitions, each arguing for a structural arrangement that best meets their own needs instead of organizationwide interests—all the time, of course, couching their arguments and their preferred criteria in terms of organizational effectiveness. In such an environment, politics will determine the criteria and preferences of decision makers. What kind of structure will emerge? It depends on who has the power to effect the decision.

COALITIONS FIGHT FOR POWER

While organizations are made up of individuals, it may be more valuable to think of organizations as coalitions of interests. These coalitions flourish largely because of the ambiguity surrounding goals, organizational effectiveness, and what is thought to be rational.

> It is difficult to think of situations in which goals are so congruent, or the facts so clear-cut that judgment and compromise are not involved. What is rational from one point of view is irrational from another. Organizations are political systems, coalitions of interests, and rationality is defined only with respect to unitary and consistent orderings of preferences.[7]

Coalitions form to protect and improve their vested interests. Employees in the marketing department have a common special interest, ensuring that they obtain their share of the organization's resources and rewards. But they are not alone. Accounting, finance, purchasing, and every department will have their coalitions. These coalitions, of course, are not limited to horizontally differentiated units. Plant managers will have their coalitions, as will different levels of middle managers and even the top management cadre.

The power-control view proposes that these coalitions wrestle in a power struggle to control the organization. Notice that this power struggle comes about because there is dissention concerning preferences or in the definition of the situation.[8] Without this dissention there would be no room for judgment, negotiation, and the eventual politicking that occurs.

[7]Ibid., pp. 11–12.

[8]Jeffrey Pfeffer, "Power and Resource Allocation in Organizations," in Barry M. Staw and Gerald R. Salancik, eds., *New Directions in Organizational Behavior* (Chicago: St. Clair Press, 1977), p. 240.

What does this mean in terms of an organization's structure? Dissension and the existence of self-serving coalitions ensure a fight for control over organizational design decisions. Varied structural designs do not foster neutral responses from coalitions. The location of the coalition in the structure will determine such things as its influence in planning, choosing its technology, selecting the criteria by which it will be evaluated, allocating rewards, controlling information, and determining its proximity to senior executives. Moreover, powerful coalitions will be in a position to determine in large part their own internal structure—how much complexity, formalization, and centralization there will be. Size, technology, and environment will act as general constraints on structure to narrow decision-making choices. However, after acknowledging these constraints, there is still a lot of room left for negotiating, especially since structural choices only have to satisfice. Since organizational effectiveness is a problematic state, "the critical question becomes not how organizations should be designed to maximize effectiveness, but rather, whose preferences and interests are to be served by the organization."[9]

Figure 10–2 depicts how power-control advocates perceive that an organization's structure comes to be. The choice of a structure is constrained by the organization's strategy, size, technology, environment, and the required minimal level of effectiveness. These forces combine to establish the set of structural alternatives from which the decision will be made. Who will make the decision? The most powerful or dominant coalition. How will this dominant coalition make the decision? By imposing its self-interests on the criteria and preferences in the decision. The result is the organization's emergent structure.

FIGURE 10–2 The power-control model

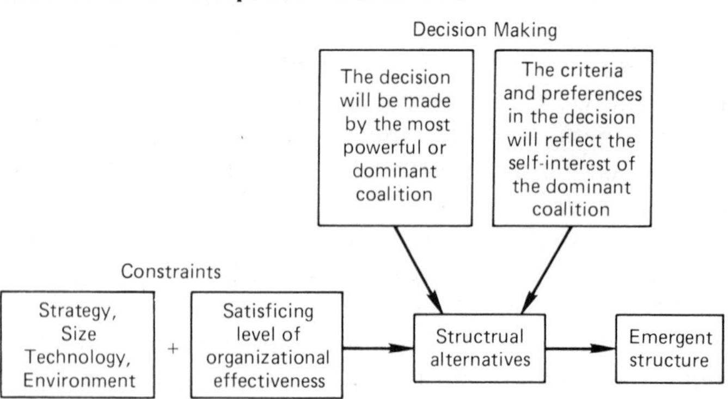

[9]Pfeffer, *Organizational Design*, p. 223.

STRATEGIC-CHOICE VERSUS POWER-CONTROL

The similarities and differences between the strategic-choice perspective offered in Chapter 6 and the power-control position should now appear considerably clearer. Both assume goals and managerial discretion. But the strategic-choice argument assumes the rational pursuit of organizational goals. It assumes further that the choice will be made by top management. The power-control position replaces the organization's goals with the coalition's goals. Additionally, the decision will be made by the dominant coalition that usually is, but need not be, the same as the top management group. As we discuss in a moment, authority and power are not the same thing, and to assume that those high in authority will be the ones making structural design choices may be naïve.

Who Makes up the Dominant Coalition?

The dominant coalition is the one that has the power to affect structure. In a small company, the power coalition and the owners are typically one and the same. In large organizations, top management usually dominates. But not always. Any coalition that can control the resources on which the organization depends can become dominant. A group with critical information, expertise, or any other resource that is essential to the organization's operation can acquire the power to influence the outcome of structural decisions and thus become the dominant coalition. A fuller explanation of the source of such power appears later in this chapter.

Authority versus Power

The terms "authority" and "power" are consistently confused by students of management. In no area is this confusion more likely to cause problems than in comparing the strategic-choice imperative with that of power-control.

In Chapter 5, we defined authority as the right to act, or command others to act, toward the attainment of organizational goals. Its unique characteristic, we said, was that this right had legitimacy based on the authority figure's position in the organization. Authority goes with the job. You leave your managerial job and you give up the authority that goes with that position. When we use the term "power," we mean an individual's capacity to influence decisions. As such, authority is actually part of the larger concept of power; that is, the ability to influence based on an individual's legitimate position can affect decisions, but one does not require authority to have such influence.

Figure 10–3 depicts the difference between authority and power. The two-dimensional hierarchical arrangement of boxes in Figure 10–3A indicates that there are levels in an organization and that the rights to make decisions increase as one moves up the hierarchy. Power, on the other hand, is conceptualized best as a three-dimensional cone. The power of individuals in an organization depends on their vertical position in the cone and their distance from the center of the cone.

Think of the cone in Figure 10–3B as an organization. The center of the cone will be called the power core. The closer one is to the power core, the more influence one has to affect decisions. The existence of a power core is the only difference between A and B in Figure 10–3. The vertical hierarchy dimension in A is merely one's level on the outer edge of the cone. The top of the cone is equal to the top of the hierarchy; the middle of the cone is equal to the middle of the hierarchy; and so on. Similarly, the functional groupings in A become wedges in the cone. This is seen in Figure 10–4, which depicts the same cone in Figure 10–3B, except that it is now shown from above. Each wedge of the cone represents a functional area. So, if the second level of Figure 10–3A contains the marketing, production, and administrative functions of the organization, Figure 10–4's three wedges are the same functional departments.

The cone analogy allows us to consider these two facts: (1) the higher one moves in an organization (an increase in authority), the closer one automatically moves toward the power core; and (2) it is not necessary to have authority to wield power, because one can move horizontally inward toward the power core without moving up.

Ever notice that secretaries of high-ranking executives typically have a great deal of power but very little authority? As gatekeepers for their bosses, they have considerable say as to who can make appointments and

FIGURE 10–3 Authority versus power

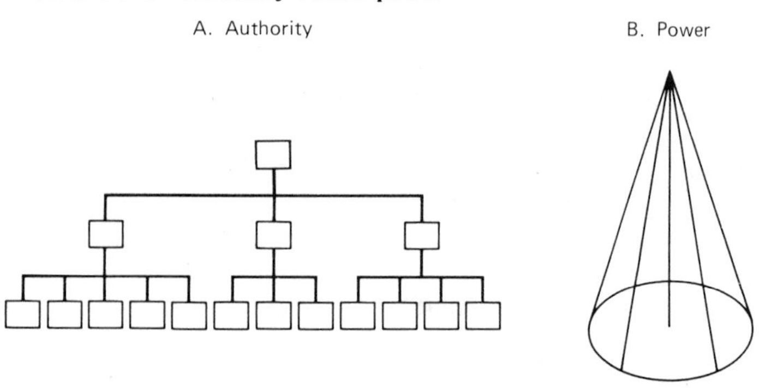

FIGURE 10–4 Aerial view of the organization conceptualized as a cone

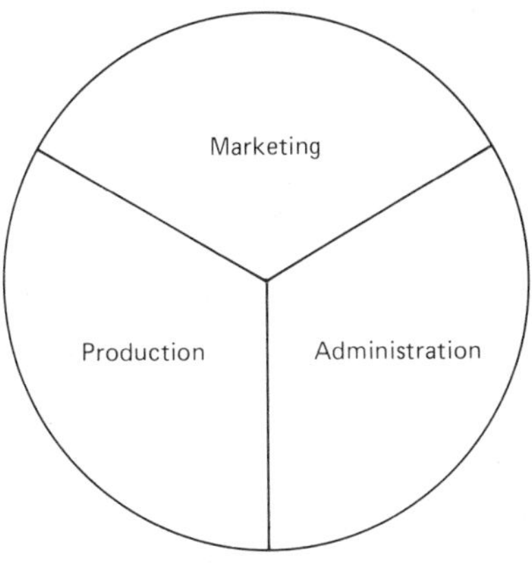

who cannot. Additionally, because they are relied upon regularly to pass on information to their bosses, they have some control of what is heard. It's not unusual for $60,000-a-year middle managers to tread very carefully so as not to upset their boss's $20,000-a-year secretary. Why? Because this secretary has power! She is low in the authority hierarchy, but she is close to the power core. Low-ranking employees who have relatives, friends, or associates in high places may be close to the power core. So, too, may be the lowly production engineer, with twenty years of experience in the company, who is the only one in the firm who knows the inner workings of all the old production machinery. When pieces of this old equipment break down, no one but this engineer understands how to fix it. Suddenly, this engineer's influence is much greater than would ever be construed from assessing his level in the vertical hierarchy.

The separation of authority and power is obviously very important to understanding the power-control perspective and to differentiate it from strategic-choice. It reminds us that those with formal authority may have the clout but, then again, that others in the organization may have created strong power bases that allow them to have even greater influence over decisions. Moreover, because those with the capacity to influence decisions will select criteria and preferences that are consistent with their own self-interests, choices are likely to be highly divergent from those that would occur under strategic-choice conditions. In other words, the power-control position argues that not only will structural decisions be made against different goals but, in contrast to the strategy imperative, they may be made by a coalition other than those senior executives with the greatest amount of formal authority.

THE ROADS TO POWER

How does an individual or group gain power? There are many roads that can be taken, but most of them fall into one of two categories. They either represent attempts to *control resources* or to *reduce uncertainties* that may impinge on the organization's performance.

Control of Resources

If you have something that others want, you can have power over them. But the mere control of a resource is no guarantee that it will enhance your power. The resource must be both scarce and critical.[10]

Unless a resource is scarce within the organization, it is unlikely to be a source of power. When gasoline was plentiful, your neighborhood service-station owner had little ability to influence you. In the summer of 1979, when many of us sat in lines for three hours to get $5.00 worth of gas for our cars, that station owner suddenly had increased clout. He said "Jump," and we said "How high?" The same concept applies in organizations. The mere possession of a resource means nothing if that resource is not scarce.

If resource scarcity increases the power of the resourceholder, then the proximity of relevant substitutes for the resource should also be considered. That is, a resource for which there is no close substitute is more scarce than one that has high substitutability. Skills represent an example. Organizations rely on individuals with a wide range of special skills to perform effectively. Those who possess a skill that the organization needs but that no one else in the organization has will obviously be in a more influential position than will one whose skills are duplicated by hundreds of other employees. This describes Johnny Carson's influence at NBC in the early 1980s. Probably the most powerful man in American television, Carson negotiated a new contract in 1981 that increased his salary to an estimated $5 million a year and required him to work less time. He also issued barbed attacks at his boss at the time, NBC president Fred Silverman. How could Carson negotiate such an attractive contract or dump on his boss publicly and survive? Because his show draws over 12 million viewers a night and is the single most lucrative entity at NBC, earning an estimated $60 million a year for the network. Most important, the people at NBC believe—rightly or wrongly—that Carson is the scarce and critical resource responsible for generating these high earnings and that there is no close substitute for him.

Similarly, a labor union's power relative to management's is largely

[10]Pfeffer, "Power and Resource Allocation in Organizations," pp. 248–249.

a function of its members' ability to restrict management's options. If the organization is highly labor intensive, it will rely heavily on people to get the jobs done. If a company cannot hire someone unless, at the time of hiring, he or she is already a member of the union, the union could hold the firm captive to its demands. That is why "closed shops" are illegal. Unions obviously would like to hold considerable control over the firm's labor supply. This explains why unions so strongly dislike so-called right to work laws that make it illegal for any collective bargaining agreement to contain clauses calling for compulsory union membership.

These examples indicate another requirement for a resource to give its holder power: the organization must need it! Just being scarce isn't good enough; the resource must also be important. The more a resource approaches criticality for the organization, the more power it gives its holder. To return to a previous example, there may be no gasoline sources anywhere in your town except at one station. The person or persons who control that gasoline—probably the owner or station manager—has power only to the degree that you need gasoline. If you do not own a car, the scarce supply of gasoline means nothing to you. However, if you are a salesperson who goes on the road, lives in a Sunbelt city where public transportation options are minimal, and your livelihood depends on having enough gasoline to make your regular calls, that service-station owner has a great deal of power. It is just such instances that led to reports of customers paying black market prices of $5 and up per gallon of gas. When you are desperate, you do what you must. Conversely, when others are desperate for what you have, you can use your power to exact a high price for your resource.

Managers in organizations hold control over evaluating the performance of subordinates. They also frequently have considerable say over the rewards (salary increases, promotions, desirable work assignments, etc.) allocated to those subordinates. As such, the authority inherent in a manager's job provides a considerable power base. But, of course, there are resources that are scarce and important and that are certainly not the sole province of managers. Control and access to information is an example that falls in that category. If I know something that the organization needs, I have power. My power actually lies in my ability to withhold that information. If I am a senior executive in a firm, I am likely to have access to important information, but it is rarely scarce. Lots of other managers also have access to that same information. So "where you sit" has less bearing on your power than "what you know." This explains why expertise leads to power in organizations. It also explains why many employees go to considerable extremes to cloud what they do in a shroud of secrecy.

Expert knowledge or the possession of special skills is a powerful source of influence, especially in a technologically oriented society. As jobs become more specialized, experts become more indispensable. Therefore, anyone who can develop an expertise that is scarce and important will have power. This increasingly includes jobs such as computer specialists, tax accountants, solar engineers, and industrial psychologists. But remember that expertise need not be associated with professionalization. It can be localized knowledge that has little transferability. For instance, suppose that the order clerk in one company (call it XYZ) had developed close ties with a senior purchasing executive at one of the company's major customers (call it ABC). Based on years of telephone contact, the purchasing executive at ABC had instituted the practice of bypassing XYZ's sales personnel who were responsible for the ABC account. Million-dollar orders were just called in directly to the order clerk at XYZ. This frustrated the sales group at XYZ to no end, but they got credit for the sales and they were not about to upset this prize customer by making him follow XYZ's procedures. The order clerk, meanwhile, capitalized on the situation. He became increasingly knowledgable of ABC's needs. He even made suggestions to the ABC executive on product modifications that XYZ could make to better service ABC. On the other hand, the salesperson assigned to the ABC account knew nothing of ABC's needs nor had he developed any contacts with key ABC personnel. The result was that this order clerk had become a very powerful figure at XYZ. No one, particularly in the sales department, dared upset him. When he wanted a few extra weeks of vacation, he got them with no questions asked. When he suggested his new son-in-law for a vacancy in the product design department, the application went through and an offer was made in record time, with noticeable expediting coming from a senior manager in the sales department.

Information, per se, can be a power source. Again, of course, the information must be scarce and important. Secrecy or the limitation of access to information is used by individuals and groups within the organization to enhance and maintain influence.[11] The information used to make the decision may be kept secret. If others do not know what information went into making a decision, the decision makers can always say that those who did not like the final decision were not privy to all the facts. In effect, as long as information is controlled, it is virtually impossible for anyone to challenge the decision. This describes much of the power attributed to David Stockman, the director of the Office of Management and Budget in the Reagan administration. In the winter of 1981, for instance, Stockman advised the other cabinet secretaries that he intended to slash their budgets. On paper, all the cabinet posts were equal. But they were not. Stockman's influence in the cabinet was greater than his authority. Part of his power was due to the full support he had from the president. But a greater source

[11]Ibid., p. 246.

of his power was the information he controlled. All federal agencies had to filter their requests for funds through Stockman's office. There it was studied by his staff of over three hundred examiners who then forwarded the recommendation to the OMB director. Stockman's control of information about the bureaucracy and his willingness to read the data available turned him into what *Time* magazine called "the greatest human repository of information on the U.S. government" in Washington. Stockman used his control of information to exercise power in the federal government.

In addition to maintaining secrecy over the information used in the decision, it is also possible to keep the decision-making process itself secret or occasionally even the results of the process secret. The former may involve not divulging the names of the decision makers or the process of deliberation. The latter is exemplified best by the practice, in many organizations, of keeping salaries secret.

This discussion of using expertise and information as power tools provides insights into employee actions that are often seen as irrational. When placed in the context of controlling scarce and important resources, behaviors such as destroying the procedure manuals that describe how your job is done, refusing to train people in your job or even to show others exactly what you do, creating specialized language and terminology that inhibits others from understanding your job, or operating in secrecy so that the tasks you perform will appear more complex and difficult than they really are suddenly appear to be very rational actions.

Reduce Uncertainties

To the degree that you can reduce the organization's uncertainties, you will have power in the organization.[12] Uncertainty, as we discussed in the previous chapter, is something that management seeks to avoid. Those individuals or groups that can cope with these uncertainties increase their value to the organization. Of course, our previous comment about importance and substitutability has application here too. Power will be greatest for those who can absorb the organization's critical uncertainties and for which few other alternative sources for uncertainty reduction exist.

The "ability to reduce uncertainty creates power" argument appears to explain the background of chief executive officers. In the 1930s and 1940s, the critical contingencies facing organizations were production related, and, therefore, individuals with production backgrounds tended to rise to the CEO position. In the 1950s, marketing-related issues became the

[12]David J. Hickson, Christopher R. Hinings, Charles A. Lee, Rodney E. Schneck, and Johannes M. Pennings, "A Strategic Contingencies' Theory of Intraorganizational Power," *Administrative Science Quarterly*, June 1971, pp. 216–229.

greatest uncertainty facing organizations, and marketing people increasingly filled CEO positions. In the 1960s, financial issues created the greatest uncertainties, and finance people found themselves in the fast track. The 1970s, with increased government legislation confronting organizations, people with a knowledge of the law were best able to cope with the critical uncertainties. Some predict that personnel will be in the power seat in the 1980s as organizations attempt to increase productivity and design human resource systems that meet equal employment opportunity requirements.

This reasoning can also be used to explain differences in departmental power between organizations. At IBM, for instance, critical uncertainties tend to be concentrated in technical and innovative areas. The success of IBM is *most* dependent on a continued string of new products. At IBM, therefore, research and development people are extremely powerful. In contrast, Procter & Gamble's critical uncertainties lie in marketing. At P&G, the marketing people are most powerful.

A study of production plants in France found that the people who controlled the factories' critical uncertainties acquired the most power.[13] In one plant, specifically, the researcher observed that the maintenance engineers exerted a great deal of influence even though they were not particularly high in the organizational hierarchy. The researcher concluded that, in this plant, the breakdown of the machinery was the only remaining uncertainty confronting the organization. The maintenance engineers were the only personnel who could cope with machine stoppage, and they had taken the pains to reinforce their power through control of information. They avoided written procedures for dealing with breakdowns; they purposely disregarded all blueprints and maintenance directions; and so on. Not even the supervisors in the plant had adequate knowledge to check on these engineers.

We can even predict, based on the uncertainty-reduction theme, that those holding power will occasionally resort to inventing problems that they can handle just to remind others in the organization how critical they are to the organization's success.[14] In the French factory, if the machines never broke down, the maintenance engineers would have no opportunity to demonstrate the organization's dependence on them. This reasoning can explain why industrial relations departments occasionally allow a strike to occur when an impasse could be resolved. What better way is there to remind everyone within a company just how important the industrial relations department is than to have a strike that closes most of the company down and *requires* the skills of the industrial relations labor negotiators to resolve the conflict?

[13]Michel Crozier, *The Bureaucratic Phenomenon* (Chicago: University of Chicago Press, 1964).

[14]Pfeffer, "Power and Resource Allocation in Organizations," p. 257.

Certain positions in the organization are more likely to confront critical uncertainties and be able to absorb them than are others. Boundary-role jobs are clearly well positioned. Boundary roles are more critical and visible. Even if, in fact, boundary roles are not critical, they are frequently perceived as such because their activities are less predictable and less routinized. The degree of routinization has been the frequent object of analysis. "Research and observation suggest that the most important source of power is absence of routinization . . . the task that is routinizable, that is, highly predictable and regularizable, has less power."[15] While this may be an overstatement, we should not forget that routinization of activities and power in the organization are inversely related.

POWER-CONTROL AND STRUCTURE

It is now time to translate our insights from the power-control perspective into implications for the structuring of organizations. We begin by considering a power-control interpretation of technology and environment's role on structure.

Technology and Environment

"The picture of the organization as an adaptive, responsive entity, proximately affected by the demands of technology or environment, is probably as misleading as the parallel portrait of the competitive organization in classical economic theory."[16] Power-control advocates argue that an organization's structure, at any given time, will be one that allows those in power to maintain the control they have. In terms of technology and environment, therefore, the dominant coalition can be expected to seek routine technologies and attempt to manage their environment to reduce uncertainty. Let us expand briefly on each of these points.

Technology does not *cause* structure. It is chosen. The choice of a domain tends to constrain the organization's technology, but the domain is also chosen. Within a given domain, a range of technologies almost always exists. Which type of technology will be selected? That which is most routine and relies most heavily on mechanization and automation. Routine technologies make individual workers more substitutable for each other and hence more easily replaceable. Routinization also serves the interest of top management by facilitating centralization of power. Given that technology is chosen, routine technologies will be most prevalent because they enhance control.

[15]Leonard R. Sayles *Leadership: What Effective Managers Really Do and How They Do It* (New York: McGraw-Hill; 1979), p. 95.

[16]Pfeffer, *Organizational Design*, p. 225.

The organization will seek to manage its environment to reduce uncertainty. This point was elaborated on in the previous chapter. Remember that there are ways for organizations to respond to uncertainty. They can insulate their technologies to reduce the impact of uncertainty; they can establish more favorable relationships with those elements in the environment that pose potential difficulties; or they can shift to a more favorable environment by changing domains. The view that structure is a response to the environment implies that changes in structure occur to improve organizational effectiveness. When the organization responds to external demands, it usually does so under extreme duress. "The organization that appears to be innovative or responsive is so, we would argue, because such a course of action enhances the influence and resource position of those in control of the organization's activities."[17]

Stability and Mechanistic Structures

These comments lead us to additional extensions. Because organizations seek routinization and management of uncertainty, structural change should be minimal. We can expect those in power to try to maintain their control. If the current structure is effective in maintaining control, why should they want to change? They will not, except when forced. The argument made by power-control advocates is that significant changes represent, in effect, quasi-revolutions.[18] They are likely to occur only as a result of a political struggle in which new power relationships evolve. This rarely occurs. When it does, it usually follows a major shake-up in top management or indicates that the organization is facing obvious and direct threats to its survival. When changes in structure occur, they are more typically incremental.[19] Incrementalism maintains stability by keeping changes small and never deviating much from the previous structural arrangement. A look at the organization structures of General Motors, the U.S. Air Force, or *The New York Times* in 1950 and 1980 shows each substantially unchanged over the thirty-year period and that change has been evolutionary rather than revolutionary.

The power-control view of structure predicts that not only will structural arrangements be relatively stable over time but that mechanistic structures will dominate. This is consistent with the conclusions drawn in Chapter 9. If stability, routinization, and centralized control are sought, it seems logical that mechanistic structures will rule. And observations of structures, as we noted in Chapter 9, concur with this prediction. Those in power will choose structures that maintain their control—ones that minimize com-

[17]Ibid.

[18]Ibid., p. 176.

[19]Ibid., p. 14.

plexity and maximize formalization and centralization. This anticontingency position flies in direct opposition to the "there is no one best way to organize" theme. The contingency advocates' "no one best way" theme uses performance as the standard. The mechanistic structure *is* the "one best way," if *best* refers to "maintenance of control" rather than performance.

Complexity

Increased differentiation—horizontally, vertically, or spatially—leads to difficulties in coordination and control. Management would prefer, therefore, all things being equal, to have low complexity. But, of course, all things are not equal. Size, technology, and environmental factors do make high complexity efficient in many cases. So compromise is required. The "imperatives" set the parameters. Management can then be expected to choose the lowest degree of complexity (to maximize control) consistent with the satisficing criterion for organizational effectiveness.

It has been noted that information technology can permit the development of more elaborate and complex structures without necessarily foresaking management's control.[20] Sophisticated information systems utilizing computer technology allow senior executives to receive ongoing communications. Management can monitor a large range of activities many levels down the hierarchy or thousands of miles away and still maintain close control over those activities. The fact that an executive in Atlanta can punch eight keys on the computer terminal at his desk and get an immediate readout on the current status of an inventory item in a company warehouse in Seattle means that this executive can monitor inventories closer than managers in Seattle could have twenty years ago.

Formalization

Those in power will influence the degree of rules and regulations under which employees work. Because control is a desired end for those in power, we can expect organizations to have a high degree of formalization.

If technology were nonroutine or if environmental uncertainty could not be managed, we would expect that high formalization—while desired by those in control—could not be implemented without disasterous effects on organizational performance. But as we have concluded, management will make extensive efforts to routinize tasks and manage uncertainty. Since technology and environments are chosen by those in power, we can expect them to select ones that are compatible with high levels of formalization and maintenance of control. In those cases where factors require low for-

[20]Ibid., pp. 73–75.

malization—because of an extremely turbulent environment that cannot be managed or highly professionalized personnel—those in power can be expected to rely on sophisticated information technology as a control device that can be substituted for rules and regulations.

Centralization

From earlier discussions on centralization, we know that it is preferred when mistakes are very costly, when temporary external threats exist, or when it is important that decisions reflect an understanding of the "big picture." To these we can add, when those in control want to make the decisions. In fact, decentralization should occur infrequently. Even when it does, it may be pseudodecentralization. That is, top management will create the appearance of delegating decisions downward but use information technology for feedback. This feedback allows those in control to monitor lower-level decisions closely and to intercede and correct at any time the decisions they do not like.

> If persons are allowed discretion, but are permitted the opportunity to make decisions because their performance can be rapidly and accurately assessed, it seems that there has been no real sharing of control, influence, or power in the organization. It is conceivable, then, that the introduction of information technology can make possible the appearance of decentralization while maintaining effective centralized control over organizational operations.[21]

It can also be argued that those in power maintain control in decentralized situations by defining the parameters of decisions. For example, university faculty members perceive themselves as operating in a heavily decentralized environment. Important decisions, such as hiring, are made by faculty members at the department level. But the decision that a vacancy exists typically lies with the college- or university-level administrators. The president decides which departments will be given new positions to staff and also decides the disposition of slots that open up as a result of resignations or retirements. While its true that department members select their colleagues, top-level university administrators maintain considerable control through their power to allocate positions among campus units and their ultimate rights to veto candidates of whom they do not approve.

SUMMARY

No more than 50 to 60 percent of the variability in structure can be explained by strategy, size, technology, and environment. The remainder can be attributed to organizational politics; more specifically, to the power-control view of structure, which states that an organization's structure is the result

[21] Ibid., pp. 72–73.

of a power struggle by internal constituencies who are seeking to further their interests.

The previous determinants of structure assumed rationality. However, for rationality to prevail an organization must have either a single goal or agreement over the multiple goals. Neither case exists in most organizations. As a result, structural decisions are not rational. The structure decision is a power struggle between special-interest groups or coalitions, each arguing for a structural arrangement that best meets their own needs. Strategy, size, technology, and environment define the minimal level of effectiveness and set the parameters within which self-serving decision choices will be made.

Power is the central theme in the power-control perspective. Structural choices will be made by those who hold power. This is usually the senior management, but it need not be. Power can be acquired by controlling resources that are scarce and critical in the organization or by reducing uncertainties that may impinge on the organization's performance.

The argument is made that both technology and environment are chosen. Thus, those in power will select technologies and environments that will facilitate their maintenance of control. Organizations, therefore, should be characterized by routine technologies and environments in which uncertainities are relatively low. To enhance control further, those in power will seek to choose structures that are low in complexity and high in both formalization and centralization.

FOR REVIEW AND DISCUSSION

1. "Strategy, size, technology, and environment are irrelevant in explaining an organization's structure." Do you agree or disagree? Discuss.
2. How do human and organizational limitations constrain the normative decision-making process?
3. What conditions must exist for decisions to be rational?
4. Contrast optimizing and satisficing.
5. Who makes up an organization's dominant coalition?
6. Contrast strategic-choice and power-control.
7. How is it possible for someone low in the organization to obtain power?
8. Using the power-control perspective, describe how most organizations are structured.
9. "Power is derived from the division of labor that occurs as task specialization is implemented in organizations." Do you agree or disagree? Discuss.

10. The president of a large corporation hires an impartial consultant to analyze the organization's structure. After a long and careful analysis, the consultant submits a report to the corporation's board of directors that suggests several small changes but that leaves the current structure substantially in place. Explain the president's decision to use a consultant and the consultant's conclusion from a power-control perspective.

PART IV

ORGANIZATIONAL DESIGN: CHOOSING THE RIGHT STRUCTURAL FORM

CHAPTER

11

BUREAUCRACY

This chapter is the first of three to address the question: What alternatives exist in the design of organizations? We begin by reviewing *bureaucracy*.

What does the term bureaucracy mean to you? To many it conjures up a host of attributes, all implying inefficiency—red tape; rigid application of rules; buck-passing; impersonal; a lethargic attitude toward change; redundancy of effort; papershuffling; empire building; and the like. Forget these prejudices! Bureaucracy does not *mean* inefficiency. Think of it as a noun rather than as an adjective. It is a type of structure—*the* dominant form in organizations today. Its widespread popularity demands that we assess *exactly* what it is, its strengths and weaknesses, and under what conditions is it the preferred structure.

WEBER'S DEFINITION OF BUREAUCRACY

The classic perspective on bureaucracy was proposed by German sociologist Max Weber (pronounced *Vay-ber*) at the beginning of this century.[1] He sought to describe an ideal organization—one that would be perfectly rational and would provide maximum efficiency of operation. The following characteristics form the essence of Weber's ideal organization. Keep in mind, however, that Weber's bureaucratic model was a hypothetical rather than a factual description of how most organizations were structured:

[1]Max Weber, *The Theory of Social and Economic Organizations*, ed., Talcott Parsons, trans., A. M. Henderson and Talcott Parsons (New York: Free Press, 1947).

Division of labor. Each person's job is broken down into simple, routine, and well-defined tasks.

Well-defined authority hierarchy. A multilevel formal structure, with a hierarchy of positions or offices, ensures that each lower office is under the supervision and control of a higher one.

High formalization. Dependence on formal rules and procedures to ensure uniformity and to regulate the behavior of jobholders.

Impersonal nature. Sanctions are applied uniformly and impersonally to avoid involvement with individual personalities and personal preferences of members.

Employment decisions based on merit. Selection and promotion decisions are based on technical qualifications, competence, and performance of the candidates.

Career tracks for employees. Members are expected to pursue a career in the organization. In return for this career commitment, employees have tenure; that is, they will be retained even if they "burn out" or if their skills become obsolete.

Distinct separation of members' organizational and personal lives. The demands and interests of personal affairs are kept completely separate to prevent them from interfering with the rational impersonal conduct of the organization's activities.

These characteristics illustrate Weber's "ideal type" of rational and efficient organization. Goals are clear and explicit. Positions are arranged in a pyramidal hierarchy, with authority increasing as one moves up the organization. The authority lies in the positions rather than in the people who occupy them. Selection of members is based on their qualifications rather than on "who they know"; requirements of the position determine who will be employed and in what positions; and performance is the criterion for promotions. Commitment to the organization is maximized and conflicts of interest eliminated by providing lifetime employment and separating members' off-the-job roles from those required in fulfilling organizational responsibilities.

Sounds good, doesn't it? No politicking, no emotional involvement with individual personalities, no conflicts over goals or criteria for defining effectiveness, decisions based solely on objective criteria, and nice clear lines of authority. Does this jive with the bureaucracies you know? Probably not! But remember: Weber was not describing the average or typical organization. He was defining the characteristics that established the "ideal type," the ultimate efficiency machine. As Weber said:

> Experience tends universally to show that *the purely* bureaucratic type of *administrative* organization . . . is, from a *purely technical point of view,* capable of attaining the *highest degree of efficiency* and is in this sense

> formally the most rational known means of carrying out imperative control over human beings. It is superior to any other form in precision, in stability, in the stringency of its discipline, and in its reliability. It thus makes possible a particularly high *degree of calculability* of results for the heads of the organization and for those acting in relation to it. It is finally superior both in intensive efficiency and in the scope of its operations, and is formally capable of application to all kinds of administrative tasks.[2]

We consider the problems with bureaucracy later in this chapter—and there are certainly plenty of them—but before doing that, it is important to understand fully the implications of Weber's model. Weber's bureaucracy has some strong and positive qualities.

Positive Qualities in Weber's "Ideal Type"

Weber's bureaucracy included a number of characteristics that, it can be argued, are highly desirable. Specifically, we can single out the attempt to eliminate the use of irrelevant criteria for choosing employees; the use of tenure to protect employees against arbitrary authority and changes in skill demands and declining ability; the establishment of rules and regulations to increase the likelihood that employees will be treated fairly and to create stability over time; and the creation of a vertical hierarchy to ensure that clear lines of authority exist, that decisions are made, and that accountability over decisions is maintained.[3]

Weber's model seeks to purge the organization of favoritism. He fought against prejudice and discrimination more than half a century before civil rights legislation. One major plus of bureaucracy, therefore, is that it sought to bring objectivity to employee selection by reducing nepotism and other forms of favoritism by decision makers and replacing it with job competence criteria.

The idea of giving employees security through tenure is often attacked on the grounds that it makes employees complacent. Why work hard when your job is literally guaranteed? The potential costs of complacency are real, but they must be compared with the benefits that tenure provides. These benefits include commitment to the organization, protection against arbitrary actions of senior management, and inducement to master skills that may have limited marketability. By offering employees security in employment, they can pursue those activities and learn those skills that may have little value outside the organization but that, nevertheless, are

[2]Ibid., p. 337. (Author's emphasis)

[3]The following discussion is adapted from Charles Perrow, *Complex Organizations: A Critical Essay* (Glenview, Ill.: Scott, Foresman, 1972), pp. 8–44.

important for the organization's success. You are much more likely to accept spending a year or more learning the idiosyncracies of your firm's accounting system if you recognize that the firm is committed to providing you a career regardless of whether the accounting system changes or there is a significant decline in the company's business. A glance at the historical management-labor relationship in Japan supports the value of tenure. Japanese employees have traditionally been granted permanent employment, regardless of the business cycle. In response, Japanese firms have some of the most loyal and productive employees in the world.

Rules and regulations may be constraints on what you can and cannot do, but they reduce ambiguity and increase uniformity of actions. Without a policy, for instance, how does a manager know when he can make a decision? Absence of policy, therefore, leaves him open to reprimand for any decision he makes, however trivial. Similarly, if I do something wrong, I want to be assured that I am not unduly penalized. Bureaucracy's high formalization provides the mechanism with which to facilitate this standardization of discipline practices.

Finally, while the vertical hierarchy may be seen as a vehicle for "buck-passing," its positive qualities are often overlooked. It answers such questions as: To whom do I take my problems? How much authority does that manager have? Who do I have to see to get this decision made? The importance of these issues is revealed in a survey of managers in industrial firms. They were found to be decidedly "in favor of more, rather than less, clarity in lines of authority, rules, duties, specification of procedures, and so on."[4] These managers recognized that only when the structure and relationships are clear can authority be delegated.

Why Bureaucracies Work: An Example

Bureaucracies work because they are the best way in which to organize large numbers of people who perform a diverse set of activities. This can be illustrated by looking at how an organization designed originally as an alternative to bureaucracy evolves eventually into the bureaucratic form as it grows and prospers.

Celestial Seasonings, Inc. was started in 1971 as the brain child of two fellows in their early twenties who were looking for something to do during the summer.[5] Mo Siegel and John Hay lived in Boulder, Colorado. Both were "free spirits." But even free spirits have to eat, so Mo and John decided to make and sell herb teas. They wanted to create something that

[4]Cited in Perrow, *Complex Organizations,* p. 37.

[5]Eric Morgenthaler, "Herb Tea's Pioneer: From Hippie Origins to $16 million a Year," *The Wall Street Journal,* May 7, 1981, p. 1.

would provide them with a living, without the structure of typical 9-to-5 jobs. So began Celestial Seasonings.

When the organization started, there were no job descriptions, production lines, or the like. Mo, John, and whoever else they could rustle up would pick herbs in the mountains. Wives and girlfriends would sew the muslin bags to hold the tea. Everyone would pitch in to mix and blend the teas. The completed product would then be sold to natural foods stores in the Boulder area. Decision making was consistent with the organization's origins. Informal meetings were held once a week. It was not unusual for these meetings to last eight hours, while participants dwelled on topics such as the philosophical attributes of tea bags.

But Celestial Seasonings was not destined to remain a free and flexible organization. Something began to happen very soon after its founding that changed its structure dramatically. The company's products began to sell! Demand for its teas increased. More people had to be hired. When Celestial Seasonings had been just a half a dozen friends and relatives, it could adjust rapidly to new conditions, because everyone knew everyone else's job. Communication was easy because the staff was small and operating out of little more than a single room. But when the staff grew to fifteen, then twenty, then thirty, and so on, it became obvious to the founders that the looseness that was effective before would no longer work.

Activities had to be divided up. Departments were formed. Production lines were created and jobs were standardized. Job descriptions were written. Rules and regulations were introduced. Professional managers from such companies as Procter & Gamble and Coca-Cola were hired. Vertical differentiation expanded. The organization also took on other characteristics associated with bureaucracy. The company now purchases herbs from thirty-five countries, makes forty different kinds of herbal teas, and is predicting revenues of $50 million a year by mid-1986. The irony is that Celestial Seasonings has become what many of its early members hoped to avoid. It is a bureaucracy. The structure of Celestial Seasonings today much more closely approximates the structure of Thomas J. Lipton or the Maxwell House division of General Foods than it does a countercultural alternative organization. Why? Because bureaucracy works. For doing certain types of tasks, it is superior to all other forms of organization that we know. For all but a few large organizations, bureaucracy is the most efficient form.

Summarizing Weber's Contribution

The central theme in Weber's bureaucratic model is standardization. The behavior of people in bureaucracies is predetermined by the standardized structure and processes. The model, itself, can be dissected into three groups of characteristics: those that relate to the structure and function of the organization, those that deal with means of rewarding effort, and those that deal with protections for individual members.[6]

Weber's model stipulated a hierarchy of offices, with each office under the direction of a higher one. Each of these offices was differentiated horizontally by division of labor. This division of labor created units of expertise, defined areas of action consistent with competence of unit members, assigned responsibilities for carrying out these actions, and allocated commensurate authority to fulfill these responsibilities. All the while, written rules governed the performance of members' duties. This imposition of structure and functions provided a high level of specialized expertise, coordination of roles, and control of members through standardization.

The second group of characteristics in Weber's model related to rewards. Members received salaries in relation to their rank in the organization. Promotions were based on objective criteria such as seniority or achievement. Since members were not owners, it was important that there be a clear separation of their private affairs and property from the organization's affairs and property. It was further expected that commitment to the organization was paramount, the position in the organization being the employee's sole or primary occupation.

Finally, Weber's model sought to protect the rights of individuals. In return for a career commitment, members received protection from arbitrary actions by superiors, clear knowledge of their responsibilities and the amount of authority their superior held, and the ability to appeal decisions that they saw as unfair or outside the parameters of their superior's authority.

MACHINE VERSUS PROFESSIONAL BUREAUCRACIES

Bureaucracy, by definition, is well suited to producing standard outputs because it uses standardized processes. All bureaucracies are designed to operate in stable environments where contingencies can be predicted. But there are two types of bureaucracies.[7] There is the traditional one, which Weber described. We call this a *machine bureaucracy.* In addition, there is a second type that, while still bureaucratic, is more effective with highly skilled employees. This structure, which relies on extensive decentralization, is called a *professional bureaucracy.*

[6]Ibid., p. 59.

[7]Henry Mintzberg, "Structure in 5's: A Synthesis of the Research on Organization Design," *Management Science,* March 1980, pp. 332–335.

The Machine Bureaucracy

Large organizations that face simple and stable environments and utilize highly routine technology are most effective when they have a machine bureaucracy. This machine bureaucracy is characterized by highly routine operating tasks, very formalized rules and regulations, tasks that are grouped into functional departments, centralized authority, decision making that follows the formal chain of command, and an elaborate administrative structure with a sharp distinction between line and staff activities.

Where are you likely to find machine bureaucracies? In mass-production firms such as those in the automobile and steel industries; service organizations with simple, repetitive activities such as prisons or insurance and telephone companies; government agencies with routine work such as post offices and tax collection departments; and organizations that have special safety needs, such as airlines and fire departments. All these organizations have highly routine and standardized activities. Most of their contingencies have occurred many times before and are, therefore, predictable and amenable to formalized procedures. You would not, for instance, want to fly with an airline that was not organized as a machine bureaucracy. How comfortable would you be if you knew the "maintenance men did whatever struck them as interesting instead of following precise checklists, and the pilots worked out their procedures for landing in foggy weather when the need arose?"[8]

The Professional Bureaucracy

Organizations can be bureaucracies without being centralized. When would such a structure be preferred? When the operating work is standardized and predictable but also complex. This complexity of the work requires that it be done by individuals whose knowledge and skills are highly developed. Such structures are staffed by trained specialists—professionals—who maintain considerable control over their own work. Because the work that these professionals do cannot be regulated easily, the professional bureaucracy is characterized by decentralized decision making and less formalization than in the machine bureaucracy.

Notice that, while both machine and professional bureaucracies rely on standardization, their source of this standardization is different. In the former, the standards are developed inside the organization. Management designs work standards for operatives and then gives line managers the

[8]Henry Mintzberg, *The Structuring of Organizations* (Englewood Cliffs, N.J.: Prentice-Hall, 1979), p. 332.

responsibility for enforcing them. The standards in the professional bureaucracies, on the other hand, originate largely outside the organization. The educational institutions and associations that the professionals have attended and belong to establish the standards. The professionals then apply those standards in their jobs. "So whereas the Machine Bureaucracy relies on authority of a hierarchical nature—the power of office—the Professional Bureaucracy emphasizes authority of a professional nature—the power of expertise."[9] The professional, in contrast to his counterpart in the machine bureaucracy, controls his own work. Authority is decentralized. The professional, therefore, is relatively autonomous. Typically he works with his own clients, subject only to the collective control of his colleagues, who were trained and indoctrinated similarly and who reserve the right to censure him for malpractice.

The professional bureaucracy typically appears in organizations that confront environments that are both complex and stable. "Complexity demands the use of skills and knowledge that can be learned only in extensive training programs, while stability ensures that these skills settle down to become the standard operating procedures of the organization."[10] These conditions are likely to be evident in school systems, universities, social work agencies, general hospitals, public accounting firms, and craft manufacturing firms.

It should be noted that professional bureaucracies usually exist in conjunction with machine bureaucracies. A university, for instance, typically has a democratic administrative hierarchy for professionals and a second centralized machine bureaucracy for the support staff. Faculty, librarians, and researchers are in the first; departmental secretaries, cafeteria workers, and personnel in the admissions and records office are examples of the second.

DYSFUNCTIONAL CONSEQUENCES OF BUREAUCRACY

Bureaucracies have received more than their share of unfavorable publicity. In this section, we review these criticisms.

Goal Displacement

Bureaucracy is attacked most frequently for encouraging the displacement of organizational goals by subunit or personal goals. This general theme has been packaged in a number of forms.

[9]Ibid., p. 351.
[10]Mintzberg, "Structure in 5's," p. 334.

The most general argument has been proposed by Robert Merton.[11] After acknowledging that bureaucratic rules and impersonality produce a high degree of reliability and predictability, he pointed out that conformity can be detrimental because it reduces flexibility. Rules and regulations become so emphasized that they take on a symbolic meaning of their own. The rules become more important than the ends that they were designed to serve, the result being goal displacement and loss of organizational effectiveness. Occasionally you will see this phenomenon in large retail clothing stores. Rules about keeping shelves fully stocked and neat, instituted to increase sales, can be followed so compulsively by the sales personnel that customers are ignored. Similarly, people in the registrar's office in some colleges become so enamoured with making students follow the rules for adding and dropping courses that they forget that they are there to help students get the class schedule they want and clear the path to getting their degrees.

Philip Selznick also believed that means could become ends through goal displacement.[12] He emphasized that specialization and differentiation create subunits with different goals. The goals of each separate subunit become primary to the subunit members. What happens as a result of the conflict between these subunits is that achievement of subunit goals becomes more important than accomplishment of the organization's goals. This was illustrated in one manufacturing firm, where marketing secured a very large and profitable order. The sale came with a tight deadline and required production personnel to give the order special handling outside the normal routine. Despite the profits that this sale would bring to the company, the production manager balked because the order would disturb his unit's efficiency ratios. He succeeded in dragging his feet long enough so that the order was lost to a competitor.

A third perspective on goal displacement was offered by Alvin Gouldner.[13] Gouldner proposed that rules and regulations not only define unacceptable behaviors, but also that they define *minimum* levels of acceptable performance. If the organization's goals are not internalized and made a part of the employee's behavior, the rules encourage apathy. That is, people will do just the bare minimum to get by. The rules, therefore, become interpreted as setting the minimum standards for performance rather than identifying unacceptable behaviors. You will see this phenomenon operating when students take a course on a "pass-fail" basis rather than for a

[11]Robert K. Merton, "Bureaucratic Structure and Personality," *Social Forces,* May 1940, pp. 560–568.

[12]Philip Selznick, *TVA and the Grass Roots: A Study in the Sociology of Formal Organizations* (Berkeley: University of California Press, 1949).

[13]Alvin W. Gouldner, *Patterns of Industrial Bureaucracy* (New York: Free Press, 1954).

letter grade. The instructor's cutoff separating passing from failing becomes the point of attention. Students rarely exert more effort than is necessary to just get into the passing range.

A final goal-displacement argument has been proposed by Victor Thompson.[14] Thompson sees the highly formalized bureaucracy as creating insecurities in those in authority that lead to what he has called "bureaupathic behavior."[15] Decision makers use adherence to rules to protect themselves from making errors. Instead of high formalization facilitating decision making, the rules and regulations provide protection to hide behind: "Don't blame me. I was just following the rules!" Thompson suggested that, as persons in hierarchical positions become increasingly dependent upon lower-level specialists for achievement of organizational goals, they tend to introduce more and more rules to protect themselves against this dependency.

Inappropriate Application of Rules and Regulations

Related closely to the problem of goal displacement is the undesirable effect of members' applying formalized rules and procedures in inappropriate situations; that is, responding to a unique situation as if it were routine, resulting in dysfunctional consequences. Merton suggested that, over time, bureaucracies breed such devotion to rules that members blindly repeat decisions and actions that they have made a number of times before, unaware that conditions have changed.[16] Of course, actions and decisions based on past training and experience may be very inappropriate under different conditions. This leads, as many of us have observed firsthand in dealing with government agencies, to errors. The clerk who processes drivers' license applications in a state motor vehicle office may know how to handle applicants who have never driven before, renewals, and out-of-state applications. When confronted with an applicant who had a valid foreign license, your author found the clerk handling it as if it were an out-of-state application. Only six weeks later did I find, upon receipt of a letter from the state capitol, that the clerk had failed to use a special procedure for applicants who are coming from out of the country. We can conclude that bureaucracies' high formalization makes it difficult to respond to changing conditions.

[14]Victor Thompson, *Modern Organizations* (New York: Knopf, 1961).
[15]Ibid., p. 154.
[16]Merton, "Bureaucratic Structure and Personality."

Employee Alienation

A major cost of bureaucracy is employee alienation. Members perceive the impersonality of the organization as creating distance between them and their work. As a "cog in the wheel," it is frequently difficult to feel committed to the organization. High specialization further reinforces one's feeling of being irrelevant—routine activities can be easily learned by others, making employees feel interchangeable and powerless. In professional bureaucracies, formalization must be lessened; otherwise the risk of employee alienation is very high.[17]

Concentration of Power

The concentration of power in senior executives of bureaucracies has been targeted by some. Although this criticism is subjective—it depends on whether one considers concentration of power undesirable or not—undoubtedly it flies in the face of those social scientists who want to equalize power in organizations to make them more humanistic.[18] It is a fact that bureaucracy generates an enormous degree of power in the hands of a very few. If you perceive this as undesirable or counter to the values of a democratic society, as some do, you will find this attribute a negative consequence of the bureaucratic form.

Nonmember Frustration

The last negative consequence that we address relates to those outside the organization who must deal with the bureaucracy. Members are remunerated for their work in bureaucracies. If it takes six weeks to process an internal requisition for a dozen typewriter ribbons, it may be frustrating to the employee who needs those ribbons. But he or she is paid to be in the office forty hours a week—and that pay is received whether the ribbons are there or not. So, while bureaucracies may alienate some of their members—in the name of efficiency—the members' compensation is some salve for the wounds. But clients and customers of bureaucracies must meet the impersonal "monster" and its occasional hassles without being paid to do so. If the bureaucracy is a business firm, with viable competitors, you can always take your business someplace else if the bureaucracy fails to satisfy

[17]George A. Miller, "Professionals in Bureaucracy, Alienation Among Industrial Scientists and Engineers," *American Sociological Review,* October 1967, pp. 755–768.

[18]See, for example, Chris Argyris, *Personality and Organization: The Conflict Between System and the Individual* (New York: Harper & Row, 1957).

your needs. But reality reminds us that, in all probability, the competitors also use the bureaucratic form. Moreover, if the organization is a government agency or a regulated monopoly (such as the telephone company), you have little choice. When you move and need to have your phone installed or the gas turned on, you deal with the bureaucracy on its terms. They will not tell you, as so often happens, when exactly they will be at your residence other than to say it will be between 8 A.M. and 5 P.M. on a given day. So *you* stay home and wait, although they profess that they exist to serve you. Every college student who has undergone the rigors of registration and has confronted the school's impersonal and rule-dominated "system" can relate to the frustration that nonmembers feel who must deal regularly with bureaucracies.

IS BUREAUCRACY A STRUCTURAL DINOSAUR?

"Bureaucracy had its time, but those days are gone. If bureaucracy is not already dead, it is gasping its last breath." "Bureaucracy is alive and well. It is still the most efficient way in which to organize activities."

These positions reflect two perspectives on bureaucracy. Which is correct? Let us present the arguments; you be the judge.

The Coming Death of Bureaucracy

One of the best known arguments presented against the machine bureaucracy was made by social psychologist Warren Bennis.[19] While published more than fifteen years ago, and since modified,[20] it nevertheless represents a succinct analysis of the antibureaucracy attack. The following summarizes Bennis's argument that bureaucracy has become obsolete.

Every age develops an organizational form appropriate to its needs, and the one that dominated in the latter part of the nineteenth century and first half of the twentieth century was known by sociologists as bureaucracy and by most business managers as "damn bureaucracy." That form is now out of step with contemporary realities.

The bureaucratic model was developed as a reaction against the personal subjugation, nepotism and cruelty, and the capricious and subjective judgments that passed for acceptable managerial practices during the early

[19]Warren G. Bennis, "The Coming Death of Bureaucracy," *Think*, November–December 1966, pp. 30–35. With permission.

[20]See Warren G. Bennis, "A Funny Thing Happened on the Way to the Future," *American Psychologist*, July 1970, pp. 595–608, and "Conversation: An Interview with Warren Bennis," *Organizational Dynamics*, Winter 1974, pp. 50–66.

days of the Industrial Revolution. Bureaucracy emerged out of the organizations' need for order and precision and the workers' demands for impartial treatment. It was an organization form ideally suited to the values and demands of the Victorian era. Today's conditions are inconsistent with those values and demands. At least four factors are direct threats to bureaucracy:

1. *Rapid and unexpected change.* Bureaucracy's strength is its capacity to manage efficiently routine and predictable activities that take place in a stable and predictable environment. Bureaucracy, with its nicely defined chain of command, its rules and its rigidities, is poorly adapted to the rapid change the environment now demands.

2. *Growth in size.* While in theory there may be no natural limit to the height of a bureaucratic pyramid, in practice the element of complexity is almost invariably introduced with great size. Increased administrative overhead, tighter controls, greater impersonality, outmoded rules—all are examples of what happens in bureaucracy as size increases—act to hinder organizational growth.

3. *Increasing diversity.* Today's activities require persons of very diverse, highly specialized competence. Hurried growth, rapid change, and increased specialization are incompatible with bureaucracy's well-defined chain of command, rigid rules and procedures, and impersonality.

4. *Change in managerial behavior.* Managers are undergoing a subtle but perceptible change in philosophy. These changes are undermining the ideology that surrounded and supported bureaucracy. Specifically, managers have (a) a new concept of *man,* based on increased knowledge of his complex and shifting needs, which replaces an oversimplified, innocent, push-button idea of man; (b) a new concept of *power,* based on collaboration and reason, which replaces a model of power based on coercion and threat; and (c) a new concept of *organizational values,* based on humanistic-democratic ideals, which replaces the depersonalized mechanistic value system of bureaucracy.

In summary, Bennis saw the bureaucratic structure as too mechanical for the needs of modern organizations. He argued that the structure has become obsolete because it is designed to deal with stable environments, whereas the contemporary need is for a structure that is designed to respond effectively to change.

The Greatly Exaggerated Death of Bureaucracy

Robert Miewald has offered a counterargument to Bennis.[21] His major contention is that bureaucracy can adapt to changing and dynamic environments. The following summarizes Miewald's response.

Warren Bennis has caught the fancy of many by describing conditions that, he argues, are bringing about the death of bureaucracy. Certainly there can be no doubt that the organization is changing, but these changes are not leaving bureaucracy behind. In fact, the forces of bureaucracy have never been stronger.

Our perspective on bureaucracy has been influenced strongly by the characteristics identified by Max Weber. Genius though he was, Weber was not a soothsayer. He could not have foreseen all the many forms that the essence of bureaucracy could take. His formulation of the concept of bureaucracy provided an invaluable tool for the analysis of organizational problems in a society that was making the adjustment to industrialization. However, rather than make the superficial assumption that "postindustrial" means "postbureaucratic," it might be wiser to inquire whether bureaucracy can adjust to the so-called "New Age." Is bureaucracy restricted to the mechanical? In many cases it would appear that external bureaucratic controls have simply been replaced by more subtle influences on the individual. The end result in either case is the same: a high degree of predictability about human behavior in large, complex organizations.

Weber never implied that his ideal type was the universal, eternal form. His intention, rather, was to make the affairs of people more amenable to rational calculation. Given the technology of the nineteenth century and his familiarity with the authoritarian tendencies of the Germans, it is little wonder that Weber described bureaucracy as he did. He would hardly be surprised, however, to learn that more sophisticated means of controlling behavior have been invented. All he wanted was a scientifically derived concept of efficiency and certainly would not be aghast to find that his model had been modified to reflect new ways in which to improve on efficiency. At the peak of its influence, machine bureaucracy was the most efficient means for applying rationality to organizational life. Of all social structures, it promised the maximization of scientifically correct decision making.

Is the so-called postbureaucratic situation of today really different from the conditions implied in Weber's model? No! It does not differ at all in any significant sense, and one might go on to argue that, in the most

[21]Robert D. Miewald, "The Greatly Exaggerated Death of Bureaucracy," *California Management Review,* Winter 1970, pp. 65–69. With permission.

critical areas, the postbureaucratic system is nothing more than the Weberian model with all the most sophisticated modifications. Despite the contortions through which organizational theorists have put themselves in the twentieth century, the remarkable fact remains that there has been no substantial change in their basic premises. The guiding belief is still that regularities exist that, on one level or another, may be learned and acted upon.

Bureaucracy is not dead. If Weber were here today, he would conclude that bureaucracy is still very much alive and well. Specific elements of his model are poorly adjusted to our times and must be modified. But that is a reasonable concession to the fact that conditions do change. It is one thing to say that bureaucracy must be *eliminated* and another to admit that it has *changed with the times.*

How has it changed? Most obviously it had to develop an alternative to deal with organizations where authority is based on knowledge. The professional bureaucracy is a clear example of such a modification. Rational discipline, rather than imposed externally, is internalized through the professionalization of employees. Authority from above is replaced with self-regimentation. This, of course, does not result in the end of bureaucracy. One can argue, in fact, that the professional bureaucracy has merely substituted the arrogance of high training for the arrogance of high office.

In summary, Miewald has argued that Weber never meant bureaucracy's characteristics to endure for eternity. Weber's major objective was to create a rational and efficient form. That *form* is bureaucracy. Whatever form is required to maintain rationality and efficiency results in bureaucracy. The development of the professional bureaucracy is a perfect example of bureaucracy's characteristics being modified to represent the most rational and efficient way in which to structure knowledge-dominated organizations.

WHEN IS BUREAUCRACY THE PREFERRED STRUCTURE?

We have described bureaucracy—machine or professional—as a highly efficient structural form. Weber's "ideal type" represents a standard, a benchmark for defining bureaucracy. Of course, no real organization can be as pure as Weber's model. Bennis and Miewald imply this. Observation confirms it. In spite of efforts by organization designers to eliminate all unwanted extraorganizational influences upon the behavior of employees, people are more complex than the assumptions inherent in Weber's model. "They track all kinds of mud from the rest of their lives with them into the organization, and they have all kinds of interests that are independent of the organization."[22] Nevertheless, bureaucracy exists. In actuality, its form may deviate from the perfectly efficient standard, but real-life bureaucracies are reasonable facsimiles of the picture painted by Weber. So we have reached the point where it's necessary to ask: When is bureaucracy the preferred structural form? Our answer depends on whether the bureaucracy is machine or professional.

The machine bureaucracy is most efficient when matched with large size, a simple and stable environment, and a technology that contains routine work that can be standardized. You see its effectiveness when you go into the main public library in any major city. Employees are assigned specific responsibilities. Procedures govern the way in which books are to be gathered, stacked, and replaced on shelves. Procedures also direct the way in which books are to be checked out. Librarians insist that the rules be followed. Change comes painfully slowly. When change does come, as in the early 1960s when most libraries converted from the Dewey decimal system to the Library of Congress cataloging system, large leadtimes are expected. Even with that leadtime, however, most of these libraries took years to convert. Why? Their structure is not conducive to making changes rapidly or efficiently. On the other hand, the structure is extremely efficient for providing quick access to materials and for processing the "lending" of books.

The professional bureaucracy is at its best when matched with large size, a complex and stable environment, and a routine technology internalized through professionalization. The organization's operating core will be dominated by skilled professionals who have internalized difficult-to-learn but nevertheless well-defined procedures. The complex and stable environment means that the organization requires the use of difficult skills that can be learned only in formal education and training programs, but there is enough stability for these skills to be well defined and standardized. This professional bureaucracy rarely describes the entire organization; it is usually coupled with a supporting machine bureaucracy structure.

The offices of the "Big 8" public accounting firms in major metropolitan areas combine professional and machine bureaucracies. The accountants—who may number a hundred or more—perform standardized auditing, tax advisory, and other services. They have acquired their skills through years of studying for college degrees and their CPA certificates. These professional accountants perform their activities relatively autonomously, but the structure is high in complexity and there are lots of rules and regulations; only the formalization is internalized rather than imposed by the organization itself. Complementing this structure is a machine bureaucracy of support staff—secretaries and clerks—who assist the professionals.

[22]Perrow, *Complex Organizations*, p. 5.

YOU CANNOT IGNORE THE OBVIOUS: BUREAUCRACIES ARE EVERYWHERE!

Despite the criticism directed at bureaucracy, you cannot ignore the obvious. Bureaucracies are everywhere! The vast majority of large organizations are predominantly bureaucratic in structure, and, for all but a few, bureaucracy represents the most efficient way for them to organize.[23]

This conclusion runs counter to what *should* prevail if, as some claim, we now live in times where change is ongoing and dynamic, standardized technologies have been replaced by customized processes, and humanistic practices and the goal of reducing employee alienation demand the elimination of the rigidities of bureaucracy. Why is it, then, that the bureaucratic form is thriving? There appears to be no simple answer to this question. We can propose half a dozen possible explanations:

1. *It works.* Forgetting the contingency factors that would predict nonbureaucratic structures, for a moment, it is obvious that bureaucracy works. Regardless of technology, environment, and so on, bureaucracies are effective in a wide range of organized activities: manufacturing, service firms, hospitals, schools and colleges, the military, and voluntary associations. As one proponent remarked, bureaucracy is "a form of organization superior to all others we know or can hope to afford in the near and middle future."[24]

2. *Large size prevails.* Organizations that succeed and survive tend to grow to large size. And we know that bureaucracy is efficient with large size. Small organizations and their nonbureaucratic structures are more likely to fail, so over time, small organizations may come and go but large bureaucracies stay. It may also be that size is the dominant criterion determining structure and, therefore, that increased size may *cause* bureaucracy.

3. *Societal values are unchanging.* A counterpoint to Bennis's position that management's philosophy is shifting to greater humanism is that North American values favor order and regimentation. North Americans have traditionally been goal oriented and comfortable with authoritarian structures. Parents are controlling in the home; the church seeks order and rationality in parishioner behaviors; and schools reinforce order, regularity, and being part of the "system." Employees in organizations look with disfavor on jobs that are ambiguous and where job responsibilities are vague. While North Americans believe strongly in individual freedoms, it

[23]Ibid., p. 5.
[24]Ibid., p. 7.

is generally acknowledged that freedom requires obedience to a set of rules and regulations. "Your freedom to swing your fists ends where my nose begins." Bureaucracy is consistent with the values of order and regimentation.

4. *Environmental turbulence is exaggerated.* As discussed in Chapter 9, environments may not be as dynamic as assumed. The media projects that "the times, they are a 'changin.' " A more correct observation might be that (a) changes are no more dynamic now than at any other time in history and (b) the impact of uncertainties in the environment on the organization are substantially reduced as a result of managerial strategies.

5. *The professional bureaucracy has emerged.* The professional bureaucracy provides the same degree of standardization and control as does Weber's machine bureaucracy. The increased need for technical expertise in organizations and the rapid expansion of knowledge-based industries has been handled neatly by the professional bureaucracy. The bureaucratic form has demonstrated the ability to adjust to its greatest threat—the knowledge revolution—by modifying itself. The goal of standardization has proven to be achievable by more than one path.

6. *Bureaucracy maintains control.* High standardization, preferably with centralized power in the hands of the dominant coalition, is desired by those in control. Bureaucracy obviously meets that end. From the power-control perspective, therefore, we would predict bureaucracy to be the preferred structure because it is the most effective mechanism structurally for maintaining control. Consistent with this conclusion is the observation that a moderate degree of routineness pervades all organizations.[25] Since technology is chosen, it is logical to conclude that those in power would select technologies (and a matching structural form) that would maintain and enhance their control.

The elements listed, when taken together, lead us to the inevitability of bureaucracy. It is the dominant structural form in North America, and the probability of doing away with it or significantly changing it in our lifetime is very likely close to zero.

SUMMARY

Bureaucracy refers to a type of organizational structure characterized by division of labor, a well-defined authority hierarchy, high formalization, impersonal relations, employment decisions based on merit, career tracks

[25]Ibid., p. 175.

for employees, and distinct separation of members' organizational and personal lives. This definition originated from the work of German sociologist Max Weber.

There are basically two types of bureaucracy. The one identified by Weber is what we would now call machine bureaucracy. It is characterized structurally by high complexity, high formalization, and centralization. Professional bureaucracy, the other type, is preferred when the organization employs highly skilled professionals. The professional bureaucracy achieves the same end as the Weberian model, but it relies on extensive decentralization and the replacement of external formalization with internalized professional standards.

The strength of the bureaucratic form lies in standardization. The organization is more efficient because employee behavior is controlled and predictable. Organizational members benefit by knowing that they will be treated fairly.

The critics of bureaucracy have argued that it results in goal displacement, inappropriate application of rules and regulations, employee alienation, the concentration of power in the hands of a few, and frustrations for the clients and customers who must deal with the impersonality and rule-bound behavior of bureaucrats.

The machine bureaucracy is most efficient when matched with large size, a simple and stable environment, and a routine and standardized technology. The professional bureaucracy is at its best when matched with large size, a complex and stable environment, and a routine technology internalized through professionalization.

Our conclusion is that bureaucracy is both the dominant organizational form in society and that it has achieved its distinction because it works best with the type of technologies and environments that most organizations have. Importantly, it is also consistent with maintaining control in the hands of the organization's dominant coalition.

FOR REVIEW AND DISCUSSION

1. Define bureaucracy. How does this compare with the layperson's definition of the term?
2. As an employee in a bureaucracy, with what benefits does this structural form provide you?
3. "Bureaucracy is the ideal type of organization." Do you agree or disagree? Discuss.
4. Contrast the machine and professional bureaucracies.
5. "Providing employees with permanent employment leads to ambivalence and eventually organizational ineffectiveness." Build an argument to support this statement. Then refute your argument.

6. Describe an organization you are familar with that is *not* a bureaucracy. Explain why it has not taken on bureaucratic characteristics.
7. What conditions foster the development of (a) a machine bureaucracy? (b) a professional bureaucracy?
8. Give an example of goal displacement in a bureaucracy that you have observed personally.
9. "There are only two types of organizations: those that are newly formed and bureaucracies." Do you agree or disagree? Discuss.
10. How do you explain the popularity of the bureaucratic form?

CHAPTER

12

ADHOCRACY

A major New York management consulting firm employs several hundred consultants. These employees are assigned to consulting jobs as they are contracted. Consultants in this firm have varied talents—some are financial experts, some are computer professionals, still others design production systems. When a job is assigned to a project leader, he reviews the consulting firm's inventory of consultants and selects his team based on available consultants who he believes will be able to assist in the completion of the project. In this firm, consultants are paid whether they are assigned to projects or not. However, if a consultant is consistently passed over by project leaders when they are creating their teams, the partners conclude that the employee is not able to carry his or her weight, and the employee will be terminated. Internally, this consulting firm allows the "survival of the fittest" doctrine to determine who stays and who goes or who works on project X or project Y. The good consultants are sought and fought over by project leaders. Those who have been on projects and have made marginal contributions find their services in considerably less demand. Importantly, in this firm, there are no *permanent* assignments of consultants to projects or even specialized departments such as finance, production, planning, or systems.

When Steven Spielberg or George Lucas go about making a film, they bring together a diverse group of professionals. This team—composed of producers, scriptwriters, film editors, set designers, and hundreds of other specialists—exists for the singular purpose of making a single movie. They may be called back by Spielberg or Lucas when they begin another film, but that is irrelevant when the current project begins. These professionals frequently find themselves with overlapping activities because no formal rules or regulations are provided to guide members. While there is a production schedule, it often must be modified to take into consideration unforeseen contingencies. The film's production team may be together for a few months or, as happened when Francis Ford Coppola made *Apocalypse Now,* three years or more. But the organization is temporary. In contrast to General Motors or the U.S. Department of Health and Human Services, the New York consulting firm and the film-making organizations have no entrenched hierarchy, no permanent departments, no formalized rules, and no standardized procedures for dealing with routine problems.

These are examples of adhocracies. In this chapter, we shift from bureaucracy to the other extreme along the structural design continuum. Flexible, adaptive, responsive, innovative—these are the type of terms associated with adhocratic structures. What bureaucracy was to the mechanistic form, adhocracy is to the organic form.

A note of caution before we begin. Keep in mind that adhocracy is a model. It is an abstraction. Just as there is no such thing in the real world as a "pure bureaucracy," you will also find that there is no such thing as a "pure adhocracy." An organization's structure may be *generally* adhocratic or *moving toward* adhocracy, but no organization will have all the characteristics attributed to the pure adhocracy model. Later in the chapter, when we offer examples of adhocracies, you will see that they represent modifications of the pure form—having lost something in the translation. With that caveat, let us clarify what we mean by the term "adhocracy."

DEFINING ADHOCRACY

An adhocracy has been described as a "rapidly changing, adaptive, temporary system organized around problems to be solved by groups of relative strangers with diverse professional skills."[1] A more meaningful understanding of adhocracy, however, can be gained by dissecting it and ascertaining its key characteristics.

In terms of our three structural dimensions, adhocracies would be characterized as having moderate to low complexity, low formalization, and decentralized decision making. Let us elaborate on each of these components.

Adhocracies have a high degree of horizontal differentiation based on formal training. Since adhocracies are staffed predominantly by professionals with a high level of expertise, horizontal differentiation is great. But vertical differentiation is low. The many levels of administration found in a bureaucracy are absent. Why? First, the organization needs flexibility,

[1]Warren G. Bennis, "Post-Bureaucratic Leadership," *Transaction,* July–August 1969, p. 45.

and lots of levels of administration would restrict the organization's ability to adapt. Second, the need for supervision is minimal because professionals have internalized the behaviors that management wants.

We have already found professionalization and formalization to be inversely related. The adhocracy is no exception. There are few rules and regulations. Those that exist tend to be loose and unwritten. Again, the objective of flexibility demands an absence of formalization. Rules and regulations are effective only where standardization of behavior is sought. In this context, it may be valuable to compare the professional bureaucracy with adhocracy. Both employ professionals. The key difference is that the professional bureaucracy, when faced with a problem, immediately classifies it into some standardized program so that the professionals can treat it in a uniform manner. In an adhocracy, a novel solution is needed so that standardization and formalization are inappropriate.

Decision making in adhocracies is decentralized. This is necessary for speed and flexibility and because senior management cannot be expected to possess the expertise necessary to make all decisions. So the adhocracy depends on decentralized "teams" of professionals for decision making. Employees of the organization are assigned to temporary work units on an "as needed" basis. They are a part of that team until the unit's objectives are achieved. As long as they are part of the team, employees participate actively in its key decisions. Democratic decision processes are prevalent, in contrast to bureaucracy's hierarchical decision making. That is, influence in an adhocracy is based on the power of expertise rather than on the authority of position.

The adhocracy, therefore, takes on the form of a very adaptable structure. Multidisciplinary teams are formed around specific objectives. The departmental stability found in a bureaucracy is replaced by constantly changing units. Teams are forming regularly within the organization to pursue specific objectives. At the same time, other teams are dissolving as their objectives have been achieved. Individuals within the adhocracy find their responsibilities in a continual flux, adjusting as they move from assignment to assignment. Additionally, responsibilities are not delineated clearly as they are in the bureaucracy. Professionals do those tasks that are necessary to fulfill their team's objectives. Thus there are times in an adhocracy when there will be an overlapping of activities.

ADHOCRACY: ITS STRENGTHS AND WEAKNESSES

If any conclusion should be clear by this point in the book, it is that there is no such thing as a perfect structure "for all occasions." Every structural form has its own set of strengths and weaknesses. Adhocracy is no exception. Let us take a look at adhocracy's strengths and weaknesses.

Strengths

The history of adhocracy can be traced to the development of task forces during World War II, when the military created ad hoc teams that were disbanded after completion of their missions. There was no rigid time span for their existence: teams could last a day, a month, or a year. Roles performed in the teams were interchangeable, and, depending upon the nature and complexity of the mission, the group could be divided into subunits, each responsible for different facets of the job to be performed. The advantages of these ad hoc teams included their ability to respond rapidly to change and innovation and their facilitating the coordination of diverse specialists. Forty years have passed since World War II, but the advantage of ad hoc teams, or what we call adhocracy, continues today. When it is important that the organization be adaptable and creative, when individual specialists from diverse disciplines are required to collaborate to achieve a common goal, and when tasks are technical, nonprogrammed, and too complex for any one person to handle or for individual supervision, the adhocracy represents a viable alternative.

Weaknesses

Conflict is a natural part of adhocracy. There are no clear boss-subordinate relationships. Ambiguities exist over authority and responsibilities. Activities cannot be compartmentalized. In short, adhocracy lacks the advantages of standardized work.

Adhocracy also creates social stress and psychological tensions for its members. It is not easy to set up and quickly dismantle work relationships on a continuing basis. Some employees find it difficult to cope with rapid change, living in temporary work systems, and having to share responsibilities with other team members.

In contrast to bureaucracy, adhocracy is clearly an inefficient structure. It lacks the precision and expediency that the mechanistic model offers. So why would it ever be used? Because its inefficiences, in certain circumstances, are more than offset by the need for flexibility and innovation.

THE MATRIX: ADHOCRACY IN ACTION

The most popular application of adhocracy is the *matrix structure.* In simplistic terms, the matrix is a combination of deparmentation by function and by product or project.

Figure 12-1 shows a matrix structure in an aerospace firm. Along the top are the traditional functional departments: Design Engineering, Manufacturing, Contract Administration, Purchasing, Accounting, and Personnel. Overlapping this structure is a second structure of projects. Each

FIGURE 12-1 A matrix organization in an aerospace firm

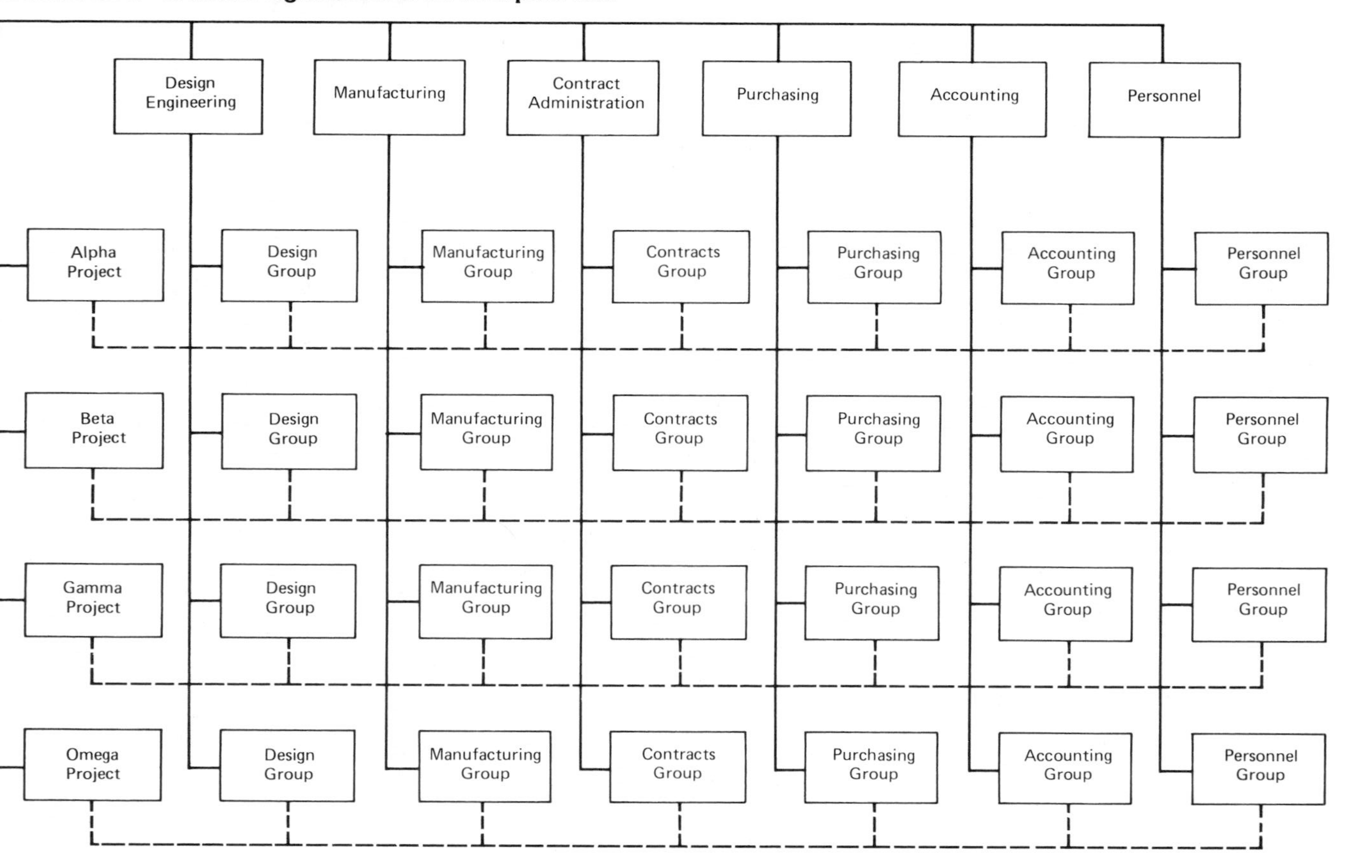

project is directed by a manager who staffs his or her project with people from the functional departments. The unique characteristics of the matrix now become evident.

What Is Unique About the Matrix?

The matrix breaks the unit of command concept—a cornerstone of bureaucracy—that requires every employee to have one and only one boss to whom he or she reports. Employees in the matrix have two bosses—their departmental manager and their project manager. The matrix has a dual chain of command. There is the normal vertical hierarchy within functional departments, which is "overlayed" by a form of lateral influence. So the matrix is unique in that it legitimates lateral channels of influence. Project managers have authority over those functional members who are part of that manager's project team. The purchasing specialists, for instance, who are responsible for procurement activities on the Gamma project, are responsible to both the manager of purchasing and the Gamma project manager. Authority is shared between the two managers. Generally, this is done by giving the project managers authority over project employees relative to the project's goals. Decisions such as promotions, salary recommendations, and the annual review of each employee typically remain a part of the functional manager's responsibility.

The matrix is designed to benefit from the strengths of both the functional and product structures yet avoid the weaknesses of either.[2] That is, the functional structure's strength lies in putting like specialists together, which minimizes the number necessary, and it allows the pooling and sharing of specialized resources across products. Its disadvantages include having departmental goals supersede organizational goals and the difficulty of coordinating the tasks of specialists so that their activities are completed on time and within budget. The product or project structure, on the other hand, has exactly the opposite benefits and disadvantages. It facilitates the coordination among specialties to achieve timely completion and meet budget targets. Further, it provides clear responsibility for all activities related to a project. But in the pure project structure, no one is responsible for the long-run technical development of the specialties, and it results in duplication of costs. If the organization "has two projects, each requiring one half-time electronics engineer and one half-time electromechanical engineer, the pure project organization must either hire two electrical engineers—and reduce specialization—or hire four engineers (two electronics and two electromechanical)—and incur duplication costs."[3]

[2]Jay Galbraith, "Matrix Organization Designs: How to Combine Functional and Project Forms," *Business Horizons*, February 1971, pp. 29–40.

[3]Ibid., p. 30.

Two Types of Matrix Structures

The projects or products in a matrix can be undergoing change continuously or they can be relatively enduring. The first typifies the temporary matrix; the second represents the permanent matrix.

The aerospace example depicted in Figure 12-1 illustrates the temporary matrix. When new contracts are secured, project teams are created by drawing members from functional departments. A team exists only for the life of the project on which it is working. While each project might last half a dozen or more years, the fact that such companies as McDonnell-Douglas or General Dynamics may have a large number of projects operating simultaneously means that the makeup of the matrix changes constantly. New contracts demand the formation of new projects so, at any one time, you might find several projects winding down while others are in their infancy. If the New York consulting firm, discussed at the opening of this chapter, assigned personnel to functional departments and then overlayed its various projects on that structure, a temporary matrix would emerge.

The projects or products in the permanent matrix stay relatively intact over time. Large colleges of business use the permanent matrix when they superimpose product structures—undergraduate programs, graduate programs, research bureaus, and executive development programs—over the functional departments of accounting, finance, management, marketing, and the like. Directors of the product structures utilize faculty from the departments to achieve their goals. The director of the graduate business program staffs his courses with members from the various departments. Notice that the products do not change; thus we say that this is a permanent matrix. Why use this type of structure? It provides clear lines of responsibilities for each product line. The success or failure, for instance, of the executive development program in a college of business lies directly with its director. Without the matrix, it is difficult to find anyone who can coordinate and take responsibility for the effective performance of the development program.

Permanent matrix structures also are evident in some large retail chains such as Sears, Roebuck and J. C. Penney.[4] These chains create dual lines of authority when they establish store managers (equivalent to product managers) and merchandise managers (equivalent to functional managers). The former is responsible for the performance of his or her store. The latter's responsibility relates to the purchasing of appropriate merchandise for these stores. The women's lingerie buyer, for instance, will purchase merchandise for many of the company's stores. These dual lines

[4]Leonard R. Sayles, "Matrix Organization: The Structure with a Future," *Organizational Dynamics,* Autumn 1976, pp. 2–17.

of authority create two sets of permanent managers who have separate responsibilities and report up separate lines of authority.

Advantages and Disadvantages

The strength of the matrix lies in its ability to facilitate coordination when the organization has a multiplicity of complex and interdependent activities. As an organization gets larger, its information-processing capacity can become overloaded. In a bureaucracy, complexity results in increased formalization. The direct and frequent contact between different specialties in the matrix can make for better communication and more flexibility. Information permeates the organization and reaches more quickly those people who need to take account of it. Further, the matrix reduces bureaupathologies. The dual lines of authority reduce tendencies of departmental members to become so busy protecting their "little worlds" that goals become displaced.

There are other advantages to the matrix. As we noted, it facilitates the efficient allocation of specialists. When individuals with highly specialized skills are lodged in one functional department or project group, their talent is monopolized and underutilized. The matrix achieves the advanatages of economies of scale by providing the organization with both the best resources and an effective way of ensuring their efficient deployment. Further advantages of the matrix include increased ability to respond rapidly to changes in the environment, an effective means for balancing the customer's requirements for project completion and cost control with the organization's need for economic efficiency and development of technical capability for the future, and increased motivation by providing an environment more in line with the democratic norms preferred by scientific and professional employees.[5]

The major disadvantages of the matrix lie in the confusion it creates, its propensity to foster power struggles, and the stress it places on individuals.[6] When you dispense with the unity of command concept, ambiguity is significantly increased. Confusion exists over who reports to whom. Confusion and ambiguity create the seeds for power struggles. Bureaucracy reduces the potential for "power grabs" by defining the rules of the game. When those rules are "up for grabs," power struggles between functional and project managers result. For individuals who desire security and absence from ambiguity, this environment can produce stress. Reporting to more than one boss introduces role conflict, and unclear expectations in-

[5]Kenneth Knight, "Matrix Organization: A Review," *Journal of Management Studies*, May 1976, pp. 111–130.

[6]Ibid., and Stanley M. Davis and Paul R. Lawrence, "Problems of Matrix Organizations," *Harvard Business Review*, May–June 1978, pp. 131–142.

troduce role ambiguity. The comfort of bureaucracy's predictability is absent, replaced by insecurity and stress.

Applications of the Matrix

The matrix began in aerospace companies in the early 1960s, but it can now be found in a wide range of business firms, such as Caterpillar Tractor, General Telephone & Electronics, National Cash Register, Prudential Insurance, and Texas Instruments, as well as in construction companies, banks, hospitals, government agencies, universities, and professional organizations.[7] In the following pages, we review briefly how the matrix is used at General Mills and Dow Corning.

General Mills. There is no shortage of name brands at General Mills: Cheerios, Bisquick, Trix, Betty Crocker cake mixes, Stir 'n Frost, Total, Hamburger Helper, Gold Medal flour. Each of the thirty-three consumer food brands at General Mills has its own product manager, and the company has adapted this matrix structure to some of its nonfood subsidiaries such as toy-maker, Kenner Products.[8] The product managers act as business managers—they collect all the internal and external information that might affect the brand, set goals for it, and establish strategies and tactics to achieve these goals. They are responsible for identifying key issues, thoroughly reviewing their business and their competitors, and formulating an operating plan that includes a sales forecast, itemization of costs to meet the forecast, and advertising, pricing, and trade tactics. The plan is submitted to, and negotiated with, a marketing director who is responsible for several product managers.

Once a plan is approved, executing it is the product manager's responsibility. But with that task goes almost no formal authority. He has control over his budget, but little else. He, therefore, must be a master of persuasion. If the product manager needs special support from the sales force or increased output from the plant to gear up for a big advertising campaign, he has to sell the idea to people who report to functional managers in charge of sales and manufacturing. Similarly, if he thinks that his product needs different packaging, a more focused television commercial, or a reformulation of ingredients, he must impress the appropriate support groups with the importance of paying particular attention to his brand.

In summary, General Mills uses the matrix structure as a way to give brand managers a feeling of running their own show, in spite of their being part of an established, hierarchical company with sales of over $4 billion

[7]Knight, "Matrix Organization."

[8]Ann M. Morrison, "The General Mills Brand of Managers," *Fortune*, January 12, 1981, pp. 99–107.

a year. These ambitious managers, who at the time of this writing were all under 35 years of age, are given the responsibility for sales, market share, and profits for their brands. In return, they earn $30,000 to $40,000 annually, are eligible for bonuses that can add up to another $10,000 to their compensation, and have the opportunity to take a set of resources and show top management what they can do in terms of generating profits for General Mills.

Dow Corning. The products of Dow Corning are not the household names as at General Mills. Dow Corning is, however, a multibillion-dollar corporation with an established set of products. In 1967, Dow Corning decided that its traditional divisionalized form of organization required a total structural overhaul.[9] This conclusion was reached after management noticed that (1) executives did not have adequate financial information and control of their operations (marketing managers, for instance, did not know how much it cost to produce a product because prices and margins were set by division managers), (2) cumbersome communication channels existed between key functions, especially manufacturing and marketing, (3) the corporation had become insufficiently oriented to environmental changes, (4) lack of communication between divisions created separatism rather than team effort, and (5) the corporation was suffering from overstaffing and duplicated effort. Dow Corning chose a form of matrix structure, one that went even beyond the typical two-dimensional model.

Dow Corning created a four-dimensional structure. The corporation's ten businesses were divided along product lines: rubber; resins and chemicals; fluids, emulsions, and compounds; specialty lubricants; medical products; and so on. The five major functions within Dow Corning were marketing; technical service and development; manufacturing; research; and economic evaluation, control, and planning. These ten products and five functions represented the typical matrix. However, the company decided to add two more dimensions. Since its businesses varied widely from area to area, it broke down products and functions further by geographic area. Finally, the company added a space and time dimension to reflect fluidity, the fact that the organization is constantly changing, and the need for long-range planning.

How does Dow Corning's structure work? It has created a team—called a Business Board—for each of the company's ten businesses. The team's only full-time member is the manager of the business. This manager is given direct responsibility for his business's profit, but as characteristic of the product manager, he has little authority over the resources needed

[9]William C. Goggin, "How the Multidimensional Structure Works at Dow Corning," *Harvard Business Review*, January–February 1974, pp. 54–65.

to accomplish his goals. His only resources are the single representatives from each of the five functional departments that make up his Business Board. They, of course, report directly to their functional department heads.

At first, Dow Corning found that the new structure created stress. The functional specialist not only had to be concerned with maintaining and improving the professionalism in his function, but also had the job of helping to develop profits for his business. However, as these specialists' understanding of their business goals increased as did their comprehension of the workings of the other functions, the stress began to dissipate. Teamwork began to replace jurisdictional jousting.

After five years of experience with the matrix, management considered it a success. The company was able to identify a number of positive results, many of which was attributed to the new structural form: higher profits; increased competitiveness based on technological innovation and improved product quality; improved communication; sound, fast decision making; better balancing of authority among businesses, functions, and areas; progress in developing broadly based short- and long-range planning; resource allocations that are proportionate to expected results; and accountability that is related more closely to responsibility and authority.

OTHER EXAMPLES OF ADHOCRACIES

While the matrix is the most popular form of adhocracy, it is not the only type. The design of adhocratic structures is limited only by the creativity of the designers. Three further examples of adhocracies are the task force, the committee structure, and the collegial structure.

The Task Force

The task force is a temporary structure formed to accomplish a specific, well-defined, and complex task that involves a number of organizational subunits. It can be thought of as a scaled-down version of the temporary matrix. However, rather than being a full structure applicable to an entire organization, the task force is an appendage to a more traditional hierarchical structure. Members serve on the task force until its goal is achieved, at which time the task force is disbanded. Then the members move on to a new task force, return to their permanent "home" department in the organization, or leave the organization.

When an organization is confronted with a task whose success is critical to the organization, which has specific time and performance standards, is unique and unfamiliar, and requires functions that are interdependent, a task force can be desirable. These conditions explain why General Motors went to the task force concept in the 1970s to mastermind the downsizing (shrinking) of their automobiles.[10]

For GM to meet federally mandated mileage standards, it was evident to the corporation's top executives that their automobiles—produced by five divisions (Chevrolet, Pontiac, Oldsmobile, Buick, and Cadillac)—would have to undergo a major reshaping. The task force structure was used to coordinate the development of new body lines among the various automobile divisions—a complex task in normal times but an extremely complex undertaking when, for example, all full-sized cars had to be changed radically. A task force was established for each major project: one for the full-sized cars, one for the intermediates, and so forth. For instance, the A-body task force tackled the development problems in downsizing GM's intermediates. The group worked on parts and engineering problems common to all divisions, such as frames, electrical systems, steering gear, and brakes. The A-body task force ran from late 1975 through the fall of 1977, at which time its goal was accomplished and the group was disbanded. Note the major advantage of the task force: it allowed GM to be adaptive yet, at the same time, maintain its efficient bureaucracy. By attaching task force structures to the mechanical mainframe, organizations get the best of both worlds: flexibility and efficiency.

The task force is also a common tool of consumer product firms. In addition to using the matrix—as General Mills did with its brand managers—on a permanent basis to oversee product lines, consumer product firms use the task force to design and develop new products. When Procter & Gamble, for instance, decides to create a new toothpaste, people with expertise from finance, manufacturing, marketing, product design, research, and other relevant functions are brought together to formulate the product, design its package, determine its market, compute its manufacturing costs, and project its profit. Once the problems have been worked out of the product and it is ready to be mass produced, the task force disbands and the toothpaste is integrated into the permanent structure. In fact, it is most likely that the toothpaste will be assigned a brand manager and become part of Procter & Gamble's own matrix structure.

The Committee Structure

Another example of adhocracy is a committee form of organization. When it is desired that a broad range of experience and backgrounds be brought to bear on a decision, when those who will be affected by a decision are allowed to be represented, when it is believed desirable to spread the work load, or during periods of management transition when no single individ-

[10]Charles G. Burck, "How G.M. Turned Itself Around," *Fortune*, January 16, 1978, pp. 92–96.

ual is ready to lead the organization, committee structures may be highly effective.

Committees may be temporary or permanent. A temporary committee typically is one and the same with a task force. Permanent committees, however, facilitate the bringing together of diverse inputs such as the task force, plus the stability and consistency of the matrix. When permanent committees are established at the top level of the organization, we frequently refer to the positions as forming a plural executive. Such a structure brings diverse perspectives into top-level decision making and permits the heterogeneous tasks of the chief executive's job to be divided up and parceled out according to the background and skills of the plural executive group. DuPont, for example, has utilized the plural executive concept for a number of decades. Westinghouse and General Electric, similarly, use a three-person management committee at the top. Each person still retains certain lines of authority, but all work as a group on planning and attacking long-range strategic problems of a nonoperating nature. Some universities and state governments have also introduced the plural executive committee. A number of universities have an "office of the president" rather than the position of president, whereas several states have an "office of the governor" instead of a singular position.

The Collegial Structure

A structural form of adhocracy fashionable in universities, research labs, and other highly professional organizations is the collegial structure. Its unique characteristic is full democracy in the making of all important decisions. This is in contrast to the task force or committee structures that utilize representative decision making.

The best example and most widespread use of the collegial structure is the design of academic departments in major universities. All key decisions are made by the department as a whole. Typically, even the department head carries no more weight than his or her one vote. The selection of new members, contract renewals, allocation of teaching assignments, performance appraisals, granting of tenure, modifications in curriculum, grading policies, and similar decisions are made by the department as a whole.

The collegial structure represents the utmost in decentralization. In universities, faculty members act with only minimal guidelines. These guidelines—university policies and procedures—tend to allow a great deal of leeway for departmental discretion. In the research units at Eastman Kodak or Bell Labs, you similarly find a structure that provides employees with extremely high autonomy, a minimum of formalization, and collegial decision making, which allows highly skilled professionals to adapt rapidly to the changing needs of their work.

WHEN IS ADHOCRACY THE PREFERRED STRUCTURE?

The adhocracy is certainly not every organization's "cup of tea." The factors that determine when adhocracy will be effective are the organization's strategy, technology, environment, and life stage.[11]

The adhocracy is associated with strategies of diversity, change, and/or high risk. Such strategies demand the flexibility inherent in adhocracy.

The technology in an adhocracy will be nonroutine. A nonroutine technology must be used to respond to the changing strategies that the organization will be employing. The technology will contain little formalization, relying on the expertise of professionals to provide the "right" response. Additionally, the technology will be complex in that it will draw on the talents of diverse specialties. This, in turn, requires coordination and integration of specialized and heterogeneous skills. The adhocracy is the preferred mechanism for facilitating this integration.

The adhocracy's environment will be dynamic and complex. This is because innovative work, being unpredictable, is associated with a dynamic environment and because innovative work, which is sophisticated, links with a complex environment—one that is difficult to interpret and comprehend.[12]

Finally, the adhocracy form is preferred in the early years of an organization's life cycle. Why? This is the time when the organization needs the greatest flexibility as it attempts to identify its market niche and determine precisely how it is going to go about achieving its goals. Innovation is high in an organization's formative years as it struggles to survive. Of course, the lack of prior precedents and entrenched vested interests fosters trying new and different approaches. It has been argued that adhocracy is most evident in those industries that are relatively young—ones that basically developed since World War II.[13] This would include several that we have referenced throughout the chapter: aerospace, electronics, consulting, and research.

"IT'S NICE IN THEORY, BUT . . ."

Do you see a disparity between the conclusions drawn about bureaucracy and the direction of this chapter? Regarding bureaucracy, we said that it was thriving, inevitable, and "the dominant structural form in North America." In this chapter, however, we have described a variety of organizations that use adhocracy and have implied that it is found in virtually all organ-

[11]Henry Mintzberg, "Structure in 5's: A Synthesis of the Research on Organization Design," *Management Science*, March 1980, pp. 336–338.

[12]Henry Mintzberg, *The Structuring of Organizations* (Englewood Cliffs, N.J.: Prentice-Hall, 1979), p. 449.

[13]Mintzberg, "Structure in 5's," p. 338.

izations that have developed in the past four decades. Both these observations are correct. However, they are not contradictions.

Usage in a wide *range* of organizations should not be confused with wide *acceptance*. First, adhocracies are the dominant structure in only a small minority of industries. Second, the form is used most popularly as an adjunct to bureaucracy. Finally, where adhocracy is found, it would be more accurate to conceive of it as a "vehicle" propelling the organization toward bureaucracy or failure rather than as an ongoing structure.

One must be careful in generalizing from a few examples. It is true that many small electronic firms, some large aerospace companies, most research laboratories and advertising agencies, and almost all "think tank" consulting firms are organized as adhocracies. But these examples also comprise basically the entire set of adhocracies. In terms of impact—whether you use sales, number of personnel employed, or any other standard criterion—these industries are not the mainstay of organized activity in North America.

Adhocracy is most likely to emerge as an addendum to the bureaucratic form. Survival will demand, at times, that the bureaucratic organization respond rapidly to change. As described at General Motors, adhocracy is the ideal instrument to use in fostering innovation and flexibility while allowing those in power to maintain control.

Finally, and perhaps most important, when adhocracy does emerge as the dominant structure in an organization, don't expect it to stay that way long. Success and progression in its life cycle drive the organization toward stability and standardization. This was evidenced in our discussion of Celestial Seasonings, Inc. in the previous chapter. As an organization settles in on what it does best, it is encouraged to repeat these activities. Standardization, differentiation, and formalization result. Of course, there is another alternative. The organization may die. Adhocracies will exist in dynamic environments where, unfortunately, the risk of failure is great. Changes in consumer tastes, breakthroughs by competitors, and the like are threats to survival. Adhocracies, therefore, are more vulnerable than are bureaucracies.

At the societal level, organizations that succeed take on bureaucratic characteristics. Those that fail may be summarized best by this antecdote. Chris Argyris, a consistent proponent of democracy in organizations, studied two hundred American companies. After looking at his results, he was disheartened to find them all authority conscious. Commenting on the findings, one of his colleagues remarked: "Chris, did it ever occur to you that the reason you didn't get a chance to study the organizations which are democratic is because they didn't stay in business long enough?"[14]

Our conclusion from the previous chapter still holds: bureaucracies

[14]"McClelland: An Advocate of Power," *International Management*, July 1975, p. 28.

are the dominant structural form. Adhocracies are few in number and, in spite of those who believe that adhocracy is the structure best adapted to the technologies and environments of the last half of this century,[15] there is no reason to believe that the adhocractic form is anything other than a structural design that is right for certain organizations at a certain stage in their life cycles or as an addendum to a bureaucracy. Our analysis suggests that adhocracy should rarely be an organization's dominant structure. Observations confirm this prediction.

SUMMARY

What bureaucracy was to the mechanistic model, adhocracy is to the organic. An adhocracy is a rapidly changing, adaptive, temporary system organized around problems to be solved by groups of relative strangers with diverse professional skills. It is characterized structurally as moderate to low in complexity, low in formalization, and decentralized.

Adhocracies are excellent vehicles for responding rapidly to change, facilitating innovation, and coordinating diverse specialists. However, they create internal conflicts and tend to be inefficient.

Examples of adhocracies include the matrix, the task force, committee structures, and collegial structures. When should these types of designs be considered? With diverse, changing, or high-risk strategies or where the technology is nonroutine and the environment is both dynamic and complex. It is also the preferred structural form when an organization is in the formative years of its life cycle.

Despite the attention given to adhocracies in recent years, it continues to be an atypical organizational form. Adhocracies are the dominant structure in only a minority of industries. When used, it is usually as an adjunct to bureaucracy. Finally, organizations that are adhocracies in their early years either evolve into bureaucracies or die off.

FOR REVIEW AND DISCUSSION

1. What characterizes an adhocracy?
2. Describe the type of organizations that might be organized as adhocracies. Why?
3. Contrast the professional bureaucracy to adhocracy.
4. Present the advantages and disadvantages of the matrix.
5. Is your college organized along bureaucratic or adhocratic lines? How did you draw your conclusion? What were the critical determinants affecting your college's structure as it is?

[15] See, for example, Alvin Toffler, *Future Shock* (New York: Random House, 1970).

6. Some people would rather work in a bureaucracy; others prefer adhocracy. What individual characteristics might separate those who choose one over the other? In which would you prefer to work? Why?
7. Why would an adhocracy be inefficient where the organization utilized a routine technology and faced a stable environment?
8. "The adhocracy rates low on all three structural components." Do you agree or disagree? Discuss.
9. Is adhocracy compatible with large size? Support your position.
10. "Adhocracy is the organizational structure of the twenty-first century." Build an argument to support this position. Then build an argument to refute this position.

CHAPTER

13

OTHER STRUCTURAL FORMS

In one way, organizations are like fingerprints. Each has its own unique structure. Yet, no structure is truly unique. It has common elements that allow us to generalize about it and place it into one or more structural categories. As you review the potpourri of forms discussed in this chapter, keep in mind that, when they are added to our previous coverage of bureaucracy and adhocracy, they create a framework and labeling system that describes almost all types of structural forms. Every organization may not fit neatly into one of our categories. Some may appear to belong in several. Others may deviate in various ways from the pure form that is presented. Overall, however, you should find the structural forms described in Chapters 11 and 12 and those pages that follow to be a valuable schema for labeling and understanding structural forms.

THE SIMPLE STRUCTURE

What do a small retail store, an electronics firm run by a hard-driving entrepreneur, a new Planned Parenthood office, and a city in the midst of a race riot have in common? They probably all utilize the *simple structure.*

The simple structure is said to be characterized most by what it is not rather than what is is. The simple structure is not elaborated.[1] It is low in complexity, has little formalization, and has authority centralized in a single person. The structure is depicted best as a flat organization, with an organic

[1]Henry Mintzberg, "Structure in 5's: A Synthesis of the Research on Organization Design," *Management Science,* March 1980, p. 331.

FIGURE 13–1 Organization chart for Fashion Flair stores

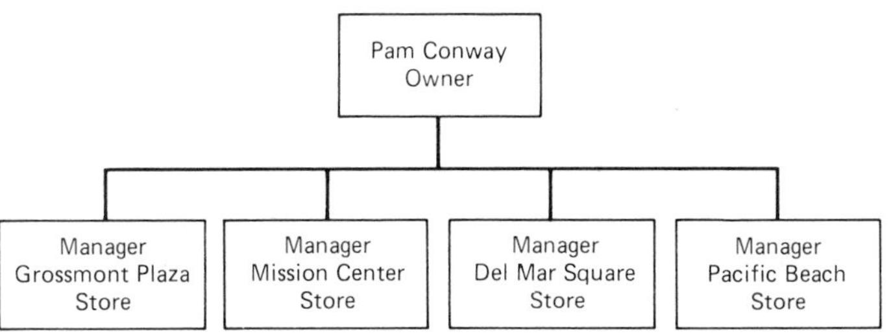

operating core and almost everyone's reporting to the one individual in whom the decision-making power is centralized. Figure 13–1 illustrates the simple structure. Notice that this organization, Fashion Flair retail stores, is flat. Decision making is basically informal—all important decisions are centralized in the hands of the senior executive who, because of the low complexity, is able to obtain key information readily and to act rapidly when required. This senior executive is the owner-manager at Fashion Flair. The senior executives in the simple structure typically have a wide span of control.

Strengths and Weaknesses

The strength of the simple structure lies in its simplicity. It's fast and flexible and requires little cost to maintain. There are no layers of cumbersome structure. Accountability is clear. There is a minimum amount of goal displacement because members are able to identify readily with the organization's mission and it is fairly easy to see how one's actions contribute to the organization's goals.

The simple structure's predominant weakness is its limited applicability. When confronted with increased size, this structure generally proves inadequate. Additionally, the simple structure concentrates power in one person. Rarely does the structure provide countervailing forces to balance the chief executive's power. Therefore, the simple structure can easily succumb to the abuse of authority by the person in power. This concentration of power, of course, can work against the organization's effectiveness and survival. The simple structure, in fact, has been described as the "riskiest of structures, hinging on the health and whims of one individual."[2] One heart attack can literally destroy the organization's decision-making center.

[2]Henry Mintzberg, *The Structuring of Organizations* (Englewood Cliffs, N.J.: Prentice-Hall, 1979), p. 312.

When Should You Use It?

When are you likely to find a simple structure? If the organization is small or in its formative stage of development, if the environment is simple and dynamic, if the organization faces high hostility or a crisis, if the senior manager is also the owner, or if the senior executive either wants to hoard power or his subordinates thrust the power upon him.

The simple structure is effective when the number of employees is few. Small size usually means less repetitive work in the operating core, so standardization is less attractive. Informal communication is convenient. As long as the structure remains small, the "one-man show" can effectively oversee all activities, be knowledgeable about key problems, and can carry out all important decisions.

As with adhocracy, the simple structure meets the needs of organizations when they are in their formative years. "The *new organization* tends to adopt the Simple Structure, no matter what its environment or technical system, because it has not had the time to elaborate its administrative structure."[3] Almost all organizations, therefore, pass through the simple structure stage. For those that remain small in size, the simple structure may be permanent rather than transitory.

Simple and dynamic environments tend to be associated with the simple structure's flat organization with centralized decision making and organic operating core. Why? A simple environment is comprehended easily by a single individual and, therefore, enables that individual to control decision making effectively. A dynamic environment requires an organic structure so that it can react to its unpredictable contingencies.

Regardless of size, when an organization suddenly confronts a hostile environment, management is likely to resort to the simple structure. The reason for this is logical. When survival is threatened, top management wants control. Further, since the hostility disrupts the standard operating procedures, the SOPs are likely to be suspended. The result is a temporary flattening out of the organization.

Our discussion of the power-control position in Chapter 10 leads to the prediction that the simple structure should be preferred. As a control mechanism that concentrates power in a single place, the simple structure is even superior to the Bureaucracy. Large size typically excludes the possibility of a permanent simple structure, but, among even medium-sized organizations where power is consolidated, the simple structure should be dominant. A look at most small and medium-sized owner-managed organizations confirms this prediction. Owner-managers have considerable power. They assert that power by maintaining a structure that allows them the greatest control. That, of course, is the simple structure.

[3]Ibid., p. 308.

Similarly, regardless of size, when the top executive hoards power and purposely avoids high formalization so as to maximize the impact of his or her discretion, that executive will, in effect, design a simple structure for the organization. Power and the simple structure are again correlated when organizational members defer power to the chief executive. That is, even if the senior executive does not crave power, if subordinates do not want to be involved with decision making, they force it back to the executive. The result is the same as if the power had been sought by the executive: decision making becomes centralized in one person at the top, and the organization takes on simple structure characteristics.

It has been proposed that the classic case of the simple structure is the entrepreneurial firm.[4] It continually searches for risky environments where bureaucracies hesitate to operate. These firms are usually small, so they can remain organic and their entrepreneurs can maintain tight control. Of course, the high risk translates into a high attrition rate. Thus, the entrepreneurial firm rarely stays that way long. The weak ones die. The successful ones tend to grow and become increasingly risk aversive. When this happens, the simple structure tends to be replaced by a form that is predominantly bureaucratic.

THE FUNCTIONAL STRUCTURE

"Listen, nothing happens in this place until we *produce* something," said the production executive. "Wrong," commented the research and development manager. "Nothing happens until we *design* something!" "What are you talking about?" asked the marketing executive. "Nothing happens here until we *sell* something!" Finally, the exasperated accountant responded, "It doesn't matter what you produce, design, or sell. No one knows what happens until we *tally up the results!*"

This dialogue is an undesirable result of the *functional structure.* In this section, we describe the functional form of organization, consider its strengths as well as its weaknesses, and suggest those conditions under which it is most effective.

The functional structure was alluded to in Chapter 3, in our discussion of functional departmentation, and in the previous chapter's review of the matrix structure. So the idea of the functional structure should already be familiar to you. Its major distinguishing feature is the grouping together of similar and related occupational specialties. Activities such as marketing, accounting, manufacturing, and personnel are grouped under functional executives who report to a central headquarters. Figure 13–2 shows a typical functional structure for a manufacturing organization.

[4]Mintzberg, "Structure in 5's," p. 332.

FIGURE 13–2 Functional structure in a manufacturing organization

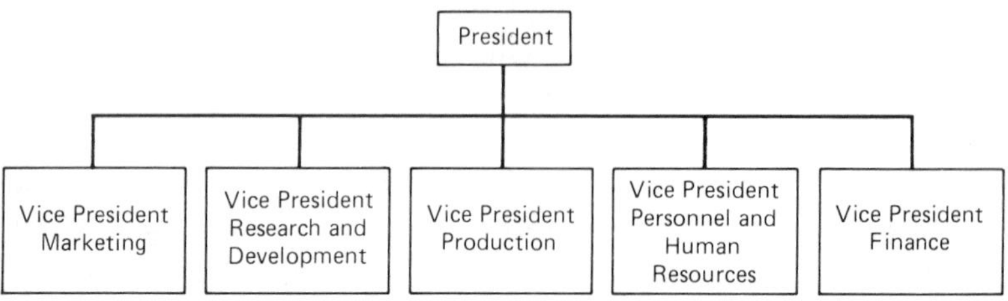

Strengths and Weaknesses

The functional structure's strengths and weaknesses were outlined when we discussed the matrix. We can summarize them briefly as follows.

Its strength lies in the advantages that accrue from specialization. Putting like specialties together results in economies of scale, minimization of duplication of personnel and equipment, and comfortable and satisfied employees who have the opportunity to talk "the same language" among their peers.

The weaknesses of the functional structure are legendary. As noted at the opening of this section, the functional form creates subunit conflicts. This, of course, can lead to goal displacement. Accountability suffers under the functional structure. No one functional group is totally responsible for end results. Coordination within units is easy, but coordination among units is difficult. This is due to the diversity of interests and perspectives that exists between units. The job of coordination falls on top management, because that is the only group that can see the whole picture. This diversity among units is a major problem made evident in Dearborn and Simon's classic study in perception.[5] Twenty-three business executives were asked to read a comprehensive case describing the organization and activities of a steel company. Six of the executives were in the sales function, five in production, four in accounting, and eight in miscellaneous functions. Each was then asked to write down the most important problem he or she found in the case. Five of the six sales executives, or 83 percent, rated sales important, in contrast to 29 percent of the others. This, along with other results of the study, led the researchers to conclude that the participants perceived aspects in the situation that related specifically to the activities and goals of the unit to which they were attached. The functional structure automatically builds in conflicts between the functional units.

Two final weaknesses of the functional structure relate to its inability to cope effectively with large size and its failure to develop top management

[5]DeWitt C. Dearborn and Herbert A. Simon, "Selected Perception: A Note on the Departmental Identification of Executives," *Sociometry*, June 1958, pp. 140–144.

generalists. Regarding size, the disadvantages of the functional structure appear to grow rapidly as size increases. The reason is that, as size expands, the need for coordination between the functional units increases. The larger the organization, the more likely the separation by function leads to goal displacement and offsets the advantages of specialization. The functional structure is also noteworthy for its inability to provide adequate preparation for functional executives to assume the organization's chief executive position. The functional managers only see a narrow dimension of the organization—that segment that deals with their function. Exposure to other functions is limited. The functional structure has no position in which a manager can learn and prepare to handle the complexities inherent in the chief executive's job. As a result, the structure is a poor training ground for developing executives with a broad perspective on the organization's activities.

When Should You Use It?

The functional structure is well adapted to smaller organizations. As noted, large size creates major coordination problems for this type of structure.

There is strong agreement among organization theorists that the functional structure is preferred when organizations deal in a single product or service. Conversely, it is poorly suited to multiproduct or multimarket organizations. As the organization diversifies by adding products or markets, the functional specialists must spread their talents. In such cases, the advantages of specialization begin to be more than offset by the problems of diversification.

It should be obvious to anyone who has not lived on a deserted island forever that the functional structure is extremely popular. You find it in small organizations and large ones as well. We make this observation in spite of our acknowledgment that it poses distinct coordination problems in large organizations. The functional structure's popularity is due undoubtedly to both its compatability with the bureaucratic model and the fact that it facilitates maintenance of power by the chief executive. This is because the structure is designed so that full information of what is going on is held only by the person or persons who occupy the very top positions in the organization. In a business firm this rarely includes more than the chairman of the board, the president, the chief operating officer, and perhaps the executive vice president. The myopia created by having separate and autonomous functions ensures that only those at the very top have access to all key information. We propose that, if the senior management of an organization wants to fortify its power, the "divide and conquer" aspects of the functional structure make it an excellent control device. The functional structure's popularity has certainly not been deterred by this fact.

THE DIVISIONAL STRUCTURE

Figure 13–3 is an adapted version of the most widely reproduced organization chart in America. It belongs to General Motors. It represents an example of the *divisional structure.*

The divisional structure, pioneered in the 1920s by General Motors and DuPont, is designed essentially to foster self-contained units. Each unit or division is generally autonomous, with a division manager responsible for performance and holding complete strategic and operating decision-making authority. At General Motors, the divisions are based on product and include such entities as Buick, Cadillac, Chevrolet, Oldsmobile, Pontiac, GMC Truck and Coach, Fisher Body, GM Assembly, AC Spark Plug, Delco Electronics, Diesel Equipment, and Hydra-Matic. Each of GM's several dozen divisions is headed by an executive who is totally responsible for results. As in all divisional structures, there is a central headquarters that provides support services to the divisions. This typically includes financial, legal, and tax services. Additionally, of course, the headquarters acts as an external overseer, evaluating and controlling performance. Divisions, therefore, are autonomous within given parameters. General Motors has followed Alfred Sloan's original dictum of "decentralized operations and responsibilities with coordinated control" for half a century. Division managers are free to direct their division anyway they see fit as long as it is within the overall guidelines set down by headquarters.

A closer look at divisional structures reveals typically that their "innards" contain functional structures. The divisional framework creates a set of essentially autonomous "little companies." Within each of these companies lies another organizational form, and it is almost always of the functional variety. While it does not show in Figure 13–3, if you were to dissect, for instance, the Chevrolet Motor Division, you would find that the division manager has functional executives responsible for marketing, production, R&D, and the like reporting to him.

Strengths and Weaknesses

One problem associated with the functional structure is the potential for the functional units to become so enamoured with their specialty that they forget the organization's overall goals. The divisional structure attempts to remedy this by placing full responsibility for a product or service in the hands of the divisional manager. This structure, therefore, focuses on end results rather than on means.

The divisional structure frees up the headquarters staff from being concerned with day-to-day operating details so they can pay attention to the long term. Big-picture, strategic decision making is done at headquarters. At GM, for instance, senior executives in Detroit can wrestle with the

FIGURE 13–3 General Motors Corporation

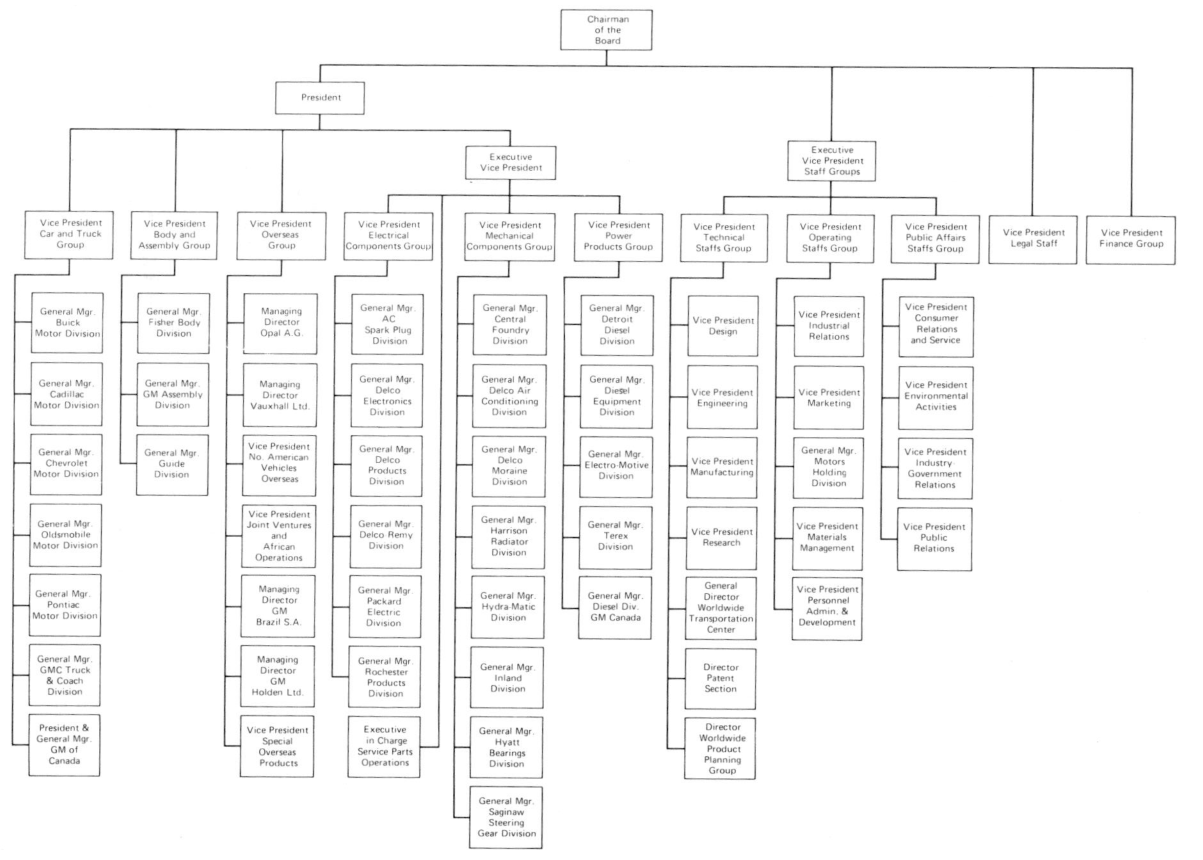

world's future transportation needs while the division managers can go about the business of producing Chevrolets and Buicks as efficiently as possible.

Consistent with this is the fact that essentially autonomous divisions allow for a wide span of control at the top. Since the divisions are relatively independent, a large number of divisions can report to one senior executive. The Car and Truck group vice president at GM has seven division general managers reporting to him. These divisions, which employ literally hundreds of thousands of people, can be overseen effectively only because they are basically autonomous. As such, they require little in the way of constant attention from the group vice president. If these units were highly interdependent and in need of close supervision by the vice president, he probably could not direct more than three or four of these huge units.

It should be obvious that the autonomy and self-containment characteristics of the divisional form make it an excellent vehicle for training and developing general managers. This is a distinct advantage over the functional structure and its emphasis on specialization. That is, the divisional structure gives managers a broad range of experience with the autonomous units. This individual responsibility and independence gives them an opportunity to run an entire company, with its frustrations and satisfactions. So a large corporation with fifteen divisions has fifteen division managers who are developing the kind of generalist perspective that is needed in the organization's top spot.

Another strength of the divisional form is that its autonomous units can be lopped off with minimal effect on the entire organization. Ineffective performance in one division has little effect on the other divisions. As such, the divisional structure spreads the risk by reducing the chance that a poorly performing part of the organization will take down other parts of the organization with it.

It's evident that the real strengths of the divisional form come from its creation of self-contained businesses "within a business." The divisions have the responsiveness, the accountability, and the benefits of specialization and are able to process information as if they were organizations unto themselves. Yet they also have the benefits of large size that allow economies of scale in planning, acquisition of capital, and spreading of risk. Returning to our example of General Motors, when the GMC Truck and Coach Division needs $100 million to modernize a production plant, GM is able to borrow that money at a rate several percentage points below what the division could negotiate if it were not part of General Motors Corporation. Similarly, that division can be provided with legal expertise that could never be available "inhouse" if the Truck and Coach Division were a separate corporation independent of General Motors.

Let us turn now to the weaknesses of the divisional structure, of which there is no shortage. First, is the duplication of activities and resources. Each division, for instance, may have a marketing research department. In the absence of autonomous divisions, all the organization's marketing research might be centralized and done for a fraction of the cost that divisionalization requires. So the divisional form's duplication of functions increases the organization's costs and reduces efficiency.

Another disadvantage is the propensity of the divisional form to stimulate conflict. There is little incentive with this structural design to encourage cooperation among divisions. Further conflicts are created as divisions and headquarters argue about where to locate support services. The more the divisions succeed in having these services decentralized to their level, the less dependent they are on headquarters and, hence, the less power headquarters' personnel can wield over them.

The autonomy of the divisions, to the degree that it is more theory than practice, can breed resentment in the division managers. While the structure gives general autonomy to the divisions, the autonomy is exercised within constraints. The division manager is being held fully accountable for results in his unit, but because he must operate within the uniform policies imposed from headquarters, he is likely to be resentful and argue that his authority is less than his responsibility. The Buick Motor Division general manager has a valid case if he complains that he is charged with responsibility for Buick's performance yet a number of basic decisions that are critical to his division's performance, such as the number, size, and weight of his product line, are dictated by the corporation's policy committee.

Finally, the divisional form creates coordination problems. Personnel are frequently unable to transfer between divisions, especially when the divisions operate in highly diverse product or service markets. DuPont employees in the Remington Arms Division, for instance, have little transferability to the Textile Fibers or Petro-Chemicals divisions. This reduces the flexibility of headquarters' executives to allocate and coordinate personnel. Additionally, the divisional form may make coordination of customer relations and product development a problem. If the divisions are in competing or closely adjoining markets, they may compete with each other for the same sale. To many prospective automobile buyers, Chevrolets and Pontiacs are nearly interchangeable products. Yet, since the two have substantially distinct dealer networks, competition to get the sale is as intense between Chevrolet and Pontiac as between Chevrolet and Ford. Similarly, the competition between divisions over product development can be dysfunctional. The classic illustration is the NDH—not developed here—syndrome. An innovation developed by one division and then authorized by headquarters to be instituted in all divisions frequently fails because it was NDH. This rivalry and territorial protectionism by the individual divisions can make coordination by headquarters extremely difficult.

When Should You Use It?

The primary criterion determining the use of the divisional structure is product or market diversity. When an organization chooses a diversification strategy—to become a multiproduct or multimarket organization—the divisional form becomes preferable to a functional structure. When an organization diversifies, conflicts along the horizontal dimension between functions become too great and a change in structural design becomes necessary.

Other contingency factors include size, technology, and environment. As size increases, it becomes more difficult to coordinate functional units and to keep members' attention focused on the organization's goals. Organizational size and goal displacement appear to be highly correlated. So increases in size encourage movement to the divisional structure. All technologies are not compatible with the division form. To be applicable, the organization's technology must be divisible. "Divisionalization is possible only when the organization's technical system can be efficiently separated into segments, one for each division."[6] Thus, it is difficult, for instance, for U.S. Steel to divisionalize because economies of scale and the commitment of hundreds of millions of dollars to very high fixed-cost technical systems basically precludes divisibility. Finally, the environment affects preference for the divisional form. The divisional structure works best where the environment is neither very complex nor very dynamic. Why? Highly complex and dynamic environments are associated with nonstandardized processes and outputs, yet the divisional form is a lot like the machine bureaucracy in its emphasis on standardization. So the divisional form tends to have an environment that is more simple than complex and more stable than dynamic.

THE SECTOR STRUCTURE

The latest addition to the organization design offering is the *sector structure.* Introduced in 1977 by General Electric, it places an additional layer of management between the divisional managers and the corporate executive office.[7] Each sector represents a set of common businesses that have a clearly defined industry identity. As such, each sector is actually analogous to a "superdivision." For instance, General Electric has created six sectors, responsible for Consumer Products and Services, Industrial Products and Components, Power Systems, Technical Systems and Materials, International Operations, and Utah Mining International (see Figure 13–4). 3M

[6]Mintzberg, *The Structuring of Organizations,* pp. 397–398.

[7]See, for example, "GE's New Billion-Dollar Small Businesses," *Business Week,* December 1977, pp. 78–79; and Robert R. Frederick, "Sector Executives: Management Evolution," *Management Review,* October 1978, pp. 29–30.

FIGURE 13–4 Sector structure at General Electric.

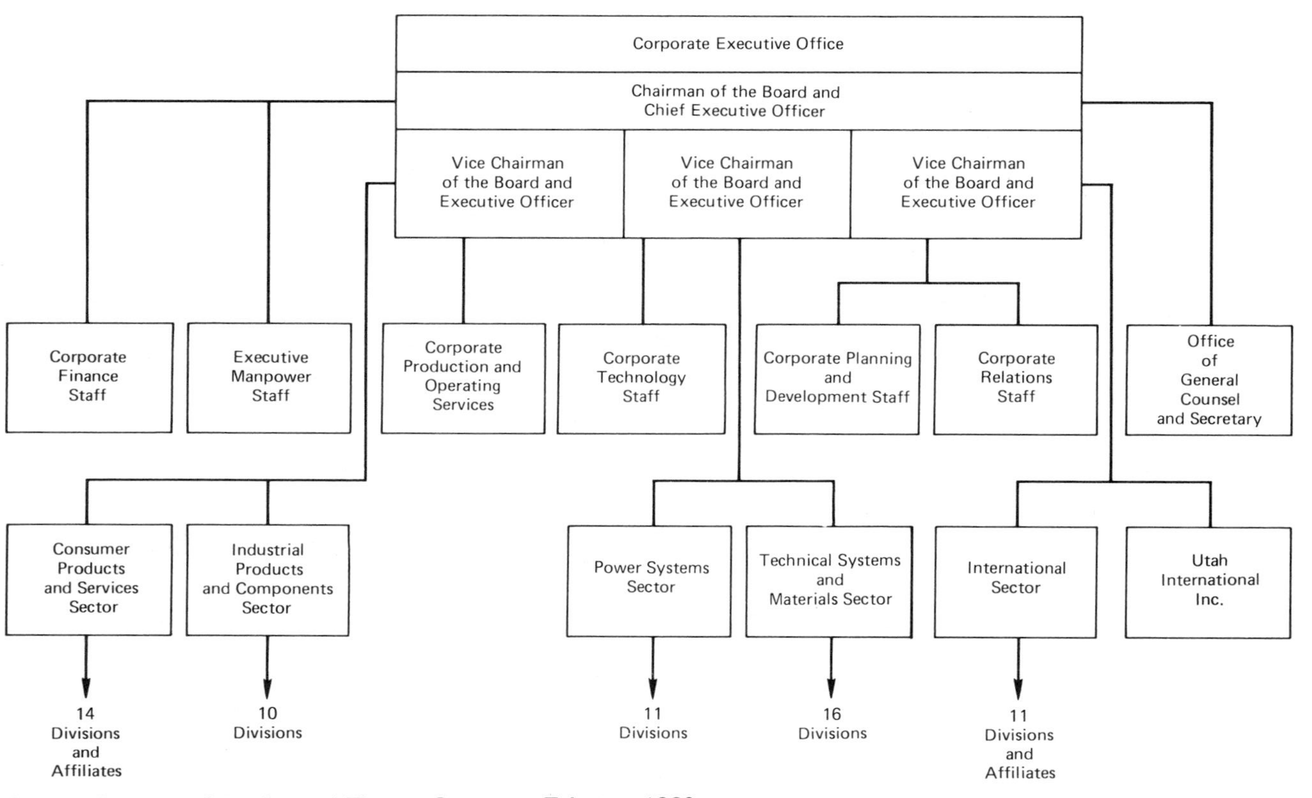

Source: Courtesy of the General Electric Company, February 1980.

Co., which has recently implemented the sector structure, has consolidated its ten divisions under four sector groups: Industrial and Consumer Products, Life Sciences, Electro and Communications Technologies, and Imaging Sciences.[8]

3M's decision to go to a sector structure was a result of the increasing recognition that the divisional form was ineffective in facilitating one of the company's primary goals—to be a major factor in the rapidly growing automated office equipment market. Even though 3M offered a wide array of copiers, facsimile machines, and microfilm, the fact that they were produced and marketed through separate divisions severely hampered the company's effort to develop integrated office systems. As one former 3M manager noted, "The problem was, you could never get a system funded across division lines."[9] The sector structure is designed to deal with this drawback of the divisional form.

Strengths and Weaknesses

The sector structure provides a mechanism for very large organizations to grow without overburdening the top executives' span of control. It reduces the number of managers reporting to senior executives, decreases the probability that the senior executives will suffer from information overload, and frees up those at the top to focus their attention on strategic planning, including external matters such as government regulation and taxation.

Other positives for the sector structure are that the extra level of management creates additional promotion opportunities and, therefore, serves as a motivating force and that the positions as sector executives are the ideal training ground for assuming the top job in the organization. GE has three vice chairmen and six sector-level executives who are gaining the type of experience necessary to assume the chief executive officer's position.

The major disadvantages of the sector structure are those associated with an additional layer of management: communication problems and increased costs. The sector executives create another barrier between middle managers and the executive cadre. This may result in some of the dysfunctional aspects, as discussed in Chapter 3, that parallel increased vertical complexity. The cost factor, while relevant in absolute dollars, is probably negligible for a large corporation. However, it should be noted that the addition of five or six sector executives can easily increase the annual corporate payroll costs by $2 million or more.

[8]"3M looks Beyond Luck and Fast Profits," *Business Week*, February 23, 1981, p. 44.

[9]Ibid.

When Should You Use It?

The newness and limited use of the sector structure makes the identification of conditions when it is preferred speculative. Given this caveat, the following predictions seem reasonable. The sector form is desirable for very large organizations that are pursuing growth strategies. It accommodates growth—through the addition of new divisions—without increasing the span of control for top management. As a case in point, notice in Figure 13–4 that new divisions can be added under the sector executives at GE with no change in the upper structure. Further, even though the organization is large and pursuing a growth strategy, its products must have some common industry identity. If the organization has, for instance, fifteen divisions, each of which operates in a distinct and unrelated industry, the use of the sector concept would make little sense. It is the linking together of similar product lines that allows each sector executive to be top management's corporate spokesperson for an industry.

THE CONGLOMERATE STRUCTURE

The last structural form we will discuss is the *conglomerate.* A product of the 1960s, when it was highly popular, its continued use requires that it receive attention.

The unique characteristic of the conglomerate structure is that there are no important interdependencies among its units or divisions, except for pooling of resources. The conglomerate, therefore, is similar to the divisional structure, only the units are completely independent. Management purposely seeks a diverse set of divisions so as to smooth out the boom-and-bust cycles to which the single-domain organization is susceptible.

The role of headquarters in the conglomerate depends on whether management is active or passive. In the former, the headquarters staff would be small (in contrast to the other structural forms we have discussed) and would engage in allocating resources among the divisions and monitoring each one's performance, total corporate planning, and the financial analysis necessary to make acquisition and divestiture decisions. When a conglomerate's management is passive, there results a holding company with little or no headquarters staff. This fragmented structure, in effect, is no longer a single organization but merely an artificial frame to hold together a set of totally independent companies. The rest of our discussion will be directed to the actively managed conglomerate.

Two prominent examples of the conglomerate are ITT and the Signal Companies. The ITT structure includes such diverse companies as Federal Electric, Sheraton Hotels, Grinnell, Rayonier, Continental Baking, Qume

FIGURE 13–5 The Signal Companies organization chart.

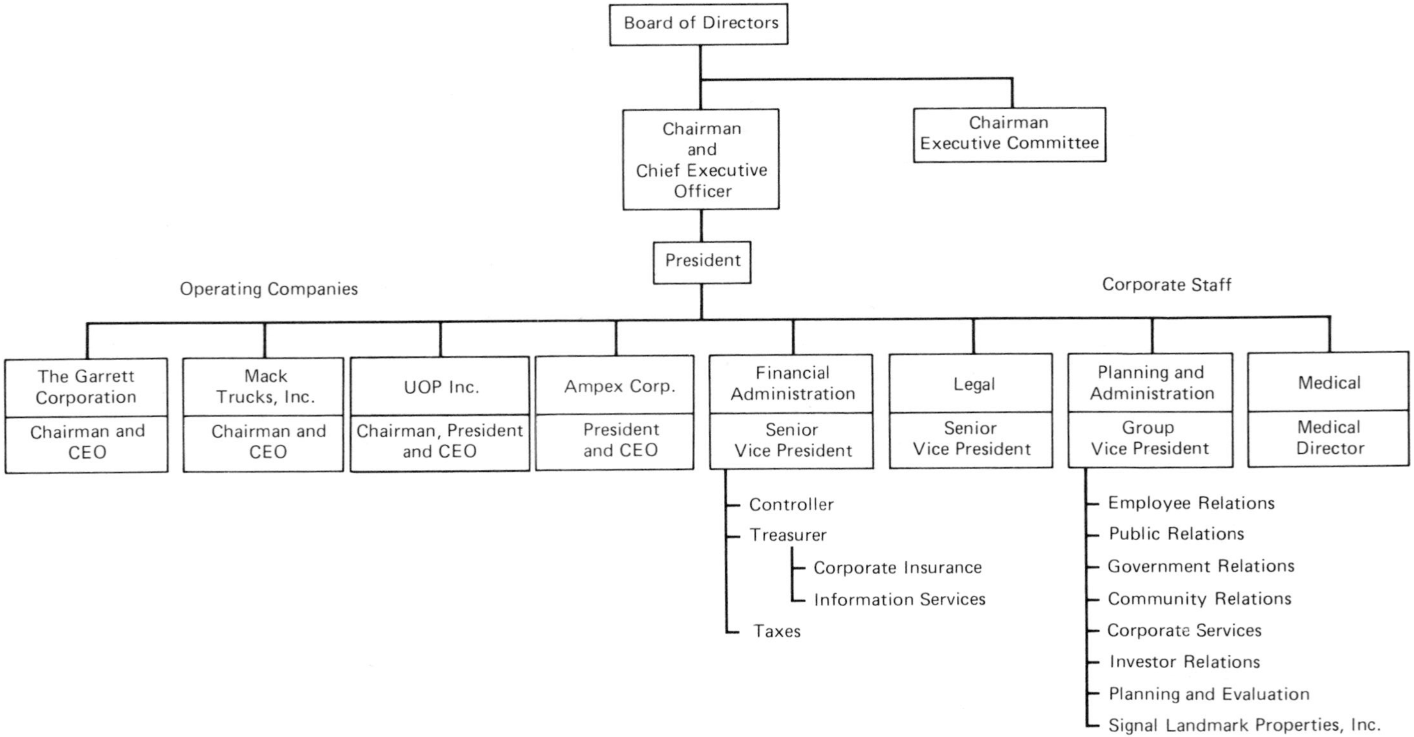

Board of Directors

Chairman and Chief Executive Officer

Chairman Executive Committee

President

Operating Companies

The Garrett Corporation — Chairman and CEO

Mack Trucks, Inc. — Chairman and CEO

UOP Inc. — Chairman, President and CEO

Ampex Corp. — President and CEO

Corporate Staff

Financial Administration — Senior Vice President

- Controller
- Treasurer
  - Corporate Insurance
  - Information Services
- Taxes

Legal — Senior Vice President

Planning and Administration — Group Vice President

- Employee Relations
- Public Relations
- Government Relations
- Community Relations
- Corporate Services
- Investor Relations
- Planning and Evaluation
- Signal Landmark Properties, Inc.

Medical — Medical Director

Source: Courtesy of the Signal Companies, January 1981.

Corp., and Eason Oil. Figure 13–5 presents the organization chart for the Signal Companies. As shown, this conglomerate's companies are Garrett Corporation, Mack Trucks, UOP Inc., and Ampex Corporation.

Strengths and Weaknesses

The conglomerate's divisions are treated as fully autonomous units. As such, its basic strength is that it is not attached operationally or emotionally to any one of its divisions. They can be bought and sold independently to enhance the overall organization's financial goals. The mere size of the conglomerate also implies advantages in acquiring financial resources.

The weaknesses of the conglomerate structure are the results of detachment. The fact that the divisions are fully autonomous means that there are no operational economies of scale. It also means duplication of activities since there is no sharing of skilled personnel or sophisticated equipment and facilities. And, of course, the conglomerate's top management cannot be knowledgable of any division's operations beyond the impersonal reports that the divisions are required to submit regularly to headquarters. Unless the control system is extremely tight, the conglomerate form places power (via control of information) into the hands of the division management. This may explain why, in a study of thirty conglomerates, over half had solidified the power of top management by significantly increasing the emphasis placed on each division's long-range planning, monthly budget reviews, monthly narrative reports on operations, formal goal-setting systems, and the performance evaluation of unit executives.[10]

When Should You Use It?

As with the sector structure, the key requirement for using the conglomerate form is a growth strategy. Furthermore, the growth is usually strongly biased toward enhancing the organization's financial position rather than, say, operational economies.

At Signal, for example, its strategy is to emphasize internal growth while constantly analyzing external opportunities.[11] This strategy has proven successful: between 1976 and 1980, the organization showed 18 percent annual real growth. Sales in 1980 reached nearly $5 billion. What criteria does Signal use for assessing acquisitions? In the spring of 1981, any new addition had to be a high-technology company; have a high

[10]Stephen A. Allen, "Organizational Choices and General Management Influence Networks in Divisonalized Companies," *Academy of Managemnt Journal*, September 1978, pp. 341–365.

[11]"Conglomerates' Growth Explained," *San Diego Union*, April 3, 1981, p. 46.

growth rate, a strong market position, and at least $100 million of annual sales; be involved in the international market, not be petroleum dependent; and have a product that runs countercyclical to the organization's large Mack Truck division.[12]

SUMMARY

The five structural forms presented in this chapter are elaborations and extensions of the bureaucracy and adhocracy models introduced in the previous chapters. The functional, divisional, sector, and conglomerate structures are all consistent with bureaucratic characteristics, particularly high complexity. On the other hand, the simple structure is closest to adhocracy. It is not elaborate. It is highly organic—low on complexity and formalization—but high on centralization. The simple structure is recommended for small organizations, for those in their formative stage of development, for organizations in environments that are simple and dynamic, for firms during times of crisis, or when those in control desire power to be centralized.

The functional structure groups similar and related occupational specialties together. It is preferred by smaller organizations that deal in a single product or service.

The divisional structure is made up of self-contained and autonomous units. It is applicable to organizations with product or market diversity, large size, divisible technologies, and neither very complex nor very dynamic environments.

The sector structure combines divisions into common business groupings. It is recommended for very large organizations that are pursuing a growth strategy and have divisions with some common industry identity.

The conglomerate structure's divisional units are the most autonomous of the designs discussed. The units are completely independent. This structural form should be used with growth strategies.

FOR REVIEW AND DISCUSSION

1. Describe the simple structure. When would you use it?
2. Describe the functional structure. When would you use it?
3. Describe the divisional structure. When would you use it?
4. Describe the sector structure. When would you use it?
5. Describe the conglomerate structure. When would you use it?

[12]Ibid.

6. During the 1960s, the conglomerate structure was extremely popular. Not so, in the 1980s. What do you think brought about its decline in popularity? Does this suggest that a major determinant of an organization's structure is what others are doing; that is, what is currently in vogue? Discuss.
7. Contrast the simple structure and adhocracy.
8. Explain, in power-control terms, the popularity of the functional and divisional structures.
9. What differences, if any, are there between bureaucracy and a functional structure?
10. Which structural designs are best for developing future top managerial talent?

PART V

APPLICATIONS: CURRENT ISSUES IN ORGANIZATION THEORY

CHAPTER

14

MANAGING JOB DESIGN

The jobs that people do, on a day-to-day basis, are both the building blocks of organizational design and the most visible representation of organizational structure.[1] The discussion of such diverse topics as horizontal specialization, span of control, formalization, decentralization, or technology all have a common denominator—they revolve around the way in which employee tasks and responsibilities are organized, coordinated, and controlled. Yet, to this point in the book, we have paid little attention to the content of jobs. The purpose of this chapter is to correct this omission.

The content and design of jobs has interested engineers and economists for centuries. Until approximately thirty years ago, this interest was quite narrow in focus. Job design was substantially synonymous with job specialization. In 1776, for instance, Adam Smith articulated in his *Wealth of Nations* the economic efficiencies that could be achieved by dividing jobs into smaller and smaller pieces so that each worker could perform a minute and specialized task. At the turn of this century, Frederick Taylor and others in the scientific management movement touted the advantages of systematizing and proceduring of jobs. The dominant view of job design was that specialization increased efficiency. Jobs, therefore, should be specialized, simplified, standardized, and routinized. Beginning in the late 1940s and early 1950s, as a result of insights from psychologists, sociologists, and other social scientists, attention began to shift to consider the human needs of employees. The reason was that the social scientists were

[1]Warren B. Brown and Dennis J. Moberg, *Organization Theory and Management: A Macro Approach* (New York: John Wiley, 1980), p. 136.

finding that a good thing could be taken too far. Extreme specialization had its drawbacks—being increasingly associated with boring tasks, unchallenging work, and employee alienation. High specialization produced handsome economic returns, but it often left behind work assignments that had little meaning to people. When carried too far, the economies of specialization could be more than offset by the diseconomies of employee dissatisfaction. The shift toward considering the human issues in job content led to the development of alternative methods of job design besides specialization. These alternatives sought to make work less routine and more meaningful. Today we describe these alternatives as quality of work life (QWL) programs.

THE QWL MOVEMENT

The search to make work more meaningful was not based on altruism. While many of those involved in the QWL movement held strong humanistic values, it should be obvious that, if job redesign programs are to move from academic theories to organizational practice, they must provide some economic payoff. Otherwise, managers have no motivation to implement them. Certainly the majority of managers have a social conscience, but pragmatics dictate that no enduring effort to improve jobs can be sustained merely by offering managers happier and more satisfied employees. Management will not and cannot implement programs that undermine the organization's economic effectiveness just to increase employee satisfaction. QWL must, therefore, blend employee welfare goals with economic goals. Along with increases in employee job satisfaction, there needs to be improved productivity or reduced absence and turnover. Interestingly, improved job satisfaction and economic effectiveness are interrelated. Research demonstrates that satisfied employees are late to work less often, have fewer absences, and are less likely to quit.[2] So, even if a job redesign program has no direct impact on an employee's productivity, it has an indirect influence if it increases employee satisfaction, because this is associated with decreases in tardiness, absenteeism, and turnover.

ARE TODAY'S EMPLOYEES DISSATISFIED WITH THEIR JOBS?

Before we assess management's structural options for making employees' jobs more meaningful, let us take a look at the problem. Certainly there are workers who are dissatisfied with jobs, but what is the extent of this

[2]See, for instance, Arthur H. Brayfield and Walter H. Crockett, "Employee Attitudes and Employee Performance," *Psychological Bulletin*, September 1955, pp. 396–428; and Victor H. Vroom, *Work and Motivation* (New York: John Wiley, 1964).

dissatisfaction? Do we have an ailment that afflicts 5 percent of the labor force or 90 percent?

Regardless of what evidence one cites, it is extremely difficult to build an argument that we presently face a crisis regarding the state of employee dissatisfaction with their work. The media have given considerable attention to the problem—television networks and national news magazines run features regularly on work alienation in America—but the evidence suggests that the vast majority of workers are generally satisfied with their jobs. Let us look at the figures.

The most popular measure of satisfaction is to ask workers, "How satisfied would you say you are with your job?" Surveys conducted by the University of Michigan Survey Research Center, the National Opinion Research Center, and the University of California Survey Research Center covering the years 1958 through 1977 found that the percentage of workers who reported that they were satisfied with their jobs never fell below 80 percent. In 1977, 88.4 percent of the respondents said they were "very" or "somewhat" satisfied with their jobs.[3]

However, when more elaborate measures are used to measure satisfaction, the evidence indicates both a substantial decline in job satisfaction during the 1970s and the relatively frequent mention of problems concerning job content as a source of this decline.[4] Between 1969 and 1977, data indicate that there has been a pervasive decline in job satisfaction, affecting all demographic and occupational classes surveyed. While the majority of work-related problems reported by respondents in 1977 focused on such issues as inadequate pay and fringe benefits, health or safety hazards, and rigidities in work schedules, problems relating to job content received frequent mention as well. Some 36 percent reported that they had some skills from their experience and training that they would like to use but could not on their present jobs. Similarly, 37 percent reported unpleasant working conditions. Interestingly, lack of control over conditions of work was very often seen as a problem, not the conditions themselves. For example, lack of control over days worked (77 percent) was a problem more frequently than was working on days that did not suit the worker (12 percent), and lack of control over one's own job assignment (54 percent) was a more frequent problem than not being able to use one's skills in a present job assignment (36 percent). Apparently, a large segment of workers desire *control* over those job conditions that impact upon them directly.

These findings are not insignificant. While most workers seem to be

[3]U.S. Department of Labor, *Job Satisfaction: Is There a Trend?* Manpower Research Monograph, No. 30 (Washington, D.C.: Manpower Administration, 1974), p. 4; and "Many Found Less Content on Jobs," *The New York Times*, December 17, 1978, p. 1.

[4]Graham L. Staines and Robert P. Quinn, "American Workers Evaluate the Quality of Their Jobs," *Monthly Labor Review*, January 1979, pp. 3–11.

satisfied with their work, moderate or high dissatisfaction plagues at least 10 to 15 percent of the workplace. And the trend in job satisfaction is downward. Justification for QWL efforts to make work more meaningful needs to be placed in perspective. If only 10 percent of the U.S. work force is dissatisfied with their jobs, we are still talking about more than 11 million real people! If we can make a fraction of these people's jobs more meaningful through job redesign and, at the same time, produce economic benefits for the organization, we will have achieved a worthwhile end. So, while we may have no crisis on our hands, we certainly have room for improvement.

THE JOB CHARACTERISTICS MODEL

The most complete and best known framework for guiding job redesign efforts is the job characteristics model.[5] It identifies five job characteristics, their interrelationships, and their impact on employee productivity, motivation, and satisfaction. According to the model, any job can be described in terms of five core job dimensions, which are labeled and defined as follows:

> *Skill variety.* The degree to which a job requires a variety of different activities so that one can use a number of different skills and talents.
>
> *Task identity.* The degree to which a job requires completion of a whole and identifiable piece of work.
>
> *Task significance.* The degree to which a job has a substantial impact on the lives or work of other people.
>
> *Autonomy.* The degree to which a job provides substantial freedom, independence, and discretion to the individual in scheduling the work and in determining the procedures to be used in carrying it out.
>
> *Feedback.* The degree to which carrying out the work activities required by a job results in the individual's obtaining direct and clear information about the effectiveness of his or her performance.

Figure 14–1 presents the model. Notice how the first three dimensions—skill variety, task identity, and task significance—combine to create meaningful work. That is, if these three characteristics exist in a job, we can predict that the person will view his or her job as being important, valuable, and worthwhile. Notice, too, that jobs that possess autonomy give the job incumbent a feeling of personal responsibility for the results and that, if a job provides feedback, the employee will know how effectively he or she is performing. From a motivational standpoint, the model says

[5]J. Richard Hackman and Greg R. Oldham, "Development of the Job Diagnostic Survey," *Journal of Applied Psychology*, April 1975, pp. 159–170.

FIGURE 14–1 The job characteristics model

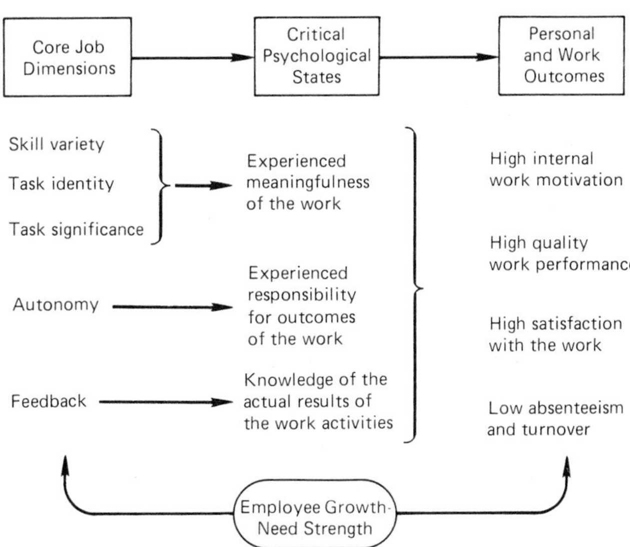

Source: J. Richard Hackman, "Work Design," in J. R. Hackman and J. L. Suttle, eds., *Improving Life at Work* (Santa Monica, Calif.: Goodyear Publishing, 1977), p. 129.

that internal rewards are obtained when one *learns* (knowledge of results) that one *personally* (experienced responsibility) has performed well on a task that one *cares about* (experienced meaningfulness).[6] The more these three conditions are present, the greater will be the employee's motivation, performance, and satisfaction and the lower his or her absenteeism and likelihood of turnover. As the model shows, the links between the job dimensions and the outcomes are moderated or adjusted for by the strength of the individual's growth need; that is, the employee's desire for self-esteem and self-actualization. This means that individuals with a high growth need are more likely to experience the psychological states when their jobs are enriched than are their low-growth-need counterparts and will respond more positively to the psychological states, when they are present, than will low-growth-need individuals.

The core job dimensions have been analyzed and combined into a single index shown in Figure 14–2. Jobs that are high on motivating potential must be high on at least one of the three factors that lead to experiencing meaningfulness, plus they must be high on both autonomy and feedback. If jobs score high on motivating potential, the model predicts

[6]J. Richard Hackman, "Work Design," in J. R. Hackman and J. L. Suttle, eds., *Improving Life at Work* (Santa Monica, Calif.: Goodyear Publishing, 1977), p. 129.

FIGURE 14–2 Computing a motivating potential score

$$\text{Motivating potential score} = \left[\frac{\text{Skill variety} + \text{Task identity} + \text{Task significance}}{3} \right] \times \text{Autonomy} \times \text{Feedback}$$

that motivation, performance, and satisfaction will be positively affected, whereas the likelihood of absence and turnover is lessened.

While the job characteristics model is still undergoing testing, the preliminary results have been supportive. Specifically,

1. People who work on jobs with high core job dimensions are more motivated, satisfied, and productive than are those who do not.
2. People with strong growth needs respond more positively to jobs that are high in motivating potential than do those with weak growth needs.
3. Job dimensions operate through the psychological states in influencing personal and work outcome variables rather than influencing them directly.[7]

As an example of the model's potential, an application of it at the Travelers Insurance Company led to some impressive results.[8] Compared with a control group, redesign changes made to make jobs high on the core job dimensions led to significant improvements in employee attitudes and work quantity as well as to decreases in error rates and absenteeism. The changes saved Travelers over $90,000 a year.

VIABLE REDESIGN OPTIONS

If we are concerned with managing job design, we need to assess our options. How can management make work more meaningful through job redesign? The following topics represent the more viable options.

Job Rotation

Job rotation allows workers increased skill variety by permitting them to shift jobs periodically. When an activity is no longer challenging, the employee would be rotated to another job, at the same level, that has similar skill requirements. The shifts can include as few as two people, the rotation being merely an exchange of jobs. However, the organization can provide much more elaborate rotation designs where a dozen or more employees

[7]Ibid., pp. 132–133.

[8]J. Richard Hackman, G. R. Oldham, R. Janson, and K. Purdy, "A New Strategy for Job Enrichment," *California Management Review*, Summer 1975, pp. 57–71.

are involved. That case would describe, for instance, the practices in the headquarters of some of the largest U.S. banks. Bright, young college graduates are hired with the idea that in three or four years they will be able to assume managerial positions in the bank. Their training consists of spending four to six months in all the key areas of the bank—operations, lending, trusts, and so forth. At about the time they have gained a reasonable understanding of an activity, they are rotated to a new area.

The strength of job rotation is that it reduces boredom through diversifying the employee's activities. Of course, it can also have indirect benefits for the organization since employees with a wider range of skills give management more flexibility in scheduling work, adapting to changes, and filling vacancies. The drawbacks to job rotation center on costs, disruptions, and its rather limited impact on enhancing job meaningfulness. Shifting people around has costs. Even though the same skill levels are assumed, productivity is typically adversely affected in the short term. The efficiencies derived through experience, much of which are lost as a result of job rotation, can be substantial. Job rotations also create disruptions. Members of the work group have to adjust to the new employee. The supervisor may also have to spend more time answering questions and monitoring the work of the recently rotated employee. Finally, rotation is a weak solution to jobs that score low on motivating potential. Since job rotation does not really change the job, merely the job-employee mix, the employee is unlikely to have experienced greater meaningfulness from his or her work by having done four boring jobs during a given year instead of one.

Work Modules

If you can conceive of extremely rapid job rotation, to the point where one would assume new activities every few hours, you can comprehend the technique of work modules. It has been suggested as a solution to meet the problem of fractionated, boring, and programmed work, at an acceptable price, with undiminished quality and quantity of product.[9]

Robert Kahn, of the University of Michigan, has defined a work module as a time-task unit equal to approximately two hours of work at a given task. A normal forty-hour-a-week job would then be defined in terms of four modules a day, five days a week, for between forty-eight and fifty weeks a year.

Through the use of modules, it is possible to increase work diversity and give employees a greater opportunity to determine the nature of their jobs. Employees could request a set of modules that together would constitute a day's work. Additionally, those tasks that are seen as undesirable

[9]Robert L. Kahn, "The Work Module," *Psychology Today*, February 1973, pp. 35–39.

could be spread about, for example, by having everyone take a module or two each day. The result would be that people would change activities through changing work modules.

The benefits of work modules include letting employees pick their work tasks, thus taking into account individual job preferences. Further, it provides a way for the more boring and undesirable tasks to get completed without totally demoralizing those who must do them. Finally, since employees would be allowed some say in the choice of modules, the job would be constructed to meet the needs of the individual rather than to force people to fit a particularly defined job.

However, work modules would present the same cost and disruption obstacles as job rotation. Considerable time and money are involved in planning and executing the changeover. Bookkeeping and payroll computation costs increase. Conflicts can also develop over the question of equity and allocation of modules.

Have any organizations tried work modules? If there are, they have received no notoriety. The closest approximation with which your author is familiar is the practice in some firms of allowing workers in a specific group of jobs to trade activities each day after lunch. But these are isolated practices representing fewer than one hundred employees in corporations that employ tens of thousands.

Job Enlargement

When a job is expanded horizontally, we use the term job enlargement to describe the process of adding related tasks. The effect of enlargement is to give increased skill variety and more meaningful task identity to the worker by adding similar tasks to an existing job. For instance, at one oil company, the clerks who processed the credit-card applications had been separate from the person who took phone calls from people inquiring as to the status of their application. Management decided to enlarge the jobs of the processing clerks by having the switchboard operator direct inquiries to the appropriate clerk based on the caller's last name (one processor handled A to C, another D to F, and so forth).

When a job is enlarged so that one employee performs an entire task cycle, as when an assembly-line worker puts together a complete unit independently, enlargement also provides feedback on performance. But enlargement, like job rotation and work modules, is still an inadequate response to work that inherently lacks meaning. As one worker so eloquently commented, "Before I had one lousy job. Now, through enlargement, I have three lousy jobs." What is needed is a redesign option that expands a job vertically and gives the employee more say and control over what he or she does. Such an approach is job enrichment.

Job Enrichment

The technique that has received the widest attention in the search to improve the quality of work life is job enrichment.[10] As we shall see, in contrast to the previous redesign concepts, enrichment fulfills almost all the requirements for high motivation potential in the job characteristics model.

A job is enriched by allowing the worker to assume some of the tasks executed by his or her supervisor. Enriched jobs are expanded vertically so that the employee takes on additional responsibility to plan, execute, and inspect that work. If a job is enriched successfully, in addition to increasing responsibility, it should also increase the employee's freedom and independence, organize tasks so as to allow workers to do a complete activity, and provide feedback so that individuals will be able to correct their own performances.

A successful job enrichment program should increase employee satisfaction. But, since organizations do not exist to create employee satisfaction as an end, there must also be direct benefits to the organization. There is evidence that job enrichment produces lower absenteeism and reduced turnover costs, but on the critical issue of productivity, the evidence is inconclusive. In some situations, job enrichment has increased productivity; in others, productivity has decreased. However, when it decreases, there appears to be consistently conscientious use of resources and a higher quality of product or service. In other words, in terms of efficiency, for the same input a higher quality of output is obtained.

To get a better idea of an enriched job, we review a job enrichment experiment at the Buick division of General Motors.[11]

The Buick Product Engineering group decided in the early 1970s to analyze the job of assembler for enriching. An assembler is a skilled hourly mechanic, responsible for performing experimental changes in fleet cars as ordered by the design engineers and for keeping the fleet cars in top operating condition. The Product Engineering Group employed forty-five assemblers.

The assemblers' content of daily tasks was restructured and redefined, but the job description itself was not changed. Job modifications included such things as allowing the assembler to

[10]See, for example, F. Herzberg, B. Mausner, and B. Snyderman, *The Motivation to Work* (New York: John Wiley, 1959); Louis E. Davis, *Design of Jobs* (London: Penguin, 1972); and R. N. Ford, *Motivation Through the Work Itself* (New York: American Management Association, 1969).

[11]F. J. Schotters, "Job Enrichment at Buick Products Engineering," *GM Personnel Development Bulletin,* no. 22, June 4, 1973.

Correct any deficiencies discovered and to record the action on a work sheet (this job modification was selected as the most practical for initial introduction).

Choose own work assignment.

Contact the design engineer directly.

Inspect own work.

Establish own completion dates and job-hour content.

Presentations concerning the proposed job restructuring were made to departmental management, the design engineers, and the union. An informal approach was used to introduce the program to the assemblers. Each supervisor handled implementation according to his assessment of the best way in which to approach the employees. He determined the feelings in his own group and in most cases introduced additional job modifications on a one-to-one basis. Acceptance of the project was fostered by the assemblers themselves, who often "sold" the program to each other through informal discussions.

One way for each supervisor to track project progress was by recording the reactions from the assemblers. In some cases implementation of the job modifications was too fast and negative feedback occurred: "How come I have to write these tickets? Did they take all the pencils away from the engineers?"

During the early stages of the program, some design engineers also expressed objections to the redefined duties. However, as communication between assemblers and design engineers improved and as additional phases of job restructuring were introduced, most difficulties were worked out through face-to-face discussion.

This interpersonal approach prevented the program from becoming a "management directive" and resulted in management credibility and in employee acceptance of the project.

Since implementation of the job enrichment program, the following changes have been observed by Product Engineering supervision:

Productivity has increased nearly 13 percent (as measured by increased work tickets per assembler per month).

Petty grievances (where no discipline is assessed) have been virtually eliminated.

Fleet cars are kept in better mechanical condition because assemblers have shown initiative in discovering and repairing such discrepancies as rattles, steering gear whine, defective exhaust systems, and engine starting problems.

Departmental morale has improved considerably, along with increased pride and interest in the work.

Communication and personal relationships between and among assemblers, supervisors, and design engineers have increased and improved. (Assemblers now call or visit engineers to discuss projects personally.)

Integrated Work Teams

If job enlargement is practiced at the group rather than at the individual level, integrated work teams result. For jobs that require teamwork and cooperation, this approach can increase diversity for team members.

What would an integrated work team look like? Basically, instead of performing a single task, a large number of tasks would be assigned to a group. The group then would decide the specific assignments of members and be responsible for rotating jobs among the members as the tasks required. The team would still have a supervisor who would oversee the group's activities. You see the frequent use of integrated work teams in such activities as in building maintenance and construction. In the cleaning of a sizable office building, it is not unusual for the supervisor to identify the tasks to be completed and then let the maintenance workers, as a group, choose how the tasks will be allocated. Similarly, a road construction crew frequently decides, as a group, how its various tasks are to be completed.

Autonomous Work Teams

Autonomous work teams represent job enrichment at the group level. The work that the team does is deepened through vertical integration. The team is given a goal to achieve and then is free to determine work assignments, rest breaks, inspection procedures, and the like. Fully autonomous work teams even select their own members and have the members evaluate each other's performance. As a result, supervisory positions take on decreased importance and may even be eliminated. The autonomous work team concept has been applied at a General Foods pet food plant in Topeka, Kansas, and a plant of Shaklee Corp. in Norman, Oklahoma, that manufactures health powders and pills.

The Topeka pet food plant was built in 1971, especially to accommodate the autonomous work team concept.[12] Teams have from seven to fourteen members and hold collective responsibility for large segments of the production process. The team's responsibilities include the traditional functional departmentation in a plant: maintenance, quality control, industrial engineering, and personnel. For instance, teams do their own screening of applicants to locate replacements that are qualified and who

[12]Richard E. Walton, "From Hawthorne to Topeka and Kalmar," in E. L. Cass and F. G. Zimmer, eds., *Man and Work in Society* (New York: Van Nostrand Reinhold, 1975), pp. 118–119.

will fit into the teams. Workers make job assignments, schedule coffee breaks, and even decide team members' pay raises.

A unique feature at the Topeka plant is the absence of job classification grades. All operators have a single classification and earn pay increases based on their ability to master an increasing number of jobs. No limits are placed on how many team members can qualify for the higher pay brackets, thus encouraging employees to teach each other their jobs.

When the experiment began, team leaders were appointed to facilitate team development and decision making. However, after several years, the teams became so effective at managing themselves that the team leader positions were being eliminated.

What impact did this work environment have on the employees' and the plant's performance? Several years following its introduction, employees were generally praising the variety, dignity, and influence that they enjoyed; and they liked the team spirit, open communication, and opportunities to expand their mastery of job skills. While the experiment was not without detractors, it was generally believed that the work system as a whole was better than any other they knew about. From the management side, the plant operated with 35 percent fewer employees than did similar plants organized along traditional lines. Additionally, the experiment resulted in higher output, lower waste, absence of shutdowns, lower absenteeism, and lower turnover.

Shaklee Corp. adopted a similiar job design format in 1979 at its Oklahoma plant that produces nutritional products, vitamins, and other pills.[13] About 190 of the plant's production employees were organized into teams with three to fifteen members. As with the Topeka operation, the team members set their own production schedules, decide what hours to work, select new team members from a pool approved by the personnel department, and even initiate discharges if necessary. The results have been impressive. The company reports that units per labor-hour are up nearly 200 percent over those of other plants, two-thirds of which they attribute to the autonomous work team concept (the rest is explained by better equipment). Management states that the Oklahoma plant can produce the same volume as their more traditional facilities but at 40 percent of the labor costs.

Quality Circles

The most recent addition to job redesign alternatives has been the quality circle. Originally begun in the United States and exported to Japan in the 1950s, it has recently been imported back to the United States.[14] The quality

[13]"The New Industrial Relations," *Business Week,* May 11, 1981, p. 96.

[14]Ibid., p. 86.

circle concept, in fact, is often mentioned as one of the techniques that Japanese firms utilize that has allowed them to make better quality products at lower costs than their American counterparts. To get an idea of the quality circle's popularity in Japan, one expert estimates that approximately one out of every nine Japanese workers is involved in a quality circle.[15]

What is a quality circle? It is a voluntary group of workers, primarily a normal work crew, who have a shared area of responsibility.[16] They meet together weekly, on company time and on company premises, to discuss their quality problems, investigate causes, recommend solutions, and take corrective actions. They take responsibility for solving quality problems, and they generate and evaluate their own feedback. Of course, it is not presumed that employees inherently have this ability. Therefore, part of the quality circle concept includes teaching participating employees group communication skills, various quality strategies, and measurement and problem-analysis techniques.

Quality circles are expanding rapidly in the United States, in large and small companies alike. In the fall of 1981, about 1,000 organizations were using them, up from about 150 a year earlier.[17] Honeywell, Inc., for instance, has 350 quality circles involving about 4,000 employees.[18] Hughes Aircraft attributes quality circles for saving $45,000 a year from reduction of defects and another $48,000 from redesign suggestions made by a quality circle group.[19]

The quality circle integrates job redesign with the behavioral idea of extensive employee participation. In terms of the job characteristics model, the concept increases skill variety, task identity, autonomy, and feedback.

Summary

Table 14–1 summarizes the redesign options we have discussed in terms of their ability to meet the criteria identified in the job characteristics model.

All the concepts increase skill variety. Whether they increase task significance is difficult to say without knowing more about the work content in question. Table 14–1 indicates that job enrichment, autonomous work teams, and quality circles are significantly superior to the other options *in terms of the job characteristics model.* Of course, management may decide to redesign jobs in addition to increasing their motivation potential for other reasons; and there is nothing in Table 14–1 to indicate cost-benefit consid-

[15] "A Quality Concept Catches on Worldwide," *Industry Week,* April 16, 1979, p. 125.

[16] Ed Yager, "Quality Circle: A Tool for the '80's," *Training and Development Journal,* August 1980, p. 62.

[17] *The Wall Street Journal,* September 22, 1981, p. 25.

[18] "The New Industrial Relations," *Business Week,* p. 92.

[19] "A Quality Concept Catches on Worldwide," p. 125.

TABLE 14–1 Job characteristics provided by various job redesign concepts

	SKILL VARIETY	*TASK IDENTITY*	*TASK SIGNIFICANCE*	*AUTONOMY*	*FEEDBACK*
Job rotation	X		?		
Work modules	X		?	X	
Job enlargement	X		?		
Job enrichment	X	X	?	X	X
Integrated work teams	X		?		
Autonomous work teams	X	X	?	X	X
Quality circles	X	X	?	X	X

erations. The various options we have proposed differ significantly in their implementation costs. Obviously, autonomous work teams must generate considerably more benefits than job rotation if they are to justify the greater time, effort, and cost to implement them.

DON'T FORGET INDIVIDUAL DIFFERENCES!

No job design is ideal for every person. Any effort at redesign, therefore, must take into account individual differences. Efforts toward integrating this reality into job redesign is evident in the job characteristics model—it states explicitly that the impact of the core job dimensions on personal and work outcomes is moderated by employee growth-need strength. The greater this need, the more likely the employee will obtain meaningfulness and the other psychological states when the core job dimensions are present.

There tends to be consistent evidence that higher-order need strength is an important individual difference that predicts success of job redesign programs. However, a number of other individual difference factors may also suggest when redesign efforts will be successful.[20] The age of the employees should be considered. Younger workers tend to accept change more readily. Older employees tend to prefer more repetitive jobs because they have made the adjustment to them and know how to do them well. Education may also be relevant. Generally, the higher the employees' ed-

[20]See, for example, J. Richard Hackman and E. E. Lawler, III, "Employee Reactions to Job Charcteristics," *Journal of Applied Psychology*, April 1971, pp. 259–286; John P. Wanous, "Individual Differences and Reactions to Job Characteristics," *Journal of Applied Psychology*, October 1974, pp. 616–622; and Arthur P. Brief and Raymon J. Aldag, "Employee Reactions to Job Characteristics: A Constructuve Replication," *Journal of Applied Psychology*, April 1975, pp. 182–186.

ucation, the greater the preference for autonomous and challenging jobs. Similarly, self-assurance has shown success as a moderator. The greater the self-confidence, the greater assurance the employee has that he or she can learn more exacting tasks. Individuals who favor the Protestant work ethic—hard work, efficient time utilization, assumption of responsibility—can also be expected to accept QWL redesign options more readily.

Although often overlooked by the zealous advocates of QWL, some workers are actually happier with repetitive, monotonous, and boring jobs. When given the opportunity to assume a job with demanding and rewarding tasks, some workers will opt to remain in their highly repetitive and low-skill jobs. Are they weird or abnormal? No! They merely do not have strong needs for growth and autonomy or have chosen to satisfy their needs off the job. Many workers look to their jobs as providing the *means* to allow them to do more gratifying activities outside the work context. To ignore this diversity in the work force is foolhardy. Efforts to redesign everyone's job in an organization to improve its motivation potential—where employees experience the work as inherently meaningful, feel personal responsibility for the outcomes of the work, and receive consistent feedback about the results of their work activities—will undoubtedly lead to making some people less happy and less productive.

THE FUTURE OF JOB REDESIGN

An appropriate conclusion to this chapter is to ask: What is the likelihood that job redesign ideas, such as those we've discussed, will be widely implemented in organizations? One author has considered this question carefully.[21]

When the topic of quality of work life arises, individuals tend to make one of two diverse assumptions. The first holds that many employees are presently underutilized and unchallenged at work. Proponents of this assumption are not saying necessarily that this is even the majority of employees. Rather, there are simply millions—maybe tens of millions—of workers whose jobs are neither challenging nor a personally fulfilling part of their lives. The second assumption proposes that people are much more adaptable than we often assume. Regardless of the setbacks in our lives, the vast majority of us survive. How? We adapt. Otherwise, we would face constant feelings of distress and dissatisfaction. This adaption capability also applies to work. When faced with challenging tasks or dull ones, we tend to make the best of them.

Each of these assumptions leads to different directions in job design. The first—call it route 1—should lead to fitting jobs to people. Management

[21]This section has been adapted from J. Richard Hackman, "The Design of Work in the 1980's," *Organizational Dynamics*, Summer 1978, pp. 3–17.

would make jobs more meaningful. Employees would be given increased discretion and control over their work tasks. Jobs would be designed so as to inherently motivate job incumbents. Job enrichment and autonomous work teams would be logical design choices. The second direction—call it route 2—should reassert scientific management's goal to fit people to jobs. Specialization would be emphasized. Decisions over what is to be done and how it is to be done would clearly reside with management. Control would come from above as management closely monitored employee actions. Since jobs themselves would have little in the way of intrinsic motivation properties, extrinsic rewards such as money, fringe benefits, and security would be emphasized.

Does the future lie with route 1 or route 2? Regardless of one's personal preference, evidence indicates that route 2 will undoubtedly win out. Why? There are a number of factors that lean in route 2's favor.[22]

First, managers tend to go with what they know. They know how to operate according to route 2 rules and feel comfortable traveling its path. Second, route 2 solutions fit nicely with the traditional bureaucratic hierarchy. Third, route 2 is the least threat to those in power. It maintains managerial control. Finally, route 1 is an enigma and a threat to union leaders. It is seen typically as diminishing the appeal of unionism. In unionized organizations, therefore, the unions themselves will represent a force pushing for route 2.

SUMMARY

Job design, up until thirty years or so ago, was basically concerned with increasing efficiency through specialization. Attention in recent years has been focused on making jobs less routine and more meaningful for workers. This attention is justified by the statistics that support that millions of employees are dissatisfied with their jobs.

The job characteristics model provides a guideline for job redesign. Specifically, it proposes to identify those core job dimensions that impact on employee productivity, motivation, and satisfaction. Job redesign options should be held up against this model in the assessment of their effectiveness.

Viable job redesign options include job rotation, work modules, job enlargement, job enrichment, integrated work teams, autonomous work teams, and quality circles. In terms of the job characteristics model, job enrichment, autonomous work teams, and quality circles are preferred.

Efforts at job design should not be implemented without considering individual differences among employees. Not *all* employees want chal-

[22]Ibid.; and George W. Bohlander, "Implementing Quality-of-Work Programs: Recognizing the Barriers," *MSU Business Topics*, Spring 1979, pp. 33–40.

lenging, meaningful jobs. An individual's growth need, age, education, level of self-assurance, and Protestant work ethic attitude all moderate the impact of design changes on employee attitudes and behavior.

The future of job redesign suggests people will be fitted to jobs rather than the other way around.

FOR REVIEW AND DISCUSSION

1. What is QWL?
2. If only 10 to 15 percent of the work force is dissatisfied with their work, why does the media give this issue so much attention?
3. What is the job characteristics model?
4. To score high on motivating potential, why must a job have both autonomy and feedback?
5. "Employees should have jobs that give them autonomy and diversity." Build an argument to support this statement. Then build an argument to refute this statement.
6. What is job enrichment? Compare it with job enlargement.
7. Which of the core job dimensions do you value most? Do you think that most of your friends or parents and grandparents would give a similar answer?
8. Do you think that in twenty years most jobs will score high on motivating potential? Discuss.
9. Why would you expect union leaders to be more supportive of route 2 than route 1?
10. "Employees who perform routine, repetitive tasks typically have little power in the organization. Assuming that these employees have a high growth need strength, their low job performance may be the result of their powerlessness rather than of the inherent characteristics of their jobs." Do you agree or disagree? Discuss.

CHAPTER

15

MANAGING CHANGE

It is taken as a truism among organization theorists that organizations are not fixed, static entities. The following quotation is representative of the reigning viewpoint held by organization theorists toward change:

> One of the major tasks facing institutions today is adaptability to change. Political, business, military, and educational organizations are continually faced with highly dynamic and interdependent situtations. It is the responsibility of management within these organizations to deal with complex conditions while improving organizational effectiveness.[1]

This sensitivity to change and arguing for its importance should come as no surprise to you. Our previous review of the literature on strategy, technology, environment, adhocracy—to take the more obvious cases—made constant reference to change. Strategies that entailed a great deal of change had different implications on structure than did those that were essentially stable. Nonroutine technologies entail more change than do routine ones, and, to ensure effectiveness, the nonroutine type requires a more flexible structure. Similarly, organizations facing rapidly changing environments will look for flexibility in their structures. Adhocracy was introduced as the model most compatible with change. Change demands

[1]Sam E. White and Terence R. Mitchell, "Organizational Development: A Review of Research Content and Research Design," *Academy of Management Review,* April 1976, p. 57.

flexibility, innovation, and rapid responsiveness. Organizations facing a high degree of change, it was argued, will be most effective with an adhocratic structure or at least a structure with a number of adhocracy's primary characteristics.

This chapter looks at what managers can do to actively facilitate change. We begin by defining "managing change," present evidence on the pervasiveness of resistance to change, introduce an organizational change model, and proceed to elaborate on the various steps in the model. The chapter concludes with a counterargument to the "change is inevitable" position. There is a small but growing set of theorists who propose that change is *not* inevitable. In fact, they argue provocatively that there are processes in organizations that make change highly unlikely. But we shouldn't get the cart before the horse. Before we review the argument that attacks the traditional view of change in organizations, we need to present that traditional view.

WHAT DO WE MEAN BY "MANAGING CHANGE"?

Change can "just happen" or it can be "planned." Change that is managed is change that we call planned.

Planned Change

The objective of planned change is to keep the organization current and viable. As long as organizations confront change—current products and services reach maturity in their life cycles and become obsolete, competitors introduce new products or services, government regulations and tax policies affecting the organization are changed, important sources of supply go out of business, a previously nonunionized labor force votes for union representation—the organization either responds or accepts the inevitable decline in effectiveness. Organizations that persist in keeping "their heads in the sand" eventually find themselves running going-out-of-business sales, in bankruptcy courts, or just phasing out of the scene. Firms such as W. T. Grant and Railway Express were billion-dollar corporations that were thriving in the 1950s and 1960s, but, because they failed to respond to a changing environment, they closed their doors forever in the late 1970s. In the 1980s, the same fate may befall Chrysler Corporation; many homebuilders, savings and loan associations, and airlines; and a large number of small private colleges that are unable to survive in a declining market. Because organizations are open systems—dependent on their environments—and because the environment does not stand still, organizations must develop internal mechanisms to facilitate planned change.

Structural Change

There are different types of change that management seeks to create. The type of change depends on the target. At the individual level, managers attempt to affect an employee's behavior. Training, socialization, and counseling represent examples of change strategies that organizations use when the target of change is the individual. Similarly, management may use interventions such as sensitivity training, survey feedback, and process consultation when the goal is to change group behavior. Individual and group change, which is typically studied in organizational behavior courses under the heading of "organizational development," is outside the province of this text. Our concern is with structural change. In this chapter, we focus on techniques that impact on the organization's structural system. This means that we will be looking at changing authority patterns, access to information, allocation of rewards, technology, and the like. Of course, because behavioral change considerations are avoided purposely should in no way diminish their importance. Managers can and should use behavioral techniques to bring about change along with structural techniques. Together, the two represent a complete "tool kit" for managing change. However, in this text we concern ourselves solely with the structural side.[2]

Organizations Are Conservative and Resist Change

Organizations, by their very nature, are conservative.[3] They actively resist change. You don't have to look far for confirming evidence. Government agencies want to continue doing what they have been doing for years, whether the need for their service changes or remains the same. Organized religions are deeply entrenched in their history. Attempts to change church doctrine require great persistence and patience. Educational institutions, which exist to open minds and challenge doctrinaire, are themselves extremely resistant to change. Most school systems are using the same teaching technology today as they were thirty years ago. Predictions in the middle 1960s that electronic teaching machines and computers would totally revolutionize the classroom and dramatically change the role of the teacher by the late 1970s never materialized. Further evidence of organizational resistance to change was seen in the Democratic Party's attempt, in 1981, to adjust to its resounding defeat at the polls in November 1980.

[2]For readers interested in behavioral change techniques, see Stephen P. Robbins, *Organizational Behavior: Concepts, Controversies, and Applications*, 2nd ed. (Englewood Cliffs, N.J.: Prentice-Hall, 1983), pp. 481–89.

[3]Richard H. Hall, *Organizations: Structure and Process*, 2nd ed. (Englewood Cliffs, N.J.: Prentice-Hall, 1977), p. 346.

The party and its leadership were strongly committed to liberal positions, yet faced an American public that apparently had shifted its political allegiance to the right. A hundred years of liberal thinking cannot be thrown out the window and replaced by a "new, improved, conservative Democratic Party." The success of the Democrats at the polls in future elections will depend more on the public's political tastes moving back to the left than on the party's undergoing a significant change in its philosophical position. Finally, in support of our case, we offer the consistent difficulty that American industries have had in adapting to change. The railroads, steel companies, and automobile manufacturers in the United States represent very visible examples of organizations that resisted changes introduced from outside—new forms of competition, lower labor costs in foreign countries, changes in consumer tastes, rapid increases in the price of gasoline.

Why do organizations resist change? Certainly, there are a number of contributors to resistance, but a large part of the explanation lies in the people who make up organizations. These people resist change as a response to real and imagined threats to their self-interests.

Any change can be an actual threat to a member or group's power, prestige, or security. The greater the threat, the greater the resistance. One way in which to envision this is to think in terms of a member's investment. The more investment one has in the status quo, the greater is the threat of change. For instance, why do older people tend to resist change more than younger ones? Because older people have generally invested more in the current system and, therefore, have more to lose by adapting to a change. If you have spent twenty years of your adult life as a mail sorter with the post office, you can be expected to resist automatic mail sorters more vigorously than a recent high school graduate who has been performing the job for only six months. Having invested relatively little time and effort in developing his skills as a mail sorter, the latter has little vested interest in the old system and is less threatened by automation.

A threat need not be real to create resistance. If management reassures the accounting department that the new computer system will not reduce the size of its staff or the importance of its function, even if management is correct in its appraisal, resistance can still arise as a result of a perceived threat. Misunderstandings due to lack of information or inaccurate information, lack of trust in what management says, and different assessments of the same set of data can all lead to increased employee resistance.

These considerations should not be interpreted as applying only to nonmanagerial employees. Managers are interested in protecting their self-interests as much, or maybe more so, than are operative employees. Many a change effort has been sabotaged by a manager who perceived that a disturbance of the status quo would result in negative consequences for his or her unit or career path.

The traditional position is that "organizations can and do change."[4] We discuss in the following sections various mechanisms that can help to facilitate that change. But the purpose of this section has been to acknowledge that there are forces that will attempt to inhibit change efforts. These forces include members of the organization who are threatened by the change. The regimentation and standardization within the system, too, make change more difficult. As you will learn later in this chapter, the more entrenched the procedures and regulations governing the way things should be done, the more difficult it is to introduce changes in those patterns.

A MODEL FOR PLANNED ORGANIZATIONAL CHANGE

Figure 15–1 represents a model for organizational change. It can be broken down into a set of steps. Planned change is initiated by certain forces. These forces are acted upon by a change agent. Depending on the forces instigating change and the change agent's perception of his or her role, the change agent selects an intervention strategy. Implementation of the strategy contains two parts: *what* is done and *how* it is done. The *what* requires three phases: unfreezing the status quo, making the change, and institutionalizing the change through refreezing. The *how* refers to the way in which the agent chooses to operationalize the change process. The change itself, if successful, improves organizational effectiveness. Of course, changes do not take place in a vacuum. A change in one area of the organization is likely to initiate new forces for other changes. The feedback loop in Figure 15–1 acknowledges that this model is dynamic. The need for change is both inevitable and continual.

FIGURE 15–1 Model for planned organizational change

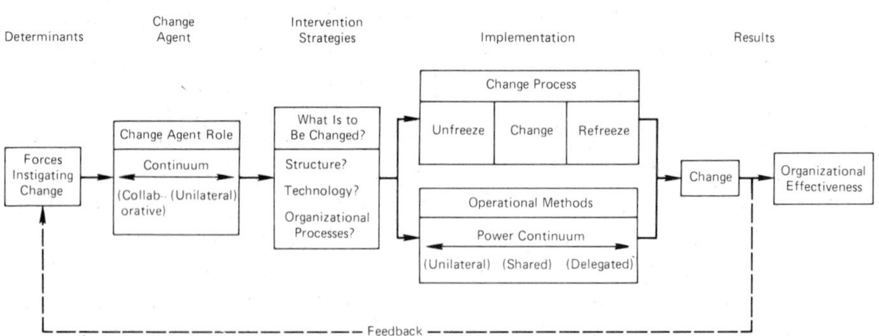

Source: Adapted from Larry E. Short; "Planned Organizational Change," *MSU Business Topics*, Autumn 1973, p. 56.

[4]Ibid., p. 349.

Determinants of Change

How does an organization know that change is necessary? It may be the identification of an opportunity upon which management wants to capitalize. More often, however, it is in anticipation of, or in reaction to, a problem. These opportunities and problems may exist inside the organization, outside the organization, or both.

The factors capable of initiating structural change are countless. While it is tempting to create several categories in which most of the factors can fall neatly, such efforts dramatize quickly that the impetus for change can come from anywhere. A more meaningful approach is just to list a number of the more visible reasons for an organization's considering a change in its structure.

1. *Change in objectives.* When an organization's objectives or mission change, its structure will typically be redesigned too. This is consistent with the strategic imperative discussed in Chapter 6. For instance, if an organization chooses to move from being an innovator to being a follower, its structure will likely become more mechanistic: the technology should become more standardized and the need to monitor the environment, through boundary-spanning roles, should increase.

2. *Purchase of new equipment.* The purchase of new equipment, when it is used in activities done previously by human labor, makes the organization more capital intensive. When this happens, specialization tends to be replaced by standardization. When the major U.S. automobile companies, in the mid-1970s, began significantly increasing the number of robots on the assembly line, technology changed and so did structure. For instance, fewer supervisors were needed to get the same output because an increased number of activities were now being done by mechanical devices.

3. *Scarcity of labor.* When an important skill that the organization depends upon is scarce, structural change frequently occurs. During World War II, Henry Kaiser was able to build warships without the traditional shipwrights (who were off fighting the war) by training women to do very small and simple segments of the jobs that the skilled craftsmen did. Many more employees were necessary, the technology was dramatically different, and so too was the structure. Complexity, formalization, and centralization all increased. In more recent years, the shortage of tax lawyers, systems analysts, and the like has forced managers to make the structures in which these individuals work more organic. The tight labor market increased the power of many of these employees to negotiate a greater voice in decision making, less direct supervision, and fewer rules and regulations to follow.

4. *Implementation of a sophisticated information processing system.* When organizations introduce sophisticated information processing, the centralization dimension of structure is typically altered. As noted in earlier chapters, improved information processing allows top management to decentralize authority yet at the same time maintain control.

5. *New government regulations.* An obvious impetus to structural change is new government regulations. An excellent example of this was the creation by firms of affirmative action offices in response to Equal Employment Opportunity legislation. Similarly, the passages of the Occupational Safety and Health Act in 1970 resulted in many firms' creating a new management position to coordinate health and safety programs within the organization, whereas others increased the importance of the position by giving it higher rank in the hierarchy. In some cases, the position was given vice presidential status, all as a result of OSHA legislation.

6. *Unionization.* Obviously, when an organization's employees become unionized, structural modifications become necessary. If the organization is dispersed geographically, with plants and offices throughout the country, unionization could be expected to result in the centralization of labor relations activity. This allows for the effective coordination of plant and office labor problems and negotiation of companywide collective bargaining agreements.

7. *Increased pressures from consumer advocate groups.* As consumer groups have organized and increased their power, many of those organizations that confront these groups have changed their structure to respond more appropriately. Examples include the creation or expansion of the public relations department and the upgrading in authority of personnel in the quality-control function.

8. *Mergers or acquisitions.* No major merger or acquisition can take place without reorganization. Duplicate functions must be eliminated. New coordinating positions must be created. Many of the structural effects due to increases in size can be expected when companies merge with others or grow through acquisition.

9. *Rapid changes in price or availability of raw materials.* When there is instability in the flow of inputs, management can be expected to introduce structural changes to reduce the effect of the instability. A large homebuilder, when confronted with major fluctuations in the price of lumber, may add one or more persons whose job it is to forecast price patterns, recommend when to make purchases, and suggest how much the inventories should be allowed to expand. This type of environment is also likely

to create changes in the purchasing function, possibly resulting in an increase in staff or recognition of purchasing's increased importance by promoting the senior purchasing executive to vice presidential status.

10. *Actions of competitors.* One southern company found itself with increased competition in its traditional urban markets. The company chose to change its marketing strategy to emphasize the penetration of rural markets. This change, however, would dramatically increase the company's cost of maintaining its sales staff. To generate the same amount of sales, more personnel would be necessary and the cost of supporting each salesperson on the road was estimated to be approximately 40 percent higher than when the sales personnel were concentrated in urban areas. The company decided to eliminate its own sales staff and rely on jobbers and distributors to call on its clients. The commissions paid to these jobbers and distributors amounted to less than half the cost of supporting a company-based sales staff. In this case, an action of a competitor initiated changes in strategy and structure.

11. *Decline in morale.* We have seen a number of instances, in this text, in which structural modifications were suggested as ways in which to deal with morale problems. It was most evident, for instance, when dealing with professionals. These individuals were depicted as preferring jobs that were low in formalization and low in horizontal differentiation and allowed for considerable decision-making discretion. Changes in structure—such as making the organization more organic—may be a way for management to reverse a decline in morale. Similarly, a redesign of jobs following the job characteristics model might improve morale. Consistent with structural redesign being a solution to morale problems, we see companies that have created the position of ombudsman to arbitrate employees' grievances and others that have introduced job enrichment.

12. *Increase in turnover.* An unsatisfactory level of employee turnover can also initiate structural changes. If an organization is losing employees that are good performers and who are difficult to replace, management frequently turns to structure for the solution. Job redesign may be an answer. Possibly the reward system needs to be modified. Wages and salaries may be too low. The creation of a performance-based incentive plan might prove to be an effective solution.

13. *Sudden internal or external hostility.* It has been mentioned in several chapters that a temporary crisis is typically met by a temporary structural change. Management tends to centralize in times of crisis and complex structures suddenly become simple.

14. *Insufficient supply of internal executive candidates.* When organizations find that their current structure is not providing an adequate supply of candidates to fill future executive positions, major structural changes may be imminent. As noted in Chapter 13, certain structures, such as the divisional and sector forms, offer extremely good training for future chief executives. An organization that is faced with a shortage of individuals with the ability to assume the top management slot may decide to "grow its own" by choosing to redesign its structure and creating "little" companies within the company.

15. *Decline in profits.* When a corporation's profits drop off, management frequently resorts to a structural shake-up. Not only will personnel be shuffled and replaced, but frequently the structure itself will be changed to bolster weak performance areas in the firm. Departments are typically added and deleted, new authority relationships defined, and decision-making patterns significantly altered. When Burroughs Corp., the computer manufacturer, was financially troubled in the early 1980s, its chairman launched a massive reorganization to decentralize its marketing and product development operations. Over half the company's four hundred eligible executives took early retirement, and nearly a quarter of its officers resigned or retired.[5]

As noted, this listing is far from comprehensive. The seeds of structural change can come from an unlimited set of sources. But there should be no doubt in your mind that changes in strategy, size, technology, environment, or power can be the source of structural change.

The Change Agent

Who makes structural changes? The change agents! But who are *they?* Those in power and those who wish either to replace or constrain those in power.[6] Occasionally, they are even outside consultants brought in by those in power to advise, oversee, or directly initiate the change.

Figure 15–1 depicts the change agent as the intermediary between the forces instigating change and the choice of an intervention strategy. He is important for who he is and what interests he represents. He is also important in that he selects the role that other employees will play in choosing the intervention strategy.

As our discussions of organizational effectiveness and the power-control perspective demonstrated, decision making in organizations is *not*

[5] "Will a Shake-up Revive Burroughs?" *Business Week,* May 4, 1981, p. 53.

[6] Daniel Katz and Robert L. Kahn, *The Social Psychology of Organizations,* 2nd ed. (New York: John Wiley, 1978), p. 679.

value free. You should expect, therefore, that every change agent will bring along his or her own self-interests. What one manager considers a situation "in need of change" may be fully within the acceptable range for another. It is not unusual for employees in any given function to politick actively for someone from their area to be selected for the organization's top spot. If successful, they can typically expect favored treatment. A CEO who rose through the ranks of the marketing staff can be expected to be more receptive to marketing's problems. He is also more likely to recognize marketing's contribution to the organization's effectiveness. As long as effectiveness is appraised in terms of who is doing the evaluating, the background and interests of the change agent are critical to the determination of what is perceived as a condition in need of change.

The change agent also is in the position of choosing the role he will play. He may "view his role as boss with absolute authority and responsibility for making and implementing decisions or as a partnership collaborating jointly with other employees in deciding on solutions to problems."[7]

Intervention Strategies

The term "intervention strategies" is used to describe *what* is to be changed. Strategies tend to fall into one of four categories: people, structure, technology, and organizational processes. Since we are concerned with structural issues in this volume, rather than with behavior, we can omit from our discussion the topic of changing people.

Structure. The structure classification includes changes affecting the distribution of authority; allocation of rewards; alterations in the chain of command; degree of formalization; and addition or deletion of positions, departments, and divisions. General Electric's sector innovation was a reorganization change that added another vertical level and reduced the span of control at the top. This reduced top management's involvement in day-to-day operating activities, created greater flexibility for growth, and provided more opportunities for training those candidates most likely to assume the company's top slot.

Technology. The technology classification encompasses modifications in the equipment that employees use, interdependencies of work activities among employees, and sociotechnical changes.

For instance, the business faculty at a junior college in the Midwest decided that all introductory courses—basic management, marketing, finance, accounting—would be converted from the lecture format to self-

[7]Larry E. Short, "Planned Organizational Change," *MSU Business Topics*, Autumn 1973, p. 53.

paced video cassette learning modules. Each course required students to listen to forty one-hour cassette tapes and complete a programmed learning text designed especially for the course and coordinated with the tapes. Faculty members designed the courses, made the tapes, wrote the accompanying texts, provided one-on-one tutorials, and devoted an increased amount of time to preparing for and teaching more advanced courses. This major change in technology dramatically reduced the need for new faculty, altered the characteristics required of new faculty in that new members needed greater specialization to handle the advanced courses, eliminated the variance in the information that students received when they took the same course from different instructors, and allowed department heads to supervise a greater number of faculty effectively.

Organizational processes. The final strategy considers changing organizational processes such as decision making and communication patterns. If a change agent, for instance, introduces task forces into a mechanistic bureaucracy with the intent of improving the transmission of information between functional units and allowing representatives from each unit to participate in decisions that will affect each of them, the change agent will have altered the organization's decision-making processes.

Implementation

Referring again to Figure 15–1, once forces for initiating change exist, someone has assumed the change agent role, and it has been determined what it is that is to be changed, we need to consider *how* to implement the change. We begin by looking at the steps in the change process. Then we turn our attention to the power distribution in implementation.

The change process. Successful change requires *unfreezing* the status quo, *changing* to a new state, and *refreezing* the new change to make it permanent.[8] Implicit in this three-step process is the recognition that the mere introduction of change does not ensure either the elimination of the prechange condition or the fact that the change will prove to be enduring.

The management of a large oil company decided to reorganize its marketing function in the western United States. The firm had three divisional offices in the West, located in Seattle, San Francisco, and Los Angeles. The decision was made to consolidate the divisions into a single regional office to be located in San Francisco. The reorganization meant transferring over 150 employees, the elimination of some duplicated managerial positions, and the institution of a new hierarchy of command. As you might guess, a move of this magnitude was difficult to keep secret.

[8]Kurt Lewin, *Field Theory in Social Science* (New York: Harper & Row, 1951).

The rumor of its occurrence preceded the announcement by several months. The decision itself was made unilaterally. It came from the executive offices in New York. Those people affected had no say whatsoever in the choice. For those in Seattle or Los Angeles, who may have disliked the decision and its consequences—the problems inherent in transferring to another city, pulling youngsters out of school, making new friends, having new co-workers, the reassignment of responsibilities—their only recourse was to quit. This actual case history of an organizational change will be used to illustrate the unfreezing-changing-refreezing model.

The status quo can be considered an equilibrium state. To move from this equilibrium—to overcome the pressures of both individual resistance and group conformity—unfreezing is necessary. This can be achieved in one of three ways. The *driving forces,* which direct behavior away from the status quo, can be increased. The *restraining forces,* which hinder movement from the existing equilibrium, can be decreased. A third alternative is to *combine the first two approaches.*

Using the reorganization example cited, management can expect employee resistance to the consolidation. To deal with that resistance, management can use positive incentives to encourage employees to accept the change. For instance, increases in pay can be offered to those who accept the transfer. Very liberal moving expenses can be paid by the company. Management might offer low-cost mortgage funds to allow employees to buy new homes in San Francisco. Of course, management might choose to unfreeze acceptance of the status quo by removing restraining forces. Employees could be counseled individually. Each employee's concerns and apprehensions could be heard and clarified specifically. Assuming that most of the fears are unjustified, the counselor could assure the employees that there was nothing to fear and then demonstrate, through tangible evidence, that restraining forces are unwarranted. If resistance is extremely high, management may have to resort to both reducing resistance and increasing the attractiveness of the alternative if the unfreezing is to be successful.

Once unfreezing has been accomplished, the change itself can be implemented. This is where the change agent introduces one or more intervention strategies. In reality, there is no clear line separating unfreezing and changing. Many of the efforts made to unfreeze the status quo may, in and of themselves, introduce change. So the tactics that the change agent uses for dealing with resistance may work on unfreezing and/or changing.

Six tactics have been suggested for use by managers or other change agents in dealing with resistance to change.[9] Let us review them briefly.

[9]John P. Kotter and Leonard A. Schlesinger, "Choosing Strategies for Change," *Harvard Business Review,* March–April 1979, pp. 106–114.

1. *Education and communication.* Resistance can be reduced through communicating with employees to help them see the logic of a change. This tactic assumes basically that the source of resistance lies in misinformation or poor communication. If they receive the full facts and get any misunderstandings cleared up, the resistance would subside. This can be achieved through one-on-one discussions, memos, group presentations, or reports. Does it work? It does, provided that the source of resistance is inadequate communication and that management-employee relations are characterized by mutual trust and credibility. If these conditions do not exit, it is unlikely to succeed. Additionally, against its advantages must be considered the time and effort that this tactic involves, particularly where the change affects a large number of people.

2. *Participation.* It's difficult for individuals to resist a change decision in which they participated. Prior to making a change, those opposed can be brought into the decision process. Assuming that the participants have the expertise to make a meaningful contribution, their involvement can reduce resistance, obtain commitment, and increase the quality of the change decision. However, against these advantages are the negatives: potential for a poor solution and great time consumption.

3. *Facilitation and support.* Change agents can offer a range of supportive efforts to reduce resistance. When employee fear and anxiety are high, employee counseling and therapy, new skills training, or a short paid leave of absence may facilitate adjustment. The drawback to this tactic is that, as with the others, it is time consuming. Additionally, it is expensive, and its implementation is no assurance of success.

4. *Negotiation.* Another way for the change agent to deal with potential resistance to change is to exchange something of value for a lessening of the resistance. For instance, if the resistance is centered in a few powerful individuals, a specific reward package can be negotiated that will meet their individual needs. In the oil companies' reorganization, acceptance of the transfer and reshuffling of duties by several highly valued middle managers was "bought" by providing them with larger staffs in their new jobs and by allowing them to live on company expense for nearly six months while they and their wives "looked" for acceptable permanent housing accommodations. Negotiation, as a tactic, may be necessary when resistance comes from a powerful source. Yet one cannot ignore its potentially high costs. Additionally, there is the risk that, once a change agent negotiates to avoid resistance, he or she is open to the possibility of being blackmailed by others with power.

5. *Manipulation and cooptation.* Manipulation refers to covert influence attempts. Twisting and distorting facts to make them appear more attractive, withholding undesirable information, or creating false rumors to get employees to accept a change are all examples of manipulation. If corporate management threatens to close down a particular manufacturing plant if that plant's employees fail to accept an across-the-board pay cut, and if the threat is actually untrue, the management will be using manipulation. Cooptation, on the other hand, is a form of both manipulation and participation. It seeks to "buy off" the leaders of a resistance group by giving them a key role in the change decision. The coopted's advice is sought not to result in a better decision but only to get their endorsement. Both manipulation and cooptation are relatively inexpensive and easy ways to gain the support of adversaries, but the tactics can backfire if the targets become aware that they are being tricked or used. Once discovered, the change agent's credibility may drop to zero.

6. *Coercion.* Last on the list of tactics is coercion; that is, the application of direct threats or force upon the resisters. If the corporate management, mentioned in the previous paragraph, were really determined to close the manufacturing plant if employees did not acquiesce to a pay cut, then coercion would be the label attached to their change tactic. Other examples of coercion include threats of transfers, loss of promotions, negative performance evaluations, or a poor letter of recommendation. The advantages and drawbacks of coercion are approximately the same as those mentioned for manipulation and cooptation.

Assuming that a change has been implemented, if it is to be successful, the new situation needs to be refrozen so that it can be sustained over time. Unless this last step is attended to, there is a very high likelihood that the change will be short lived and employees will attempt to revert to the prior equilibrium state. The objective of refreezing, then, is to stabilize the new situation by balancing the driving and restraining forces.

How is refreezing done? Basically, it requires systematic replacement of the temporary forces with permanent ones. It may mean formalizing the driving or restraining forces: for instance, a permanent upward adjustment of salaries or the permanent removal of time clocks to reinforce a climate of trust and confidence in employees. The formal rules and regulations governing behavior of those affected by the change should be revised to reinforce the new situation. Over time, of course, the group's own norms will evolve to sustain the new equilibrium. But until that point is reached, the change agent will have to rely on more formal mechanisms.

Are there key factors that determine the degree to which a change will become permanent? The answer is "Yes." A review of change studies identified a number of relevant factors.[10] The *reward allocation system* is critical. For instance, if rewards fall short of expectations over time, the change is likely to be short lived. If a change is to be sustained, it needs the support of a sponsor. This individual, typically high in the management hierarchy, provides legitimacy to the change. Evidence indicates that, once *sponsorship is withdrawn* from a change project, there are strong pressures to return to the old equilibrium state. People need to know what is expected of them as a result of the change. Therefore, *failure to transmit information* on expectations should reduce the degree of refreezing. *Group forces* is another important factor. As employees become aware that others in their group accept and sanction the change, they become more comfortable with it. *Commitment* to the change should lead to greater acceptance and permanence. As noted earlier, if employees participate in the change decision, they can be expected to be more committed to seeing that it is successful. Change is less likely to become permanent if it is implemented in a singular unit of the organization. Therefore, the more *diffusion in* the change effort, the more units affected and the greater legitimacy the effort will carry.

These factors remind us that the organization is a system and that planned change will be most successful when all the parts within the system support the change effort. What is more, successful change requires careful balancing of the system. The consolidation of three divisional units into a singular regional office obviously carries with it a wide range of reverberating effects. But the impact of even small changes (i.e., when a multibillion-dollar consumer product firm creates a new Department of Public Affairs staffed with only a handful of personnel) can be expected to be widespread. Other departments and employees will be threatened. Still others will feel that a portion of their responsibilities has been taken from them. All changes, regardless of how small, will have an impact outside the area in which they were implemented. No change can take place in a vacuum. A structural modification in unit A will impact on other structural variables within unit A, as well as affect structural variables in units B, C, and so forth. This system perspective makes it imperative that change agents consider any or all interventions as potentially impacting on a far greater territory than the specific point where the change was initiated.

Power distribution. Paralleling the change process in the implementation stage is the decision as to the degree to which power over the process is to be shared with those affected by the change. The oil company reorganization example presented earlier illustrates a case of top manage-

[10]Paul S. Goodman, Max Bazerman, and Edward Conlon, "Institutionalization of Planned Organizational Change," in Barry M. Staw and Larry L. Cummings, eds., *Research in Organizational Behavior*, vol. 2, (Greenwich, Conn.: JAI Press, 1980), pp. 231–242.

ment's making structural changes unilaterally. Change can be accomplished, however, by using various power distributions. One researcher identified seven approaches, which he categorized under three alternative uses of power.[11]

I. Unilateral Power

1. *The decree approach.* A one-way announcement originating with a person with high formal authority and passed on to those in lower positions.

2. *The replacement approach.* Individuals in one or more key organizational positions are replaced by other individuals.

3. *The structural approach.* In decreeing or injecting new blood into work relationships, management changes the structure of roles and required relationships among subordinates.

II. Shared Power

4. *The group decision approach.* Participation by group members in selecting and implementing alternatives that are generated by others. Emphasis is on obtaining group agreement on a particular course of action.

5. *The group problem-solving approach.* Greater latitude is given participants by allowing them to identify and solve problems rather than to merely select from a previously identified set of alternatives.

III. Delegated Power

6. *The data discussion approach.* Presentation and feedback of relevant data to the client system either by an external change agent or by change agents within the organization. Organizational members are encouraged to develop their own analyses of the data, presented in the form of case materials, survey findings, or data reports.

7. *The sensitivity training approach.* Members are trained to be more sensitive to the underlying processes of individual and group behavior. Changes in work patterns and relationships are assumed to follow from changes in interpersonal relationships.

The choices of how change is to be implemented can be thought of as lying on a continuum. At one end is the unilateral approach, in which power tends to be concentrated in the hands of top management. It is top management who decides what is to be changed and how it is to be done. At the other extreme along the continuum is the delegated approach, in which subordinates are substantially in control of problem identification

[11]Larry E. Greiner, "Patterns of Organization Change," *Harvard Business Review*, May–June 1967, pp. 119–130.

and solution selection. In between is the shared power approach. This middle-ground position still retains authority at the top but allows participation by subordinates.

Results

The model in Figure 15–1 culminates with change taking place and a resulting effect on organizational effectiveness. Whether that effect is positive, negative, temporary, or permanent depends on each of the earlier steps. Regardless of the outcome, the model is dynamic. The need for change is continuous; hence the need for the feedback loop. The successful change agent has little time to sit back and reflect on his or her achievements. New forces will already be working to make additional changes necessary. The change model we have proposed, therefore, is never at rest.

PREDICTING CHANGE FROM STRUCTURAL DIMENSIONS

Organizations can have similar goals and environments, but they differ significantly in the rate at which they initiate change. A growing body of evidence indicates that the structure of these organizations may offer insights into how likely they are to change themselves.

Hage and Aiken studied *program change,* which they defined as the addition of new services or products.[12] The organizations they investigated varied, although most of their findings come from their research in welfare agencies. Their research looked specifically at the relationship between the structural variables and the rate of program change. Hage and Aiken's findings will be the centerpiece of our predictions. Bonoma and Zaltman have also looked at the structure-change relationship.[13] They have proposed a number of ideas that, though not tested empirically, are consistent with related research in the published literature. The following sections evolved out of these two sources.

Complexity

Hage and Aiken found that the greater the complexity, the greater the rate of program change. Why does this occur? Probably because increased complexity creates coordination problems and conflicts between differentiated

[12]Jerald Hage and Michael Aiken, *Social Change in Complex Organizations* (New York: Random House, 1970).

[13]Thomas V. Bonoma and Gerald Zaltman, *Psychology for Management* (Boston: Kent Publishing, 1981), pp. 315–322.

specialists and because specialists are likely to keep abreast of advances in their areas and want to implement them. All these factors lead to a greater impetus for change.

Bonoma and Zaltman concur with Hage and Aiken. Additionally, they offer the following postulates:

1. *There is less risk and uncertainty associated with change if the organization is relatively complex and many departments and units are involved in the decision.* Increased complexity allows the blame to be spread if the change is unsuccessful. Also, input from different specialties makes everyone more confident about the decision.

2. *The change agent's effort to communicate to varying groups the real or potential value from accepting the change must be greater when the complexity is greater.* The greater the complexity, the greater the potential variation in values, experiences, and needs in the organization. If unfreezing is to take place, communications must respond effectively to the varying needs of potential resistance groups. Conversely, low complexity implies greater homogeneity among members, so the change agent's communications can be more uniform.

3. *Changes with potential for impact on many areas of the organization are less likely to be adopted by complex organizations and will involve a longer decision process than will changes with impact on fewer areas.* Increased complexity typically means more groups stand to be affected by a change; hence the higher the likelihood of the effect's being adverse. This fear of adversity in turn increases the number of sources of resistance in the organization.

4. *Changes that offer unique relative advantages for different subgroups are more likely to be adopted than are those that give advantage to a single subgroup.* The more a given change satisfies a wide constituency, the greater will be the support for that change.

5. *A more divisible change strategy in terms of where it can be used in the organization is more likely to be tried.* Divisibility allows one group to try a change without the need of cooperation with other subgroups.

6. *The greater the complexity of the organization, the more susceptible the change strategy must be to modification if adoption is to occur.* The greater the ease with which a change can be adapted to different needs or circumstances, the more likely it is to be adopted on a sustained basis.

Formalization

Hage and Aiken found formalization and propensity to change inversely related; that is, the greater the degree of formalization, the lower the rate of program change. This, of course, is completely consistent with what one would expect. The greater the number of rules and regulations, the greater the rigidity and inflexibility within the organization. High formalization discourages new ways of doing things. Further, high formalization stabilizes the organization and reinforces the status quo. The organization is more reliable and predictable, but it is also less responsive to the forces of change.

Bonoma and Zaltman agree that high formalization hinders the initiation of change. Again, they offer some further insights:

1. *A more formalized organization is more likely to have a mechanism for dealing with radical changes.* A radical change is one that differs significantly from available alternatives. The greater the divergence, the more radical the change. Decision makers are not likely to consider, never mind adopt, a radical change unless it can be legitimated by the organization's formal regulations. In this way, if the change fails, they can share responsibility with the system of rules and procedures.

2. *High formalization makes those changes most attractive that are easily reversed and divisible.* Reversibility allows the organization to reinstitute the rules and regulations dropped or altered as a result of enacting a change. Divisibility enables the organization to keep most of its rules and regulations intact by limiting the change to only part of the organization.

3. *The greater the degree of commitment a change requires and the more formalized the organization, the longer is the decision-making period, and the less likely is full adoption.* High formalization creates barriers. If a change is to be adopted, it must clear these barriers, which is a time-consuming process.

4. *High compatibility of a change to an organization's rules and regulations makes its adoption more likely.* Resistance will be lowest to changes that are the least radical.

Centralization

Hage and Aiken found centralization to be inversely related to program change. Consistent with the power-control perspective, those in power typically find that it is in their best interest to fight change, since structural changes redistribute power.

Bonoma and Zaltman concur with this conclusion and propose two additional ideas:

1. *Changes that require strong and widespread commitment if they are to be effective are likely to be more successful with decentralized decision making.* This postulate is consistent with the comments made earlier in this chapter about the value of participation. Increased participation widens the set of members able to provide input and enhances commitment.

2. *Highly centralized structures are more important and efficient the less divisibile, the less reversible, and the broader the impact of the change.* Units low in the organization hierarchy are reluctant to make unilateral decisions that will affect other groups in the organization on a relatively permanent basis or that will disrupt the organization as a whole if the change is implemented and then discontinued.

IN THE BATTLE BETWEEN CHANGE AND STABILITY, BET ON STABILITY!

Early in this chapter we described organizations as conservative, with strong tendencies to resist change. Consistent with our attempt throughout this book to make its contents realistic, we need to reiterate the conservative nature of organizations.

Planned organizational change gets a lot more attention in textbooks than it gets in practice. The reason for the divergence between theory and practice is explained by the power-control perspective. Essentially it is this: those in power have little reason to initiate change. The current structure maintains control and furthers the interests of the powerholders. Since effectiveness is defined in terms of those doing the evaluating, the rational textbook assumption that "changes in structure will be implemented as needed to ensure high performance" is probably little more than a myth. In reality, the structural changes that do occur are neither planned nor in response to facilitate technical efficiency or demands of the environment.[14]

Change is most likely a response to pressing demands created by internal and external parties interested in the organization. That is, it is reactive rather than anticipatory. In practice, "planned" change is typically a process of (1) change, followed by (2) the planning that legitimates and ratifies this change. As noted about goals in Chapter 10, meaning is attributed to an action, but usually *after* it has occurred. So, while change is made in response to demands by powerful interest groups, it is packaged

[14]This section has been adapted from Jeffrey Pfeffer, *Organizational Design* (Arlington Heights, Ill.: AHM Publishing, 1978), pp. 190–192.

and sold in a more legitimate form: it is rationalized as being consistent with the goals of enhanced organizational effectiveness.

The power-control position offers important insights into organizational change in practice. It recognizes that the pressures for stability are extremely great in organizations. Those who argue for the highly dynamic nature of organizations, and hence the need for continual change, make assumptions about goals and effectiveness measures that are not consistent with reality. So change, planned or otherwise, is not nearly as prevalent as theorists would predict. Of course, changes do occur. Pressures for change will come from outside the dominant coalition, and, if those in power are not able to keep those pressures in check, changes will be implemented. It may not be what the dominant coalition wants, but at that point, they have lost control. When the changes are implemented, in response to outside pressures, you should expect it to be conveyed as planned and consistent with the organization's goals of improved performance. An example may help to clarify some of these points.

The business school at a specific university had experienced very rapid growth. In a period of four or five years, the number of faculty increased from approximately fifteen to thirty-five. Most of these new members were young, having recently finished their own graduate studies.

The dominant power coalition was made up of the dean and his department heads. All the department heads had been at the university for many years and ruled with considerable strength. Although the dean had come from another university and been in his position only a few years, he was in his late fifties and had been handpicked by the department chairmen because he was seen as someone who would *not* "shake up the ship." What the dominant coalition had overlooked, however, were the facts that there were now more young faculty than "old-timers" and that the university's top administrators believed that the future of the business school resided with the new young faculty. Conditions were right for a revolt. The young faculty knew that they had the numbers to overthrow the dominant coalition. The top administration's concern with keeping them at the school enhanced their power. Here is what took place.

Several of the young faculty went to the university's vice president and outlined the business school's problems. They also presented evidence on the poor performance of the dean in dealing with these problems. A few visits with the vice president, followed by his own confirming data, resulted in the dean's being asked to tender his resignation. An acting dean was appointed. Interestingly, few of the dominant coalition saw that a revolt was brewing. It appeared that the department chairmen expected the next dean to maintain the status quo. This, of course, was fine for the chairmen. They were the "fat cats" in the system.

At a faculty meeting, several months after the dean's resignation, one of the items on the agenda was nominations to the search committee for selecting a new dean. When that item came up, the young faculty were ready. Within less than a minute, they had succeeded in nominating and seconding five of their own to the five committee positions. The nominations were closed. Suddenly, it became obvious to everyone at that meeting that the young faculty had stacked the deck. You can probably guess what happened from that point on.

The young faculty wanted the power coalition changed, and only those candidates that supported such a change became finalists for the deanship. When the new dean was appointed, the young faculty members took control. All the chairmanship positions were changed. The old-timers were replaced by members of the young faculty coalition. The business school was subsequently reorganized, and the interests of the young faculty were paramount in this structural change. These changes, it was argued, were necessary to improve the effectiveness of the business school. Whether they did is problematic. But there is no question that it furthered the interests of the young faculty by legitimating their power. The young faculty totally revamped the goals and structure of that business school in their interests. To this day, the old-timers have never recovered.

SUMMARY

Managed change is planned change. But organizations are essentially conservative and resist change. Any efforts to implement change must acknowledge this basic resistance.

A wide range of forces can instigate change. The change agent is the individual or individuals who makes the structural changes. He or she chooses from structural, technological, or organizational process intervention strategies. The implementation of change requires unfreezing the status quo, changing to a new state, and refreezing the new changes to make them permanent. Implementation also requires a decision as to how power is to be distributed in the change process.

The evidence indicates that change is more likely to occur in organizations typified as high in complexity, low in formalization, and decentralized.

Despite all the attention that planned change has received from organization theorists, a more realistic conclusion is that structural changes occur infrequently and, when they do, they are neither planned nor in response to facilitate technical efficiency or demands of the environment.

FOR REVIEW AND DISCUSSION

1. What is the traditional view of change in organizations?
2. What does "managed" change mean?
3. Why do organizations resist change?

4. Describe five determinants of change.
5. Describe the three types of intervention strategies.
6. Contrast driving and restraining forces in unfreezing.
7. Why is "refreezing" of change necessary?
8. Compare the following organizations in terms of resistance to change:
   a. Price Waterhouse accountants
   b. Scott Paper Co.
   c. American Airlines
   d. AT&T
   e. Sara Lee Foods
9. Review the various tactics for dealing with resistance to change in power-control terms.
10. Explain why organizations have an inherent bias toward stability.

CHAPTER

16

MANAGING CONFLICT

Jennifer Maher produces a situation comedy for the National Broadcasting Company in New York City. The quiet in her office was broken by the buzz on her intercom. "Ms. Maher," her secretary blurted, "there's a riot out here. There's a bunch of people who want to see you." Within seconds, a half a dozen of Jennifer's scriptwriters burst through the door. "Jenny," began the spokesperson for the group, "we've had it. You promoted Nick Crane to script supervisor three weeks ago after Christine resigned. Well, we can't work with him! With Christine, we were a team. We wrote each script together. We shared ideas. Our scripts were good, damn good, because we all participated in making them that way. Well, Nick has changed the whole thing around. He's split us into two groups, each working on a separate episode. After the three of us have roughed out the general format for the episode, he breaks us up and makes each of us work on one of its three acts. He says it makes for better accountability. He thinks he can now find out who the best writers are! Have you ever heard of anything so crazy? Jenny, if you don't do something right now, I'm telling you, we're all gonna quit!"

A thousand miles away, at the head office of a large chemical company in Chicago, the following telephone conversation is taking place between Bill Douglas and Gary Panek. Bill is vice president of sales. Gary is vice president of research and development.

"I don't care how much work you've got down there," Bill was saying, "American Steel is one of our best customers. I told them we'd have a solvent that would meet their needs within 30 days." "I appreciate your dilemma, Bill," Gary replied, "but I've got a dozen projects that have high priority. My staff has only so much time. I think I can put someone on developing a solvent for American in six or seven weeks. Tell American we'll have a product for them within 90 days. "No way," snapped Bill, "we'll lose the whole account." "I'm sorry," Gary said. "If this upsets you so much, Bill, call Henry [the company's president] and tell him, like I've been telling him for the last year, how the R&D group needs a larger staff," lobbied Gary in closing.

Both incidents have a common thread. They represent organizational conflicts. If we can generalize from a study of middle- and top-level executives by the American Management Association, the average manager spends approximately 20 percent of his or her time dealing with conflict.[1] No study of organizations, therefore, would be complete without an analysis of this topic. We propose that conflict is an inevitable part of organizational life, stemming as much from structural characteristics as from incompatible personalities. Organizations have scarce resources, employees with diverse interests and outlooks, and other attributes, which make conflict an ongoing reality.

DEFINING CONFLICT

There is no shortage of definitions for the term conflict. A sampling of the literature describes it as "that behavior by organization members which is expended in opposition to other members";[2] "the process which begins when one party perceives that the other has frustrated, or is about to frustrate, some concern of his";[3] or merely "whenever incompatibile activities occur."[4] Several common themes, however, underlie most definitions.

Conflict must be *perceived* by the parties to it. Whether conflict exists or not is a perception issue. If no one is aware of a conflict, it is generally agreed that no conflict exists. Of course, conflicts perceived may not be real, whereas many situations that otherwise could be described as conflictive are not because the organizational members involved do not perceive the conflict. For a conflict to exist, therefore, it must be perceived. Additional commonalities among most conflict definitions are the concepts of *opposition, scarcity,* and *blockage* and the assumption that there are two or more parties whose interests or *goals appear to be incompatible.* Resources—whether money, promotions, prestige, power, or whatever—are not un-

[1]Kenneth W. Thomas and Warren H. Schmidt, "A Survey of Managerial Interests with Respect to Conflict," *Academy of Management Journal,* June 1976, pp. 315–318.

[2]James D. Thompson, "Organizational Management of Conflict," *Administrative Science Quarterly,* March 1960, p. 389.

[3]Kenneth W. Thomas, "Conflict and Conflict Management," in M. D. Dunnette, ed., *Handbook of Industrial and Organizational Psychology* (Chicago: Rand McNally, 1976), p. 889.

[4]Morton Deutsch, *The Resolution of Conflict: Constructive and Destructive Processes* (New Haven, Conn.: Yale University Press, 1973), p. 10.

limited, and their scarcity encourages blocking behavior. The parties are therefore in opposition. When one party blocks the goal achievement of another, a conflict state exists.

Differences between definitions tend to center on *intent* and whether or not conflict is a term limited only to *overt acts*. The intent issue is a debate over whether blockage behavior must be a determined action or whether it could occur as a result of fortuitous circumstances. As to whether conflict can refer only to overt acts, some definitions, for example, require signs of manifest fighting or open struggle as criteria for the existence of conflict.

Our definition of conflict acknowledges awareness (perception), opposition, scarcity, and blockage. Further, we assume it to be determined action, which can exist at either the latent or overt level. We define conflict to be *a process in which an effort is purposely made by A to offset the efforts of B by some form of blocking that will result in frustrating B in attaining his goals or furthering his interests.*

TRANSITIONS IN CONFLICT THOUGHT

It is entirely appropriate to say that there has been "conflict" over the role of conflict in organizations. One school of thought has argued that conflict must be avoided, that it indicates a malfunctioning within the organization. We call this the *traditional* view. Another school of thought, the *behavioral* view, argues that conflict is a natural and inevitable outcome in any organization and that it need not be evil but, rather, has the potential to be a positive force in determining organizational effectiveness. The third, and most recent perspective, proposes not only that conflict *can* be a positive force in an organization but argues explicitly that some conflict is *absolutely necessary* for an organization to perform effectively. We label this third school the *interactionist* approach. Let us take a closer look at each of these views.[5]

The Traditional View

The early approach assumed that conflict was bad and would *always* impact organizational effectiveness negatively. Conflict was used synonymously with such terms as violence, destruction, and irrationality. Since conflict was harmful, it was to be avoided. For managers, part of their responsibilities was to rid the organization of any conflicts. This traditional philosophy dominated the management and organizational literature during the late nineteenth century and continued to the mid-1940s.

[5]This section, and significant parts of this chapter, have been adapted from Stephen P. Robbins, *Managing Organizational Conflict: A Nontraditional Approach* (Englewood Cliffs, N.J.: Prentice-Hall, 1974).

The Behavioral View

The traditional approach was followed by the behavioral view. The behavioralists' position argued that conflict was a natural occurrence in organizations. By their very nature, organizations have built-in conflicts. Disagreements over goals clearly exist. Sections compete for recognition. Departments compete for prestige. Other units compete to increase their boundaries. All compete for power. Since conflict is inevitable, the behavioralists advocated "acceptance" of conflict.

The behavioral view rationalized the existence of conflict: it can not be eliminated, and there are even times when it may benefit an organization's performance. Note, however, that this approach represented, at best, superficial acceptance of conflict. The behavioralists seem to be grasping for supportive evidence to defend the existence of conflict. Although encouragement of conflict was occasionally alluded to, nowhere did those who hold this view actively seek conflict or introduce the idea that management should consider the positive creation of the conditions that breed conflict. So, while the behavioralists accepted conflict as inevitable, when they referred to *managing* conflict, all they meant was *resolving* conflict. From a historical perspective, the behavioral view dominated management and organization theory from the late 1940s through the mid-1970s.

The Interactionist View

The current theoretical perspective on conflict is the interactionist approach. While the behavioral view *accepted* conflict, the interactionist approach *encourages* conflict. That is, a harmonious, peaceful, tranquil, and fully cooperative organization is prone to becoming static, apathetic, and nonresponsive to needs for change and innovation. Conflict can stimulate new ideas, improve intragroup cohesiveness, result in better decisions through the input of divergent opinions, allow for venting of frustrations, and offer other similar benefits to the organization. Specifically, the interactionist approach differs from the behavioral in that it

1. Recognizes the absolute necessity of conflict.
2. Explicitly encourages functional opposition.
3. Defines conflict management to include stimulation as well as resolution methods.
4. Considers the management of conflict as a major responsibility of all managers.

The interactionist viewpoint implies that conflict is neither all good nor all bad. Those conflicts that support the goals of the organization and improve its performance are functional. Those that hinder performance are dysfunctional. The manager's role, therefore, is to create an environment in which conflict is healthy but not allowed to run to pathological extremes. As shown in Figure 16-1, it is undesirable for conflict levels to be too high or too low. Situation B represents the optimal level. The area from A up to but not including B requires the manager to stimulate conflict to achieve full benefits from its functional properties. The area to the right of B demands resolution efforts to reduce the conflict level.

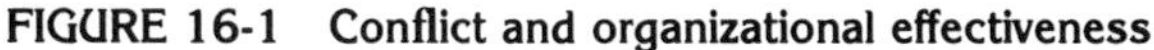

FIGURE 16-1 Conflict and organizational effectiveness

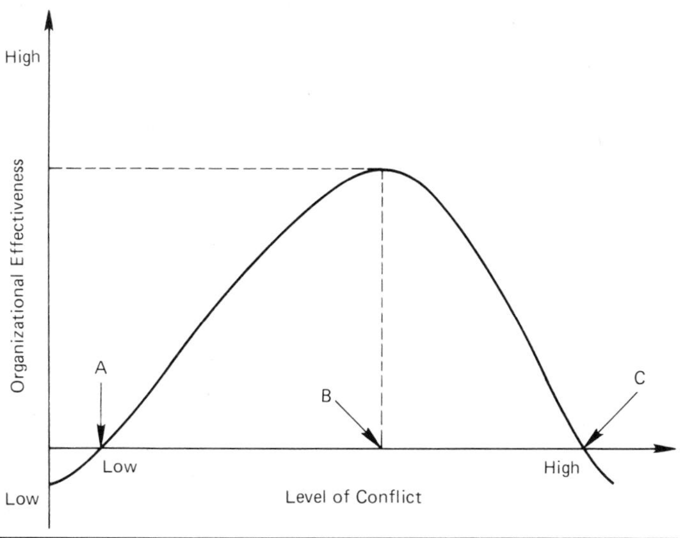

SITUATION	LEVEL OF CONFLICT	TYPE OF CONFLICT	ORGANIZATION'S INTERNAL CHARACTERISTICS	ORGANIZATIONAL EFFECTIVENESS OUTCOME
A	Low or None	Dysfunctional	Apathetic Stagnant Nonresponsive to change Lack of new ideas	Low
B	Optimal	Functional	Viable Self-critical Innovative	High
C	High	Dysfunctional	Disruptive Chaotic Uncooperative	Low

ANTICONFLICT VALUES PERMEATE OUR SOCIETY

It would be naïve to assume that most managers today practice the interactionist approach. Although there is an increasing body of research that attests to the value of conflict, most managers still follow the traditional approach. The interactionist view, therefore, is undoubtedly prescriptive rather than descriptive.

Why is it that managers are uncomfortable with conflict? The answer lies in the fact that tolerance of conflict is counter to most cultures in developed nations. The U.S., Canadian, and advanced European cultures have successfully engendered in their inhabitants a "fear of conflict" and a desire for at least the appearances of agreement and cooperation. Most organizations today reinforce this sentiment. Let us take a closer look at the sources of these anticonflict values.

We are most susceptible to influence in the early years of our development. From the time we reach an age of understanding through the primary school years, we have been inculcated with the value of getting along with others and avoiding conflicts. The home, school, and church are the three major institutions that share the responsibility for reinforcing anticonflict values during the developing years of a child.

Historically, the home has reinforced the authority pattern through the parent figure. Parents knew what was right and children complied. Conflict between children or between parents and children has generally been discouraged actively. The traditional school systems in developed countries have reflected the structure of the home. Teachers had *the* answers and were not to be challenged. Disagreements at all levels were viewed negatively. The last major influencing institution, the church, also has supported anticonflict values. Church doctrines, for the most part, advocate acceptance without questioning. The religious perspective emphasizes peace, harmony, and tranquility. This is examplified best by the teachings of the Roman Catholic Church. According to its beliefs, the Pope's word on religious matters is infallible. Such dogma has discouraged questioning the teachings of the church.

In addition to the influence of the three institutions mentioned, entire countries such as the United States have further fostered an anticonflict image by developing a national pride as a peace-loving nation. Multibillion-dollar expenditures are made each year for defense, not offense. Preparation to fight is made only because others may initiate force and therefore protection is justified. If it is survival of the fittest, America will be prepared, although the striving for the attainment of peace dominates the thinking of the nation's people.

We are still operating under the influence of the traditional view of conflict. Any type or form of conflict is seen as bad. The vast majority of us have been influenced at home, in school, and through the church to eliminate, suppress, or avoid conflict. Further, it has made us uncomfortable to be in its presence. Abraham Maslow expressed this view vividly in describing our society as one in which there generally exists "a fear of conflict, of disagreement, of hostility, antagonism, enmity. There is much stress on getting along with other people, even if you don't like them."[6]

The term conflict has a negative connotation for many in our society. The semantic problem has resulted in viewing conflict only from a negative perspective—as destructive or annihiliatory. As we already recognize, conflict has a positive side that is repressed in our culture. We are inculcated with anticonflict views from childhood, and as a result most of us grow up with mores that sanction unquestioned authority. Disagreement is considered unacceptable; all conflicts are bad. An American Management Association study supports this contention.[7] An overwhelming majority of two hundred managers agreed that the most important single skill of an executive is his or her ability to get along with people.

We live in a society that has been built upon anticonflict values. Parents in the home, teachers and administrators in schools, teachings of the church, and authority figures in social groups all traditionally reinforce the belief that disagreement breeds discontent, which acts to dissolve common ties and leads eventually to destruction of the system. Certainly we should not be surprised that children raised to view all conflict as destructive will mature into adults who will maintain and encourage the same values.

Too few managers accept, and almost none attempt to stimulate, conflict. It is true that conflict is uncomfortable and that it can be a source of problems. But it is additionally true, and this is what is paramount to the manager, that conflict is absolutely necessary in organizations if they are to maintain their viability and to increase the probability of their surviving. One may speculate that the reason that managers are paid the highest salaries in organizations is to compensate for their supposed acceptance of conflict. A good part of their remuneration may be viewed as "combat pay" to work in an environment that is, and must be, constantly uncomfortable.

The predominant view of conflict held by most individuals is demonstrated in an enlightening study illustrating the extent to which anticonflict sentiments permeate our society.[8] Series of groups were formed to study a problem, some containing a deviant who challenged and questioned dominant positions, others without. As we might expect, in every case, the group containing a deviant developed a richer analysis of the

[6]Abraham Maslow, *Eupsychian Management* (Homewood, Ill.: Irwin, 1965), p. 185.

[7]As quoted in Garret L. Bergen and William V. Haney, *Organizational Relations and Management Action* (New York: McGraw-Hill, 1966).

[8]Elise Boulding, "Further Reflections on Conflict Management," in Robert L. Kahn and Elise Boulding, eds., *Power and Conflict in Organizations* (New York: Basic Books, 1964), pp. 147–148.

problem and a more elegant solution. When each group was then asked to drop one member, in every group that had a deviant member, it was the deviant who was ousted. When given the opportunity, the childhood socialization that conflict was undesirable arose and the confronting force was eliminated, regardless of its positive value. Our desire for consensus and agreement influences us more than the desire for effective performance.

Both the traditional and behavioral approaches to conflict confuse the study of conflict resolution with conflict management.[9] These "great peacemakers" have made a weak basic assumption. They accept the notion that, since conflict does exist in organizations, it *must* be in excess of the level that is desired. They assume that it is the manager's role to reduce tensions. Their conclusion then is to initiate actions to reduce conflict. But the goal of management is not harmony and cooperation—it is effective goal attainment! Elimination of conflict is not realistic in complex organizations, nor would such elimination be desirable. As one author has noted, "the individuals or groups who are most vocal in advocating 'harmony and happiness' in an environment devoid of conflict may only be protecting their vested interests in the *status quo*."[10]

SOURCES OF ORGANIZATIONAL CONFLICT

A number of diverse factors can precipitate organizational conflict. Some factors—such as incompatible personalities—are psychological. That is, the conflict is due to the individual characteristics of employees. All that this is really saying is that some people have difficulty getting along with each other and that this difficulty has nothing to do with their job requirements or formal interactions. Our concern, however, is with structurally derived conflicts. The following review reflects the most frequently cited structural sources of conflict.[11]

Mutual Task Dependence

Mutual task dependence refers to the extent to which two units in an organization depend upon each other for assistance, information, compliance, or other coordinative activities to complete their respective tasks effectively. This would describe, for instance, the interactions between the

[9]Stephen P. Robbins, " 'Conflict Management' and 'Conflict Resolution' Are Not Synonymous Terms," *California Management Review*, Winter 1978, pp. 67–75.

[10]Leonard Rico, "Organizational Conflict: A Framework for Reappraisal," *Industrial Management Review*, Fall 1964, p. 67.

[11]A number of these sources were categorized originally in Richard E. Walton and John M. Dutton, "The Management of Interdepartmental Conflict: A Model and Review," *Administrative Science Quarterly*, March 1969, pp. 73–84.

programming and market analysis groups at a large FM radio station. They depend on each other to determine the right balance in their music format.

The linkage between mutual task dependence and conflict is not direct. What we know is that the former raises the intensity of interunit relations. When forced to interact, there is a definite escalation in the potential for conflict. However, the interaction does not have to lead to conflict. It can also lead to friendly and cooperative relations. If there is a history of antagonism between the units, mutual task dependence will intensify it. Similarly, it will intensify friendly relations as well.

One-Way Task Dependence

The prospects for conflict are much greater when one unit is unilaterally dependent on another. In contrast to mutual dependency, one-way dependency means that the power balance has shifted. The prospects for conflict are decidedly higher because the dominant unit has little incentive to cooperate with the subordinate unit.

The conflict potential in one-way task dependence takes on greater meaning when we recognize that it is far more prevalent in organizations than is mutual dependence. Assembly-lines have one-way dependency. This can lead to conflict when "one department's shoddy or incompleted work is left for the next department to complete, with the dependent unit in no position to retaliate."[12] Cooks and waitresses in restaurants are not mutually dependent—the waitress depends more on the cook than vice versa. In business firms, marketing is typically dependent on the credit department for approval of its sales. The medical examiner in a hospital is dependent on the laboratory unit for his autopsy results. In fact, almost all line-staff relations are based on one-way task dependence. The staff is required to get along with the line, understand the line's problems, and justify its own existence, whereas none of these requirements is reciprocated by the line groups.

High Horizontal Differentiation

The greater the difference between units, the greater the likelihood of conflict. If units in the organization are highly differentiated, the tasks each does and the subenvironments each deals with will tend to be dissimilar. This, in turn, will lead to significant internal differences between the units. Evidence indicates, for instance, that high horizontal differentiation leads to different goals, time orientations, and management philosophies between units.[13] In a manufacturing firm, the people in production will tend

[12]Howard E. Aldrich, *Organizations and Environments* (Englewood Cliffs, N.J.: Prentice-Hall, 1979), p. 94.

[13]Paul R. Lawrence and Jay W. Lorsch, *Organization and Environment* (Homewood, Ill.: Irwin, 1969).

to have a short-term perspective. In contrast, laboratory researchers in the same firm will tend to have a longer-term orientation. Why? Their training has instilled a different time perspective and the demands of their jobs accentuate these orientations. There is truth to the belief that marketing people and accounting people see the organization's "world" through different eyes. It is a natural by-product of specialization. Of course, high differentiation does not automatically lead to conflict. Other factors such as interdependence of tasks and rewards can act to retard or stimulate the latent potential for conflict.

Low Formalization

Rules and regulations reduce conflict by minimizing ambiguity. High formalization establishes standardized ways for units to interact with each other. Role definitions are clear so that members of units know what to expect from the other. Conversely, where formalization is low, the potential for jurisdictional disputes increases. Departments, for example, jockey for resources and other power bases. Interactions between units, because they are not regulated formally, are characterized by negotiation. In this type of environment, conflicts between units are likely to flourish. Conflicts can still breed in highly formalized structures; however, they are likely to be more regulated and less subversive. As in a hockey game, the rules do not eliminate conflicts. Rather, they allow spectators to better anticipate when conflicts are likely to break out.

Dependence on Common Scarce Resources

Conflict potential is enhanced when two or more units depend on a common pool of scarce resources such as physical space, equipment, operating funds, capital budget allocations, or centralized staff services such as the typing pool. The potential is increased further if unit members perceive that their individual needs cannot be met from the available resource pool when other units' needs are satisfied. When units perceive the situation as "zero-sum"—anything you get comes out of my hide—you can expect inter-unit conflicts, empire-building, monopolizing of resources, and other behaviors that decrease organizational effectiveness.

Differences in Evaluation Criteria and Reward Systems

The more the evaluations and rewards of top management emphasize the separate performance of each department, rather than their combined performance, the greater the conflict. We see evidence of this in organizations all the time.

The preference of production units for long, economical runs with its accompanying rewards are in opposition to the rewards provided to sales units from quick delivery to good customers. Production is rewarded for fewer runs that minimize costs, whereas sales is rewarded for speed, which frequently entails the need for a greater number of runs. Similarly, sales is rewarded for selling as much as possible. The credit unit, however, is typically rewarded for minimizing losses. This objective is achieved by curtailing sales to marginal accounts. Many a sales manager spends hours each week trying to convince the credit executive in his firm that what the credit department considers a financially unworthy customer is actually "marginally acceptable."

Line-staff conflicts can also stem from differing evaluation criteria and reward systems. Staff units value change, for this is the major way in which they justify their existence. The systems department that suggests no changes is a likely target for elimination. But line units value stability. To line units, change has undesirable repercussions for their operations. Not only is change inconvenient but it also degrades current methods. Any change suggested by a staff unit implies that the current methods are inadequate, an obviously degrading implication. For further evidence of the conflict that staff units can create, spend a few weeks as an auditor or a quality-control inspector in a manufacturing firm. You don't develop a lot of cooperative relations with personnel in units where you are evaluated and rewarded for finding errors in their work!

Participative Decision Making

The evidence finds that joint decision making, where those who will be affected by a decision are made part of the decision-making body, promotes conflict.[14] The participative process permits a greater opportunity for the expression of existing disputes and allows more occasions for disagreements to arise. This is especially likely to occur when true value differences exist among the participants. The research suggests that the high interaction incurred in participation acts to solidify differences more than facilitate coordination and cooperation. The result is greater differences of opinion and greater awareness of conflict. In many cases, the conflict intensity may be no greater after participation than before, but it tends to move the conflict from latent to overt.

[14]See Meyer Zald, "Power Balance and Staff Conflict in Correctional Institutions," *Administrative Science Quarterly*, June 1962, pp. 22–49; and George Strauss and Eliezer Rosenstein, "Workers Participation: A Critical View," *Industrial Relations*, February 1970, pp. 197–214.

Heterogeneity of Members

The more heterogenous members are, the less likely they are to work smoothly and cooperatively together. It's been found that personal dissimilarities, such as background, values, education, age, and social patterns lowered the probability of interpersonal rapport between unit representatives and in turn decreased the amount of collaboration between their respective units.

Consistent with this notion, we would expect the average tenure of a group to be inversely related to conflict. That is, the longer the group members have worked with each other, the more likely they are to get along well together. Research confirms this hypothesis. For instance, in a school setting, it was found that conflict was highest among the younger and shortest-tenure faculty members and lowest among the older members.[15] We could expect, therefore, that recently established units with all new personnel or those units that have experienced high turnover among members should be more conflict prone.

Status Incongruence

Conflict is stimulated where incongruencies occur in status gradings or from alterations in the status hierarchy. For instance, an increase in conflict was found when the degree to which personal status, or how one perceives oneself, and the level of departmental representation differed in rank ordering of status dimensions.[16] These dimensions include length of service, age, education, and pay. Similarly, in an organization where it was generally acknowledged that research had more prestige than engineering, patterns of initiation and influence were accepted as long as they followed this status ordering. But when this order was abandoned, as for example when low-status industrial engineers needed to direct the higher-status researchers in the implementing of tests, conflict resulted.[17] Further evidence that status inconsistencies lead to conflict is found in William Whyte's classic study of the restaurant industry.[18] Conflict was found to result when low-status waitresses gave "orders" to high-status cooks. Due to the incongruity between initiation and status, cooks were being perceived in a lower-prestige grade.

[15]Ronald G. Corwin, "Patterns of Organizational Conflict," *Administrative Science Quarterly*, December 1969, pp. 507–520.

[16]John A. Seiler, "Diagnosing Interdepartmental Conflict," *Harvard Business Review*, September–October 1963, pp. 121–132.

[17]Ibid.

[18]William F. Whyte, *Human Relations in the Restaurant Industry* (New York: McGraw-Hill, 1948).

Role Dissatisfaction

Closely akin to status incongruence is role dissatisfaction. Role dissatisfaction can come from a number of sources, one of which is status incongruence. When someone feels that he deserves a promotion to reflect his record of accomplishments, he suffers from both role dissatisfaction and perceived status incongruence. In this section, however, we want to emphasize that the ways in which people perceive themselves in their positions can significantly affect their performance and thus the potential for conflict between them and their peers in their own and adjoining units. When people accept a role, they bring to it a set of hopes and aspirations. When these expectations are not met—for instance, when their work does not prove challenging or the rewards they receive are seen as inadequate—these individuals may display their frustrations in a number of directions. Some resign. Some reduce the effort they exert on the job. Still others choose to fight. This last group can become continuous conflict stimulators—looking for problems, spreading rumors, twisting and distorting facts to instigate disturbances, and similar actions. Such people, and all large organizations have at least one, seem to enjoy upsetting the system. To the degree that they establish allies in their cause, they can become a major source of conflict.

Communication Distortions

One frequently cited source of conflict is communication difficulties. An obvious case is vertical communications. As information is passed up and down the hierarchy, it is susceptible to ambiguity and distortion. But distortions also occur at the horizontal level. For instance, one researcher argued that the less the differing units know about each other's jobs, the less the collaboration that will take place. And this lack of knowledge can lead to unreasonable interunit demands.[19] Animosities observed by your author between a county welfare department and other county agencies in a southern California community appeared to be attributable directly to ignorance on the part of each agency as to the nature of duties of other agencies. In contrast, smooth coordination and relations existed where nonwelfare agency members were familiar with the welfare department's responsibilities and contributions.

Semantic difficulties are a frequent problem in organizations. They impede communication essential for cooperative efforts between units. Semantic difficulties can be attributed to the different training, background,

[19]E. J. Miller, "Technology, Territory, and Time," *Human Relations*, August 1959, pp. 243–272.

and socialization processes that members of units have undergone. It has been reported that the difference in training of purchasing agents and engineers contributes to their conflict.[20] As with physicians and professional hospital administrators, their academic training and orientations differ significantly. Differences in training develop disparate vocabularies and jargon, which impede the effective movement of ideas.

Pragmatism suggests that we also mention that a source of communicative conflicts is the willful withholding of information by one unit from another. As we have noted in previous chapters, information can facilitate the attainment of power. It is only realistic, therefore, to acknowledge that, when important information is deliberately kept secret, conflicts can ensue.

If inadequate, distorted, or ambiguous information is a source of conflict, the existence of complete or perfect knowledge might be expected to result in little or no conflict. Interestingly, it does not seem to work that way. Studies demonstrate that interdepartmental conflict increases when departments possess a great deal of knowledge of each other's activities.[21] Why does this occur? Complete knowledge makes each party's self-interest fully visible and reveals any and all inequities. Imperfect knowledge, on the other hand, clouds self-interest, diminishes disparities, and makes coordination easier. We can conclude that communication extremes can be sources of conflict. Inadequate or unclear communications stimulate conflict. So, too, does perfect or complete information.

RESOLUTION TECHNIQUES

When the forces of conflict are too great, we say that it is dyfunctional. It has a negative impact on organizational effectiveness. Something needs to be done, therefore, to bring the conflict down to an acceptable level. The following represent structural techniques for reducing conflict intensity.

Superordinate Goals

A superordinate goal is a common goal, held by two or more units, that is compelling and highly appealing and cannot be attained by the resources of any single unit separately.[22]

[20]George Strauss, "Work-Flow Frictions, Interfunctional Rivalry, and Professionalism: A Case Study of Purchasing Agents," *Human Organization*, Summer 1964, pp. 137–149.

[21]See, for example, Richard E. Walton, John M. Dutton, and Thomas P. Cafferty, "Organizational Context and Interdepartmental Conflict," *Administrative Science Quarterly*, December 1969, pp. 522–542.

[22]Muzafer Sherif, "Experiments on Group Conflict and Cooperation," in Harold J. Leavitt and Louis R. Pondy, eds., *Readings in Managerial Psychology* (Chicago: University of Chicago Press, 1964), p. 410.

A superordinate goal initiates with a definition of a shared goal and the recognition that, without the help of the contending parties, it cannot be attained. While each unit desires them, they are unattainable to any single unit. Superordinate goals are highly valued, unattainable by any one group alone, and commonly sought. They must, to be effective, supersede other goals that the units may have individually. They act to reduce conflict by requiring the disagreeing parties to work together in achieving those goals they mutually seek.

After extensive research of resolution techniques, one researcher has concluded that, in those instances where conflict has developed from mutually incompatible goals, the use of superordinate goals, based on mutual interdependence, should increase cooperation.[23] The cooperative environment grows as effort is directed away from concern with separate and independent units to recognition that the conflicting units are part of a larger group, a synergy developing from the collaboration of forces.

A union-management dispute illustrates the functioning of the superordinate goal. In times of economic plenty, unions are frequently adamant in their demands. But in cases where an organization's survival has been seriously threatened by economic pressures, some unions have accepted pay reductions to keep the organization in business. Once this crisis is overcome, demand for higher wages returns. A compelling and highly valued goal—survival—has preceded other individual goals and has temporarily resolved the labor conflict. Evidence supports that, when used cumulatively, superordinate goals develop long-term "peacemaking" potential, thereby reinforcing dependency and developing collaboration.

Reduce Interdependence Between Units

When mutual and one-way interdependence creates conflicts, reduction of this interdependence should be considered as a possible solution. Buffers, for example, can be introduced to reduce interdependence. If the output of department X is department Y's input, then Y is dependent on X. When X is behind schedule, Y will also look bad. Conversely, if X is producing output faster than Y can process it, the latter again looks bad. One solution involves creating an inventory of X's output as a buffer. The interdependency of X and Y is thus reduced.

Coordination positions can also be effective in reducing interdependence between units. On occasion, when industrial firms have interunit conflicts, such as between accounting and engineering departments, they will seek an individual with both an accounting and engineering back-

[23]Muzafer Sherif, *In Common Predicament: Social Psychology of Intergroup Conflict and Cooperation* (Boston: Houghton Mifflin, 1966), p. 93.

ground and then create the position of coordinator for him. Because he speaks the language of both, he functions as an integrator between the separate units.

Expanding Resources

When conflict is predicated upon the scarcity of a resource, the easiest manner in which to resolve the confrontation, and the one most satisfying to the conflicting parties, is through expansion of the available resources. Although it may be most undesirable to other parties outside the conflict, its greatest strength as a resolution tool is in its ability to allow each conflicting party a victory.

If the purchasing department in a moderately sized school district is allocated only $400 for monthly salary increases, to be distributed among the department's four members, any individual's gain above $100 is at the expense of others in the unit. If each of the four departmental members expects a $150 a month raise, then there is a conflict: demand for the fixed resource exceeds its supply. One solution is to allocate more money for salary adjustments. An increase of $200 in the allocation would resolve the conflict.

This technique was used effectively in 1969, when the presidency of the Ford Motor Company was left vacant by the departure of Semon Knudsen. Three vice presidents were candidates for the position. The decision of who would be promoted to the presidency rested with the company's chairman, Henry Ford, II, but a decision to give one of the aspirants the position would have resulted in only one winner and two losers. Hence, the three vice presidents' desire for a limited resource, the company's presidency, created a conflict. Henry Ford's decision to create an Office of the President resolved the conflict through expansion. Each of the three aspirants became president over a specific jurisdiction. By increasing the scarce resource, supply was expanded to meet the demand. This solution resolved the conflict by directly altering its source and thus creating three winners.

Expanding resources as a resolution method is extremely successful because it leaves the conflicting parties satisfied. But its use is restricted by the nature of its inherent limitations that organizational resources rarely exist in such quantity as to be easily expanded.

Mutual Problem Solving

Mutual problem solving has been described as the soundest method for resolving intergroup conflicts.[24] This technique requires the conflicting par-

[24]Robert R. Blake, Herbert A. Shepard, and Jane S. Mouton, *Managing Intergroup Conflict in Industry* (Houston: Gulf Publishing, 1964), pp. 99–100.

ties to come face to face with the underlying causes for their conflict and share responsibility for seeing that the solution works. The purpose is to solve *the* problem rather than merely to accommodate different points of view.

Mutual problem solving requires that the conflicting units have "the potential to achieve a better solution through collaboration."[25] Although this may be a difficult requirement to meet, where it exists, it relies on seeking fundamental points of difference rather than on determining who is right, who is wrong, who wins, or who loses. Further, through sharing and communicating, the problem is mutually defined. The participants, or at least their representatives, consider the full range of alternatives, and similarities in views become emphasized. Through this process, the causes of doubt and misunderstanding that underlie the conflict become outwardly evident.

Problem solving additionally attempts to "accentuate the positive" by highlighting the commonly held views of the parties. This recognizes an often overlooked side of any conflict—that there exists in almost every instance some issues on which the dissenting parties are in agreement. These similarities are too frequently bypassed and result in what has been referred to as Gresham's law of conflict,[26] which states that similar views and those that work to increase cooperation are pushed out by those views that accentuate differences. Bad forces push out the good. Problem solving seeks to emphasize the similar views and avoid those that breed a hostile climate.

The attempt to resolve differences through the mutual problem-solving approach as described is frequently used, and unfortunately, evidence indicates that it frequently fails. How often we hear someone who is aware of the existence of a conflict say, "What they need to do is sit down and discuss the situation." But problem solving is limited in the types of conflict with which it can deal effectively. Its failures are closely related to its misapplication. Clearly, it is most successful in semantic conflicts. Oppositions that develop from misunderstandings lend themselves to the in-depth analysis of problem solving, definition of terms, and thorough understanding of the opposing parties' ideas.

Appeals Systems

The resolving of conflicts can be handled by creating formal channels for grievances to be heard and acted upon. If an employee or group of employees believes that their rights have been jeopardized by the actions of a superior or a peer, an appeals system provides the right of formal redress.

[25]Ibid., p. 86.

[26]James S. Coleman, *Community Conflict* (New York: Free Press, 1957), p. 14.

The appeal may be made to one's boss's boss, an executive several levels higher in the organization, or a third-party arbitrator.

Unionized organizations present an excellent illustration of the appeals technique. In their grievance procedure, unions have established an elaborate appeals system to resolve conflicts with management. If an aggrieved union member cannot find satisfaction through discussion with a superior, the aggrieved may proceed to appeal the grievance upward through the employing organization; a frequent route in an industrial firm may include presenting the case to the area supervisor, shift supervisor, plant superintendent, industrial relations manager, plant manager, and eventually to a neutral, third-party arbitrator, if necessary.

A few organizations, however, have created the position of ombudsman to arbitrate differences. For example, colleges and universities have used the ombudsman to hear and resolve problems among and between faculty, students, and staff. The ombudsman typically begins by using the mutual problem-solving technique. If this fails, the ombudsman may attempt negotiation or suggest that a senior administrator in the organization—one with authority over both of the conflicting parties—resolve the differences by enforcing a solution.

Formal Authority

The authority that superiors have over the conflicting parties is important enough and its usage spread so widely that it can be singled out as a separate resolution technique.

A disagreement between two nurses that cannot be resolved between them is taken to their supervisor or head nurse for a decision. Similarly, when a conflict develops between sales and production units within a manufacturing firm, it is referred to the two immediate executives responsible for each function and who possess the authority to resolve the differences. If an agreement cannot be reached at this level, the authority of their mutual superior will act as the ultimate judge and, in the majority of cases, will be accepted by both parties.

Individuals in organizations, with rare exception, recognize and accept the authority of their superiors as an acceptable way of resolving conflicts. Although they may not be in agreement with these decisions, they abide by them. Thus, formal authority is highly successful in achieving reductions in conflict.

Increasing Interaction

All other things held equal, the more people interact with each other, the more likely they are to find common interests and bonds that can facilitate cooperation.[27] Certainly, if parties with distinctly opposing values are

[27]Sherif, "Experiments on Group Conflict and Cooperation," pp. 408–421.

forced to interact regularly, there is a high probability of conflict. But our point is that continued interaction should reduce the conflict. It may never be as low as management might desire, but the direction should be downward. This can be achieved through transference or exchange of unit members.

By transferring people into or out of a unit, we change its internal structure. The forces that caused conflict in that unit or between that unit and other units may be dissipated by "shaking up" the internal common bonds. Transferring someone out of his or her unit and into an adversary unit can cross-fertilize those areas in conflict and force contact between members.

Cross-fertilization may be achieved more effectively by requiring some personnel in the conflicting units to exchange jobs. Previous organizational barriers are often reduced. A manager at a production plant for a major U.S. aluminum company used employee exchange to reduce conflict in his accounting department. The plant controller attributed the dysfunctional behavior between his general accounting and cost accounting sections to the lack of an information flow between each group. The two units were frequently at odds with each other. To reduce misunderstandings, he had the supervisors of both sections switch jobs for a six-month period. The move expanded the perspective of each supervisor and promoted greater understanding and reduced interunit conflict as the modified views filtered down through each's section.

Organizationwide Evaluation Criteria and Reward Systems

If separatism in evaluations and rewards creates conflicts, management should consider performance measures that evaluate and reward units for cooperation. Elimination of zero-sum situations should be beneficial. Ensuring, for instance, that quality-control, auditing, and other policing functions are evaluated for their preventive contributions rather than for their success in finding errors will reduce conflicts. Additionally, instituting an organizationwide profit-sharing or bonus plan should assist in reminding people that the organization's primary concern is with the effectiveness of the entire system, not with any singular unit.

Merging Conflicting Units

A final suggestion for resolving conflict is for one of the conflicting units to expand its boundaries and absorb the source of its irritation. This merger technique is exemplified by the solution applied to the conflicts generated when a college of business's curriculum must rely heavily upon the economics courses offered in the economics department. Historically, economics was located in the college of arts and sciences or liberal arts. The philosophical conflicts that often develop between business and economics can be reconciled through expansion of the business program to include the economics department. The result is the frequently encountered "College of Business and Economics." Elementary and secondary school systems utilize this same technique when they allow persons critical of the curriculum to participate in the review and evaluation of the system's programs and policies. They coopt their critics by merging them into the system.

STIMULATION TECHNIQUES

The interactionist view recognizes that conflict may, at times, be too low as well as too high. When its too low, managers need to stimulate opposition—to create functional conflict.

Unfortunately, from a theoretical standpoint, we know a great deal more about how to resolve conflicts effectively than we know about stimulating them. This is simply a result of the fact that the notion of stimulating conflict is a relatively recent idea and is just beginning to receive attention by organizational researchers. The following pages contain some potential stimulation techniques. They have been derived from reviewing the sources of conflict presented earlier in this chapter. They are far more sketchy than our previous discussion of resolution methods; however, do not confuse brevity with unimportance. Stimulation techniques are no more or less important than their resolution counterparts—we just know less about them.

Communications

Managers can manipulate communication messages and channels in such ways as to stimulate conflict. Ambiguous or threatening messages encourage conflict. Information that a plant will close, that a department is to be eliminated, or that a layoff is to be incurred will accelerate conflict intensity. These kinds of messages can be transmitted through the formal authority hierarchy or informal channels. The latter includes all loosely knit and ill-structured networks. "Rumors on the grapevine" refer to unsubstantiated communications following the informal channels. By careful selection of the messages to be distributed through the grapevine and the individuals to carry them, the manager can increase conflict. He can purposely manipulate receivers and message content to add, negate, or make ambiguous the communications that are carried by formal means. How, you may ask, would this produce beneficial results for the organization? It might, for example, reduce apathy, force members to confront their differences, or encourage the reevaluation of current procedures and stimulate new ideas.

Heterogeneity

One way in which to "shakeup" a stagnant unit is to add one or more individuals whose background, experience, and values vary significantly from those currently held by members in a unit. Heterogeneity can be synthetic as well as real. The infiltrator may play the role of the proverbial "devil's advocate," who though sharing similar views with other unit members, is assigned the task to question, attack, inquire, and otherwise resist any homogeneity of views. Either way, the status quo has been disturbed by introducing heterogeneous people.

Competition

Management can stimulate conflict by creating competitive situations between units. Of course, where the stakes in the competition are zero sum, you can expect the conflict to be that much more intense. For instance, when city fire units compete against each other to win the "best firehouse" award, the result is generally a more effective firefighting organization. Equipment is kept in top condition, units respond rapidly to alarms, and teamwork is high. Many companies that continually promote sales contests within their sales staff believe that this competition leads to a more effective sales force.

Changing the structure by increasing horizontal differentiation has been suggested as an excellent way in which to create conflict.[28] The example is offered of a school of business made up of just a few departments—accounting, economics, and business administration. The last department includes all the faculty who teach management, marketing, and finance courses. This department of business administration is large, having thirty-two members, with a single chairperson who reports to the dean. When a new dean was hired, he perceived apathy. Faculty members were comfortable with their structural arrangement, sufficiently so that many members were stagnating. As a result, the dean began entertaining the idea of splitting up the unit into separate departments of management, marketing, and finance, each with eight to twelve members and a chairperson. The dean's logic is fully consistent with the interactionist view and the value of stimulating conflict. By increasing horizontal differentiation, each area of specialization will be more homogeneous. But there will be differences between units. They will be forced to compete with each other for resources, students, faculty, and the like. If you believe in Darwin's "survival of the fittest" doctrine, then you should find structural decisions like this to be an attractive conflict stimulation device.

[28]James L. Gibson, John M. Ivancevich, and James H. Donnelly, Jr., *Organizations: Behavior, Structure, Processes*, 3rd ed. (Dallas: Business Publications, 1979), p. 177.

SUMMARY

Conflict is a process in which an effort is purposely made by one person or unit to block another that results in frustrating the attainment of the other's goals or the furthering of his or her interests. Views toward conflict can be labeled as traditional, behavioral, and interactionist. The traditional views all conflict as bad. The behavioral accepts conflict. The interactionist encourages conflict. The interactionist perspective is currently in vogue among theorists, but the traditional perspective dominates in practice.

The most frequently cited structural sources of conflict are mutual task dependence, one-way task dependence, high horizontal differentiation, low formalization, dependence on common scarce resources, differences in evaluation criteria and reward systems, participative decision making, heterogeneity of members, status incongruence, role dissatisfaction, and communication distortions.

Resolution techniques include superordinate goals, reducing interdependence between units, expansion of resources, mutual problem solving, appeals systems, formal authority, increased interaction, organizationwide evaluation criteria and reward systems, and merging of conflicting interests. Stimulation of conflict can be achieved through manipulating communication messages and channels, creating heterogeneous units, or creating competition between units.

FOR REVIEW AND DISCUSSION

1. Contrast traditional, behavioral, and interactionist views of conflict.
2. What forces make the traditional perspective dominant in practice?
3. In what ways can conflict be functional?
4. How does formalization affect conflict?
5. What is the relationship between participative decision making and conflict.
6. What are superordinate goals? Give an example where they could be used to reduce conflict.
7. Compare appeal systems and formal authority as conflict resolution techniques.
8. Give some examples of ways in which to stimulate conflict.
9. What is the relationship between clarity of communication and conflict?
10. "Bureaucracies are mechanisms that simultaneously resolve and stimulate structural conflicts." Do you agree or disagree? Discuss.

CHAPTER

17

MANAGING GROWTH AND DECLINE

The preponderance of theoretical material in this book arose from research and publications produced between the mid-1940s and the mid-1970s. Coincidentally, this same three-decade period was one of relatively uninterrupted growth. It should not be surprising, therefore, to find that the organization theory literature is heavily growth oriented, focusing almost exclusively on problems or benefits associated with expansion.

It's easy to overlook the fact that growth is only one side of the growth-decline cycle that organizations experience. If organizations are all growing, then growth should be getting the bulk of the attention. But, obviously, all organizations are not in a continual growth pattern. So the consideration of decline should receive some attention even if growth is the dominant pattern. Two facts, closely intertwined, have recently surfaced that now make it imperative that the growth perspective be balanced by an analysis of the organization when it is in its decline cycle. These facts are (1) the primary conditions that fostered the growth decades no longer exist and (2) the increasing body of literature that indicates that managing organizational decline is not merely reversing what one has done during growth. These two facts require that we look at such topics as the growth bias, how Americans view stagnation and decline, and the potential problems that organizational decline creates for managers.

AMERICAN VALUES FAVOR GROWTH

Traditional American values include optimism about the future. In America, any young person can grow up to be president. You can become rich and successful regardless of the economic status of your family. Parents expect that their children will have more of "the good life" than they have. These notions, while under some attack in the last decade, are relatively accurate descriptions of Americans' fundamental confidence that the future will be better than the present. These optimistic values have permeated our ideas on organizations. Managers and researchers, alike, have allowed the goal of growth to become a means to express this confidence in an organizational context. Growth came to represent a way in which to make tomorrow's organizations better than today's.

Bigger Is Better

One of the strong forces for growth has been the "bigger is better" notion in America. Large organizations were desirable, as were large cars and large homes. But large size, when applied to organizations, could also be justified in economic terms. Growth was desirable because with increases in size came economies of scale. Bigger, in fact, was frequently more efficient.

The "bigger is better" notion, it should be pointed out, still dominates the securities markets. Growth rates continue to be a primary determinant of a stock's value. Stocks that show compounded sales growth rates of 20 percent and higher year after year become the darlings of Wall Street. They frequently carry price-earnings ratios of 30, 40, or higher. However, let that growth curve flatten, and the stock's price can be expected to dive. Why does this happen? Growth serves as an indicator of an organization's fitness for the future.[1] Since an optimistic future influences the extent to which the organization can obtain continued or increased support from its specific environment, managers are motivated to seek growth.

Growth Increases the Likelihood of Survival

In our discussion of organizational effectiveness, we acknowledged the paramount status accorded to survival. If the organization does not survive, other issues become purely academic. Growth becomes desirable, then, because it increases the likelihood of survival.

Large organizations are not permitted to go out of existence as are small organizations.[2] Lockheed received government support when it got into financial difficulty. The bankruptcy of Lockheed would have had dire consequences on such places as California and Georgia where the firm had manufacturing facilities, and politicians in these locales brought strong

[1]James D. Thompson, *Organizations in Action* (New York: McGraw-Hill, 1967), p. 89.

[2]Jeffrey Pfeffer, *Organizational Design* (Arlington Heights, Ill.: AHM Publishing, 1978), p. 114.

pressure to bear on the federal government to help Lockheed out. Similarly, Chrysler Corporation's large size alone assures it of strong constituencies to fight for its survival. Your community drugstore or laundromat certainly does not attract that kind of support. This same logic, of course, holds for hospitals, colleges, and government agencies. In times of economic crisis, the State of Massachusetts is far more likely to close down Framingham State College, with its 2,500 students and 120 faculty members, than it is the University of Massachusetts, with its 18,000 students and more than a thousand faculty!

In addition to providing a large constituency, growth facilitates survival by having more resources with which to buffer itself against uncertainty. Larger organizations can make errors and live to talk about them. General Motors, for instance, has a greater margin for error than does Avanti Motors. A $100 million mistake at General Motors is an annoyance. The same mistake at Avanti Motors would be a catastrophe. Similarly, more resources provide a buffer in times of setbacks. Growing organizations have slack resources that can be cut more easily than do small or stable organizations. The growing organization that has to reduce its budget by 10 percent can often cut fat without threatening its survival. The stagnant organization is often forced to cut bone. Cosmetic surgery in the first case becomes life-threatening major surgery in the second.

Growth Becomes Synonymous with Effectiveness

What is success? If an organization is getting bigger, it is common to assume that it is being managed effectively.[3]

Business executives flaunt the fact that "sales are up significantly." Hospital administrators produce charts showing that they are handling more patients than ever. College deans brag about having record enrollments. As one business dean remarked, "We must be doing something right. Our enrollments are up more than 15 percent for the fourth year in a row." These examples all illustrate how organizations use, rightly or wrongly, growth as a synonym for effectiveness. If those in the specific environment on whom the organization depends for continued support also equate growth with effectiveness, managers will obviously be predisposed to the values of growth.

The interlacing of growth and effectiveness is seen explicitly in the systems concept, which we discussed in Chapter 1. If you remember, organizations were described as open systems. In this context, organiza-

[3]David A. Whetten, "Organizational Decline: A Neglected Topic in Organizational Science," *Academy of Management Review*, October 1980, p. 578.

tions are analogous to living organisms, maintaining themselves by acquiring inputs from, and disposing of its output to, the environment. The systems approach favors growth. Growth is sought because it connotes youth and vitality.[4] Growth is evidence that the organization is in good health. And expansion, again consistent with the systems perspective, increases the likelihood that the organization will survive.

Growth Is Power

The arguments that growth can be consistent with economies of scale, can be used by the specific environment to assess the organization's effectiveness, and can increase the likelihood of survival are all economically rational explanations for the pro-growth bias. Now we want to present a political argument in favor of growth.

Growth is almost always consistent with the self-interest of the top management in the organization. It increases prestige, power, and job security for this group. It should certainly be more than of passing interest to know that growth is undoubtedly linked to executive compensation. The evidence indicates that profit rates generally increase in business firms until the organization achieves a reasonably moderate size. Then, the profit rate remains stable or declines. As we learned in Chapter 7, size—especially large size—does not necessarily generate economies. The costs of coordination can exceed the benefits from economies of scale. But, and this is what is relevant from a power-control perspective, executive salaries are related to size. Size, in fact, is a better predictor of executive salaries than is profit margin.[5] Should we not expect, therefore, for top business executives to be motivated toward expanding their firms?

Growth also provides the organization with more power with respect to other organizations and groups in its environment.[6] Larger organizations have more influence with suppliers, unions, large customers, government, and the like.

This leads us to the obvious conclusion that growth is not a chance occurrence. It is the result of conscious managerial decisions. Growth typically provides both economic benefits to the organization and political benefits to the organization's executive decision makers. As such, strong forces are continually encouraging organizations to grow and expand.

[4]William G. Scott, "The Management of Decline," *The Conference Board Record,* June 1976, p. 57.

[5]Jeffrey Pfeffer and Gerald R. Salancik, *The External Control of Organizations* (New York: Harper & Row, 1978).

[6]Jeffrey Pfeffer, *Organizational Design,* p. 115.

DECLINE IS ALIEN TO AMERICAN VALUES

If growth is as American as apple pie, the concept of decline is alien to American values. Before we look at why decline has a negative following, its important to define the term.

When we refer to "organizational decline," we mean a prolonged decrease in the number of personnel in an organization. It is not meant to describe temporary aberrations in an organization's growth curve, though it is often used in this context.

One researcher has distinguished two types of organizational shrinkage: decline as stagnation and decline as cutback.[7] The first is treated in the literature as a reflection of poor management or noncompetitive market conditions. The second is seen as the consequence of environmental scarcity. Decline as stagnation describes an organization that is losing market share. In contrast, decline as cutback characterizes those situations where the entire market is shrinking. This, for instance, might characterize many federal agencies in the early 1980s or colleges whose sole function has been the training of elementary and secondary school teachers. Organizational death prompted by stagnation is viewed as suicide; death due to cutback is treated as homicide. In our discussion of decline, we will be emphasizing the cutback typology. We have always had to confront the reality that some organizations stagnate while their competitors flourish. The more recent phenomenon, and one that many believe is responsible for the current interest in the management of decline, is the recognition that a number of industries are confronting cutbacks resulting from a shrinking pie and the increasing likelihood that everyone will have to live with a smaller piece of the pie.

Declines due to cutback run directly counter to the optimistic, pro-growth values that have dominated thinking in the United States since the end of World War II. It is counter to Americans' optimism about the future. As we point out at the end of this chapter, prolonged organizational decline creates a number of potential problems for managers. These problems are derived basically from the frustration that organizational members feel with having to cope with the reality that tomorrow is unlikely to be as good as today. Its probably accurate to conclude that, until very recently—within the past ten years—whenever an organization faced decline, it was treated as an aberration. As one author noted, "incidents of decline were treated with characteristic optimism. They were temporary periods of consolidation, forerunners to future expansion."[8] Managers are increasingly coming

[7]David A. Whetten, "Sources, Responses, and Effects of Organizational Decline," in John Kimberly and Robert H. Miles, eds., *The Organization Life Cycle: Issues in the Creation, Transformations, and Decline of Organizations* (San Francisco: Jossey-Bass, 1980), pp. 342–374.

[8]Scott, "The Management of Decline," p. 56.

to recognize that this might not be true for their organizations. More and more managers are having to face the reality that their jobs entail overseeing the continuing saga of an organization in the throes of contraction.

WHY THE RECENT CONCERN WITH MANAGEMENT OF DECLINE?

The pro-growth bias suggests that managers would not be concerned with trying to understand the implications of organizational contraction if they, figuratively speaking, did not have "a gun to their heads." Railroad executives have been facing declining organizations for decades, but they have been treated almost universally as a special case. Beginning in the mid-1970s, however, evidence led increasingly to the conclusion that many industries and individual organizations were entering the decline side of their life cycles.

The incredible escalation in oil prices, initiated by the Organization of Petroleum Exporting Countries' decision in October 1973 to raise the price of oil from $2.25 to $11.00 per barrel, began a series of events culminating in the contraction of Ford Motor and Chrysler. The lower labor costs and more modern equipment of Japanese steel producers forced cutbacks in U.S. steel firms. The increasing popularity of smaller families and childless marriages contributed to the drastic decline in school enrollments and the contraction of many school districts across North America. Taxpayer revolts in California, Massachusetts, Michigan, and other states have brought severe cutbacks in government services. The election of Ronald Reagan on a platform of less government has brought the same treatment to the federal bureaucracy.

These examples illustrate an increased need to better understand some of the problems unique to managing in a declining organization. One writer has gone as far as to suggest that the traditional values that underlie organization theory need to be rethought. As a beginning to such a rethinking, he proposed a radical model with a very different set of values.[9]

The traditional values of organization theory have supported growth, abundance, and consensus. It is believed that material growth is a desirable end, material abundance is limitless, and consensus is the natural manner by which individuals relate. These values reflect optimism, which in turn is rooted in an abundant environment. That is, growth creates organizational abundance, or surplus, which is then used by management to achieve consensus by buying off potentially conflicting interest groups that compete for the organization's resources.

Radical values would be those that are opposite to growth, abun-

[9]William G. Scott, "Organization Theory: A Reassessment," *Academy of Management Journal*, June 1974, pp. 242–254.

dance, and consensus, namely, stability or decay, scarcity, and conflict. The management of decline appears to be more compatible with these radical values. Our contention is—and this will be built upon later in this chapter—that, when environmental resources are scarce, some organizations will be forced into contraction. The contraction process, in turn, stimulates conflicts both between organizations fighting for these resources and among powerful interest groups within the organization trying to ensure that they are not the victims of any cutbacks.

IS MANAGING DECLINE THE REVERSE OF MANAGING GROWTH?

There is very little research on the decline process. This is undoubtedly due to the growth bias and the reality that organizations undergoing contraction rarely can afford the luxury of sponsoring reflective research nor do their managements see much to gain by permitting outsiders to chronicle their organization's decline.[10] We are left, therefore, with a research vacuum that must be filled with a great deal of speculation.

We begin with the proposition that the management of decline is not merely composed of reversing the process of managing growth. An organization cannot be reduced piece by piece by simply reversing the sequence of activity and resource building by which it grew.[11] While the research is scant, there does appear to be enough evidence to conclude that activities within the same-sized organization during periods of growth and decline will not correspond directly. As a generalization, there is a lag that typifies the rate of change in structure during prolonged decline that is not evident in growth.[12] As discussed in Chapter 7, changes in size have a significant impact on structure. But those conclusions were drawn from organizations that were all changing in the growth direction. During decline, size has an impact on structure, but it is not a reverse parallel of the growth pattern. This lag results in the level of structure being greater in the same organization for a given level of size during decline than for the same level of size during growth.[13] Referring to Figure 17–1, the lag thesis would state that at a given size, X, points a and b are not equal. More specifically, at point b in time, the organization should have a greater degree of structure. For instance, we could expect a lag in the degree of formalization. Typically, when an organization goes from 100 employees

[10]Whetten, "Organizational Decline," p. 579.

[11]C. H. Levine, "More on Cutback Management: Hard Questions for Hard Times," *Public Administration Review*, March/April 1979, pp. 179–183.

[12]Jeffrey D. Ford, "The Occurrence of Structural Hysteresis in Declining Organizations," *Academy of Management Review*, October 1980, pp. 589–598.

[13]Ibid., p. 592.

FIGURE 17–1 The organization's life cycle

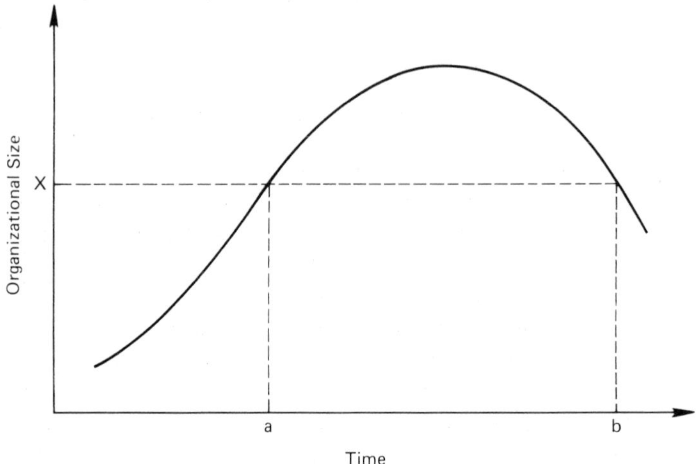

to 1,000, there is an increase in formal rules and regulations. But this is not easily reversible. We predict, therefore, that, when an organization is contracting, it would tend to have a higher degree of formalization at each size level than it had at the same level in its growth stage. This lag factor is most evident, however, in recent studies of the administrative component in declining organizations.

The Administrative Component Revisited

As described in Chapter 7, the administrative component refers to the number of people in an organization who engage in supportive activities. If there is a lag in decline, one would expect the administrative component to shrink at a slower rate than the whole organization. Studies of over eight hundred school districts confirm this expectation.[14] In some cases, evidence has been found that the administrative component actually increased while organizations declined.[15] Although the exact nature of the relationship is not well established, it is clear that the relationship between size and the administrative component is different during decline than during growth. Interestingly, either a lag or an increase would be consistent with the conclusion that organizational politics distorts the decline

[14]John H. Freeman and Michael T. Hannan, "Growth and Decline Processes in Organizations," *American Sociological Review,* April 1975, pp. 215–283.

[15]Jeffrey D. Ford, "The Administrative Component in Growing and Declining Organizations: A Longitudinal Analysis," *Academy of Management Journal,* December 1980, pp. 615–630.

process's effect on the administrative component.[16] The administrative support group, because of its power, is more effective in resisting cutback pressures. As a result, the ratio of supportive staff to operatives will be higher at the same level of total organizational size in the decline stage.

An Enhanced Case for Power-Control

Organizational size is a major factor in determining an organization's structure during growth, but not during decline. So our conclusions in Chapter 7 on the size-structure relationship appear to be relevant only on the upside of an organization's life cycle.

While the evidence is sketchy, we offer the following hypothesis. Size is a key determinant of structure during growth, but it is replaced by power-control in decline. During growth, the actions of vested interest groups to maintain or enhance their power is not nearly as visible as it is in decline. Slack resources minimize conflicts. Confrontations can be resolved by all parties' winning. When the organization is contracting, scarce resources are most dear. Administrative rationality, which can explain the size-structure relationship in growth, is replaced by a power struggle. In decline, therefore, structure is more likely to reflect the interests of those in power, for they are best able to weather a political struggle.

Declines Follow Stages

A final speculation on the decline structure relationship is based on the assumption that organizations are most likely, initially, to confront what will become a prolonged decline as if it is merely an aberration. If true, prolonged declines should find management treating it in stages. First, the decline is ignored or denied. Second, when the facts of decline are evident, it will be reacted to as if it is a temporary crisis. Then, over time, management will begin realistically to make decisions as if they are confronting a prolonged contraction. Management can be expected to make different structural decisions in the second stage than in the third.

In the temporary crisis stage, we would predict management to centralize decision making and resort to a simple structure. This is consistent with the findings presented in Chapters 11 and 13. When under attack, management wants control. But this approach cannot result in effective organizational performance when the decline is of a long-term nature. As we learn later in this chapter, one of the major problems that management must face during organizational decline is the propensity for the best em-

[16]Michael T. Hannan and John H. Freeman, "Internal Politics of Growth and Decline," in Marshall W. Meyer and Associates, eds., *Environments and Organizations* (San Francisco: Jossey-Bass, 1978), pp. 177–199.

ployees to leave the organization. To reduce turnover and maintain high levels of employee morale and commitment, management must decentralize and give up autocratic control. When the decline has been diagnosed properly as the long-term variety, management will have to resort to giving employees an increased role in decision making. Increased participation should improve the organization's ability to hold employees and to get necessary input for changes that will almost certainly be necessary. We propose, then, that structure will change during decline. Once it is recognized, structure will become centralized and take on simple characteristics. However, as it becomes clear that the decline is not temporary, the structure will move toward decentralization.

A CASE STUDY IN DECLINE: CHRYSLER CORPORATION

During the late 1970s and early 1980s, Chrysler Corporation has literally become a textbook example of an organization in decline.[17] Always the smallest of the Big 3 U.S. automobile manufacturers—behind General Motors and Ford—Chrysler never was a money-making machine as GM had been. But it had a loyal segment of the U.S. car-buying public—about 16 percent of the market in the early 1970s. Their loyalty to Chrysler products allowed the company to survive through the good times and the bad. Several factors combined to gang up on Chrysler in the 1970s and force management to change the company drastically. It should be noted that management had no real choice. After a staggering $1.7 billion loss in 1980, Chrysler had to become a much smaller and more viable organization or it would never survive. Of course, even the changes that management was forced to make would provide no guarantee of Chrysler's survival.

The decline of Chrysler Corporation is not due to any single cause. The steep rise in gasoline prices led to the public's massive switch to small fuel-efficient cars. This hit Chrysler particularly hard because Chrysler was basically a large-car manufacturer. The small cars it did sell through its dealers were imported from Japan and England. The 1974–1975 recession led to an internal decision at Chrysler that would later prove shortsighted. As a result of a steep drop in sales, management decided to make massive cuts in capital spending and in staff, including engineers and designers. From that point on, Chrysler's new-model introductions were plagued by delays and by launch and quality problems. For instance, Chrysler's much publicized K-car came out a full eighteen months after GM's comparable

[17]Much of the information in this case came from "Chrysler Goes Back to the Well," *Time,* December 29, 1980, p. 53; "Chrysler Is Barreling Toward the Brink Again," *Business Week,* December 29, 1980, p. 43; and Irwin Ross, "Chrysler on the Brink," *Fortune,* February 9, 1981, pp. 38–42.

X-car. The 1980 recession added further to Chrysler's problems. Record-setting interest rates made the purchase of a new car postponable for many potential buyers.

These factors all worked against Chrysler. By 1980, with its precarious financial situation, the company asked for and received nearly $2 billion of federally backed loan guarantees. But, as part of the loan guarantee, Chrysler had to accept a radically different role for itself in the U.S. automobile industry. It lacked the resources to develop new products, while GM and Ford were now commiting unthinkable sums into the development of new compacts, subcompacts, minicompacts, specialty cars, and full-sized and luxury models. As an example, GM spent $8 billion in 1981 on new plant and tooling, whereas Chrysler spent only about $1.3 billion. It was obvious to Chrysler's management, suppliers, unions, and lenders and to government officials that Chrysler could no longer compete as a comprehensive, full-line automobile manufacturer. This reality probably hit Chrysler's chairman, Lee Iacocca, as hard as anyone. Fired from the presidency of Ford in 1978 and subsequently hired to lead Chrysler, Iacocca wanted very badly to go one-on-one against his former employer and win. By the end of 1980, it was obvious to Iacocca that the goal was no longer to overtake Ford in the automobile industry but merely to survive.

By late 1980, Chrysler's share of the U.S. market was down to less than 9 percent. From the tenth largest U.S. industrial corporation in 1975, in terms of sales, the company had fallen to seventeenth in 1979 and thirty-second in 1980. The contractions required to survive hit almost every area of Chrysler's operations.

Its overall size was cut drastically. Between August 1979 and December 1980, the company shrank from 141,000 to 79,000 employees. This compared with 218,000 in 1975. The white-collar payroll, while not cut as deeply, was trimmed about 30 percent—to 21,000 employees—during 1980. The company's goals have been narrowed substantially. Chrysler no longer is a full-line producer. In mid-1981, it was basically a small-car manufacturer, with about 70 percent of its sales in this category. With the change in goals and size came a reduction in complexity. Consistent with efforts to cut costs and improve efficiency, Chrysler reduced the number of vertical levels in its hierarchy. The number of levels between the manufacturing floor and the vice president for manufacturing was cut from seven to five. As a practical example of the open-systems philosophy, it is important to see how Chrysler's problems affected the critical elements in its specific environment. To cut 1981 operating costs by more than $1 billion, the company first cut product plans to save $550 million and then turned for help to its environment. Specifically, Chrysler asked for and got help from the United Auto Workers, suppliers, and lenders.

The UAW accepted a two-year freeze on all cost-of-living increases and a slight reduction in fringe benefits for its Chrysler members. This amounted to a savings of approximately $600 million. The company asked its 20,000 suppliers to cut prices 5 percent during the first quarter of 1981 and a freeze for the rest of that year, which saved $90 million. Chrysler's 175 lenders were asked to contribute by converting $570 million in debt to preferred stock, thereby reducing interest payments by $100 million a year.

The Chrysler case illustrates some of the issues with which management must concern itself when faced with a prolonged decline. In the next section, we address the more important problems that managers may confront when their organization is declining that are either absent or of smaller magnitude in periods of expansion.

POTENTIAL MANAGERIAL PROBLEMS WHEN ORGANIZATIONS DECLINE

Some like the challenge of managing in adversity. Others merely find themselves in a leadership position when facts dictate that the organization has entered its decline phase. While it is undoubtedly easier to manage an organization during growth than during decline, the fact remains that decline is a reality, and, when it occurs, managers must be prepared to cope with its consequences. The remainder of this chapter looks at some of the potential problems with which managers should be prepared to deal when an organization's size begins to shrink.

Increased Conflict

A manager has the opportunity to really test his or her conflict management skills during organizational decline. As we have noted before, growth creates slack that acts as a grease to smooth over conflict-creating forces. Management uses this slack as a currency for buying off potentially conflicting interest groups within the organization. Conflicts can be resolved readily by expanding everyone's resources. However, in the decline phase, conflict over resources increases because there is less slack to divvy up. For instance, conflict has been found to be higher in declining school districts than in growing districts.[18]

Consistent with our approach to conflict in Chapter 16, we are not suggesting that the increased conflict evident in decline is necessarily dysfunctional. If managed properly, it can be directed toward slowing the decline. Out of the conflict can come changes that may revitalize the organization: selection of a new domain, the creation of new products or services, and cost-cutting measures that can make the shrunken organization more efficient and viable.

[18]Hannan and Freeman, "Internal Politics of Growth and Decline."

Increased Politicking

Less slack also translates into more politicking by self-interest groups. As we noted earlier in this chapter, structural changes during decline are more likely to be determined by which coalitions win the power struggle for organizational control than by rational determinants such as size, technology, or environment. Politically naïve managers will find their jobs difficult, if not impossible, if they are unable to adjust to the changing decision-making criterion. In a "fight-for-life" situation, the standard rules are disregarded. Critical data for decisions are twisted and interpreted by various coalitions so as to further their groups' interests. This was evident, for instance, in Chrysler's use of profit projections when lobbying the federal government for its loan guarantees. The company consistently offered projections that were extremely hopeful and confident and that proved rapidly to be totally erroneous. One reporter questioned Chrysler's executive vice president in late 1980 about these projections. When the reporter pointed out how the projections presented to the government to support Chrysler's ability to pay back its loans had proven extremely overly optimistic, the executive exclaimed, "You didn't really take that stuff seriously?"[19]

Increased Resistance to Change

The organization responds more slowly to environmental change in decline than in growth.[20] In its effort to protect itself, the dominant coalition fights hard to maintain the status quo and its control. Vested interests thwart change efforts.[21] The unfreezing stage in the change process becomes extremely difficult. Resistance to change seems to be related to the previously discussed "stages of decline."[22] Early in the decline, individuals follow a pattern of "weathering the storm." This is characterized by intensified efforts to follow the old, established procedures. This may result in slowing the decline, but if it is truly of the prolonged variety, this at best can only delay the inevitable. So the early part of decline is a period of high resistance to change. Resistance should reduce as it becomes clear that the decline is not temporary.

[19]Quoted in Ross, "Chrysler on the Brink," p. 40.

[20]Hannan and Freeman, "Internal Politics of Growth and Decline."

[21]John Gardner, "Organizational Survival: Overcoming Mind-Forged Manacles," in John F. Veiga and John N. Yanouzas, eds., *The Dynamics of Organization Theory: Gaining a Macro Perspective,* (St. Paul, Minn.: West Publishing, 1979), pp. 28–31.

[22]B. L. T. Hedberg, Paul C. Nystrom, and William H. Starbuck, "Camping on Seesaws: Prescriptions for a Self-designing Organization," *Administrative Science Quarterly,* March 1976, pp. 41–65.

One writer has noted that a major force for resisting change during the initial phase of decline will be those vested interests who have benefited most from growth.[23] Since their power base is challenged, they are motivated to continuing to push for growth-related policies, even though it no longer makes sense. The writer described research demonstrating this effect in cities that have actively pursued growth—as might have characterized Phoenix, Houston, Orlando, and San Diego during the 1970s. Such cities competed with one another for new industry and other preconditions of growth by advertising their low crime rates, low taxes, large labor forces, abundant natural resources, and other favorable features. This growth orientation tended to attract to politics people who had a vested interest in growth—real estate developers, local business people, educational leaders. These people, in turn, reinforced the drive to increase city size so as to enlarge their share of the local resource pool. They argued, for instance, that growth would increase employment, despite evidence to the contrary; namely, that fast-growing metropolitan areas tend to have higher unemployment rates than do slow-growing ones. Pro-growth advocates attempt to push for growth because it supports their interest well beyond the point where the diseconomies of growth overshadow its benefits. If these cities are to change their policies, say, toward stabilizing the population, it will be necessary to dislodge the growth advocates from their power positions and replace them with a new cadre of leaders with a different set of vested interests.[24]

Increased Turnover

A major potential problem occurring with organizational decline is that of retaining valuable employees. Some of the first people to leave an organization when it enters the stage of decline are the most mobile individuals such as skilled technicians, professionals, and talented managerial personnel. These, of course, are typically the individuals that the organization can least afford to lose.

Managers are particularly prone to "jump ship" when it is clear that the growth days are over. The opportunities for advancement and increased responsibilities are obviously reduced greatly during decline. The upwardly mobile executive will look for organizations where his or her talents are more likely to be utilized. This suggests that senior management will be challenged to provide incentives to ambitious junior managers if they are to prevent a long, slow decline from snowballing into a rapid descent.

[23]Whetten, "Organizational Decline," p. 582.

[24]H. Molotch, "The City as a Growth Machine: Toward a Political Economy of Place," *American Journal of Sociology*, September 1976, pp. 309–332.

Decaying Employee Motivation and Morale

Employee motivation and morale are different when an organization is contracting than when it is enjoying growth. On the growth side, motivation can be provided by promotional opportunities and the excitement of being associated with a dynamic organization. During decline, there are layoffs, reassignments of duties that frequently require absorbing the tasks that were previously done by others, and similar stress-inducing changes. It's usually hard for employees to stay motivated when there is high uncertainty as to whether they will still have a job next month or next year. When their organization is experiencing prolonged decline, managers are challenged to function effectively in an organizational climate typified by stagnation, fear, and stress.

SUMMARY

The study of organization theory must address both the growth and decline sides of the organization's life cycle. Yet the organization literature has had a growth bias. "Bigger is better" is consistent with the growth bias. So, too, are the beliefs that growth increases the likelihood of survival, is synonymous with effectiveness, and represents power. The facts suggest that the primary conditions that fostered growth no longer exist and that managing organizational decline is not merely reversing what was done during growth.

There is a lag that typifies the rate of change in structure during prolonged decline that is not evident in growth. This lag causes the level of structure to be greater in the same organization for a given size during decline than during growth. This projects into a large administrative component during decline; the increased importance of the power-control perspective in explaining structure; and the tendency for management to, first, ignore decline, then to treat it as an aberration and, only to respond appropriately after some delay.

The management of decline requires managers to confront higher levels of conflict, increased politicking, increased resistance to change, higher levels of turnover, and decaying employee motivation and morale.

FOR REVIEW AND DISCUSSION

1. Define "organization decline."
2. Why do American values favor growth?
3. How does growth increase survival?
4. Contrast the traditional and radical values of organization theory.

5. Why does the administrative component in decline differ from that in growth?
6. Describe the three stages of "response to decline."
7. What has happened since 1981 to the fortunes of Chrysler Corporation? How have these conditions affected the company's structure?
8. Why might a manager prefer to work in a growing organization than in one that is in decline?
9. Relate the organizational life-cycle concept presented in Chapter 2 to the subject of organizational growth and decline.
10. Contrast the role of the imperatives in determining an organization's structure (discussed in Part III) during growth and during decline.

CHAPTER

18

MANAGING JAPANESE STYLE: THE THEORY Z ORGANIZATION

Imagine an organization at which, before starting the day's work, employees gather in the parking lot for an inspirational speech, hear someone read the names of those employees who are absent, sing the company song, and then participate in five minutes of group calisthenics. Sound strange? Maybe in North America, but this is the beginning of a typical workday in Japan.

This scenario describes one of the more visible differences between Japanese organizations and their North American counterparts. The fact that Eastern and Western organizations are different has been well known for decades. Few, for instance, have failed to hear about Japanese employees' having permanent or lifelong employment. Until recently, however, it was assumed that the North American efficiency model of bureaucratic structure was the standard. The difference, if it was to be eradicated, would be done by the Japanese accepting the North American style of organization. In fact, Japanese business managers have been regular readers of North American management books and periodicals.[1] Lately, however, the direction of attention has been changing.[2] North American management and organizational researchers have begun to analyze the Japanese system to assess whether it can explain the fact that the rate of productivity increases in Japan have been two to three times that of the

[1]"How the Japanese Manage in the U.S.," *Fortune,* June 15, 1981, p. 103.

[2]See, for instance, William G. Ouchi, *Theory Z: How American Business Can Meet the Japanese Challenge* (Boston: Addison- Wesley, 1981); and Richard T. Pascale and Anthony G. Athos, *The Art of Japanese Management* (New York: Simon & Schuster, 1981).

United States over the past three decades, while absenteeism has been low, organizational commitment high, and turnover rates about half those of the United States.[3] In this chapter we take a look at the Japanese system of management, with particular attention to the structural characteristics of Japanese organizations.

EXPLAINING THE SUCCESS OF JAPANESE ORGANIZATIONS

To what can we attribute the relative success of the Japanese system? Most answers center on their technology, culture, or management system.

Japanese manufacturers generally have newer and more technologically advanced equipment than do their North American counterparts. Forced to rebuild almost from scratch following World War II, the Japanese were able to install highly sophisticated equipment. In an industry such as steel, where North American equipment dates in many cases to 1920 or earlier, the Japanese have a distinct advantage. Yet the explanation of the success of Japanese organizations has to go beyond merely technology. In some industries, such as automobiles, they had no significant technological advantage over their North American competitors, but they still were more efficient and achieved a far higher quality of output. The Japanese also showed themselves to be more efficient in technologies that were not capital intensive. Apparently factors other than technology were contributing to their success.

Does the Japanese culture create a different, more productive, employee than the U.S. culture? For instance, do Japanese workers have different personality traits or significantly different attitudes toward their work from U.S workers? We know, for instance, that the Japanese are less individualistic and more tolerant of excessive authority than are Americans,[4] but this in itself should not make Japanese organizations more efficient unless the organization structures and management systems are especially designed to take advantage of these individual characteristics. While the Japanese culture is undoubtedly different from its Western counterpart, and this difference has influenced the attitudes and behavior of Japanese employees, we cannot attribute the success of Japanese organizations to their national culture alone.

The most substantive explanation for the success of Japanese organizations is their management system. They have developed a comprehensive system that combines structure and people in a way that, when integrated with the Japanese culture, generates a highly productive and

[3]R. E. Cole, *Work, Mobility, and Participation* (Berkeley: University of California Press, 1979).

[4]Chie NaKane, *Japanese Society* (Berkeley: University of California Press, 1970).

efficient organization. The fact that major parts of this system have been transferred successfully to the United States—examples of which we describe later in this chapter—suggests that the Japanese model is not culture bound.

The Japanese system is not lifelong employment, though this is a part of it. It is not consultative decision making, but this too is a part of it. Japanese organizations, especially the large ones, are different structurally from comparably sized U.S firms, but this also is only part of the Japanese system. In the following section, we describe the many facets that make up the Japanese management system.

THE JAPANESE MANAGEMENT SYSTEM

The Japanese management system is shown in Figure 18–1. It has three levels of attention: an overall focus, general strategies, and specific techniques. Let us look at each of these.[5]

Focus

The essence of management in large Japanese organizations is its focus on human resources. In most of these organizations, management considers its human resources, more than its financial or physical resources, to be *most* important in the search for long-run success. While this focus is frequently articulated by managers in the United States, the Japanese commit more than lip service to their concern for human resources. They back it up with a well-integrated system of strategies and techniques that translate ideology into reality.

Strategies

The concern for human resources is manifested in three interrelated strategies. First, employees are offered long-term and secure employment. This is an overt demonstration that the organization is committed to its people through good times and bad. Second, explicitly articulated organizational philosophies emphasize concern for employee needs and the values of cooperation and teamwork. Third, close attention is given to hiring new employees who will fit well into the organization and to ensuring that this fit is maintained and enhanced throughout the employee's work life.

Long-term employment. The U.S. view toward employees is that they share in the ups and downs that the organization experiences. When

[5]The following has been adapted from Nina Hatvany and Vladimir Pucik, "An Integrated Management System: Lessons from the Japanese Experience," *Academy of Management Review*, July 1981, pp. 469–474.

FIGURE 18–1 The Japanese management system

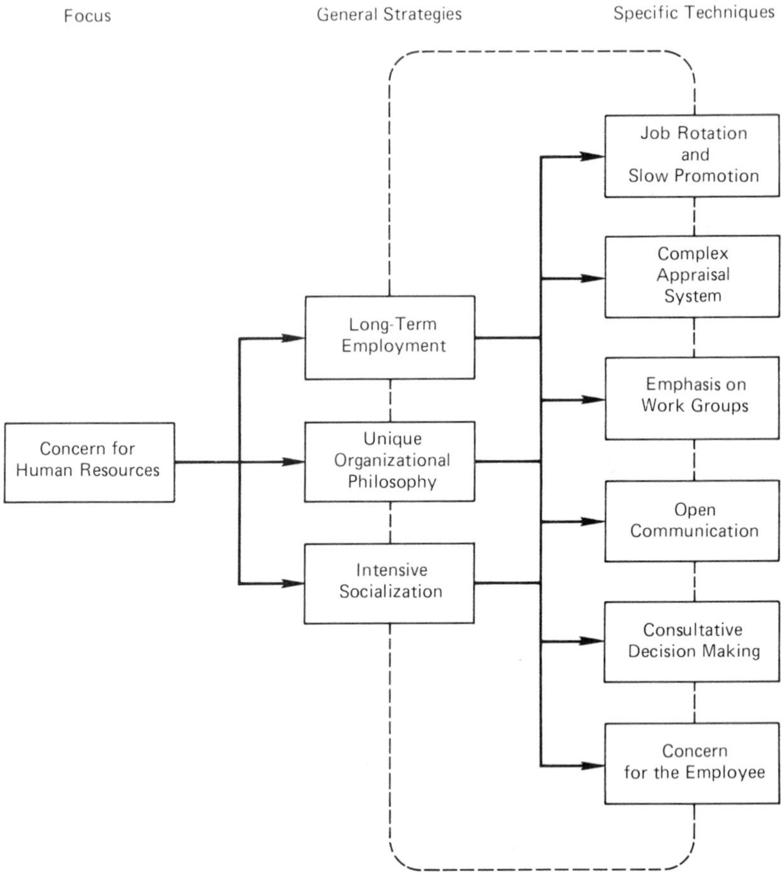

Source: Adapted from Nina Hatvany and Vladimir Pucik, "An Integrated Management System: Lessons from the Japanese Experience," *Academy of Management Review,* July 1981, p. 470.

times are bad, employees are laid off or fired. In Japan, except in the most severe economic circumstances, employees are assured of permanent employment.

Usually new employees are hired fresh out of high schools or universities. The organization then trains them, makes promotions from their internal pool, and emphasizes seniority in the allocation of rewards. Because employees are trained to do jobs that are organization specific (thus having minimal transferability value), they are rewarded based on seniority; and because they are typically recruited "untarnished" out of school, they have limited mobility. Since promotions are from within, everyone starts at the bottom. Once an individual's career takes hold, no other employer is likely to hire him.

Long-term employment results in employees with high morale. From the organization's standpoint, turnover is low, training costs are lower, and organizational cohesiveness is higher. The approach also reduces hostility to labor-saving technology or organizational changes that are likely to surface when employees fear that changes might cost them their jobs. Of course, there are also drawbacks, the most evident being the lack of flexibility. Instead of hiring in good times and firing in bad, Japanese organizations have to adjust in other ways. In bad times, there may be freezes on new hires, solicitations of voluntary retirement made attractive by adding extra benefits, across-the-board pay cuts, or across-the-board reduction in hours worked. In good times, employees may work overtime, temporaries may be hired (typically women), or work may be subcontracted to outsiders. The net effect, however, is a stable and committed labor force.

Organizational philosophy. Each Japanese organization has a specific philosophy that presents a clear picture of its objectives and values. This philosophy both directs and constrains the behavior of managers and employees alike. The philosophy acts as sort of a superordinate goal—a shared and unifying goal with which all organizational members can identify, support, and place above any one person's individual goals.

While these philosophies purportedly are unique for each organization, ranging from the extent of the organization's concern for employees' work lives to the quality of service to the customer, a common theme among Japanese companies is a heavy emphasis on cooperation and teamwork. Members of the organization are part of a family, and, in this sense, every family is unique. The family analogy holds for entrance and withdrawal: admittance is highly selective and members do not leave, even if they are dissatisfied with some aspect of "family" life. The team spirit and cooperation characteristic of a family, of course, would be impossible without the security provided by the strategy of permanent employment.

Intensive socialization. The third major strategy used by Japanese organizations is a socialization process that indoctrinates the organization's philosophy into every employee.

Applicants are carefully screened to ensure that all hires will endorse the philosophy and values of the organization and to select out those who will not fit in. The basic criteria for hiring are moderate views and a harmonious personality. Ability on the job is obviously also a requirement, but competent applicants may be screened out if it appears that they cannot get along well with others or if they hold radical views. This screening process favors applicants who have no prior work force experience; in this way, no unfreezing of previous philosophies needs to be done.

Once hired, employees undergo an initial training program that may last up to six months. This program's major purpose is to familiarize the employee with the organization. It is followed by a long series of job transfers—mostly lateral—that add to the employees' skills but also immerse him in the organization's philosophy and culture and help him to become the proverbial "organization man." The Japanese employee, in contrast to many U.S. employees, is socialized first and foremost to be committed to the organization. His technical skills are secondary. Again, the organization is able to achieve this employee commitment as a result of its reciprocal commitment to the employee. When employees have no fear of being fired, even if their skills become obsolete, they are willing to do those things that are in the best long-term interests of their organizations.

Techniques

The previous general strategies are translated into six specific management techniques. Let us review each of these techniques.

Job rotation and slow promotion. Lifetime employment results in organizations where rapid promotions are unlikely unless the organization is expanding at a very rapid rate. In the United States, for instance, the voluntary and involuntary movement of employees between organizations and the frequent practice of filling middle and top management slots from the outside means that ambitious employees can move up in their organizations. If they perceive their movement up the hierarchy as too slow, they may achieve their promotion by going to work for another organization. In Japan, lifetime employment means limited upward mobility. Movement, therefore, is predominantly lateral, through job rotation. Promotions, when they come, are based on seniority.

Job rotation in Japan is planned and widely adopted. This is in contrast to the U.S. practice, where an ad hoc response to an organizational need is more typical. When coupled with slow promotion, it results in a work force made up of generalists rather than of specialists. Additionally, it reinforces the emphasis on teamwork and cooperation. As generalists, employees are less likely to engage in protective infighting. They are also less likely to have interorganization mobility. This encourages internal cooperation and loyalty to the employer. Widespread job rotation also fosters informal communication networks that help to coordinate work activities across functional areas and reduce interunit conflicts.

Complex appraisal system. Japanese employees are appraised against a number of criteria, only one of which is current output or performance. For instance, personality traits such as creativity, honesty, seriousness, maturity, and cooperation with others are heavily weighted.

The intent of these appraisals is to downplay the short term. Occasional mistakes by lower-level employees are considered part of the learning process. Managers are more willing to take calculated risks because they do not have to show results in the next quarter or fiscal year. Appraisals also emphasize group as well as individual performance, which again reinforces teamwork and cooperation.

The Japanese appraisal system is designed to generate diverse information on employees. Because promotion is slow and employees rotate extensively among jobs, the organization obtains evaluations on a candidate from a number of supervisors. Each employee is compared with and ranked against others in his or her appropriate age and status group. But, since the appraisals evaluate criteria beyond immediate job performance, employees are motivated to demonstrate loyalty and commitment by their attitudes and actions such as exerting a high level of effort or volunteering for overtime. When a promotion opportunity develops, management has a large number of appraisals by supervisors from which to evaluate candidates. And, since the appraisals consider personality traits and attitudes as well as job competence, those who are promoted are assured of fitting in and continuing to support the organization's basic philosophy.

Emphasis on work groups. The Japanese system gives far greater attention to organizing tasks around groups than around individuals. Autonomous work teams, as described in Chapter 14, are the rule rather than the exception in Japan. Tasks are assigned to groups, and the group members then decide among themselves the best way for performing the tasks.

Group autonomy is enhanced by avoiding any reliance on experts to solve operational problems. Autonomy is, however, clearly constrained by management who carefully coordinates group activities and determines the size of the group, the amount of job rotation, and the appraisal of members.

Open communication. U.S. organizations frequently seek to foster open communication. The Japanese system is inherently designed to achieve this end. Job rotation and the heavy emphasis on groups means that employees build an informal network that facilitates extensive face-to-face communication. Much of this takes place between vertical levels and lateral groups.

The physical work setting is also designed to foster communication. Open work spaces are crowded with individuals at different hierarchical levels. Subordinates can do little that goes unobserved by their supervisors and vice versa. Even high-ranking office managers rarely have private, enclosed offices. Partitions, cubicles, and small side rooms are used for conferences with visitors or small discussions among staff members.

Consultative decision making. Decision making in Japan is not "participative" in the American sense of the term. That is, it is not characterized by frequent group meetings and negotiations between manager and subordinates. In the Japanese model, the manager discusses and consults informally with all who may be affected. When all are familiar with the proposal, a formal request for a decision is made, and, as a result of the previous informal preparations, it is almost always ratified. The key is not so much agreement with a decision as it is for those concerned to have the opportunity to be advised about it and to have their views heard fairly. The final outcome, therefore, does not imply consensus but merely inclusion of input from any individual or group who might be influenced. The position taken in Japanese organizations is consistent with a long-term perspective: we may not agree with your decision this time but we'll go along because we recognize that our viewpoint may carry the day the next time around.

One final point about consultative decision making in Japan: it does not diminish top management's responsibility for a decision's consequences. If a poor decision is made, heads still roll. However, the penalties are more subtle than in the West. U.S. firm's are prone to fire a manager who makes a major decision error. In Japan, the punishment is likely to be a transfer to a less prestigious unit.

Concern for the employee. The final management technique that makes up the Japanese system is a concern for the well-being of employees. Managers spend a great deal of their time talking to employees about everyday matters. Even senior managers regularly spend time with operating personnel to learn their concerns. The fact that an important part of every manager's appraisal is a measure of the quality of relations with his subordinates encourages managers to take a keen interest in his employee's personal needs and problems.

Japanese organizations, as do many American ones, offer a wide range of benefits to their employees. But beyond vacations, holiday pay, and insurance is a comprehensive offering of cultural, athletic, and recreational activities. For instance, an annual calendar of office events might include several overnight trips, monthly Saturday afternoon recreation, and an average of six office parties—all at the organization's expense. In addition, many Japanese organizations offer a smorgasbord of welfare services for their employees: subsidized family housing for married personnel, dormitories for the unmarried, nurseries for preschool children, scholarships for children, mortgage loans, and the like.

Summary

The Japanese management system is a complex set of integrated and congruent strategies and techniques. Emphasis is placed on slow but continuous development of an employee's skills rather than on rapid vertical promotion. Appraisals consider a multitude of criteria other than an individual's bottom-line contribution. Work is organized around teams. Open communication is encouraged and rewarded. Information about pending decisions is circulated widely before the actual decisions are made. Management demonstrates a strong commitment to understanding and responding to personal needs and problems of employees.

There is no single principle in the Japanese system. It works because it successfully blends task design, individual goals, and organizational goals by creating an organizational culture that is concerned with and supports human resources. It results in organizational structures that are low on vertical differentiation, low on formalization, and decentralized. Jobs are designed around autonomous work groups. The security of permanent employment reduces resistance to change. Job rotation increases informal communication and, when accompanied by the training of generalists, minimizes interunit conflicts.

The structure that results gives Japanese organizations distinct efficiencies in comparison with their North American counterparts. This is evident in the automobile industry.[6] In Japan, supervisors report directly to their plant managers; in the United States, supervisors encounter three extra layers of management. At the Ford Motor Co., there are eleven layers of management between the factory worker and the chairman; Toyota Motor Co. makes do with six layers. It is this smaller administrative component that helps the Japanese to make a car and ship it to the United States for $1,500 less than it costs a U.S. automaker to produce and sell a comparable vehicle.

THEORY A AND THEORY Z ORGANIZATIONS

Several American companies, whether knowingly or not, have developed systems that have many of the characteristics evident in Japanese firms.[7] Companies such as IBM, Procter & Gamble, and Hewlett-Packard have avoided creating systems with employee specialists, relatively high turnover, and individualized decision making—characteristics that typify the

[6]"Trust: The New Ingredient in Management," *Business Week,* July 6, 1981, p. 104.

[7]William G. Ouchi and Jerry B. Johnson, "Types of Organizational Control and Their Relationship to Emotional Well-Being," *Administrative Science Quarterly,* June 1978, pp. 293–317.

Western form of organization. Instead, they emphasize employees who are generalists, low turnover, and collective decision making. Let us look at the standard American organization and see how some companies have modified it to create an American version of the Japanese-style organization.

Table 18–1 presents two theoretical organization types. The first—Theory A—is designed to control employees through a tightly monitored structural system. It is adapted to handle high rates of employee turnover. Jobs are defined narrowly, and employees are required to specialize. An employee's specialized skills lend themselves to transferability between organizations, thus encouraging mobility. If employees become frustrated, they have ready alternatives in employment opportunities with other organizations. Similarly, organizations can hire employees from other firms and give them considerable responsibility and competitive salaries because these individuals' skills are transferable, allowing them to become quickly productive for their new employer.

In a system where members are transient, it is important to minimize interdependencies. Therefore, Theory A organizations individualize decision making and responsibility.

High levels of turnover also create regular vacancies. Opportunities for promotion are plentiful. Because supervisors know little about their employees beyond their job-related activities, appraisals tend to be formalized and impersonal and relate only to specific measures of job performance. These appraisals, made on at least an annual basis, then become the input from which promotion decisions are made.

When employees come and go quickly, are required to assume individual responsibilities, pursue specialized career paths, and are appraised on impersonal criteria, they have little motivation to identify with the organization or to exert energy toward forming friendships. The organization responds to this individualistic ethic by treating people as just another input cost. Employees, then, are not significantly different from a

TABLE 18–1 Two theories of organizations

THEORY A	*THEORY Z*
Short-term employment	Long-term employment
Specialized career paths	Nonspecialized career paths
Individualized decision making	Collective decision making
Frequent appraisal	Infrequent appraisal
Explicit, formalized appraisal	Implicit, informal appraisal
Rapid promotion	Slow promotion
Segmented concern for people	Comprehensive concern for people

drill press or a fork-lift truck. You purchase them to obtain utility of service and can discard them if they break or become obsolete.

The Theory Z organization is quite different, and that difference is essentially a function of low turnover. When employees are hired with the belief that the marriage is a permanent one, management can justify developing an organization in which control is maintained through the socialization process. While this is a much slower process, it results in a structure that is much more likely to mirror an adhocracy than the mechanistic bureaucracy that Theory A creates.

Long-term employment means that management can take the time to develop an employee's talent and do those things that foster teamwork. Jobs can still be specialized, but, instead of keeping people in their narrow areas of specialization, they can be rotated laterally. This lateral movement, in turn, gives employees job diversity and allows them to understand other parts of the organization and to make friends with members throughout the structure. Theory Z organizations can therefore acquire the same horizontal differentiation as practiced in Theory A firms, while maintaining low individual specialization.

While a Theory Z organization is at a clear disadvantage in that it loses many of the benefits of individualized expertise, coordination problems are reduced significantly. When employees relate to the overall organization rather than to their area of specialization, communicate with members of other departments with little friction, share actively in the decision-making process, and are appraised not only on individual performance but how well they are able to work with others, there is less need for high vertical differentiation. Theory Z organizations, therefore, tend to be flat structures.

The Theory A-Theory Z dichotomy suggests that U.S. managers have choices. The Theory Z model, though presently existing in very few Western firms, is a distinct alternative to the dominant Theory A model. The success of firms such as IBM, Procter & Gamble, and Hewlett-Packard—designed along Theory Z lines—is evidence that the characteristics of the Theory Z model can result in high organizational effectiveness. But certainly Theory Z is not applicable to all organizations. In fact, its application potential may be quite restricted. Under what conditions might North American management consider implementing a Theory Z organization?

IMPLEMENTING THE THEORY Z ORGANIZATION

The discussion of implementing Theory Z should probably begin by looking back to Chapter 10. Is Theory Z compatible with the power-control perspective? If not, then all the attention lavished on this organizational type may be wasted effort.

A major theme of this book has been that those in power will use their discretion in organizational design to create a structure that will maintain and enhance their control. In some ways, Theory Z is incompatible with this objective. In other ways, it is highly compatible.

The commitment of permanent employment provides employees with increased security. They need not fear the threat of being fired. Those in power, therefore, lose the influence base that comes from being able to demand compliance to a boss's wishes out of fear of losing one's job. The decentralized nature of the Theory Z organization is also counter to the best interests of those in power. The fact that most job-related decisions are made by the work teams takes some power away from management.

A careful look at the characteristics of the Theory Z organization, however, reveals many attributes that should be appealing to those in power. To begin with, the employee's psychological commitment to the organization for his work life makes him more likely to tolerate conditions that he might otherwise complain about. Given that his appraisal emphasizes his ability to fit in and get along with others, the employee in the Theory Z organization is less prone to stimulate conflicts and more likely to conform to the behaviors that management seeks.

Certainly the fact that Theory Z employees are trained as generalists is important from a power-control perspective. Employee power is reduced because the employees do not acquire the kinds of specialized expertise on which the organization becomes dependent. While individuals gain specialized knowledge, they hold no monopoly on it. Remember, as generalists, employees are substitutable for each other. Additionally, as long as the majority of organizations follow the Theory A model, Theory Z employees will have reduced mobility because their generalist orientation makes them less valuable to other employers.

Remember, too, that management in Theory Z organizations chooses the size of work teams, the members who will be on each team, and the job rotation patterns between teams. This power ensures management that no individual or team will obtain any significant degree of influence in the organization.

A final consideration is the lack of middle management in Theory Z organizations. Tall organizations reduce the power of top management because middle managers gain control over information. Middle managers know more about what is going on at the operating level. They also can filter information before passing it up to top management. Theory Z organizations, because they tend to be flat, enhance top management's power by increasing their control over information.

This indicates that, while Theory Z organizations present both advantages and disadvantages to those in power, the advantages appear to more than offset any disadvantages. Should we expect, therefore, the Theory Z model to gain popularity in North America? Not necessarily.

It's been noted that a common characteristic among Theory Z organizations is technological and environmental stability.[8] These organizations appear consciously to stay out of highly volatile markets, to subcontract out necessary but unstable tasks, and to reduce voluntary turnover by offering attractive working conditions and by engaging in strategies that allow them to manage their environments. For organizations that can not stabilize their technologies or specific environments, which undoubtedly covers a large segment of organizations, the Theory Z model will be inappropriate.

Where Theory Z organizations are being implemented, the ideal characteristics identified in Table 18–1 are undergoing modification. Although Theory Z represents an Americanization of the Japanese model, even some of Theory Z's characteristics are proving to be incompatible with the realities of North American life. The result is a mixed Theory A-Theory Z system.

The Japanese system, in attempting to ensure that employees fit in properly, overtly discriminates. Culturally dissimilar types, particularly women and minorities, are selectively excluded from the mainstream. Such a practice is illegal in the United States. Theory Z organizations in the United States, therefore, contain a less homogeneous work force than do their Japanese counterparts. Unions, too, in the United States are larger and more militant than are unions in Japan. Company unions in Japan tend to develop loyalties and commitment to the company. Unions in the United States cut across organizations, thus tending to emphasize identification with the union over the organization itself. And, of course, any organization following Theory Z in America is in a distinct minority. Such an organization cannot ignore that it operates in an environment dominated by Theory A types. Common sense tells us, therefore, that strict adherence to infrequent appraisals and slow promotions will encourage superior employees to jump to other organizations where their talents will be recognized more quickly.

The legal and cultural differences between the West and East lead to a modified Theory Z organization.[9] Lifetime employment is replaced with stable employment. Selection is nondiscriminatory, but still emphasizes teamwork and the creation of a family atmosphere. Employees are appraised once or twice a year. Employee commitment, therefore, is achieved as much by competitive salaries, attractive working conditions, and stable employment as by socialization to the organization's philosophy and values.

[8]William G. Ouchi and Raymond L. Price, "Hierarchies, Clans, and Theory Z: A New Perspective on Organization Development," *Organizational Dynamics*, Autumn 1978, p. 40.

[9]"How the Japanese Manage in the U.S.," pp. 97–103.

THEORY Z IN PRACTICE

Two companies, one Japanese and the other American, operate Theory Z–type plants in San Diego, California. The two systems are different, but they provide some interesting insights of how Theory Z can be operationalized.

Kyocera

Kyocera International's plant in San Diego began operation in 1971. It manufactures 70 percent of the ceramic semiconductor packaging cases made in the United States. Kyocera's eight hundred employees are almost all Americans, but its organization is decidedly Japanese.

The workday begins at 7 A.M. Employees file out into the parking lot and stand on evenly spaced yellow dots painted on the asphalt. Each wears a colored jacket, different colors signifying rank. After an inspirational speech by one of the workers, a supervisor leads the group in exercises. One manager compared the exercises with the huddle of a football team—its purpose is to set the momentum of the day.

The typical workday at Kyocera is long. Most work an eleven-hour day and many work on Saturday. Overtime pay is encouraged. In addition to providing sizable weekly paychecks, this also gives management more slack to play with in times of economic adversity. Rather than laying off people, Kyocera can cut down on the number of hours worked. This is important because the plant's management is committed to its labor force. During the 1974 recession, when orders fell drastically, excess employees were kept on the payroll and put to work cleaning floors or polishing machinery. The company's position is clearly humanistic. Employees come first. As one supervisor put it, "We would cut into retained earnings if the situation became critical."[10] This philosophy is obviously appreciated by employees, as acknowledged by one young worker. "I'd like to see 'em pay a little more money here. But that no-layoff policy is worth a lot of money; you know you're secure here. None of that hire-and-fire stuff."[11]

Consensus decision making, team units, slow promotions, and comprehensive appraisals are evident at Kyocera. All decisions are made by consensus. Meetings, therefore, are a regular part of a Kyocera's employee's daily routine. The plant itself is divided into small "amoeba" units, each of which is a profit center. These units buy and sell to each other, and their performance is measured in terms of profitability. The members of a profitable unit are not rewarded with quick promotions or immediate increases in pay. The reward is public recognition at the morning meetings

[10]Richard Louv, "Two Methods Point Way to Future for Industry," *The San Diego Union*, September 8, 1981, p. A-8.

[11]Ibid.

and the personal satisfaction from accomplishment. Performance appraisals are done semiannually and are comprehensive. Job knowledge and performance are considered, but they are secondary to attitude. Acceptance of Kyocera's commitment to spirit, loyalty, zeal, and cooperation is essential.

Does all this work? In spite of unspectacular salaries, carpets and furniture that are worn and old, and limited promotion opportunities, the plant has developed a productive and loyal work force. Labor turnover, for instance, is one-third the typical rate for U.S. factories. A 35-year-old employee, who once studied to be a minister, may have summed it up best, "See, we literally think about preserving this company for posterity, for our children or someone else's children. I'd like to think I'm not substituting one religion for another."[12]

Hewlett-Packard

Hewlett-Packard, an electronics company, was founded in 1939; the firm was committed early on to give meaning to work as well as to making a profit. Part of that commitment was to provide lifetime employment and establish a generous profit-sharing plan. The H-P plant in San Diego, which designs and manufactures computer plotters, follows that original H-P commitment.[13]

In many ways, the H-P plant is not much different from its neighbor, Kyocera. Both are committed to not laying off employees. For instance, in the early 1970s, during a recession, everyone at H-P took a 10 percent pay cut. As a result, no one was laid off. Both downplay authority. Both strongly support group decision making. H-P employees, for example, meet weekly in quality circles to resolve production problems. But the H-P plant seeks to blend the American concern for individualism with the Japanese collectivism. There are no morning inspirational speeches or calisthenics. No one wears a uniform to identify rank. Employees are not expected to work long hours. Pay raises are based on merit and seniority. Performance appraisals occur four times a year, and evaluations are based on teamwork and ability to meet or exceed individual quotas. H-P's pay structure is one of the highest in San Diego. The plant itself is modern and antiseptically clean.

H-P plants are held to under 2,000 employees to keep them manageable. The San Diego facility employs 1,500. The environment is informal. Everyone, including management, dresses casually. Managers and oper-

[12]Ibid.

[13]"Hewlett-Packard's San Diego Division," a research paper prepared by Leslie Beams, Susan Eubanks, and Arthur Turner, under the supervision of Professor Stephen P. Robbins. San Diego State University, 1981.

atives alike are addressed on a first-name basis. Flexible work hours are used so that employees can adjust their hours individually. Machines are set up to allow individuals to work at their own speeds. The work areas are open, with Personnel being the only office in the plant that has a door. If employees have a problem, they are encouraged to air it openly. Employees can take their grievance to anyone, up to and including the plant's general manager. Stories circulate that some employees have even called H-P's president with a problem.

H-P's approach appears highly successful. The company's turnover is low, and sales have been tripling every two years. H-P has developed a unique mix of the American and Japanese systems. As do Kyocera and other Japanese firms, they place a priority on their human resources. But they have not ignored the concern for individual recognition.

SUMMARY

The Japanese organizational system has recently come under close analysis. Researchers have been looking at what characteristics make up the Japanese model to see if they contribute significantly to the success of Japanese firms and if these characteristics are transferable to North America.

The focus of large Japanese organizations is on human resources. It is manifested in three interrelated strategies: long-term employment, a unique organizational philosophy, and intensive socialization. These strategies are then translated into six specific management techniques: job rotation and slow promotion, a complex appraisal system, emphasis on work groups, open communication, consultative decision making, and concern for the employee. The success of big Japanese companies is to a large extent a result of their ability to integrate these strategies and techniques into a congruent system.

In the United States, most organizations are designed following the Theory A model. Employees are specialists, there is relatively high turnover, and decision making is individualized. Some American firms have developed organizations with characteristics that are also displayed by many Japanese companies. This ideal American prototype of the Japanese model is called Theory Z.

The Theory Z organization provides long-term employment. It emphasizes groups, collective decision making, the creation of generalists, informal and infrequent performance appraisal, and slow promotion. Structurally, it is characterized as low in vertical differentiation and high in horizontal differentiation, with pervasive job rotation, low formalization, and decentralization. The Theory Z organization loses the advantages of individualized specialization, but it has fewer interunit conflicts because it substitutes organizational identity for unit identity.

Theory Z is shown to be basically compatible with the power-control position. The ideal Theory Z model has been modified where it has been implemented in America to reflect legal and cultural differences with Japan.

Kyocera International and Hewlett-Packard both have plants designed along the lines of Theory Z operating in San Diego. The latter, however, has blended the American concern for individualism with the Japanese collectivism.

FOR REVIEW AND DISCUSSION

1. Contrast the pure Japanese organization system to Theories A and Z.
2. Compare Theory Z and adhocracy.
3. "The Theory Z organization is decentralized." Build an argument to support this statement. Now build an argument to refute this statement.
4. Explain how Theory Z is compatible with the power-control position.
5. How is permanent employment a cornerstone of the Theory Z organization?
6. Compare Theories A and Z in terms of structural conflicts.
7. "Theory Z organizations are most adaptable to change." Do you agree or disagree? Discuss.
8. Contrast job rotation in a Theory A and Theory Z organization.
9. Do you expect the Theory Z organization to become widely adopted? Explain.
10. Comparing Theory A with Theory Z organizations, which would you prefer to work in as (a) an operative? (b) a manager? Why?

PART VI

APPLICATIONS: CASES IN ORGANIZATION THEORY

CASE 1

The Larger Company (A)

 This case was prepared by Edmund P. Learned and Ralph M. Hower.

The phone rang and highly indignant words blared, "Masters, what do you mean by submitting a report to all the executives without first talking it over with the division manager!"

Masters replied, "My men made every effort to see him. They never got past his secretary. He instructed her to have them talk to the works manager."

"I don't believe a word of it. Vining is up in arms. He says the report is vindictive. What are you trying to do—embarrass the division manager? I don't believe your men ever tried to see Vining and I question the veracity of their statements!" The phone on the other end was hung up with a bang.

Masters said to himself, "Gunn must be hot under the collar or he wouldn't have called me when I was away from my own office visiting another plant."

The next day Masters's office received Gunn's letter confirming this telephone conversation and demanding an explanation. A week later Masters received a letter from Gunn's superior, a Mr. Jordan, stating: "I have read the aforementioned report and discussed it with Mr. Gunn. He has advised me that the report is essentially untrue, inaccurate, and overstated. I am not satisfied to have such wide differences of opinion and have scheduled a meeting to be held in my office on ———. I would appreciate it if you would be present."

In light of the phone call and the two letters, Mr. Masters decided to reassess all events leading to this climax.

The cast of characters is shown in Figure 1. The Larger Company had an elaborate organizational structure as a result of its scale of operations. At the headquarters office of the corporation, the president had a group of staff vice presidents in charge of functions. Mr. Masters was a staff department head reporting to the vice president of manufacturing. The headquarters staff departments assisted in policy formulation and made staff studies for the operating organization when requested. Members of such departments were encouraged to offer ideas for the good of the company. Their proposals were considered by a management committee consisting of the vice presidents at the headquarters level and the operating vice presidents in charge of product groups. Mr. Jordan of this case was the operating vice president, Product Group B.

Under the product groups there were general managers of product

FIGURE 1 The Larger Company (A) organization chart

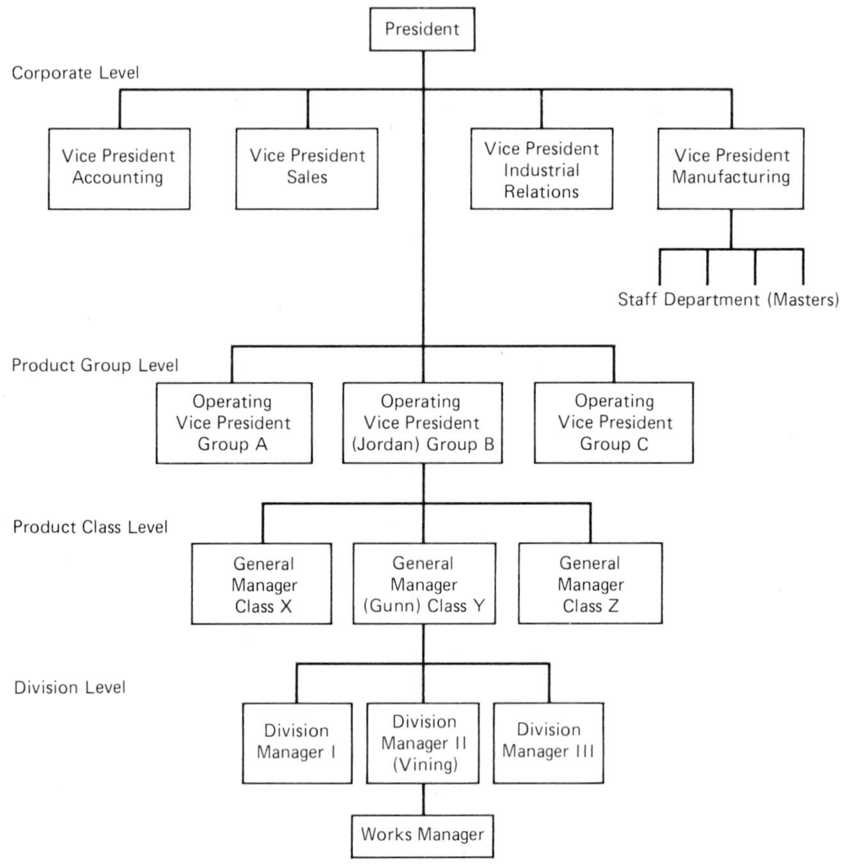

classes. They supervised the division managers, who were in charge of the sales and manufacturing operations of one or more plants. Mr. Gunn was general manager of Product Class Y. One of the four division managers under him was Mr. Vining of Division II.

Two years before this incident occurred, Mr. Masters's staff department proposed to the management committee, with the approval of the vice president of manufacturing, that representatives of Mr. Masters's office join with representatives of the vice president of accounting, to make studies in each plant of the procedures for and actual practices regarding expense control. The suggestion was approved and endorsed enthusiastically by the general managers. They sent a letter through channels to each division manager advising that periodically a team of two people would visit each plant to make a comprehensive analysis of expense-control practices and systems.

After a visit these field representatives of headquarters were to prepare a report giving findings and recommendations. They were to discuss it with the appropriate division manager and his or her staff. Thus they would be able to incorporate any specific plans of action set in motion by division managers. Next, a report was to be submitted to Mr. Masters. Both his department and the accounting office were to make comments. The final document was then to be submitted to the vice president of accounting, the vice president of manufacturing, the operating vice president of the product group, the general manager of the product class, and the division manager concerned.

This general procedure had worked smoothly within the company until General Manager Gunn of Product Class Y exploded. In the first plant studied, the two team members spent approximately four weeks examining documents, interviewing line management, interrogating industrial engineers, observing operations, and so on. The employees of this plant were very cooperative. Some of the facts revealed by them could have been embarrassing to the division manager. The team was able to make specific recommendations for improvement to the division manager. His reception of the report was good. According to him, the study had given an opportunity to review his situation and get his house in order. He intended to implement the recommendations unless they were changed in the review process at the higher level. Sixteen other plants were visited with reasonably good acceptance of the work of the team.

In his review of the Division II situation, Mr. Masters found that the team had observed all the required organization routines. Mr. Sawyer, representing Mr. Masters, had a master's degree in industrial engineering and had twelve years with the company. Mr. Peters, from the accounting office, had served that department for thirty years. Both had shown ability to gain confidences and to use them discreetly. They were considered straightforward, conscientious, and unobtrusive in their work. In Division II the team obtained from plant personnel considerable information that pointed up a number of practices and procedures requiring improvement. In the opinion of the team members, the operating organization at the lower levels sincerely wanted to make these changes. The team thought that there was some resistance at some level within the division to these suggestions and, in fact, to any from headquarters.

While the study was in process, Mr. Sawyer advised Mr. Masters about the possible impact of the information that was being collected. Mr. Masters emphasized the necessity to report to the division manager, and Mr. Sawyer promised that he and Mr. Peters would do so.

The team made several efforts to see the division manager, but his secretary informed them that he was busy. They questioned the secretary closely to learn if the manager had knowledge of the procedural requirement that he and his staff go over the report with the team. She replied that he knew the requirements but was too busy to discuss a headquarters program. He would ask his assistant, the works manager, and several staff members to go over it, and what they approved would be all right with him. Eventually this meeting was held.

The members of the local management staff took a very reasonable attitude; they admitted the bad situation portrayed in the analysis and offered their assurances that immediate steps would be taken toward improvement. The team members thought that the local management staff was glad to have their problem brought out in the open and were delighted to have the suggestions of the headquarters representatives.

When Mr. Masters reviewed the report, both team members expressed their complete dissatisfaction with the brush off they got from the division manager. Masters took this as a cue to question them extensively concerning their findings and recommendations. In view of the sensitive character of the situation and the possible controversy that it might create, he was reluctant to distribute the report. It was the consensus of the remainder of the staff and the representatives of the accounting office that the usual transmittal letter should be prepared, and distribution made. Mr. Masters signed this letter and took no other action until the telephone call came from Mr. Gunn.

Questions

1. What is the source of this conflict?
2. What does this case tell you about delegating authority?
3. Does the current procedure need changing? Support your position.
4. If you were Mr. Jordan, what would you do now?

CASE 2 Will a Shake-up Revive Burroughs?

W. Michael Blumenthal has been trying to rekindle the performance of troubled Burroughs Corp. ever since he took over as chief executive officer last September. First, he injected outside talent into the computer maker's top management, and, after he became chairman in January, he instituted an early-retirement program to clear dead wood from middle management.

Now Blumenthal has launched a massive reorganization to decentralize Burroughs's marketing and product development operations. With all this, however, it will still take a while to turn the company around.

Blumenthal's changes have been extensive indeed. Just over half of Burroughs's four hundred eligible executives took early retirement by the program's April 15 deadline. And nearly a quarter of its officers have resigned or retired. Blumenthal's moves are "very constructive," says Stephen T. McClellan, of Salomon Bros. "But they are so sweeping they will have substantial near-term impact while the transition ensues."

The reorganization, announced April 20, should erase the last vestiges of the strongly centralized operations that characterized the reign of Ray W. MacDonald, president and chairman from 1966 to 1977. Blumenthal has placed responsibility on new, lower levels of management. Moreover, the reorganization will arrange Burroughs more along the lines of International Business Machines Corp. and other competitors.

Areas of Criticism. The restructured top management aims for better coordination of product development, marketing, engineering, and customer service—all areas of criticism in the past. "It would be foolish to make these changes if we thought everything was hunky-dory," concedes Blumenthal.

Under the new structure, Burroughs will group all its product planning and software development under William P. Conlin, age 48, the new senior vice president of corporate product management. The heads of the company's four marketing groups—Business Machines, Office Products, Office Systems, and Federal & Special Systems—have been promoted from vice presidents to presidents.

Blumenthal also makes it clear that responsibility for day-to-day operations will rest with DuRay E. Stromback, president and chief operating officer since 1979. Stromback's job now includes product management, marketing, engineering, manufacturing, product distribution, and customer service. Burroughs also has shuffled its engineering and manufacturing organization by merging its Small Systems groups with the Computer Systems group, which engineers all other Burroughs computers.

"No Turmoil." Burroughs's need for some sort of remedial help became clear when the company reported its 1980 earnings. Gross revenues were up slightly from $2.8 billion to a record $2.9 billion. But net income nose-dived from $305 million in 1979 to $82 million last year.

Blumenthal blamed the slump on a general decline in business and some new-product production problems that cropped up late in the year. But the company's first quarter earnings this year, released April 14, slumped 53 percent from the same period last year to $22 million, confirming the fundamental nature of Burroughs's problems.

Some industry observers worry that Blumenthal's reorganization, which he admits will take up to two years to complete, will make it tougher for Burroughs to regain its momentum. But Blumenthal denies the suggestion. "We've spent many months preparing for this," he says. "There's no turmoil."

Questions

1. Your text argues that change takes place slowly. How do you explain the major changes at Burroughs?
2. The goals of "better coordination" and "decentralization" are incompatible. Do you agree or disagree? Discuss.
3. Blumenthal states that the reorganization will take up to two years to complete. Why might it take this long?

CASE 3 The Park Towers Homeowners Association

Especially prepared for this volume by Stephen P. Robbins.

J. J. Millman and Associates is one of the largest home and apartment builders in the northeastern United States. In 1981, it completed a home development project with more than three hundred units selling in the \$125,000 to \$175,000 price range. The firm also completed several condominium projects, one of which was the Park Towers. The Park Towers complex was a thirty-five story luxury high-rise with 412 living units. The units ranged in size from 600-square-foot studios selling for \$80,000, up to 3,200-square-foot penthouses costing in excess of \$350,000. In spite of the high cost of mortgage money in 1981, the entire complex was sold out in less than ninety days.

Millman's project manager, responsible for the Park Towers complex, had created a homeowners association that would collect fees, interpret association bylaws, and oversee the activities of the complex's property manager. The property manager, in turn, would oversee the complex's staff. Under the laws of the state in which Park Towers is located, the builder is required to create a homeowners association and calculate a fee schedule to cover maintenance of the building. Because the state's laws hold the builder responsible for any underaccruals for the first two years, Millman's project manager has computed the following monthly fee structure carefully. He believes that it will be more than adequate in covering the costs of running and maintaining the building:

Studios, $165

1 bedrooms, $205

2 bedrooms, $260

3 bedrooms, $325

Penthouses, $400

The schedule will generate approximately $100,000 a month of income. This money is to be used to maintain the large outdoor swimming pool and jacuzzi, the indoor gymnasium and racquetball courts, recreation center, garage, and the building and grounds plus cover the costs of the twenty-four-hour phone and lobby staff and insurance. Water, electricity, gas, and unit taxes are all paid by the individual unit owners.

The project manager estimates that, in addition to a property manager, the building will need at least one full-time gardener, nine lobby attendants, four maintenance engineers, two handymen, three recreation personnel, four garage attendants, four office clerical personnel, and four janitors. Additional managerial positions might also be needed.

Questions

1. What type of organization would best meet Park Towers's needs? Diagram an organization chart. What factors determined your choice?
2. Develop an organizational manual for the Park Towers Homeowners Association. Include in it
   a. the authority relationship between the association's board of directors and the property manager.
   b. guidelines as to when a service should be contracted from an outside contractor or handled by personnel "in house."
   c. job descriptions for key personnel.
   d. formalized collection procedures for monthly assessment fees.
3. How would the association's board of directors judge the effectiveness of the property manager and the association?
4. If you were the property manager, what actions could you take to enhance your power vis-à-vis the owners'?
5. If you were on the association's board of directors, what might you suggest the board do to enhance its power vis-à-vis the property manager's?

CASE 4 Supra Oil Company

 This case was prepared by Milton P. Brown and Paul Lawrence.

John Nichols, a university research worker, had a talk with Mr. Bennett[1] about the headquarters sales organization of the Supra Oil Company, one of the larger integrated oil companies in the country. Excerpts from the conversation follow:

NICHOLS: You mentioned that you're planning to make some organizational changes here at headquarters. I wonder if you could tell me something about that.

BENNETT: Well, sure I will. I don't want to take too much credit for this thing, but it sort of got started because in the last couple of years I've been doing some beefing around here about the fact that I was being kept terribly busy with a lot of operating details of the sales organization. You can see what I mean by looking at the organization chart we have been working under. (Mr. Bennett produced a chart from his desk drawer and indicated all the people who were currently reporting to him.) (See Figure 1.)

You can see that with all these people looking to me for leadership I am not in a position to give them the right kind of guidance that I think they should have on their jobs. I just couldn't take the time. It didn't work too badly some time ago, but since I've been made a member of the board of directors, those activities have taken more of my time. What with being on additional committees and things of that kind, I just couldn't give seventeen headquarters' division managers the amount of help and attention that they really need. I think one of the things that they miss is that they're not in close enough touch with me or anybody else higher up the line so that we can be in a good position to appraise their work. We hear about it from some of the field people when they are doing a lousy job, but we don't hear much about it if they're doing a good job. Occasionally a field man will report that he is getting a lot of help from some staff outfit here, but that's rather rare. So we don't have a very good basis for appraising the good things that they do. So we started talking about what might be done to straighten this out.

Our plans are taking pretty definite shape now. Let me show you what we have in mind. (Mr. Bennett sketched on a pad of paper a diagram to indicate the planned organizational changes.) (See Figure 2.) You see, we will have two regional managers instead of three. We'll be making one of the present regional managers the manager of the headquarters sales divisions. Those are the divisions that specialize in promoting and selling our different specialty products. Then we'll set up a new job for Wingate, who has been acting as an administrative assistant here at headquarters. He'll take charge of a

[1]Mr. Bennett was assistant general manager of sales.

FIGURE 1 Partial organization chart of the sales department

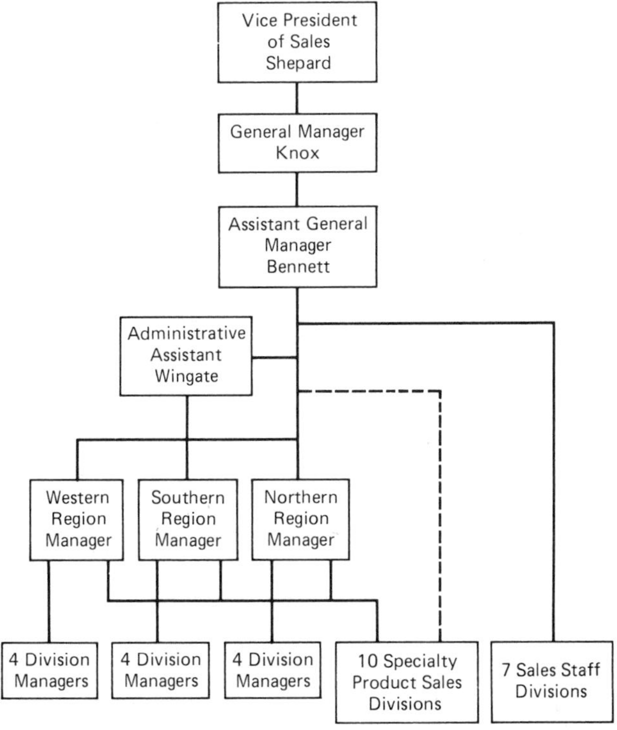

good number of headquarters sales staff divisions that were reporting directly to me. Those are staff divisions like price analysis and advertising. We will also give each of the two remaining regional managers an assistant manager. Those will be new positions too.

NICHOLS: How did you get these plans started?

BENNETT: I raised it with Shepard [vice president of sales] quite a while back.

NICHOLS: Would you say that was maybe six months ago?

BENNETT: I think it probably was six months ago. Shepard's first reaction was unfavorable. You see, I expected him to feel that way because he was the one that had the most to do with setting up our current organizational plan. But I approached him on it two or three times and complained a little bit and kept raising the question, and finally he said, "Well, I'm going to be leaving here pretty soon. You people have got to live with the organization. If you think it would work better some other way, I certainly won't object to your changing it." Well, that sort of thing gave me the green light, so then I went ahead and raised the question with Mr. Weld [president]. That is, Mr. Knox [general sales manager] and I did. The first time we went to him we talked about it just verbally in general terms. He said he thought it sounded like a pretty good idea and asked that we come back with two or three alternative

FIGURE 2 Proposed organization chart of the sales department

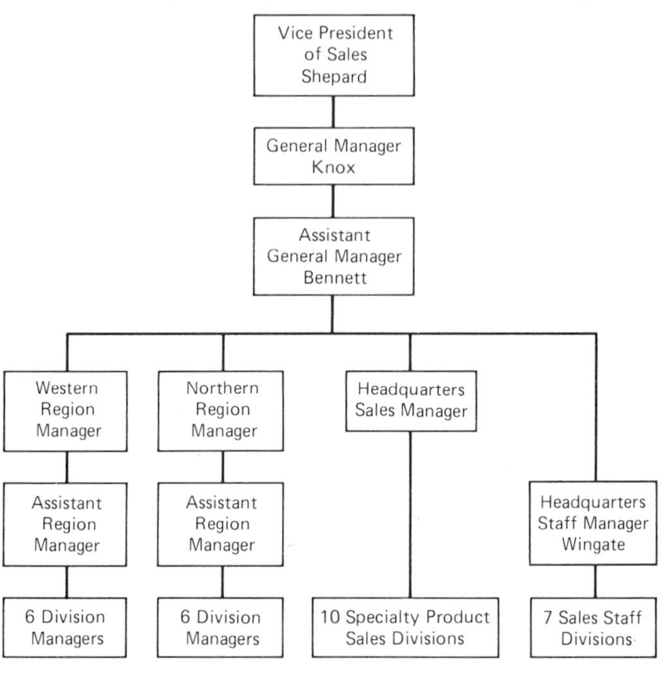

ways of doing the thing in very specific terms. We talked to him once since then and, as a matter of fact, I'm going to see him this afternoon to see if he'll give us a final OK to go ahead with these plans.

NICHOLS: If you get his approval, what would you predict—that it might be another month before the change actually takes place?

BENNETT: Well, I would say so. I think if we've got this thing going in a month that we will be doing pretty well. I'm going to want to talk to my regional managers and then to the headquarters divisional managers about this, but they should buy it all right. I think it will be a fairly simple job to sell it to them. You see, they will in effect be getting more chance to have access to their boss. I think it will work out much better, and they will see the point to it.

NICHOLS: You say that you are making one less region and making the third regional manager the head of—I guess you are calling him the headquarters sales manager. Are all three of those jobs going to continue to be on an equal level?

BENNETT: Yes, they will, but actually this job of headquarters sales manager will be sort of a training position for somebody to step into my job here as assistant general sales manager. That's what we have in mind. I think it will be a good assignment for training for my job. Then, too, we're going to be able to open up a couple of new positions here, the assistant regional managers. I think that is going to be very useful from a management development standpoint.

You see, one of our problems is that a number of the top executives here are all about the same age. You see, Knox and myself and the three regional managers are all about the same age, and then the heads of a lot of our headquarters divisions here are men of about our age who—well, they won't retire immediately, but they don't have a terribly long time to go. So we can't look to too many of those people to be our successors here at headquarters. We want to bring in some people from the field who will step in here as assistant regional managers in training for the job of regional managers.

NICHOLS: I take it then that you will be picking the people for those jobs from your field division men on the basis of talent and ability rather than on the basis of seniority.

BENNETT: Yes, that's right, we're going to pay very little attention to seniority in picking them. As a matter of fact, the two people we have in mind are two of our newest division managers, but they are both very able people. We think that this will give us a chance to give them a good training for future development here.

This change that we are proposing, however, will not drastically change anybody's status here at headquarters, and I don't think it is going to cause us much trouble to put it in. You see, nobody will be jumped over the head of anybody else ahead of them in the management line. We think it's going to help a lot to have an assistant regional manager in here because that means that both he and the regional manager will be able to spend more time out with the field organization. One will be able to cover matters here at headquarters while the other is gone.

NICHOLS: Does that mean that your field people will be getting more top-level supervision as a result of this change?

BENNETT: Well, in a sense that's true of course, but it won't be taking any authority or responsibility from the field people. We just feel that they will be in closer personal contact with the people here at headquarters. We think it is very necessary that we do more of that. You see, if our regional managers and assistant managers can get out in the field and meet with the people, they will have a better basis for appraising different people that come along, and they can make sure we get the best people in the jobs that open up. Sometimes it's pretty hard to tell here at headquarters just who some of the best people are out in the field. You see, some division may have a job open up, and they will have a candidate for that job whom they will recommend highly for the promotion. That may be all well and good, but we want to know whether or not there may be a better man in some other division whom we aren't hearing about who might be shifted over for that promotion. You can't blame the division people for that sort of thing because they will have their favorite candidate and will of course be recommending him. We've made a few mistakes along the way because of this sort of thing, and if we have more personal contact we will be able to do a better job of it.

NICHOLS: Will this mean that you will be able to spend more time in the field?

BENNETT: Yes, I do hope that it will mean that. I want to do that very much. I think I ought to get out in the field more to keep in touch with what's going on in the market. It's really pretty hard to keep in touch with things while you are spending your time here at headquarters. You know, I want to get out and talk to people and see what they are talking about and see what kind of problems they are up against.

NICHOLS: I've heard several comments on this business of getting a feel for the market by getting out in the field. I take it that is quite a different process from keeping in touch with the market on what you might call a statistical basis?

BENNETT: Well, yes, it is. You see, I can look at the reports here in the office, and I may see that some district or some division is not doing too well at all on the basis of the figures in comparison with the competition. But I don't know just what the story is behind those figures. On a personal basis I could probably begin to get some answers to it. It could be any one of a number of things. I might go out there and find that it's a temporary situation because the competition is in effect going out and buying the business away from us, or I might find out that our people are not being very smart or aggressive about promoting our products, or I might find out that they do not know some of the facilities that we have available that would help them compete for the business. You see, one way we can compete for the business is the fact that this company has available some pretty good capital resources; and if we don't have good outlets in a given district, we're often in a position to offer to put up some capital to get some better outlets. That way we can do a better job of competing for the business, and sometimes the local people don't know that those possibilities exist, or perhaps they're a little reticent about putting up proposals. Or even if they do put up proposals, if we haven't been out in the field to see for ourselves what's going on, we probably don't do as good a job of appraising the proposals they do put up.

NICHOLS: In other words, the figures tell you that maybe something ought to be checked into, but you've got to go out and talk to people to find out what is really going on?

BENNETT: Yes, that's right. You have to take a personal look. You can find out a lot faster than you can by correspondence just what is going on and what can be done about it.

NICHOLS: Won't this reorganization mean that some of the people both here and in the field will have new bosses now?

BENNETT: Yes, that's right, but it's not too drastic a change. You see, we used to have only two regional managers some time ago. I guess we shifted off that system some four or five years ago. When I was out in the field as manager of a division, I was reporting in to the northern regional manager, who was Mr. Shepard at that time. Then I was brought in here as his assistant for the whole region. It was about that time that we set up this business of having three regions and I was named one of the regional managers, and at that time Mr. Shepard became general manager.

NICHOLS: Well, it sounds as if that previous move might have been motivated somewhat by a desire to develop people and perhaps give you a chance to take over a regional managership before you might otherwise have had a chance to.

BENNETT: Yes, I think that's right. At that time, that move was the way we could open things up for further management development, and now we are sort of doing it the other way around. Everybody knows that the arrangement we are now proposing may well be changed again in a few more years.

We like to change the organization around a little bit like this from time to time just to let people know that we are not going to be static about things. Of course, we want to do it in a way so that some of our senior people do not get bypassed or jumped over by some of the younger ones, because that not only bothers the individual but it also hurts morale further down in the organization. You see, when some of the people further down see some of that sort of thing happening, they are apt to conclude that it might happen to them some day, and it's pretty discouraging to them. The way we are doing it now we can bring up some younger people without jumping over anybody's head who is senior.

I think an organization change of this kind is also useful in that it indicates to some of our younger people that they need not feel discouraged if they are in a position where someone is above them in line who shows no signs of being promoted on up. This situation might make a person feel that he is being blocked from future promotion by his boss. But he is encouraged when he sees an occasional organizational shift of this kind because it makes him realize that things can happen in the future that might shift the organization around to a point where he can be sprung loose for a move on up even though his boss may not be promotable.

NICHOLS: Then I take it that one of the predominant thoughts in this whole reorganization was one of management development?

BENNETT: Oh, that's certainly true. That was one of the prime reasons we're proposing this, because we think it will help us develop our managers and this gives us a way of doing it without upsetting the organization too much.

That afternoon Mr. Bennett kept the appointment with Mr. Weld that was mentioned in the conversation. Upon entering Mr. Weld's office, Mr. Bennett handed Mr. Weld a copy of the revised sales organization chart.

BENNETT: Here's a final version of our reorganizational plans. Do you think it's all right to go ahead on this?

Questions

1. What factors should govern the decision as to how many people report to Bennett?
2. Discuss this case in terms of the process of implementing change.
3. How is information obtained by personal observation different from information secured through a statistical report? What are the advantages of each?
4. First, Bennett argues for a new structural arrangement to increase the amount of time that he can spend supervising. Later in the case, he

argues for the new structure to develop managerial talent. A third explanation, not addressed directly, is that the new structure will increase Bennett's control. Assess each of these three positions. Which is most valid?

5. If you were Mr. Weld, how would you respond to Bennett's proposal?

CASE 5 Winthrop Hospital

Reprinted from Stephen J. Carroll, Jr., Frank T. Paine, and John M. Miner, *The Management Process: Cases and Readings,* 2nd ed. (New York: Macmillan, 1977), pp. 429–431. With permission.

Winthrop Hospital is located in a medium-sized suburban community. A general hospital, it serves a large portion of the surrounding area and is usually operating at, near, or sometimes beyond its capacity. Each floor of the hospital has its own particular structure with regard to the nurses who staff it. This formalized hierarchy runs from the supervisor (who must be a registered nurse) to registered nurses (RNs) to licensed practical nurses (LPNs) to students and nurses' aides. Professionally, there are some duties that are supposed to be performed only by the RNs; these are spelled out in the hospital manual. In practice, however, the LPNs do much of the work that is supposed to be done by the RNs. The RNs are glad for the help because they are very busy with other duties. Through time the work done by the RNs and the LPNs has meshed so thoroughly that one just does the work without thinking of whose job it is supposed to be. The hospital is normally so crowded that, even with everyone performing all types of work, there never seems to be enough time or enough help.

The procedural manual used at Winthrop Hospital was first used in 1947 and has not been revised. Everyone connected with the hospital realizes that it is extremely outdated, and actual practice varies so greatly as to have no similarity to what is prescribed in the manual. Even the courses that the student nurses take teach things entirely differently from what is prescribed in Winthrop's manual.

The vacation privileges for nurses at the hospital show extreme differences for the different types of nurses. RNs receive two weeks' vacation after nine months on the job, whereas LPNs must be on the staff for ten years before receiving their second week of vacation. The LPNs believe this to be extremely unfair and have been trying to have the privileges somewhat more equalized. Their efforts have met with little cooperation and no success. The hospital superiors have simply told them that the terms for vacation are those stated in the hospital manual and that they saw no need to change them.

Some of the individual nurses at Winthrop then began to take matters into their own hands. The LPNs on the fourth floor of the hospital decided that if they couldn't have the extra vacation because of what was written in the manual then they would follow the manual in all phases and go strictly according to the book. Difficulties surfaced as soon as the LPNs began to behave in this manner. The RNs now seemed to have more work than they could handle adequately and the LPNs were just as busy doing solely their "prescribed" duties. The same amount of effort put forth previously was being exerted, but less was being accomplished because of the need to jump around from place to place and job to job in order to work strictly according to the book. An example of this wasted effort occurred in the taking of doctors' orders. Doctors phone in the type of treatment that a patient is to receive—medicines, times for dispensing such, diet, and so forth. These doctors' orders are supposed to be taken by an RN, but in practice whoever was nearest the phone had taken the order. If an LPN took the order she had it signed by the supervisor (stationed at the desk) as a safeguard. This procedure saved the time and effort involved in getting an RN to the phone for every order. Now, however, the LPNs refused to take the doctors' orders and called for an RN. The RN had to leave the work she was doing, go to the phone, take the order, then go back to her unfinished work. This procedure wasted the time of the doctor, the RN, and the LPN who had to locate the RN. The LPNs' practice of going by the book brought about hostile feelings among both groups of nurses and among the doctors who had to work on the floor. The conflicts led to a lessening in the high degree of care that the patients had been receiving.

The conflict initiated by the difference in vacation privileges brought about more complaints from both parties. In the manual the categories for vacation privileges listed "supervisors," "RNs," "lab technicians," and "others." The LPNs resented being placed in the "others" category. They felt that they deserved a separate listing, especially because they had the same amount of training as other groups, such as the lab technicians. Adding further fuel to the fire was the fact that the lab technicians got a second week of vacation after only one year on the job. Another item of controversy was the fact that RNs were allowed to sign themselves in on the job when they reported, whereas the LPNs were required to punch in. The LPNs felt that the RNs thus could hide any incidents of lateness, whereas the LPNs had strict account kept of their time and were docked in salary for any time missed.

The RNs now complained to the hospital superiors more vehemently than ever about being understaffed. They felt that they simply needed more RNs on every floor on every shift to meet what was required of them;

this was a demand they had been voicing even before the conflict began. The shortage was especially acute at nights, when unfamiliarity with individual patients often led to mix-ups in the treatments.

The ill feelings led to arguments among the nurses. The LPNs felt that they were always doing more work than the RNs, that they spent more time with the patients because the RNs had more to do at the desk, and that they knew more about treatments because they more often accompanied doctors on their rounds. They now voiced these opinions. The RNs argued superiority on the basis of a longer period of formal training.

All these factors combined to bring about a tremendous drop in morale and a marked decrease in efficiency, and the conflict was in danger of spreading to the other floors in the hospital.

Questions

1. What is the source of the conflict?
2. If employees "work strictly according to the book" and productivity suffers, what does this tell us about formal organization?
3. "The RNs might be encouraging the conflict to further their self-interests." Explain.
4. What might be done to alleviate the problem?

CASE 6 What Makes Tandem Run?

Tandem Computers, Inc. has to be one of the biggest success stories around—even in the fast-rising minicomputer industry where dramatic growth is sometimes taken for granted. In June, the Cupertino (Calif.) company shipped its one-thousandth computer, just four years after delivering its first system. The company is growing at 100 percent annually, with revenues now running at a $100 million annual clip.

While Tandem's unique, single product still has no direct competitor, the young company's wild success is due equally to its unorthodox management style, which provides everything from Friday afternoon beer parties for its 1,100 workers to a sabbatical every four years and stock options for every employee. This "people-oriented" management style emphasizes complete informality, peer pressure, and open communications. There are few formal meetings or reviews, and the management team and organizational structure is already in place for a $500-million-plus operation. Industry experts, in fact, expect Tandem to reach easily its revenue goal of $500 million annually by 1983.

Reliability. Tandem's present prosperity is built on a "fail-safe" computer that will not lose data if any part of the system goes down. While other fail-safe systems usually require a redundant, back-up computer that lies idle unless the on-line system fails, Tandem's computer design allows dual central processors to share the data-processing work load and to take over the entire job should one break down. The system's reliability makes it especially attractive to banks, airlines, and other businesses where lost or interrupted data mean lost revenues.

Without varying its management style, the computer maker has broken through the difficult growth transitions that any young company must pass. "Tandem has done very well at getting over the management plateaus at $3 million and again at about $50 million that affect growth," notes David E. Gold, a Saratoga (Calif.) consultant. And in the year ended September 30, 1979, Tandem came within $1 million of the sales projection made in its 1974 business plan, boasts Thomas J. Perkins, Tandem's chairman and a partner in Kleiner, Perkins, Caulfield & Byers, the venture capital firm that provided the company with its initial seed money.

"When you get above $5 million, it's hard for a person to manage everything like a mother hen," say Gene M. Amdahl, founder and now chairman emeritus of Amdahl Corp. "As the company grows," Amdahl says, "it's easy to lose the entrepreneur's vision of what the company should be. But I don't believe it absolutely has to happen."

Neither does James G. Treybig, Tandem's co-founder and president, who figures that his company will need its people-oriented management philosophy more than the latest technology to continue to grow at its current pace. "The human side of the company is most important to make the $1 billion mark," declares the 39-year-old executive. Treybig says that he has "100 percent disposable time" with which to work on people projects such as his new chart of one hundred management concepts that he uses to guide the company. The chart emphasizes such notions as pushing responsibility down the employee ranks to develop managers faster, hiring the best person rather than the cheapest, and promoting from within.

The genesis of Tandem's management philosophy comes from Hewlett-Packard Co., which is not too surprising, since Treybig, along with the other three founders—Michael D. Green, John C. Loustaunou, and James A. Katzman, all vice presidents—worked at the Palo Alto computer and instrument maker before forming the company. "We learned at HP," says Katzman, "but we've extended that philosophy here."

At Tandem, for example, employees have neither the time clocks nor the name badges usually found at other high-technology companies in California's Silicon Valley. And its workers have flexible hours, a swimming pool that is open between 6 A. M. and 8 P. M., a volleyball court complete with locker room and showers, and an open-door policy that invites employees to drop in for a talk with their managers anytime.

"It's a lot of physical things," says Katzman, "but more important is our attitude that people are responsible adults and our willingness to spend money to keep people happy." One example of that corporate largesse is the six-week sabbatical—with full pay—that all employees are required to take every four years. This month, too, Tandem employees will vote on future benefits, choosing from among increased medical coverage, a retirement plan, profit sharing, or vacation privileges at resort condominiums the company would acquire.

Low Turnover. So far, Tandem's people philosophy has paid off in more than soaring revenues. "The company is able to attract really excellent people in [a geographical] area where it is supposed to be hard to get them," says Edwin B. Costello, an industry analyst with Sutro & Co., a San Francisco brokerage house. And once employees join the company, they apparently stay. Katzman claims turnover runs 8 percent annually, far lower than the industry average of 23 percent.

Tandem's reputation for hiring top employees who stay is no accident, according to the company. Job candidates are often called back three or more times for interviews lasting several hours. And salary offers are never made until a recruit accepts a job. "They've got to decide they're not just coming for the money," declares Treybig.

The company prefers to hire experienced people because they require less training, but even these people have to be indoctrinated in the corporate culture. And that is no easy task at Tandem, which is growing so fast that the average employee has been with the company for only six weeks. Treybig personally participates in most new employee orientations to spread the management gospel. And he uses peer pressure to inculcate recruits in the Tandem way. For example, a group of assemblers from the factory floor recently walked into his office to complain about their manager. "[The Manager] soon left because he didn't look on people as people," Treybig says. "Now everyone knows that that mistake was fixed, and other managers will see that if they don't do what's right, they will be fired."

Indeed, decisions are made informally, and executives get together in spontaneous meetings as problems arise. Admits Chief Financial Officer Loustaunou, "We have no scheduled reviews of things like progress reports." So far, the company has managed quite well without formal meetings. Outsiders often note that communications among the top executives flow as freely as the beer that is served every Friday afternoon. "If you ask the same question of several managers, you always get the same answer," says Alvin C. Rice, a Tandem director.

Tighter Control. Not everyone, however, is impressed with Tandem's management style. "Tandem's founders thought that HP had too many meetings, too many memos, and too much management," recalls John V. Levy, a former Tandem engineer now working for Apple Computer, Inc. "My impression," he says, "is that they did a total flip-flop."

Treybig recognizes that, as Tandem grows into a large company, ad hoc decision making will not suffice. So he is instituting more controls. In accounts receivable, for example, Loustaunou says that the company has grown too large for all the top managers to be involved with each problem account. "A year ago, we had maybe ten problem accounts," he says. "Now it is thirty to forty, and it is more appropriate to have our people tell us in writing the status of their accounts." Similarly, while the company still has no wage or salary structure, Loustaunou notes that it is only a question of time before formal review procedures are established.

But that does not mean that Tandem lacks controls on company operations. The company has rigid procedures for implementing production controls, cost standards, quality control, and management reporting systems. To handle these jobs, Tandem has eight separate in-house computer systems. "They have an informal management style imposed upon a very organized and disciplined set of business standards," says Rice. "You can't have their kind of growth without having those in place."

Treybig and his colleagues spend long hours preparing the company for the soaring growth they expect in the next few years. For instance, the executive team includes fourteen vice presidents, more than the company currently requires but necessary if it makes in three years its goal of $500 million in annual revenues. To handle that size company, Tandem has realigned its top management. Five management teams were given responsibility for marketing and production on a geographical basis.

The question remains, however, whether Tandem's Non-Stop computer can continue to be a nonstop success. While the Non-Stop still has no direct competition, Digital Equipment Corp. and several other companies are reportedly developing competitive systems. But industry observers predict that Tandem's rivals will have a difficult time duplicating the company's software developments in less than three years. "You can't have a baby in a month by making nine women pregnant," comments analyst Costello.

Confident. Treybig is even more confident of Tandem's ability to weather any competitive storm. The only inhibiting factor on Tandem's growth now, Treybig says, is the reluctance of some customers to buy computers from a vendor that has only $100 million in sales.

To raise his credibility with both customers and Wall Street, Treybig is running the company on a debt-free basis. But to do this and still grow at 100 percent annually means that Tandem has had to sell additional stock on a yearly basis. As a result, the number of shares outstanding has increased more than tenfold in the past five years to 5.2 million shares.

But James R. Berdell of Montgomery Securities in San Francisco points out that Tandem's price-earnings ratio of 36 is the highest of all of the technology stocks that he follows and almost double the computer industry average. For Treybig, such success is merely part of his long-term plan. "I never started Tandem thinking only of a $100 million company," the brash executive exclaims. "To build a $10 billion company where people loved to work would be a start."

Questions

1. How would you describe Tandem's current structure?
2. What factors best explain the current structure? The future structure?
3. Might Tandem's current structure "turn off" some prospective employees? Discuss.
4. Management implies that a structure that works for $100 million a year in sales will not be effective when sales reach $500 million. Do you agree or disagree? Why?
5. What is your opinion of the changes that management envisions necessary to reach $500 million a year? Would you propose a different set of changes?

CASE 7 Behind the Exodus at National Semiconductor

The current problems of National Semiconductor Corp. must come as a shock to any student of industry life cycles. When an industry is young and thriving, only the most blatant management mistakes cause serious bottom-line problems. But one of the first signs of maturity is the realization that demand is not limitless and that overcapacity can result in price wars, brutal competition, and the untimely death of some players. Usually, the companies that are hurt the least have high market share, low-cost positions, and in-depth product lines. Thus National, the third largest and lowest-cost producer of semiconductors, should have been relatively immune to the turmoil in the semiconductor industry.

Instead, National seems to be suffering more than its competition. Its stock price plunged from a high of $51.50 per share to $19 in less than a year, and several analysts expect that its earnings per share will be only 70¢ in fiscal 1982, compared with $2.37 in fiscal 1981. More serious, the resignation on August 28 of Pierre R. Lamond, the second ranking corporate officer and chief technologist, is but the latest in a series of defections that is assuming the proportion of an exodus. Chief Executive Charles E. Sporck, who admits that Lamond's departure "hurts," is facing the fact that his company's four years of record earnings growth are over and that he is being abandoned by much of his top staff.

Job-hopping is endemic in the fast-changing semiconductor industry, where venture capitalists and rival companies line up to lure bright executives with promises of top dollar. But at National, the roll call of managers who have left recently reads like a formidable list of potential competitors. Aside from Lamond, who says he, too, may go into competition against his former employer, the list includes

- Robert H. Swanson, vice president of the Linear Circuits Group, National's most profitable semiconductor line. He took two top circuit designers and a marketing manager with him to form a new semiconductor company.
- Fred B. Bialek, a key manufacturing talent. He became president of Dorado Micro Systems, Inc.
- E. Joseph Willits, financial vice president, and Treasurer John L. Nesheim. They were asked to resign because of vague "personality clashes," even though Nesheim was generally regarded as a strong spokesman for the company in Washington and on Wall Street.

Now, belatedly, Sporck is admitting that the management turnover cannot be entirely explained by widespread industry turmoil. And he is casting about for a new management structure not only to stanch the flow of talent but also to give the $1.1 billion company sufficient controls without compromising its division managers' abilities to remain as entrepreneurial as the new and hungry competition. Ironically, a streamlined structure was proposed by Lamond a year ago. Sporck's failure to act on that proposal was, Lamond hints, part of the reason why he became frustrated and left. Sporck himself says, "Obviously, the situation should have been resolved earlier."

National is grappling with an almost schizophrenic management structure. It has a proliferation of fiercely autonomous managers at the product level whose compensation is based in part on the performance of their own profit centers. Half of them reported to Lamond, while the other half reported to John R. Finch, another vice president. Several years ago, National centralized certain operations to gain economies of scale. For example, wafers were all manufactured at one plant in Utah, processed in several other locations, and shipped to Southeast Asia for assembly. Production, marketing, and other activities became difficult to coordinate. Lamond and Finch headed different groups that were expected to cooperate in the creation of specially priced semiconductor packages that could be sold to large customers at a discount. Because the packages required price concessions by each of the groups, the two men were often at loggerheads. As Lamond recalls it, the structure produced confusion and conflict. Decisions made within individual profit centers went smoothly, but "inter-business decisions" often had to "go all the way up," he says. Sporck would wind up settling the questions, in a red-tape-ridden process that even Sporck now admits had become untenable. "Frequently there were problems where a final decision couldn't be reached, and it would end up coming to me," he says. "That really doesn't make sense—those decisions should be made at the division level."

"Table-pounder." That is an unusual admission for Sporck. Insiders characterize him as a "table-pounder," a highly autocratic manager who could accept the concept of decentralized decision making on paper but had trouble carrying it out in practice. Indeed, for the last few years Sporck has been tightening the reins on his organization. In 1977, Lamond was put in charge of metal oxide semiconductors and other high-technology products. Finch was responsible for most other components, while Vice President E. Floyd Kvamme focused on semiconductor marketing and the company's growing computer products group. In 1979, when National acquired Itel Corp.'s computer operations, Kvamme was named president of the computer division. Rather than have the semiconductor groups coordinate marketing among themselves, Sporck took on those duties himself. Sporck also held on to direct authority for international manufacturing, which includes the assembly of nearly all of National's components, as well as European operations, which consist of computer systems and components. As a result, Sporck not only got involved in what should have been mundane pricing decisions, but kept control of production and marketing decisions as well.

Now, apparently, Sporck is finally admitting he bit off far more than he could chew, much less digest. With Lamond gone, he has turned over responsibility for the entire semiconductor division to Finch, giving him the title of general manager. Finch is in the process of consolidating several of the units to make his division more manageable. He has already cut the number of profit groups from fourteen to twelve, and he says he may ultimately combine them into eight.

Few Bonuses. That still leaves the managers who headed each of the units vying with each other to take the top spot at the remaining units, and more management talent could be lost if substantive posts are not quickly forthcoming. So far Sporck has no ready solutions other than to offer a "challenging work environment," with good pay and bonuses of up to 60 percent of salary. But bonuses could be scarce this year. In 1977, for example, when times were bad for National, some managers received no bonuses. Says Sporck, "With the large amount of venture capital out there and the fact that we have a large number of entrepreneurial managers who really have been running their own businesses, it's a problem."

There was little in the way of incentives Sporck could offer Bialek that could compare with the deal he was given. Bialek left in February after he was offered 800,000 shares of Dorado stock for $1 million, which on paper today are worth $10 million. Lamond says he was approached by four venture capital firms within 48 hours after leaving National.

The management defections, however, are just the most visible sign of National's problems. Unlike its two top competitors, it has not diversified appreciably and now finds itself in a position where semiconductors, which are providing negligible earnings, account for 72 percent of sales. Both Texas Instruments, Inc. and Motorola, Inc. derive less than 40 percent of their revenues from this line. To be sure, National's forays into computers and point-of-sale terminals for supermarkets have finally become a profitable $314 million business after years of red ink. And Sporck sees non-semiconductor sales growing to as much as 35 percent of revenues from its current 28 percent, in five to eight years.

Takeover Target? Financially, National is in good shape for the future. Capital spending will be slightly above last year's level of $150 million, despite the slump. The company is still putting 9 percent of revenues into research and development—much more than some competitors. Attrition has pared its work force by some 10 percent, and the company has cut its interest expenses in half and has pruned long-term debt to just 20 percent of equity.

But the very viability of its balance sheet, combined with its low stock price and management turmoil, may bring new problems. Analysts note that National has become a very attractive take-over target. Still, Sporck says, "If someone approached us, they would be in for one hell of a battle."

But if the management defections continue, Sporck may have to fight the battle alone. Indeed, he can use all the help he can get right now. Prices have fallen sharply in the memory sector. For 16K RAMs (random access memories that will store more than 16,000 bits of digital information), for example, price tags have dropped from $5.50 at the beginning of 1981 to less than $1 today. Analysts have revised their estimates of the dollar value of shipments as well. What they expected to be a 5 percent to 10 percent drop is now predicted to be a 10 percent to 15 percent drop.

Moreover, the Japanese are trying to capture 70 percent of the critical 64K RAM market. And semiconductor sales in Europe, which represent about one-third of National's total, "are the pits," admits Sporck. The 35 percent to 40 percent increase in the value of the dollar against European currencies is forcing National to cut prices to protect its markets.

The entire industry faces these problems. What is unique at National is that it has lost its top technologist, a key technology team, and a prized manufacturing man at what seems to be a crucial time. Still, National has built a reputation of plugging away even when times are bad. Whether it can ever again enjoy a period of growth such as it had in the past four years, when it tripled in size, will be a test of how much Sporck has learned from the management turmoil National has endured.

Questions

1. Describe National's current structure. What are its strengths? What are its weaknesses?
2. What changes is Sporck suggesting? Do you think that they will be effective? Why?
3. Is Sporck's leadership style incompatible with National's structure? If so, what is the solution?
4. Analyze this case in terms of managing growth versus managing decline.

CASE 8 What Undid Jarman: Paperwork Paralysis

When Chairman Franklin M. Jarman wrested control of Genesco, Inc. from his father, W. Maxey, to become chief executive officer four years ago, one of his primary goals was to impose a system of financial controls over the $1 billion retailing and apparel conglomerate. The 45-year-old Jarman did exactly that. His controls probably helped to save the company when it lost $52 million in 1973. But they were also chiefly responsible for his downfall last week.

Controls were an obsession with Jarman. According to insiders, he centralized management to the point of frustrating the company's executives and causing red tape and delay. Operations were virtually paralyzed by paperwork. One glaring example: Genesco's most recent annual report states that the company would spend $8 million this year to open 63 stores and renovate 124 others. Yet six months into the fiscal year, insiders report that little has been done because Jarman required more and more analysis for each project, postponing decisions.

Such delay and indecision can be particularly harmful in a company like Genesco, whose business is mostly in the fast-moving fields of apparel and retailing. Among its major product lines are Johnston & Murphy and Jarman Shoes, and its retail outlets include Bonwit Teller and S. H. Kress. "It was a classic case of the boss being in the way, and he had to go," explains one Genesco insider, who was among the more than two dozen executives participating in the palace revolt last week when Jarman was stripped of his authority.

The Undoing. Two of Genesco's inside directors, Vice Chairmen Ralph H. Bowles and Larry B. Shelton, had become alarmed by Genesco's inertia in October. At the same time many top managers complained to them that Jarman's management had been demoralizing. When Jarman seemed to be preparing to oust two key operating executives, Bowles and Shelton went to an outside director to explain how the company's fortunes were deteriorating. He in turn contacted other outside directors. Meanwhile, Bowles, Shelton, and several managers compiled for the directors a dossier of Jarman's managerial shortcomings.

Things all came together between Christmas and New Year's when Jarman was on vacation at Montego Bay. Bowles, Shelton, several managers, and four outside directors met in Washington. They called a special meeting of the board for the Monday after New Year's. With more than two dozen rank-and-file executives ready to quit if Jarman was not ousted—and waiting in the cafeteria next door on the second floor of the Genesco building in Nashville—the board did the next best thing. It took away Jarman's titles of president and chief executive officer and gave them to William M. Blackie, age 72, a retired executive vice president and former director, and told Jarman that he must take his orders from Blackie.

Jarman declined to be interviewed by *Business Week* for this article. But sources close to him and the company say that he was treated shabbily by the Genesco board and executives—many of whom owed their jobs to him. These sources say that Jarman was the victim of a conspiracy, which they say started after word got out that he was looking for a new president with marketing experience, a job for which he had hired the New York search firm of Knight & Zabriskie. According to this scenario, Bowles, age 46, and Shelton, age 42, feared that if a new president were brought in they would lose standing. Jarman came back from vacation and just before the board meeting issued a statement saying that it would be "inappropriate and contrary to the interests of the stockholders of Genesco to make any radical change in the company's management. . . . With the approval of members of the board of directors, [Jarman has] been seeking to hire a new president." Bowles and Shelton maintain that they were not among those members and that all they knew was that Jarman was looking for a senior marketing executive.

The Performance. In any case, Genesco's performance under Jarman was erratic. Although he pared many losing operations and improved the balance sheet, Genesco lost money in two of his four years as CEO. For example, last year earnings rebounded to $15.9 million, or about $1 a share, after a loss of $14.4 million the year before, but in the first quarter of this fiscal year ended October 31, earnings were off 61 percent, and Jarman had projected similarly disappointing results for the important second quarter, which includes Christmas.

Insiders are convinced there was a correlation between Genesco's earnings and the overcentralized and inflexible management style they say Jarman favored. Many criticisms of Jarman's management were chronicled by Genesco executives and by Bowles and Shelton in the form of internal memoranda. The memoranda were put in dossiers several inches thick and given to each director. The board took its action last week largely on the basis of this material.

One Genesco director thinks that this approach was amateurish and unnecessary, although he voted to oust Jarman. He says the material in the dossier consisted principally of "record memoranda—written to the files after conversations with Jarman—that were very self-serving." The memoranda, he adds, contained many inconsistencies, such as that Jarman was too involved in detail or that he was not involved enough.

An insider who has read the material says that there are inconsistencies because Jarman was an inconsistent manager. He cites the example of a new shoe store under consideration. Jarman demanded a seventy-five-page report on the $44,000 store dealing with such trifling details as whether it should have a water cooler and hot running water. On the other hand, this executive says that, if a division executive had an overwhelming personality, he could push through decisions with "no checks, no balances, not even pro forma financial statements"—as was done recently with a proposal for a new Bonwit Teller store.

As a matter of course, insiders say, Jarman got bogged down in minutiae. He delegated little real authority to his managers, even to the two vice chairmen.

"Better run it by Frank," was the company watchword for the most routine, everyday matters. He spent a great deal of time insisting that reports be bound properly in notebooks. Another criticism is that Jarman isolated himself and avoided contact with company executives. Typically, he dealt only with the four other members of the management committee, of which he was chairman and which included Bowles, Shelton, and two operating executives. Jarman, an engineer educated at the Massachusetts Institute of Technology, had come up through the financial side of Genesco and, as a director notes, "has never been good at handling people."

One executive says that, ever since Jarman had become CEO, top people in the company had been trying to get him to visit the company's many plants and offices. This executive says that Jarman did it just once. Moreover, Jarman canceled the customary annual management breakfast meetings that brought all the top executives together with the chairman. Because of Jarman's isolation from other Genesco managers, it is doubtless that the revolt against him was carried out so smoothly.

Jarman's style was to work from computer printouts, checking them for aberrations. He reportedly used to say that managing a corporation was like flying an airplane—his avocation. " 'You watched the dials to see if the plane deviated off course and when it did you nudged it back with the controls,' Jarman explained," the insider says. "At Genesco the computer printouts were the dials and Bowles and Shelton were the controls."

Sometimes, however, Jarman did not believe what the printouts said. He hired consultants to verify things, such as a division's overhead charges or the quality and pricing of its products. The footwear division, which has been consistently profitable, got this treatment several times.

Still, a Surprise. Jarman's ouster, nevertheless, took many observers by surprise. To begin with, the board had recently granted him a $105,000 raise to $285,000 a year, even though Genesco pays no common stock dividend. (The board cut Jarman to $180,000 annually last week.)

Equally surprising was the fact that Genesco's board has been structured to Jarman's specifications in recent years. Over a four-year period, it was reduced from eighteen to ten members, and many of the father's supporters were replaced by the son's choices, such as Bowles, Shelton, and Wilson, with whom Frank Jarman served on several corporate and civic boards.

To insiders, however, things were different. First, after news broke of Jarman's raise, Genesco employees signed petitions to protest. Moreover, there was overwhelming sentiment in middle management that Jarman had to go if Genesco was to survive. "You could count Jarman's supporters on the fingers of one hand," one executive said.

Last week the board started searching for an outsider to fill the presidency. Whoever lands the Genesco job will have a challenge not only to produce consistent earnings but also to gain the support of the managers, the vice chairmen, and the board of directors. "It's a slippery perch," says one corporate recruiter.

Questions

1. How does competing-values explain the measurement of Genesco's effectiveness?
2. What role did each of the following have in determining Genesco's structure?
   a. strategy
   b. technology
   c. environment
3. Assess this case from a power-control perspective.
4. Could Franklin Jarman have maintained tight control yet provided for more rapid decision making?
5. Could Franklin Jarman have prevented his ousting? If so, how?

CASE 9 A Short Shorter-Workweek Program

Especially prepared for this volume by Stephen P. Robbins.

Retail Credit Reports (RCR) operates out of Minneapolis, Minnesota. Employing approximately 125 people, the company supplies credit reports on individuals to department stores, oil companies, banks, and other organizations in Minnesota and western Wisconsin that utilize the information to make credit decisions. Firms pay a flat membership fee per year to use RCR's services plus a fee for each credit report, the cost varying with the amount of information desired.

In 1979, RCR employed seven managers, one assistant to the manager, fifteen supervisors, seventy-three service clerks, twenty secretaries, and nine investigators. Figure 1 shows the organization chart. The service clerks are organized by the last names of individuals. For instance, if a bank

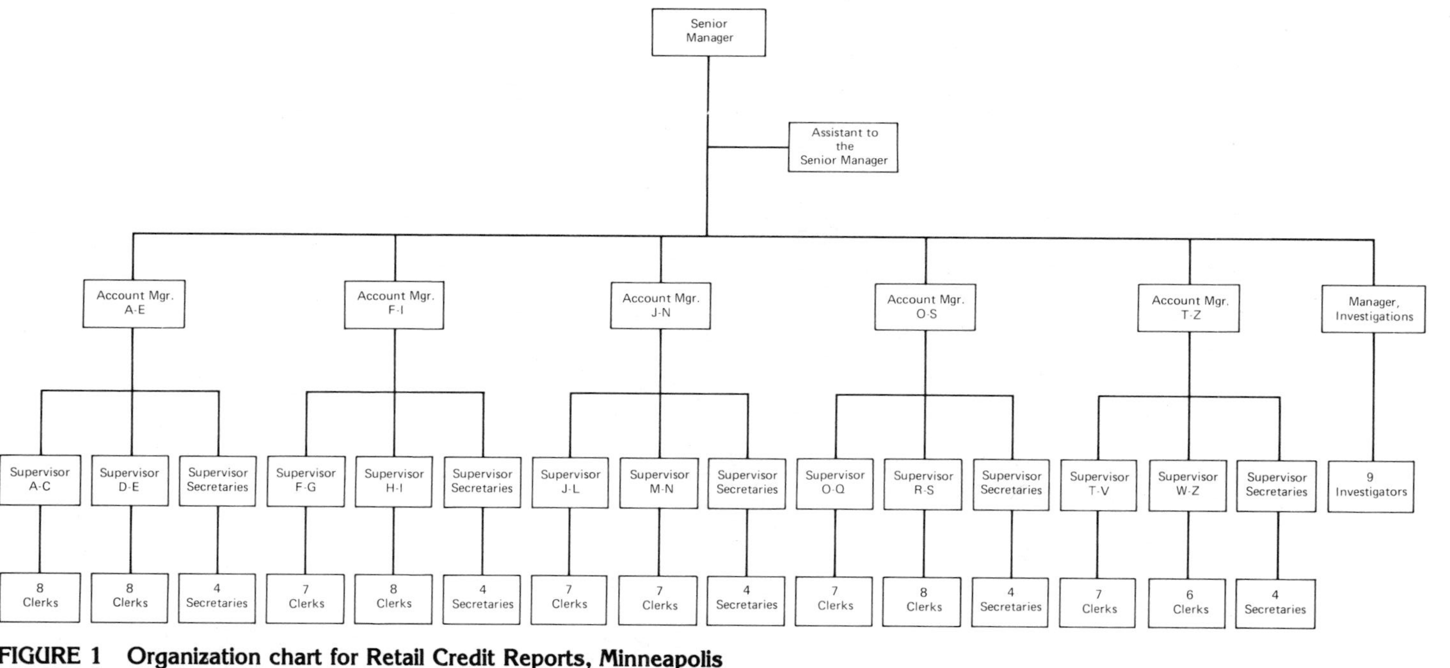

FIGURE 1 Organization chart for Retail Credit Reports, Minneapolis

wanted a credit report on Nan Greenberg, the F to I account manager would be responsible for developing the report. If the account manager needed more information than had been obtained in mail and phone reports from credit sources, she could call upon the investigations group to gather additional data. The investigations group also verified secondary data, did reference checks, and similar activities.

The structure of jobs at RCR differed within areas. For instance, the investigators typically dropped by the office every day or every other day, picked up their assignments, dropped off finished reports, and then departed. As long as they completed their assignments competently and on time, they experienced very little in terms of control. The service clerks and secretaries, on the other hand, did routine and standardized activities. Supervisors and managers monitored their on-the-job behavior closely.

The freedom that the investigators had was a sore point in the office, particularly among service clerks. In terms of education and experience, the investigators were little different from the service clerks. Even their salaries were quite similar. The continuous griping about the "soft hours that the investigators have" led Jill Friedman, the senior manager in charge of the Minneapolis office, to the decision to introduce a four-day workweek in February 1980. It would apply to all RCR employees except the investigators. The investigators could currently work a four-day week if they chose. But Jill was unsure of just what was involved and the effect that it would have on the company's performance. So she hired a consultant from a local university to help implement the program.

The consultant's strategy included tracking absence and satisfaction data before and after the shorter workweek was implemented. In this way, the consultant believed, it would be possible to assess the actual impact of the change.

The consultant had employees complete a questionnaire that assessed job satisfaction. He also reviewed employee personnel records to calculate absence figures. These became the base rates against which later figures could be compared.

Shortly after this information was obtained, employees were advised that RCR was moving to a four-day, ten-hour week. The announcement was made in a management staff meeting. It was further announced that Mondays would be the extra day off. No mention was made of the criteria for deciding whether or not the program would be continued.

One month after the 4-40 workweek went into effect, the consultant made a follow-up survey of employee job satisfaction. Absence data were also obtained. However, unbeknownst to the consultant, Jill Friedman was not pleased with how the change was working out. She was finding it increasingly difficult to schedule RCR's work activities. One month and three days after the 4-40 schedule was introduced, it was announced by Jill that RCR would be returning to the standard five-day week. The consultant, somewhat surprised, decided to make the best of the situation. He asked and received approval from Jill to do a third employee satisfaction survey. It was administered a month after the program was terminated. Absence data were also computed. This gave the consultant three sets of data. He had job satisfaction and absence data covering the period before the change was announced, a month after it had been implemented, and a month after it was terminated.

In June, the consultant provided a report to Jill giving the results he obtained. Job satisfaction improved significantly after the 4-40 was implemented. After the program was discontinued, satisfaction dropped severely, to a level well below what it was before the shorter workweek was introduced. Absence data followed a similar pattern. Using the first set of data as a base (equal to 100), absenteeism dropped to 27 a month after 4-40 was introduced but was up to 112 a month after 4-40 was terminated.

Questions

1. Redesign Figure 1 to centralize all secretarial activities directly under the senior manager. What advantages might centralization offer? Disadvantages?
2. What suggestions can you make that might improve the overall structure of RCR?
3. What factors should Jill have considered before implementing the 4-40 schedule?
4. Do you think that the final job satisfaction and absentee data would have been different if the employees had been consulted before the 4-40 program was initiated? After it was initiated, but before it was discontinued?
5. What are the implications from this case for instituting a change and then withdrawing it?

CASE 10 How Sears Became a High-Cost Operator

In 1973, when Sears, Roebuck & Co. moved its headquarters, it seemed fitting that it was placed in the world's tallest building. Sears had always been associated with superlatives—biggest, best, and sharpest. The envy of its competitors, the huge retailer was second to none in its ability to ferret out innovative products and to get suppliers to provide them at the lowest cost. Its mail-order catalog was the largest of its kind, and its 860 stores, many of which were located in the first suburban shopping centers, represented the epitome of convenience. Its staff was huge—more than 400,000 employees—and where other retailers made do with just two buyers for a single line of merchandise, Sears could seek out sources with as many as ten.

But no one is envying the giant today. It has become the highest-cost mass merchandiser in the business, with general and administrative expenses siphoning off 29 percent of its sales dollars, compared with 23 percent for J. C. Penney Co. and 19 percent for K mart Corp. One competitor estimates that Sears would need to "weed out at least $100 million a year" to be competitive with low-cost retailers such as K mart. He guesses that, with Sears's "cumbersome" cost structure, Sears needs a 50 percent markup to make a profit on items that competitors need mark up only 35 percent.

Indeed, Sears's merchandising profit margin plunged to 2.2 percent in 1979 from 3.1 percent in 1976 and is expected to fall even further when 1980 figures are tallied. Its merchandising profits have slipped precipitously to $367 million in 1979 from $439 million in 1976 on stagnant annual sales of about $17 billion in the same period. In the first nine months of 1980, earnings plunged an additional 80 percent from the same period in 1979 on sales of $12 billion. Further, its credit-card operations lost $8.1 million in the first nine months of 1980. Wall Street has graded this performance by pushing the stock near its twenty-year low.

Trial and Error. Indeed, the only bright spots in an otherwise dismal scene are Sears's insurance and real estate operations, areas that have little to do with the company's traditional retailing business. As if to underline the despair over its core business, last year Chairman Edward R. Telling reorganized Sears into a semiholding company, in effect divorcing himself from the actual management of the troubled retailing operation. The rationale was that the move would allow Telling, a merchandising executive, to concentrate on new growth opportunities. Says Telling: "Businesses with the greatest growth potential and most promise will undoubtedly be those that have first call on assets."

Still, Sears's retailing operations account for 68 percent of overall revenues, and Telling cannot cut them off at the pockets without creating a fatal wound. The new managers of the operations have invested in some significant changes, such as centralizing purchasing stations, early-retirement incentives, and store modernization. And Telling is demonstrating a willingness to enter new retail growth areas: on Jan. 22, Sears announced the opening of five freestanding business machine stores that are to be the front-runners of a network of stores geared to capitalize on the growing interest in electronic equipment from both business managers and home users.

Whether the stores are successful or not, they represent a newly focused approach to revitalizing Sears's merchandising operations and a distinct change from the series of erratic and seemingly unrelated moves that Sears's managers have made in seeking financial recovery. Indeed, Sears's apparent trial-and-error approach to managing its way out of trouble has given aid and comfort to its competitors. As K mart and Dayton Hudson's Target Stores chain solidified their reputations as savvy discounters, and specialty shops such as Herman's and Toys Я Us wooed customers with in-depth inventories of single lines, Sears lost customers. A sample of its scattershot approach includes the following:

1. An attempt to lure more affluent people into its solid blue-collar customer base by stocking expensive, high-fashion merchandise. Ignoring its own image as the provider of merchandise for America's heartland, Sears also missed one of its great opportunities: capitalizing on the back-to-nature trend characterized by the *Whole Earth Catalog*. The company neglected to use its mail-order catalog to compete with sellers of health foods and simple tools. Meanwhile, the affluent showed little interest in clothing or jewelry sporting the Sears label, and its traditional customers were turned off by the new and higher prices.

2. Sears then decided to woo the specialty stores' customers by stocking products in depth. Customers still saw no reason to buy sporting equipment at Sears rather than at Herman's, for one, and grew even more confused about why to buy at Sears at all. Sears wound up with expensive inventory nightmares and no increased sales. "We tried to be too many things to too many people and got our merchandise stretched too thin," recalls a former Sears buyer.

3. K mart's customers became the next target. In 1977, as Telling became chairman, Sears embarked on an only-too-successful price war, shooting sales up 16 percent. But when the euphoria died down, management discovered that the price cuts had destroyed profits. Earnings for the merchandise group in 1977 fell more than 10 percent.

4. Suppliers became another target of Sears's floundering tactics. Expecting that Sears's buying muscle would keep suppliers in line, Telling ordered a get-tough policy with the company's suppliers, informing them that Sears would no longer inventory products that were slow sellers in the stores. Instead, suppliers found new customers and expanded their lines of branded merchandise. For example, in 1972, Sears accounted for

61 percent of Whirlpool Corp.'s sales. In 1979, sales of refrigerators, washers, and other appliances Sears bought from Whirlpool to sell under the Kenmore name accounted for only 47 percent of Whirlpool's sales.

Of all Sears's bad decisions, the erosion of supplier relationships may be the hardest to turn around. "We historically romanced our vendors," says one former buyer. "But since Telling's tough remarks in 1978, vendors are scrambling for non-Sears business, and Sears ends up with products that are the same as everyone else's. Why should a consumer then buy a Sears product when it could buy a branded product?"

Top Heavy. At the root of most of these ill-conceived decisions lies an increasingly ponderous management structure. Sears until recently had an almost schizophrenic approach to management. It gave its field people virtual autonomy on promotional pricing, store size, product selections, and the like, yet it continually beefed up its corporate management staff in futile attempts to coordinate its diverse activities into a coherent whole. While the practice was relatively harmless during the days of unbridled growth, it created an almost knee-jerk reaction to solving problems: that of adding more managers. All through the 1970s, Sears continued to add executives, thus increasing its overhead at the same time it was superimposing a totally unwieldy hierarchy on the company.

For example, in 1976 Sears increased from five to nine its national merchandise groups, which handle buying, market development, promotion, and pricing. It created a new position, senior vice president of field, to coordinate the five territorial management teams that run Sears's vast network of stores and catalog houses. It even created a national retail sales staff to act as a liaison between headquarters and the field.

"Sears management structures on top of management structures have grown into a hindrance to timely decisions and good execution as well as an enormous cost burden," contends Louis W. Stern, a marketing professor at Northwestern University. Former Sears executives admit they and their colleagues missed the boat. "We kept expecting our sales growth to resume the 10 percent-to-12 percent rate that we took for granted in earlier years," admits one high-ranking executive who just took early retirement. "We added more and more people . . . and found ourselves with an overhead monster we couldn't control or support."

Making matters worse, while Sears was adding layers of management, its store-level work force was eroding, and its customer service was going sour along with it. Throughout the 1960s and early 1970s, Sears was able to entice experienced sales people with lucrative incentive programs based on shares of Sears stock. Once the stock started sinking, however, the incentive evaporated with it, and sales people began to leave. "With a few exceptions, you just don't find knowledgable and attentive sales people at Sears anymore," notes an industry consultant. "When I take something back that doesn't work, the Sears clerks nowadays tend to argue with me instead of readily replacing the item."

Belatedly, but nonetheless forcefully, Sears is grappling with its problems. Early last year, Telling sold his fellow directors on a massive early-retirement program aimed at managers older than 55. By year end, 1,600 of the 2,400 eligible employees took advantage of the plan, which provides three years of half pay in addition to normal pension benefits. The new vice president of field retired, and his job was eliminated. At the same time, Sears consolidated its nine merchandising groups into seven and dropped six of its forty-one buying departments and five of its forty-six field administrative units. The Southwestern territory, which employed more than three hundred people, was shut down altogether. Even the national retail sales staff was appreciably reduced. All told, by mid-1980 Sears's merchandising staff decreased to 288,000 employees. According to Telling, the reduction in executive staff will save some $125 million annually, after a write-off of $45 million.

Perhaps most significant, those that were left, combined with those hired to fill vacant positions, are much younger than their predecessors. It is no coincidence. Last year, in an attempt to infuse a more youthful orientation into what had become a stodgy management team, Telling promoted Edward A. Brennan, a 46-year-old territory manager, over the heads of several senior colleagues to become the new chairman and chief executive of the merchandise group. Brennan has, in turn, surrounded himself with a staff that is about ten years younger than the former manager's. "I think the group will be far less set in beliefs, far more willing to take risks—all the advantages that youth brings will surface," Telling predicts.

Penicillin Shots. Indeed, the new electronics stores represent a new risk, something that has been markedly absent from Sears. But the group's first priority still remains reducing operating costs. Last fall, for example, it quietly overhauled its time-worn merchandising format in which sales people rang up sales at as many as forty different locations in the store. Sears now uses centralized checkout stations in four to six clusters per store, an approach it expects will enable it to cut staff and to allow the remaining sales personnel to concentrate on serving customers.

This standardization of Sears stores is typical of what Brennan hopes to accomplish. "I feel very strongly that we need to approach the business as though we are a single store," he says. Although he insists that he recognizes that different territories do require different approaches, Brennan claims the similarities outweigh the differences. "We're not going to put together a snowblower sales program for Miami," he explains, "but we need consistency. If there is a right way to do something, then that right way should be used in New York, Los Angeles, and Miami."

Despite his protestations, however, Brennan will have to walk a very fine line between standardizing policies and removing decision making even further from the pulse of the market. Centralized decisions can easily backfire when they are applied across the board to diverse markets and operations. For example, Sears has brutally cut back on promotional programs and trimmed advertising expenses to $532 million in 1979 from $571 million in 1978. The move has cut costs on lagging items but has also made deep inroads into the sales of items that were doing well. "It was like a clinic where the doctor would find the first patient had an infection and immediately order up penicillin shots for 650 other patients in the waiting room," complains one buyer who saw profits evaporate in her department when she cut advertising.

Not surprisingly, morale on the part of formerly autonomous field managers fell to an all-time low. "When I started out working in a store, we could call a lot of the shots and felt a tremendous pressure to perform well," says one Sears veteran. "Now the temptation is to blame someone in the tower if customers don't show up. People tend to get lethargic if they don't have the responsibility for making something work."

Consolidation. Nonetheless, Brennan's apparent zeal for consolidation is rubbing off in the field, and not all managers are soured on it. William Bass, executive vice president, Eastern territory, admits that his organization was a microcosm of the parent in its staffing procedures until 1977. "Then our gross margins started to suffer, and we stopped putting people on the payroll," he says. Instead, last year existing managers for the first time started a formal planning process, coupled with a microscope approach to costs. For example, even store engineers are now expected to prepare detailed plans of how to save energy costs on an item-by-item basis.

What is more, Bass is preparing to mirror Sears's corporate move last month to consolidate two departments—traffic, dealing with retail delivery, and logistics, which handled getting merchandise to stores or warehouses—by combining his own traffic and logistics departments. Similarly, Sears has established a stronger corporate advertising department that Bass hopes will result in his being able to consolidate his own cadre of seven separate advertising staffs into a single, much smaller unit. "We've quit talking about headquarters and field, and now we're talking about Sears, about one program," he says.

Whether all field people will react with Bass's enthusiasm will probably rest on the success of Brennan's communications approach. Last fall

Brennan staged a series of two-day meetings that for the first time in thirty years put Sears's top 125 corporate buyers in the same room with more than 1,000 key field people, including every store manager. Brennan himself conducted the meetings and brought along one of Sears's latest "recruits," actress Cheryl Tiegs of the new Sears Cheryl Tiegs signature line. Even some of Sears's crustier veterans claim the meetings generated some badly needed enthusiasm. For employees who could not attend, Brennan had parts of the meetings videotaped. Brennan also taped a separate message in which he made a pitch for sales people to "act like you're happy the customer is there" and for store management to recognize that there is a "whole different world [of competition] out there selling our kinds of goods to our kinds of customers."

Polishing Its Image. But the biggest challenge facing Sears is to sharpen its fuzzy and much-tarnished image. Advertising and store displays are a vital route to accomplish this, and Brennan has turned responsibility for unifying them over to Robert E. Wood, II, aged 42, former manager of the home improvements merchandising group and grandson of General Robert Wood, the legendary head of Sears from 1928 to 1957. Wood intends to centralize the planning of local advertising as well as develop integrated national campaigns in Chicago.

Although Wood will make most of the campaign decisions, he insists that store managers will still have reasonable autonomy to promote specific items that sell well in their areas. "We have to integrate national advertising with local plans or run the risk of overkill on certain items and neglect of others," he concedes. In the past, Wood notes, local managers often interpreted plans for a national ad on a given product to mean that it is a high-priority item and should be promoted locally as well. They would thus spend local dollars on a message that was already getting to most customers. "We can't afford to duplicate what we do," he says.

But the jury is still out on whether Brennan will be able to get the proper blend of cost cutting and aggressive image rebuilding, of centralization and decentralization, of youth orientation and experience. Observers are unanimous in saying he faces a Herculean task. "Sears's reason for being was its exclusive products," says Ira Quint, a former Sears merchandising manager. "Expense controls don't give you a reason for being." And they do not attract customers, note other Sears watchers. "The company has positioned itself in such a nebulous way that I'm not sure the consumer wants to hear from Sears anymore," suggests Northwestern's Stern. Robert Kahn, a retailing consultant and director of Wal-Mart Stores, sums up: "Sears forgot its primary purpose is to please the customer by stocking the right goods and sticking by its principle of satisfaction guaranteed. Those things will be hard to regain."

Questions

1. How do you organize so as to get the economies of large-scale operations yet allow individual stores to carry merchandise that appeals to consumers in their community?
2. Why do reorganizations frequently start with massive early-retirement programs? Does this imply that experience has little value after reorganizations?
3. Are standardization and high employee morale compatible objectives at Sears? Discuss.
4. What are some of the negative side effects likely to result from Telling's efforts to consolidate and trim Sears's structure? How do these align with the issues discussed in the text associated with managing decline?

CASE 11 Finding a Place for Product Planning

Especially prepared for this volume by Stephen P. Robbins.

This Monday morning's executive committee meeting at Ontario Electronics was certain to be lively. A major decision would be made today.

In addition to being one of the largest electronic component manufacturers in Canada, Ontario Electronics was also one of the fastest growing. Between 1975 and 1980, it had achieved a 55 percent per year compounded growth rate. At its current pace, Ontario Electronics would have sales in excess of $300 million (Canadian) by 1982. Its growth, according to a recent article in a trade journal, was due primarily to heavy outlays for research that had resulted in an ever-expanding product line.

The reason that today's meeting would be interesting was easy enough to predict. At last Wednesday's board of directors meeting, the board gave unanimous approval to the president's suggestion that the company establish a product planning group. No decision was made as to where this new group would be located. This decision would be made at today's executive committee meeting. The vice presidents of marketing, production, and corporate planning each have come to the meeting prepared to argue that product planning should be placed under their jurisdiction.

"We have a major decision to make today," began the company president, Douglas Harrison. "As you know, the board has approved the creation of a product planning group. It will be the general mission of this group to identify customer needs and develop product prototypes. Exactly how far they go in terms of market research or design has not been established by the board. They told us to work that out. My preliminary budget for next year includes $650,000 for this new group. I expect when they are fully operable there will be more than a dozen people in the group."

"I think it's obvious to each of you that product planning belongs in the marketing function," initiated Veronica Duval, vice president of marketing. "The major thrust of product planning is environment scanning. It must work closely with current and potential customers to identify their product requirements. This is a marketing activity. Since we work with our customers on a daily basis, we know them and are in the best position to interpret and understand their needs."

"I agree with you, Veronica, when you say that the major thrust of product planning is environment scanning," replied Claude Fortier, head of corporate planning. "And environment scanning is precisely what we in corporate planning do on a full-time basis. It's our job to assess where the company is going. Clearly, product planning should be part of our area. Planning is planning, regardless of whether it's at the organization or product level. Our expertise, and I think the company's solid growth is a tribute to our efforts, is in scanning the environment—reading trends, assessing economic changes, evaluating the actions of competitors, and the like. The identification of customer needs is a natural extension of our current activities."

"I can't agree with either of you," was the opening comment of Mitch Jenkins, vice president of production. "The primary emphasis of this company is in production and research. Both these activities are closely related as demonstrated by the fact that production, engineering, and product research activities are all currently under my direction. This company's success is not due to marketing or corporate planning! Our success has come about because we have shown the ability to develop innovative products that meet high quality standards. I'm not going to get into a fight over whose function is more important here. The bottom line is that this is a manufacturing firm in a high-technology industry. Its success depends predominantly on generating new quality products and that's precisely what my people do. Doug, I think the decision of where we locate product planning is self-evident. It belongs under production."

Douglas Harrison looked around the table. He reaffirmed to the eight-member committee that he fully expected to resolve the issue of product planning's location at this meeting.

Questions

1. Where do you think product planning belongs? Why?
2. What insights does this case provide you about effectiveness?

3. Why do you think the three vice presidents are so determined to obtain this new group?
4. Describe how the activities of product planning might differ based on which vice president gains jurisdiction.

CASE 12 The Air Force A-7D Brake Problem

From the Hearing before the Subcommittee on Economy in Government of the Joint Economic Committee of the Congress of the United States, 91st Congress, August 13, 1969.

Mr. VANDIVIER: In the early part of 1967, the B. F. Goodrich Wheel & Brake Plant at Troy, Ohio, received an order from the Ling-Temco-Vought Co. of Dallas, Texas, to supply wheels and brakes for the A-7D aircraft, built by LTV for the Air Force.

The tests on the wheels and brakes were to be conducted in accordance with the requirements of military specification Mil-W-5013G as prepared and issued by the U.S. Air Force and to the requirements set forth by LTV Specification Document 204-16-37D.

The wheels were successfully tested to the specified requirements, but the brake, manufactured by Goodrich under BEG part No. 2-1162-3, was unable to meet the required tests.

The laboratory tests specified for the brake were divided into two categories: dynamic brake tests and static brake tests.

The dynamic brake tests basically consisted of forty-five simulated normal energy stops, five overload energy stops, and one worn-brake maximum energy stop, sometimes called a rejected take-off, or RTO. These simulated stops were to be conducted on one brake assembly with no change in brake lining to be allowed during the test. In addition, a maximum energy brake stop (or RTO) was to be conducted on a brake containing new linings, and still another series of tests called a turnaround capability test was to be performed.

The turnaround capability test consisted of a series of taxis, simulated take-offs, flight periods, and landings, and time schedule for the turn-around test was supplied by LTV to coincide with conditions under which the A-7D brake might operate on a typical mission.

Generally speaking, the brake passed all the static brakes tests, but the brake could not and did not pass any of the dynamic tests I have just described with the exception of the new brake maximum energy stop.

During the first few attempts to qualify the brake to the dynamic tests, the brake ran out of lining material after a few stops had been completed and the tests were terminated. Attempts were made to secure a lining material that would hold up during the grueling fifty-one-stop test, but to no avail. Although I had been aware for several months that great difficulty was being experienced with the A-7D brake, it was not until April 11, 1968, almost a full year after qualification testing had begun, that I became aware of how these tests were being conducted.

The thirteenth attempt at qualification was being conducted under B. F. Goodrich Internal Test No. T-1867.

On the morning of April 11, Richard Gloor, who was the test engineer assigned to the A-7D project, came to me and told me he had discovered that some time during the previous twenty four hours, instrumentation used to record brake pressure had been miscalibrated *deliberately* so that while the instrumentation showed that a pressure of 1,000 pounds per square inch had been used to conduct brake stop numbers 46 and 47 (two overload energy stops) 1,100 p.s.i. had actually been applied to the brakes. Maximum pressure available on the A-7D is 1,000 p.s.i.

Mr. Gloor further told me he had questioned instrumentation personnel about the miscalibration and had been told they were asked to do so by Searle Lawson, a design engineer on the A-7D.

Chairman PROXMIRE: Is this the gentleman who is with you now, Mr. Vandivier?

Mr. VANDIVIER: That is correct. I subsequently questioned Lawson who admitted he had ordered the instruments miscalibrated at the direction of a superior.

Upon examining the log sheets kept by laboratory personnel I found that other violations of the test specifications had occurred.

For example, after some of the overload stops, the brake had been disassembled and the three stators or stationary members of the brake had been taken to the plant toolroom for rework and, during an earlier part of the test, the position of elements within the brake had been reversed to distribute the lining wear more evenly.

Additionally, instead of braking the dynamometer to a complete stop as required by military specifications, pressure was released when the wheel and brake speed had decelerated to 10 miles per hour.

The reason for this, I was later told, was that the brakes were experiencing severe vibrations near the end of the stops, causing excessive lining wear and general deterioration of the brake.

All these incidents were in clear violation of military specifications and general industry practice.

I reported these violations to the test lab supervisor, Mr. Ralph Gretzinger, who reprimanded instrumentation personnel and stated that under no circumstance would intentional miscalibration of instruments be tolerated.

As for the other discrepancies noted in test procedures, he said that he was aware that they were happening but that as far as he was concerned the tests could not, in view of the way they were being conducted, be classified as qualification tests.

Later that same day, the worn-brake, maximum energy stop was conducted on the brake. The brake was landed at a speed of 161 m.p.h. and the pressure was applied. The dynamometer rolled a distance 16,800 *feet* before coming to rest. The elapsed stopping time was 141 seconds. By computation, this stop time shows the aircraft would have traveled over 3 miles before stopping.

Within a few days, a typewritten copy of the test logs of test T-1867 was sent to LTV to assure LTV that a qualified brake was almost ready for delivery.

Virtually every entry in this so-called copy of the test logs was drastically altered. As an example, the stop time for the worn-brake maximum energy stop was changed from 141 seconds to a mere 46.8 seconds.

On May 2, 1968 the fourteenth attempt to qualify the brakes was begun, and Mr. Lawson told me that he had been informed by both Mr. Robert Sink, project manager at Goodrich—I am sorry, Mr. Sink is project manager—and Mr. Russell Van Horn, projects manager at Goodrich, that "Regardless of what the brake does on test, we're going to qualify it."

Chairman PROXMIRE: What was that?

Mr. VANDIVIER: The statement was, "Regardless of what the brake does on test, we're going to qualify it."

He also said that the latest instructions he had received were to the effect that, if the data from this latest test turned out worse than did test T-1867, then we would write our report based on T-1867.

Chairman PROXMIRE: The statement was made by whom?

Mr. VANDIVIER: Mr. Lawson told me this statement was made to him by Mr. Robert Sink, project manager and Mr. Russell Van Horn, project manager.

During this latest and final attempt to qualify the four-rotor brake, the same illegal procedures were used as had been used on attempt No. 13. Again after thirty stops had been completed, the positions of the friction members of the brake were reversed to distribute wear more evenly. After each stop, the wheel was removed from the brake and the accumulated dust was blown out. During each stop, pressure was released when the deceleration had reached 10 miles per hour.

By these and other irregular procedures the brake was nursed along until the forty-five normal energy stops had been completed, but by this time the friction surfaces of the brakes were almost bare; that is, there was virtually no lining left on the brake. This lack of lining material introduced another problem.

The pistons that actuate the brake by forcing the friction surfaces together were almost at the end of their allowable travel, and it was feared that during the overload stops the pistons might actually pop out of their sockets within the brake, allowing brake fluid to spray the hot surfaces, resulting in fire.

Therefore, a metal spacer was inserted in the brake between the pressure plate and the piston housing.

This spacer served to make up for the lack of friction material and to keep the pistons in place. To provide room for the spacer, the adjuster assemblies were removed from the brake.

The five overload stops were conducted without the adjuster assemblies and with the spacer in place.

After stop number 48—the third overload stop—temperatures in the brake were so high that the fuse plug, a safety device that allows air to escape from the tire to prevent blowout, melted and allowed the tire to deflate.

The same thing happened after stop number 49—the fourth overload stop. Both these occurrences were highly irregular and in direct conflict with the performance criteria of the military requirements.

Chairman PROXMIRE: I understand you have a picture of this that might help us see it.

Mr. VANDIVIER: Yes.

Mr. PROXMIRE: Do you want to show that to us now?

Mr. VANDIVIER: I was going to show it here just a little bit later.

Chairman PROXMIRE: Go ahead.

Mr. VANDIVIER: For the worn-brake maximum energy stop, the adjusters were replaced in the brake and a different spacer was used between the pressure plate and the piston housing.

Now I have a copy, a picture of this brake just before it went on the maximum energy test, and here you may see at the top is the additional spacer that has been added to get sufficient braking action on the brake.

Chairman PROXMIRE: Who took that picture?

Mr. VANDIVIER: That was taken with a Polaroid camera. I am not sure—

Chairman PROXMIRE: I think it is only fair to the committee, Mr. Conable and the committee, to ask you about it later. You go ahead and we will ask questions.

Mr. VANDIVIER: All right.

In addition to these highly questionable practices, a turnaround capability test, or simulated mission test, was conducted incorrectly due to a human error. When the error was later discovered, no corrections were made.

While these tests were being conducted, I was asked by Mr. Lawson to begin writing a qualification report for the brake. I flatly refused and told Mr. Gretzinger, the lab supervisor, who was my superior, that I could not write such a report because the brake had not been qualified.

He agreed and he said that no one in the laboratory was going to issue such a report unless a brake was actually qualified in accordance with the specification and using standard operating procedures.

He said that he would speak to his own supervisor, the manager of the technical services section, Mr. Russell Line, and get the matter settled at once.

He consulted Mr. Line and assured me that both had concurred in the decision not to write a qualification report.

I explained to Lawson that I had been told not to write the report and that the only way such a report could be written was to falsify test data.

Mr. Lawson said that he was well aware of what was required but that he had been ordered to get a report written, regardless of how or what had to be done.

He stated that, if I would not write the report, he would have to, and he asked if I would help him gather the test data and draw up the various engineering curves and graphic displays that are normally included in a report.

I asked Mr. Gretzinger, my superior, if this was all right and he agreed. As long as I was only assisting in the preparation of the data, it would be permissible.

Both Lawson and I worked on the elaborate curves and logs in the report for nearly a month. During this time we both frankly discussed the moral aspects of what we were doing, and we agreed that our actions were unethical and probably illegal.

Several times during that month I discussed the A-7D testing with Mr. Line and asked him to consult his superiors in Akron to prevent a false qualification report from being issued. Mr. Line declined to do so and advised me that it would be wise to just do my work and keep quiet.

I told him of the extensive irregularities during testing and suggested that the brake was actually dangerous and, if allowed to be installed on an aircraft, might cause an accident.

Mr. Line said he thought I was worrying too much about things that did not really concern me and advised me to just "do what you're told."

About the first of June———

Chairman PROXMIRE: You skipped one line here.

Mr. VANDIVIER: Yes.

Chairman PROXMIRE: You said "I asked him"———

Mr. VANDIVIER: Yes. I asked Mr. Line if his conscience would hurt him if such a thing caused the death of a pilot and this is when he replied that I was worrying about too many things that did not concern me and advised me to "do what you're told."

About the first of June 1968, Mr. Gretzinger asked if I was finished with the graphic data and said he had been advised by the chief engineer, Mr. H. C. Sunderman, that when the data were finished they were to be delivered to him—Sunderman—and he would instruct someone in the engineering department to actually write the report. Accordingly, when I had finished with the data, I gave it to Mr. Gretzinger who immediately took it from the room. Within a few minutes, he was back and was obviously angry.

He said that Mr. Sunderman had told him no one in the engineering department had time to write the report and that we would have to do it ourselves.

At this point, Mr. Line came into the room demanding to know "What the hell is going on." Mr. Gretzinger explained the situation again and said he would not allow such a report to be issued by the lab.

Mr. Line then turned to me and said he was "sick of hearing about this damned report. Write the ——— thing and shut up about it."

Chairman PROXMIRE: Let me ask you, you had this in quotes. Did you make a note of this at the time?

Mr. VANDIVIER: Yes.

Chairman PROXMIRE: Do you have your notes with you?

Mr. VANDIVIER: No. I have notes with me, yes. I am not sure if I have this note or not, but I have notes with me.

Chairman PROXMIRE: All right.

Mr. VANDIVIER: When he had left, Mr. Gretzinger and I discussed the position we were in, and Mr. Gretzinger said that we both should have resigned a long time ago. He added that there was little to do now except write the report.

Accordingly, I wrote the report, but in the conclusion, I stated that the brake had "not" met either the intent or the requirements of the specifications and was therefore "not" qualified.

When the final report was typewritten and ready for publication, the two "nots" in the conclusion had been eliminated, thereby changing the entire meaning of the conclusion.

I would like to point out at this time the various discrepancies between the military standards and procedures and the qualification tests actually conducted:

1. Brake pressure was cut on all stops at 10 miles per hour and the wheel allowed to coast to a stop.
2. The five overload stops were conducted with a spacer between the pressure plate and the piston housing.
3. The lining carriers used for the test were specially made with an additional 0.030 of an inch lining material. This was done to assure sufficient lining material on the carriers.
4. Stators in the brake were physically reversed after stop 30 and remained in these positions throughout the test.

Mr. Chairman, the next two sentences of my printed statement contain a typographical error, words have been omitted and I would like to insert those in at this time.

5. The worn-brake RTO was conducted with an additional pressure plate between the original pressure plate and piston housing. This was done because allowable piston travel had been exceeded and without the additional pressure plate the brakes could not have been applied.
6. Prior to the worn-brake RTO [maximum energy stop], the inside diameter of the lining carriers was increased by 0.120 of an inch to alleviate the severe shrinkage of the lining carriers on the torque tube caused by overheating.

7. On stops 48 and 49 [overload stops 3 and 4], the fuse plug eutectic material—material designed to melt at a specified temperature—melted, allowing the tire to deflate.
8. The torque plate and keyway inserts for the wheel had their drive surfaces chromeplated, because of extreme wear. This was not a production process on this brake.
9. Before the start of the tests and at tear-downs the keyway inserts were sprayed with molybdenum disulfate (a lubricant).
10. After every stop the wheel and tire assembly were removed from the brake, the brake was blown out with high-velocity air, and the keyway inserts and heat shield were wiped clean.
11. After stops 10, 20, 30, 40, 45, and 50 the brake was disassembled and the expansion slots in the lining carriers were cleaned of excess lining material and opened. Excess materials removed from between the segments in the rotors and the lugs and links on the rotors were cleaned and radiused by machining processes. This in a sense is equivalent to a minor overhaul in the brake linings.

In addition there were at least four other major irregularities in the test procedure.

These, gentlemen, are only irregularities that occurred during the testing. As for the report itself, more than eighty false entries were made in the body of the report and in the logs.

Many, many of the elaborate engineering curves attached to the report were complete and total fabrications, based not on what had actually occurred, but on information that would fool both LTV and the Air Force.

I have mentioned already that the turnaround capability test that was supposed to determine what temperatures might be experienced by the brake during a typical flight mission had been misconducted through a human error on the part of the test lab operator.

Rather than rerun this very important test, which would have taken only some six hours to complete, it was decided to manufacture the data.

This we did, and the result was some very convincing graphic curves. These curves were supposed to demonstrate to LTV and the Air Force exactly what the temperatures in the brakes had been during each minute of the simulated mission.

They were completely false and based only on data that would be acceptable to the customers.

I could spend the entire day here discussing the various elaborate falsifications that went into this report but I feel that, by now, the picture is clear.

The report was finally issued on June 5, 1968, and almost immediately, flight tests on the brake were begun at Edwards Air Force Base in California.

Mr. Lawson was sent by Goodrich to witness these tests, and when he returned, he described various mishaps that had occurred during the flight tests and he expressed the opinion to me that the brake was dangerous.

That same afternoon, I contacted my attorney and after describing the situation to him, asked for his advice.

He advised me that, while I was technically not guilty of committing a fraud, I was certainly part of a conspiracy to defraud. He further suggested a meeting with U.S. Attorney Roger Makely in Dayton, Ohio.

I agreed to this and my attorney said that he would arrange an appointment with the federal attorney.

I discussed my attorney's appraisal of our situation with Mr. Lawson, but I did not, at this time, tell him of the forthcoming visit with Mr. Makely. Mr. Lawson said he would like to consult with my attorney and I agreed to arrange this.

Shortly thereafter, Mr. Lawson, went to the Dallas offices of LTV, and, while he was gone, my attorney called and said that, upon advice of the U.S. attorney, he had arranged an interview with the Dayton office of the FBI.

I related the details of the A-7D qualification to Mr. Joseph Hathaway, of the FBI.

He asked if I could get Mr. Lawson to confirm my story and I replied that I felt Mr. Lawson would surely do this.

Upon Mr. Lawson's return from Dallas, I asked him if he still wished to consult my attorney and he answered "I most certainly do."

Mr. Lawson and I went to the attorney's office, and Mr. Lawson was persuaded to speak to the FBI.

I wish to emphasize that at no time prior to Mr. Lawson's decision to speak to the FBI was he aware that I had already done so. His decision and mine were both the result of our individual actions.

Mr. Lawson related his own story to Mr. Hathaway, who advised us to keep our jobs and to tell no one that we had been to see him. I might add here that he advised us that an investigation would be made.

About this time the Air Force demanded that Goodrich produce its raw data from the tests. This Goodrich refused to do, claiming that the raw data was proprietary information.

Goodrich management decided that, since pressure was being applied by the Air Force, a conference should be arranged with LTV management and engineering staff. A preconference meeting was set for Goodrich personnel to go over the questionable points in the report.

On Saturday, July 27, 1968, Mr. Robert Sink, Mr. Lawson, Mr. John Warren—A-7D project engineer—and I met and went over the discrepant items contained in the qualification report. Each point was discussed at great length and a list of approximately forty separate discrepancies was compiled. These, we were told by Mr. Sink, would be revealed to LTV personnel the following week.

However, by the time of the meeting with LTV, only a few days later, the list of discrepancies had been cut by Mr. Sink from forty-three items to a mere three.

Mr. Chairman, during this meeting Mr. Lawson took from the blackboard at the Goodrich conference room word for word listing of all these discrepancies. This contains the forty-three items I have just mentioned. I would like to enter this into the record and also enter the subsequent list of three major discrepancies that later came out of this meeting.

Chairman PROXMIRE: Do you have copies of those documents?

Mr. VANDIVIER: Yes, I do have.

Mr. VANDIVIER: The following two-month period was one of a constant running battle with LTV and the Air Force, during which time the Air Force refused final approval of the qualification report and demanded a confrontation with Goodrich about supplying raw data.

On October 8, another meeting was held, again with Mr. Sink, Mr. Lawson, Mr. Warren, and myself present.

This was only one day prior to a meeting with Air Force personnel, and Mr. Sink said that he had called the meeting "so that we are all coordinated and tell the same story." Mr. Sink said that LTV personnel would be present at the meeting with the Air Force and our policy would be to "Let LTV carry the ball." Mr. Sink appeared to be especially concerned because Mr. Bruce Tremblay, the Air Force engineer most intimate with A-7D brake would be present at the meeting, and it was felt at B. F. Goodrich that Mr. Tremblay was already suspicious.

Mr. Sink warned us that "Mr. Tremblay will probably be at his antagonistic best." He added that the Air Force had wanted to meet at the Goodrich plant, but that we—Goodrich—couldn't risk having them that close to the raw data. "We don't want those guys in the plant," Mr. Sink said.

What happened at the meeting with the Air Force, I do not know. I did not attend.

On October 18, I submitted my resignation to Goodrich effective November 1.

I would like to read that resignation. This is addressed to Russell Line, manager of technical services:

> In May of this year I was directed to participate in the preparation of qualification report for the A7D, 26031. As you are aware this report contained numerous deliberate and willful misrepresentations, which according to legal counsel constitutes fraud and therefore exposes both myself and others to criminal charges of conspiracy to defraud. In view of this fact, I must terminate my employment with the B. F. Goodrich Company effective November 1, 1968. I regret that this decision must be made, but I am sure that you will agree that events of the past seven months have created an atmosphere of deceit and distrust in which it is impossible to work effectively and productively.

On October 25 I was told that my resignation was to be accepted immediately, and within twenty minutes I had left the Goodrich Co.

Gentlemen, I am well aware that the B. F. Goodrich Co. is a well-known and well-respected firm with an almost impeccable reputation. I am equally aware that the charges I have made are serious. However, everything I have said to you is completely true and I can prove my statements with documentary evidence.

The unfortunate part of a situation such as this is that, invariably, many innocent persons are made to suffer along with the guilty. Therefore, I should like to emphasize that three people whom I have mentioned here are, I feel, completely blameless and were implicated in this situation through no fault of their own.

Mr. Ralph Gretzinger from the very start fought this situation and tried very hard to use his influence to stop the issuance of the false report. Mr. Richard Gloor, in his own handwriting, listed the irregularities occurring during the test and was outspoken in his opposition to the report. This list was shown to B. F. Goodrich management.

Mr. Lawson, of course, was in a position similar to mine and the fact that he voluntarily disclosed the details of the A-7D test program to the FBI and GAO should stand upon its own merits. Thank you.

Chairman PROXMIRE: Thank you, Mr. Vandivier.

Mr. Lawson, you have heard the statement as read and I take it you have had a chance to see the full statement?

Mr. LAWSON: No, I have not.

Chairman PROXMIRE: The statement you have just heard read by Mr. Vandivier, do you agree with it fully or in part or do you disagree and can you tell us your reaction to it?

Mr. LAWSON: The factual data that Mr. Vandivier has presented is correct, to the best of my knowledge.

Chairman PROXMIRE: There is no statement that you heard him read with which you would disagree in any part?

Mr. LAWSON: I really don't know. I haven't read the complete text.

Chairman PROXMIRE: Would you disagree with any part of what you heard him read right now in your presence?

Mr. LAWSON: No, I don't believe there is.

Chairman PROXMIRE: Now I would like to ask you, Mr. Vandivier, you gave us a picture about which we may want to ask other witnesses, so I want to qualify that picture. As far as we know, it is a picture that you say was taken of the brake that was tested?

Mr. VANDIVIER: That is correct.

Chairman PROXMIRE: But we would like to make sure that we qualify that, because it is going to be used later.

Now would you describe again, tell us how you came to have that, when the picture was taken and so forth?

Mr. VANDIVIER: Yes. This was taken just approximately an hour and a half or two hours before the worn-brake RTO was conducted. This was for the qualification test, and I asked the plant photographer if he would take a Polaroid picture of this for me. He did so, and I took the Polaroid shot and I had it enlarged. I have a certification on this. I had the original Polaroid negative. I have the negatives that the photographer used.

Chairman PROXMIRE: Will you give us the date, the time that was taken, if you have that?

Mr. VANDIVIER: If you will give me just a moment, I can.

Chairman PROXMIRE: Meanwhile, may I ask Mr. Lawson, while Mr. Vandivier is looking up that, if you can confirm that this is in fact the picture of the A-7D brake that was undergoing qualification?

Mr. LAWSON: Yes, it appears to be.

Chairman PROXMIRE: It appears to be?

Mr. LAWSON: I would say it is.

Chairman PROXMIRE: It is. All right. Well, you can supply that a little later for the record, Mr. Vandivier.

Mr. VANDIVIER: All right.

Chairman PROXMIRE: Let me ask you this. You say you worked for Goodrich for six years?

Mr. VANDIVIER: That is correct.

Chairman PROXMIRE: What was your previous employment before you were hired by Goodrich?

Mr. VANDIVIER: I worked for the Food Machinery and Chemical Corp. at their Newport, Ind. plant.

Chairman PROXMIRE: Technical writer is a professional position that requires considerable competence and ability. What experience did you have that would qualify you to be a technical writer?

Mr. VANDIVIER: I had none.

Chairman PROXMIRE: Did you immediately go into this or did they give you a training course?

Mr. VANDIVIER: No. I had no training course. I kind of worked into the job I guess. It was—

Chairman PROXMIRE: You were not hired to be a technical—

Mr. VANDIVIER: No, I was actually hired as an instrumentation technician, and Goodrich engaged in a mass changeover of instrumentation techniques, and they wanted degreed people for this kind of work so I was switched over to the technical writing section.

Chairman PROXMIRE: How long did you work as a technical writer?

Mr. VANDIVIER: Approximately three years.

Chairman PROXMIRE: Three years. How many reports did you prepare for B. F. Goodrich?

Mr. VANDIVIER: At least 100, possibly 150.

Chairman PROXMIRE: Were any of these reports questioned in any way?

Mr. VANDIVIER: No, they were not.

Chairman PROXMIRE: Were they accepted? Did you get any reaction at all favorable or unfavorable in these reports that you wrote?

Mr. VANDIVIER: Occasionally we would get a question from the manufacturer about a wording or a clarification, and these would be supplied.

Chairman PROXMIRE: Was there any question as to the accuracy or competence of the report?

Mr. VANDIVIER: No, none whatsoever.

Chairman PROXMIRE: Were you criticized at any time that the reports were not adequate?

Mr. VANDIVIER: No, I was not.

Chairman PROXMIRE: In your statement, you say "Accordingly I wrote the report but in the conclusion I stated that the brake had not met either the intent or the requirement of the specification and therefore was 'not' qualified." Then you add "When the final report was typewritten and ready for publication the two 'nots' in the conclusion had been eliminated, thereby changing the entire meaning of the conclusion."

Now it seems to me that you have testified before this that you and Mr. Lawson constructed this report based on your instructions from your superiors, that this report was false in many ways that you knew, and that the report seemed to qualify the brakes, at least that was the impression I got, and yet you concluded, and I quote, "I stated the brake had not met either the intent or the requirement of the specifications and therefore was not qualified."

Doesn't it seem on the basis of your testimony that this is somewhat inconsistent? In other words, you had written a report that would qualify the brake and then you come in with a one-sentence conclusion in which you say it was not qualified? Do you see what I am getting at?

Mr. VANDIVIER: Yes. Mr. Chairman, this was probably one final gesture of defiance. I was so aggravated and sick at having to write this thing. I knew the words "not" would be taken out, but I put them in to show that, I do not know, they had bent me to their will but they had not broken me yet. It was a foolish thing perhaps to do, but it was showing that I still had a little spirit left. At least this is how I felt.

Chairman PROXMIRE: What did you think your superiors at B. F. Goodrich would do when they found the "not qualified" in your report, when you had been told to show the brake qualified?

Mr. VANDIVIER: I knew it would be changed probably without question. I was not worried if you are trying—I was not worried at being called on the carpet for this. I knew they would just merely change it.

Chairman PROXMIRE: Was this the only time in the three years you worked as a technical writer with Goodrich; the only time that you made false entries into a report of manufacture?

Mr. VANDIVIER: Yes it was.

Chairman PROXMIRE: So far as you know B. F. Goodrich's record is clean in every other respect with your experience?

Mr. VANDIVIER: With me—

Chairman PROXMIRE: With this single incidence being an exception?

Mr. VANDIVIER: That is right; that is correct.

Chairman PROXMIRE: They had never before asked you to do this?

Mr. VANDIVIER: No.

Chairman PROXMIRE: Do you know of any other technical writers you worked with, in which Goodrich had instructed them to take this kind of action?

Mr. VANDIVIER: If they had done this, I would know nothing of it. I could not say.

Chairman PROXMIRE: This was the only incident?

Mr. VANDIVIER: Yes, as far as I know, the only incident in which I was asked to do this.

Chairman PROXMIRE: What was the normal procedure at Goodrich when a brake failed to meet all the requirements or when normal procedures were not followed?

Mr. VANDIVIER: If for some reason or other the normal procedure was not followed or the brake simply could not meet a particular requirement, the report was written and a deviation was requested from the manufacturer, which in other words is a request to allow him to accept the brake with these noted deviations from the procedure.

I might add that there are many times that a brake just could not meet a certain requirement specified by the manufacturer, and it was always the customary procedure to ask for a deviation, and many times it was granted or some sort of a compromise was reached between the manufacturer and Goodrich.

Chairman PROXMIRE: I cannot understand what was going through the minds of Goodrich's management the way you have told the story. I cannot see what they have to gain by passing on a brake that would not meet qualifications. Somewhere along the line this is going to be shown as an unqualified brake. As you pointed out, it might be under disastrous circumstances, but in any event Goodrich would suffer and suffer badly by passing on a brake to LTV or the Air Force that was not going to work. What is their motivation?

Mr. VANDIVIER: I cannot tell you what their motivation is. I can tell you what I feel was behind this.

Chairman PROXMIRE: All right.

Mr. VANDIVIER: I feel in the beginning stages of this program someone made a mistake and refused to admit that mistake, and to hide his stupidity or his ignorance, or his pride, or whatever it was, he simple covered up, you know, with more false statements, false information, and at the time it came time to deliver this brake, Goodrich was so far down the road that there was nothing else to do.

They had no time to start over; I think it was a matter not of company policy but of company politics. I think that probably three or four persons within the Goodrich organization at Troy were responsible for this. I do not believe for a moment that the corporate officials in Akron knew that this was going on.

Questions

1. Does blind obedience to authority remove an employee from responsibility for his or her actions? Discuss.
2. Some people argue that organizations should provide both communication channels and protection for whistleblowers; that is, those who reveal wrongdoings within the organization. Do you agree? Might this undermine the traditional authority hierarchy within the organization?

3. What could the top officials of B. F. Goodrich in Akron have done to ensure that lower-level managers did not act outside the law?
4. How would you have handled this situation if you had been Mr. Vandivier?

CASE 13 The Politics of Organizational Decision Making

From *The Politics of Organizational Decision-Making* by Andrew M. Pettigrew.

From the programmers' point of view, this ambiguity of place was compounded by ambiguity of function. They were clear about their task, to design a computer system for the Stock Control Department of the Clothing Division and to program and implement it. They were much less clear about the roles to be played by other people in the Computer Department. Morgan's dual role as Bell's[1] "number one man" and supervisor of the punch-room staff seemed acceptable. After all, "data preparation was a rather routine clerical job." The problem for the programmers was trying to justify the appearance of Bill Reilly and Tim Philby, the two recruits from the Work Study Department. Bell and Morgan were much clearer about the role of these two gentlemen. Morgan remarked,

> Wilson [a company director] was most anxious that we should recruit a couple of people into the team with specialist knowledge of the affected departments. In this way we came across Reilly and Philby. Both of them were more or less spies for Wilson.

Bell seemed equally sure:

> In fact Reilly and Philby were sent to spy on us. Philby used to report what we were doing to his old boss in the Work Study Department. However, he was a great "detail" man and got so bogged down in detail that he could never see the wood for the trees. Also, Reilly's job was to police us, querying everything we did with the management.

[1]Harry Bell is head of the computer department.

Reilly's way of discussing this issue is significant. He says,

> Bell and Morgan were recruited from the furniture side of the business. Two of us were appointed from the clothing side. Tim Philby and myself. Then started what, in some respects, was a part of my working life that I could do well with forgetting. At that time Mills was in charge of the furniture division and we were working for Wilson. Really it was a typical Brian Michaels situation. Philby was a real Wilson man, everybody knew it at the time. Wilson expected Philby and myself to report exactly what Bell and Morgan were finding out and telling Mills. Really it was a terrible predicament to be in. I'd rather forget about it altogether.

The spying episode indicates clearly competition at board level between the two divisions of the company. It also reveals one of the ways in which the Michaels directors operate. Wilson was using "his men" to check on the activities of two other men from another division of the company. In addition, the case illuminates the strategy used by a Michaels director to monitor the behavior of a strange new breed of men working with a mysterious piece of technology. The strategies employed by the Michaels board to try to control the computer technologists are a topic we shall return to later. For the present, it is significant to note that Reilly, in describing this episode eleven years later, calls it "a typical Brian Michaels situation."

In this environment the Computer department was formed and the first batch of programmers appeared with their honours degrees in mathematics.

The Programmers. The arrival of programmers in Brian Michaels produced a culture shock of some magnitude. Many Michaels employees have never got over the experience. The programmers who were interviewed in the course of this study have equally vivid memories. Bell has described Michaels as

> a quill-pen firm . . . which traditionally has employed low-quality people to do low-quality work. The result is that it's the hardest of all firms to introduce change into.

While fear of what they represented may have been a major factor in explaining some of the extreme reactions toward the programmers, there were other equally pertinent reasons.

In the first place, the programmers appeared to be aliens with no interest in the firm of Brian Michaels. Like many other specialist groups, they were driven by the immediate challenge of their work. One programmer commented,

> In the early days we motivated ourselves. Getting the job on the computer was everything. The integration of the department in the company was very small indeed. As a group of people we were very independent. We had no sense of involvement in company affairs.

Another said,

> As a team we worked for an academic rather than a business interest. This was certainly true of the technical people. We were all backroom boys.

This lack of involvement even excluded interest in long-term policy matters in their own department:

> Bell never went beyond the short-term objectives. This was quite sufficient incentive for us. The major motivation was that this was a pioneering job. The problems of getting to the short-term objectives were fascinating enough.

Bell's rather closed managerial style brought praise from the programmers:

> Harry really put up the drawbridge. He kept the wolves from the door and allowed the boys to get on with the job.

Even with Bell's style and their different work patterns, the programmers would not isolate themselves totally. In fact, their strange work timetable and casual dress attracted criticism. The computer operators were the first group to pick up this ill feeling. One operator, now a senior programmer, said

> It started off with the operators; they were the first people in the company to work odd hours. They had beards, used to dress roughly, and were going home at 8:30 in the morning when everybody else was arriving. One day one of the personnel people came up and told me off for wearing a roll-collar sweater. He said to me, "You're supposed to be a young executive; you should dress accordingly."

The programmers also disrupted the company rules about clocking on and off. This, together with the rewards their market position afforded them at such a comparatively young age, created problems with the company status system. Since the Personnel Department had to deal with these issues, it was the focus of a lot of the programmers' discontent. The Personnel Department had a terrible reputation for being ruthless and inconsiderate. One senior programmer referred to its staff as the "gestapo." An operator commented,

> They were always asking us why we were late. They didn't realize we'd probably been working half the previous night. We were on overtime—some of us were earning £1200 with a base of £800, at that time a good deal more than their young executives! The fact was they tried to, but couldn't, control us in the same way as the little girls. They had a standard 8 to 5 attitude to everybody. We answered back. This had never happened to them before.

The programmers were clearly a group apart from the rest of the company. As Gerald Lane said, "There wasn't a graduate in the company. We must have stood out." They differed in education, values, work patterns, dress, and rewards from the rest of the Michaels employees. While it is understandable that a stock controller might refer to them as "long-haired, highly paid yobos," it is less clear that the conflict between the programmers and user departments was just over value differences. As Mumford and Banks have pointed out,[2] when a man is faced with change, the first question he is likely to ask is, "How will it affect me?"

The Programmers and the User Departments. To the programmers, the Personnel Department embodied all they disliked about their work situation. For the stock controllers, the computer represented a similar threat. They had no wish to become the victims of a change apparently imposed on them by a group of outsiders who knew little of their work. As a stock controller, later to join the Computer Department, recalled,

> I was very loath to join the computer setup at first. There was a great deal of anti-feeling toward the programmers that was heartily reciprocated. They called the stock controllers idiots and took the attitude that it was the programmers' job to tell them what to do. The user departments used to say *the* computer when referring to the Computer Department.
>
> I remember Kahn, who was head of stock control at that time, going into a tirade about computers when I had to see him as part of my induction course. He used to say, "These people coming into the business with the machine aren't going to tell me how to run my department." I had scars on my memory about computers before I even got near them.

Harry Bell was later asked how he got on with the stock controllers:

> I had enormous problems. Kahn was opposed to the whole system. Also, individual stock controllers were opposed to it. One man said to me, "It's taken all the interest out of the job." Another said, "Before

[2]E. Mumford and O. Banks, *The Computer and the Clerk* (London: Routledge and Kegan Paul, 1967).

> the computer I was so overworked people would tolerate my mistakes. Now everyone expects me to be right." We were tightening the controls over these people.

Although they were being asked to accept output from people who symbolized a machine they did not trust, the stock controllers were still responsible for making the kinds of decision they had made in the past. One stock controller expressed their feelings like this:

> We put so many obstacles in its way in the form of nervous argument. We didn't believe it could give us all the things we needed. We were frightened the computer would wrongly calculate something for us and we wouldn't notice this.

Essentially the stock controllers felt that, if they did not lose their jobs altogether, their skills would be diluted and their livelihood threatened. None of these things happened. In fact, the very opposite occurred. The computer eventually took much of the routine from their work and allowed them to utilize their merchandising skills more effectively. The status of the department has improved considerably since this time. Today the head stock controller acknowledges the changes in his department's fortunes but insists that in 1958–1959 "it wasn't obvious that this was going to happen."

Many people in the company attribute the user departments' early fears to the programmers' style of operating. The programmers were said to be "domineering," "arrogant," and "outside the situation of the ordinary stock controller." Even when they organized lecture courses for the stock controllers, the latter could not understand what was going on. A stock controller said,

> In the early days the programmers would give us lectures on mathematics. What we really wanted to know was what the machine could do for us and *not* the mathematical formulas behind the operations!

What eventually happened is well characterized in the following quote:

> If someone comes along from outside and just walks in without consulting people in the department, then it's only natural that staff begin to pull down the blinds.

Early in 1959, then, the programmers had mastered what was for them at that time technically an extremely complex and challenging task. They were now producing computer output for the Stock Control Department. The only problem was that the stock controllers refused to accept it. A very expensive piece of machinery was producing, from the company's point of view, irrelevant information. In this situation Jim Kenny arrived to set up an O&M Department.

The Programmers and the O&M Officers. Kenny was brought into Michaels with the encouragement of the chief personnel officer and Brian Michael himself. Somebody had to act as a link between the programmers and the stock controllers. Someone had to translate the company's needs into computer terms. O&M officers at that time were generally involved in redesigning clerical procedures. It was felt that eventually they could redefine the system of work in the Stock Control Department, set it out in the form of flow charts and reports, and then leave the programmers to translate these flow charts into a form acceptable to the computer.

Bill Reilly and two liaison officers, Tom Reagan and Harvey Peters, considered that they had been trying to do just that from within the Computer Department. They found it very difficult to convince the programmers of the value of their approach. I asked Tom Reagan how he and Bill Reilly got on with the programmers:

> Not too well. The programmers wanted to go their way. They regarded Bill's work as trivial and time wasting. They more or less dismissed his O&M work.

Harvey Peters's attitude was part admiration, part contempt:

> As a group they were highly individualistic, and at the time they struck me as being brilliant, though I wouldn't think that so much now . . . they had a tremendously selfish attitude. Anybody who was not a programmer was less than human. They were so involved in their work. I suppose it was so demanding, they had to look down a very narrow path.

Reilly described the situation in 1957–1959 as follows:

> The whole thing was a bit of a melting-pot. The only real distinction between us and the programmers was that they had no knowledge of commerce. . . . There was no doubt their mathematical training helped their logical abilities. . . . I suppose you'd expect differences between the two groups for they were down in London all the time. We were only down every other week. When they eventually came up to Wolverhampton, we had to shield them from the management.

The programmers who were interviewed did not take such an extreme stand toward Reilly, Peters, and Reagan as the latter thought that they did.

The programmers' attitude was more a matter of *we* have the skills, what is all the fuss about? Pete Taft, a senior programmer, commented,

> There was a bit of friction, but not because we couldn't talk each other's language. We were the systems analysts working with the O&M boys. The only real friction came when what we wanted and what they wanted in systems terms differed. There were no real technical arguments because we were involved in the actual systems design. They weren't in a position to argue over technical points anyway.

The analytical training the programmers had was important to them, as was the lack of this training in some of their co-workers:

> Reilly didn't have this and was therefore much less objective in problem solving than we were.

Gerald Lane expressed a similar view:

> Reilly was nothing exceptional. He was persistent and keen, but when Bell left Reilly moved over to Jim Kenny's new O&M outfit.

In spite of these differences in background, training, and work orientation, both groups in the Computer Department talked of a distinct feeling of group solidarity. Much of this was due to high involvement in their work. In 1957–1958 there were only about a dozen computers on order in Britain. Michaels purchased the first SE 100. The members of the Computer Department felt like pioneers. They were. A programmer remarked,

> In the main, relations in the Computer Department were very good. Morale was very high when we were really trying to get the system going. I can't remember a group with such high morale or of such high caliber since. They were the pioneers.

Reagan, after accusing the programmers of arrogance, noted,

> There were these differences but not enough friction to really divide the department. There was an air of enthusiasm to get things through that meant there was no real split.

Harvey Peters, the other liaison officer, pointed out the existence of an outside threat to the department which united everybody. Neil Turner, at that time a senior programmer, agreed:

> As I've said, we were very much a group. There was a slight split between the programmers and Ted Morgan's laddies but no real fric-

tion. Nobody else in the business was obviously backing computers. We were the only group interested in proving they were worthwhile. We were bound to be a close-knit group.

This feeling of group cohesiveness was well dramatized in their out-of-work activities. Reilly described the formation of a pub drinking club christened "The Fluids Society." When the team started to break up in 1960–1961, quite a few went to the London area and a "London Fluids Society" was formed. There was a tendency for members of the team, when it disbanded, to join each other in a small number of firms. Six moved to two companies in the south of England.

The Organization and Methods Department, 1959–1961. Jim Kenny arrived in Michaels in March 1959. He recruited his first four O&M officers from within the company and then offered jobs (in 1960) to Bill Reilly and Tom Reagan. They both accepted the offers. The O&M Department was situated in the company's head office in Birmingham. The stock controllers were in the same building. The Computer Department was twenty miles away in Wolverhampton.

Kenny was not impressed with the job the programmers had done:

> The computer was doing nothing but printing out some simple information. My first step was to say "let's have a look what the stock-control problem really is." Before I joined Michaels the only people who had contacted the Stock Control Department were programmers. I put in a systems team.

Kenny's early contact with the stock controllers was not trouble free. He blamed this on the backlog of discontent that had built up between the Computer Department and the stock controllers:

> Any hostility was due to the way in which they [the Computer Department] did things. They did them over the stock controllers heads. Also, the stock controllers were afraid to let the records go. I remember Kahn telling me that the stock controllers used to hide on a Friday afternoon. The department was cutting down staff and they were afraid that they'd be fired if they were seen by the management. The stock controllers regarded all their records as, if you like, acquiring evidence for the inquest.

However, the present head of stock control recalls a certain amount of ambivalence toward Kenny's own activities:

> So the first thing that happened was that Mr. Kenny came in and decided that he would do a complete study of stock control and de-

> termine what we really wanted and what we didn't. This is where the main arguments came.

The stock controllers were still very concerned about the restricted amount of information the computer was putting out compared with the manual system. There was also the issue that the output was in a different form and language from what they were accustomed to. Slowly they began to appreciate Kenny's style of operating. They began to draw comparisons with Bell's behavior:

> Bell and Co. really didn't know about stock control and they had no time to study it. But Mr. Kenny came and really studied stock control and we sat beside him and his team while they did this.
>
> I think the O&M team was rather lenient here because what they did was to slowly but surely take away from us the information we thought was required but ultimately didn't require.

By the end of 1960 the computer system was, from everybody's point of view, an acknowledged success. A week's stock had been saved. The stock controllers now had the information they needed in time to start making decisions about future stock levels. Their job increased in status. They were relieved of much of the clerical drudgery and could now act like merchandisers. As the chief stock controller recalled,

> I had always felt that the original system was like a man walking around in a street without really being able to see what was going on around him in other areas. Now with the new system it was like a man in a helicopter who had an enormous range of vision and could see for miles around.

The main task the O&M department performed in making the SE 100 computer system a viable one was to act as an intermediary between the Computer Department and the stock controllers. Between 1959 and 1961 the O&M Department had only minimal contact with the Computer Department. This was largely because the programmers were still heavily committed on the technical problems of systems design and programming for the clothing stock-control operation. In addition, at the end of 1959, the programmers had begun a new project, computerizing the stock-control function of the furniture division. The head of the programming section recalled the heavy commitments of that period:

> The Computer Department looked after clothing and furniture stock control. There was no time to do anything else. Up until 1959 we were trying to get something working. From 1959–1960 we tried to make it

operationally robust and from 1961 onward we were trying to cut it down to size. It was a full-time job in 1959–1960 just trying to get the thing going.

Summary of Programmer—O&M Officer Relations, 1957–1961[3]. A content analysis was made of the history interviews with programmers and O&M officers. Statements were coded into three categories, positive, negative, and neutral, and the intercoder reliability score for the data was .91.

Table 1 substantiates the earlier conclusion about the ultimate balancing of attitudes between the two groups in time period 1957–1961. Each group made nearly the same number of neutral comments about the other, twenty-seven as against twenty-six. As might be expected from the quotations given, the groups showed consistently strong negative attitudes toward each other. The interesting point is that the ratio of negative to positive comments is nearly the same for each group. For the O&M officers the ratio is 1.8 to 1, and for the programmers it is 2.1 to 1. There is only the slightest indication that the programmers felt more negatively toward the O&M officers than vice versa. A chi-square test revealed no significant differences in the direction of the attitudes. Clearly, the feeling of solidarity that had arisen between the two groups while they lived side by side in the Computer Department had watered down somewhat when the O&M officers moved into their own department. The important point to note at this stage is the similarity of the ratio of negative to positive statements for the two occupational categories. This ratio was soon to change radically for reasons that will presently be discussed.

While the two groups were alike in the proportion of negative attitudes they expressed toward one another, their negative feelings about Brian Michaels, its management, and user departments were not so balanced (see Table 2).

Given the comments that the programmers and the user departments made about one another, it is hardly surprising that the accumulated feel-

TABLE 1 Comparison of attitudes: O&M officers to programmers and programmers to O&M officers, 1957–1961[1]

	POSITIVE	*NEGATIVE*	*NEUTRAL*
O&M officers	20	36	27
Programmers	14	29	26

[1]No significant differences: positive-negative cells only.

[3]Note that the summary data are presented for programmers versus O&M officers and not for Computer Department versus O&M Department. The implication is that people like Reilly, Reagan, and Morgan were seen to be, and accepted that they were, doing O&M–type work within the Computer Department prior to the creation of the O&M Department.

TABLE 2 Comparison of O&M officers and programmers' perceptions of Michaels, its management, and user departments, 1957–1961[1]

	POSITIVE	*NEGATIVE*	*NEUTRAL*
O&M officers	38	71	46
Programmers	10	74	38

[1]Significant beyond .001 level with one degree of freedom: positive-negative cells only.

ings of the programmers are negative. It is a little more surprising that the O&M officers should also have negative things to say about Michaels, its management, and the user departments. This is especially so since the great majority of the early O&M officers were recruited from the Michaels Work Study or Stock Control departments. Some of the ill feeling expressed by the O&M officers was directed specifically at the company. These feelings would not have been echoed by everyone in the company. But one O&M officer said,

> Michaels is a funny place. The previous ten years had seen all sorts of purges and passions. It wasn't the sort of place where people felt secure.

Another commented that

> Michaels isn't the sort of place you'd want to retire into!

The day-to-day contacts the O&M officers had with the stock controllers brought home to them the stresses of being change agents. Reilly talked of his frequent encounters with the head stock controller, Kahn, in the following way:

> Kahn was one of the biggest cursers I've ever come across. I wouldn't like to repeat any of it now; but his general approach was, "How are you going to do it?" He'd pick a difficult one like rainwear or swimsuits and say, "Tell us the answers." We'd say: "You tell us how you do it and we'll work out how to do it on the computer." We knew he didn't know how he got his figures. They were just based on experienced hunches but he wouldn't admit it. He refused to cooperate. Kahn was afraid of his position. He was afraid the computer would affect his position.

Eventually, the Michaels directors forced Kahn to cooperate—an early signal to the user departments of where the board's allegiances lay.

The large power differential between programmers and O&M officers was soon to change. A new generation of equipment appeared that offered faster, cheaper, and more reliable service. Research was going on all the time to simplify programming. A new occupational group appeared called systems analysts, who claimed an area of task jurisdiction and a body of skills. All these factors were to affect the level of perceived hostility and the distribution of power and status among those concerned with computers in Brian Michaels. It must have been difficult for Jim Kenny to foresee all these changes and their implications in 1961. His recollection of how he felt about the programmers at that time gives a clear indication of his future strategy toward them:

> They were like a bunch of sixth-formers, sixth-form mathematicians. They were slick, witty in a sarcastic sort of way. They hid behind their technology. Trying to get to grips with them was extremely difficult. They were regarded as a lot of eggheads who lived in their own little world. The programmers were contemptuous of everybody in the business. Everybody had a nickname. They had their own language and all this was reflected in their out-of-work group they called The Fluids. They asked me to go out drinking with them but I refused. The whole thing was bloody infantile. I've no time for that sort of thing. I suppose a lot of their behavior was partly defensive. They were an odd group. They had to protect themselves.
>
> They were a little "in" group. They larked around at Wolverhampton like a bunch of school kids. I thought, I must get control of them.

Questions

1. Draw a diagram of the Brian Michaels organization in 1961. What formal relations existed among the O&M Department, the Computer Department, and the stock controllers?
2. "Those in authority at Brian Michaels are not necessarily those in power." Do you agree or disagree? Discuss.
3. Consider the activities described in this case in terms of the change process.
4. What are sources of conflict in this case? Were they resolved? If so, how?

CASE 14 Line and Staff at ITT

With the emergence of the business conglomerate in America in the early 1960s came the reemergence of centralized authority and the supervisory staff system of management.

President Ralph Cordiner's decentralized management system, as researched and perfected by the General Electric Company, was in vogue in the 1950s—cheered on by management consultants and business school deans. The staff system robbed management of its entrepreneurial prerogatives, they said. It might be satisfactory for slow, cumbersome, military-type organizations, but it was unwieldy and unresponsive in the dynamic arenas of business. All the negative adjectives were applied to centralized management. Peter Drucker was hailed as the apostle of the new decentralized, line-oriented philosophy, and the rush was on to reduce staffs to lean operating crews of specialists. Staff people of any stripe or skill were suspect.

Then along came the conglomerate—a management organization that operated like a central bank for both funds and talent. As the conglomerates gobbled up company after company and grew ever more profitable, opinions changed with respect to their management policies. Conglomerates assembled large, knowledgable staffs to audit and control the acquisitions in many diverse business activities. Companies that thought they had reached a happy medium began to doubt their staff-line relationships. As the conglomerates surged ahead, the desire to look like Litton or LTV or ITT was great enough to start the pendulum swinging. Gradually the circles of power became heavy with staff specialists, and the centralization of business management was back.

In understanding the *Darkness at Noon* atmosphere of ITT, it is necessary to understand how the staffs influenced policy. They operated like a cross between the secret police and a kindly family doctor, to a degree the staff was supreme so long as it reported all of the facts. But it was also required to confess when it was technically incompetent for a particular assignment. So staff people apologized a lot and mitigated their advice. But top ITT management knew that there was no way to run the company on the formula devised by Harold Geneen, ITT chairman and chief executive officer, without heavy emphasis on the staff role.

ITT gradually developed a unique, efficient, centralized operating system of line-staff management, both in organization and methods. In procedure it grew closer to the military general staff concept than any other major company, even to sporting an espionage organization and worldwide intelligence-gathering networks.

Unfortunately for Geneen's dreams and magnificent obsessions, ITT could never enjoy the leverage of General Motors or DuPont. It did not have the ability to dominate one or more major industries. The company seems destined to continue its piecemeal acquisition policies in diversified industries, ganging sales and profits to purchase the growth Geneen so dearly prizes. And with unrelated businesses in the assembly process at all times, management control problems become ever more complex, resulting in a tendency toward increased centralization and larger and more specialized staffs.

The ITT staffs were peppered with graduates of the management consulting profession, people who could appreciate the manipulation of power as almost an academic exercise. They seemed to have no psychic need for profit and loss responsibility and were the stuff great audit groups are made from. ITT claimed to run the largest and most efficient management consulting company in the world and continually proselytized some of the best talent away from the old-line management consulting houses.

"The only difference between a management consultant and an ITT staff man," a senior vice president said, "is that if you don't accept the consultant's advice, you leave." Another staff man said, "We get these MBAs from the Ivy League business schools all the time. But unless they learn our system, they don't last. We are taking the place of the Harvard Business School, so far as Geneen is concerned. He is proud of his Harvard tie, he lists the school's Advanced Management Program in his biography, but he balks at sending anyone back to the program. He believes that we are the trailblazers and the rest of the business world is 'sucking hind tit.'"

The staffs had taken over some functions to the point of completely emasculating company divisions management. Financial management and long-range planning were securely in staff hands. They also controlled the operations research, project management, and the market research and analysis that resulted in most of the company's acquisitions. Obviously, the staff chieftains reported directly to Geneen.

"To get to the top in this company, you've got to go through one of the staffs," Frank Deighan said. He was a graduate of Booz, Allen & Hamilton, management consultants, and had been seasoned by two tours with ITT staff groups. "You may be operating well in the field, but it will only be a matter of time before they want you back in New York. If you're going to work on the top levels, the brass must be sure of your reactions, gut and otherwise. You've got to be able to hang tough—they have to be sure. In short, you must become a known quantity. I thought the guys at Booz were ruthless until I joined H.S.G. and company. But Booz guys were little old ladies with bleeding hearts compared to these ITT guys."

As was intended, the staff struck fear into the hearts of the line management. There was a staff man always looking over your shoulder, and he was outside your jurisdiction and the control of your operating management. In fact, sometimes the staff man was outside of any authority or jurisdiction except the office of the president. The staff men were routinely rotated in assignments to avoid any rapport being achieved between division management and the staff. They were the Ogres of Operations, and headquarters intended to keep them that way.

The staff titles changed with the vogues of management policy. A fashionable one in the early 1970s was "product line manager." To read the product line manager's job description you would assume that he was a general manager, marketing manager, and financial specialist all rolled into one. And functionally his assignment was impressive, including a number of companies, usually scattered worldwide, assembled by industry or product line. But in fact the PLMs were spies, pure and simple. Their responsibility was to carry back to top management, and particularly Geneen, information concerning division operations.

The failing of these staff courtesans was often a superiority complex that allowed the line operators of the business to build up subtle defenses. Since the staff man could not know all the key factors in the operation of the business, he was always vulnerable to a technological sandbag or conflicting expert opinion. Only if he reached some kind of peace with his line counterpart would he be fed "straight dope" insofar as the real problems were concerned. So often there developed an Alphonse and Gaston relationship not unlike the deals made between top management and labor leaders. When some controversy was inevitable, the scene was rehearsed by staff and line secretly before it got to the forum of a business plan or top management review. It was amusing to sit through such meetings, in which even the friction and dissent had been contrived.

On occasion the line and staff did battle without quarter. With so many people on both sides possessing a strong instinct for the jugular, such confrontations were usually mean, ugly, and counterproductive. But stimulated by top management interrogation, the staff had to make an occasional example of some errant or cocky division president.

"You watch your boss on the staff side and you get the signal," a North American staff manufacturing specialist said. "If Geneen and Executive Vice President Bennett start zeroing in on some guy, you had better be able to pull out the sheet of embarrassing questions from your little black notebook and join in. *Au contraire,* if H.S.G. is smiling, philosophizing, and telling stories about his old days in this or that industry, then we just clam up. No matter what we have on the division boss, we make some obvious comment concerning how brilliantly the division is being operated and suggest, *sotto voce,* some minor changes. This is a totalitarian government, buddy, and we don't ever forget it."

Criteria for selecting ITT staff men indicated, by nuance, the type of man that best fitted the role: "Does he make recommendations based on a visibility of the situation not yet recognized by division management?" "Does he keep cool, even during periods of violent disagreement with line managers?"

Other requirements ranged from technical grasp to social presence but came across as being much the same as those the CIA uses to select an agent.

The system of a staff man overseeing each major line function did not encourage an entrepreneurial business climate. But the staffs did provide direction and could marshal a number of diverse technical skills very quickly to solve a problem.

Geneen's concept of forcing the divisions to constantly run their businesses "on paper" was policed by the staffs. Reports submitted by each division monthly were examined in detail by the assigned staff man. A system of marginal notations was developed by the staffs that allowed top management to analyze the problems, opportunities, danger signals, and errors contained in the reports after only a cursory glance through the thick notebooks. More than a few "red flags" meant heavy going for the division managers involved.

The disadvantage, of course, was that such star-chamber procedures often eliminated the opportunity for line people to explain their business. It was a temptation for a line manager to accept the recommendations of the staff with mild reservations, even though he might feel strongly that they were in error. By carrying out the recommendations to illogical conclusions and requesting further staff direction as the losses mounted, the situation might become embarrassing enough to drive off the staff men and allow the manager to reap the rewards of setting things right.

"I gained a hell of a lot more respect for the staff after they fried us at the business plan review," a general manager said. "Mind you, not respect for their ability. Some of them don't know their asses from a hole in the ground. But let me tell you, they know how to play the game. They sat on the other side of the table with all the questions, while my managers sat over here and tried to come up with answers, poor bastards. I'm not fool enough to put us in that situation again, let me tell you!"

With the same clarity as they recall their first sexual experience, most managers remember their maiden voyage to New York for the annual business plan review. Mr. Geneen's "show and tell" parties take place for each and every division and company in the ITT fold once every year. The Europeans are reviewed in Europe, the North Americans are reviewed in New York, and other reviews are arranged at times and places convenient to Geneen. But everyone goes under the knife.

The ITT planning process, now famous among management consultants and business historians, began as a semiformal set of directives and guidelines accumulated over the years since the early days at ITT. Geneen took the system and honed it to a fine operating edge. His reverence for facts and figures was very much in evidence. The planning process was a no-nonsense philosophy of numbers. Every division or company president was responsible for preparing such an annual business plan—a book-length document of plans, graphs, financial exhibits, and analyses. The format was standardized for all, even to the preprinting of book covers and forms. The plan was conceived, written, and presented by division management—but it was approved successively by all levels of management between the division and Geneen before it was presented to him (personally, mind you) for final approval. The work of preparation was exhaustive; the requirements for planning specialists simply to keep the plan current was a financial burden for many of the smaller divisions. Most U.S. companies cannot or do not support such a planning function or take the time to assemble all the detailed information required in the Geneen system. And not surprisingly, this is exactly where Geneen sees ITT's competitive advantage. His managers know the down, the play, the score, and even the details of the referee's sex life in that grand game called business. By comparison, competitors seem to be standing in ticket lines or still suiting up while Geneen puts points on the board.

The performance put on by division management in front of Geneen during their once-a-year confrontation is the most important mark in their overall rating. He sees and hears them, and he knows whether or not they are good disciples of the Word. During the sessions—like a Pentagon briefing, advertising agency presentation, or political rally—the results of past actions and future projections are heavily colored by the personality and charisma of the actors on stage. So the production must be carefully planned and staged to achieve the maximum favorable exposure in the short time the division will have before the gathered New York staffs, ITT top management, and Geneen himself. The mighty have risen and fallen by the flickering lights of the slide projector and the whine of the microphone.

It was cold in New York in late December when our division's first business plan was finally scheduled for review. We had been twice delayed, confirming our suspicions that the staffs were saving their best chance at a massive humiliation to the last. There was black slush on the ground, and the sky was the color of old lead. We huddled in a mid-Manhattan Hamburger Heaven, catching a quick, pre-lunch meal, which we felt might be our last of the day. The division was scheduled to be "on" at four in the afternoon, so what with preparation, waiting in the wings, the presentation, and an interrogation, the day would be filled, with no time for the niceties of dining. Binks, the division controller recently elevated from the ranks, was shaken. "Have you ever done this before?" he asked Hayden Moore, the acting general manager.

"No," Moore said weakly. "Not alone. I've carried papers to a lot of the sessions."

"So have I," said Binks. "And given testimony and wrestled graphs and all that stuff. But this is different. Boy, just the three of us. And this goddam plan—it's full of holes. Maybe you guys don't know what can happen up there. I've watched guys get torn to pieces. I've seen Geneen scream at a general manager until I thought the guy was going to crawl under the table."

"Let's ask for a bye until next year," I said. "Plead nolo. Or why don't you have a seizure? No controller, no numbers."

The cab ride to headquarters had all the hardy camaraderie of a trip to the gallows. With our slides, graphs, and hats in hand we presented ourselves to the security guards on the meetingroom floor and were duly identified and badged. We waited what seemed an interminable time in the lounge, then took our seats in the great chamber to watch the plans of other Defense Space Group companies unfold as we waited our turn.

Rumors drifted out from the business plan sessions in progress to the lounges and waiting rooms, alternately encouraging and discouraging.

"Geneen just said operations cash management is the most important consideration this year," a staff man announced. "Hope your operation's cash management plan is sound." He nudged our controller with his elbow and cackled. Binks was now blanched and shaking. I began to wonder what we would do if he couldn't see it through. A year of planning only to pass out on the stage before Geneen. A tragic prospect: Binks lying there atop his forms and ledgers.

"No negative thinking. Forget about the goddam recession, that's the word," a friendly department manager said. "Rich Bennett doesn't want any 'can't do' shit. If you're looking for things to get worse, better tone it down."

Ushered successively closer to the podium, we watched the production with a partisan interest and awe. Geneen sat like an Oriental potentate, flanked by vice presidents in descending order of importance. The hierarchy was marvelously disciplined, speaking only when called on by Geneen or the interlocutor, Executive Vice President Rich Bennett. Bennett kept the harangue and monotonous division dialogues moving with questions, invitations for staff inquiries, and an occasional attempt at levity.

Finally, our turn came. As in the Mad Hatter's tea party, we had been moving our seats closer to the speaker's rostrum, and now we were there. Moving to stage center, the middle of the table, we now faced Geneen across the ten-yard expanse of green carpet. The *Caine Mutiny* court-martial scene with Queeg on the wrong side of the green cloth.

We had been warned that everything would depend on Geneen's reactions. If he began serious questioning, the staff would be on us like a pack of hounds. We had tried to second-guess his curiosities—which areas to concentrate on and present with slide and story, where his chief interest might lie between the political and the practical. But it was impossible to cover all the holes and patches in the Cable Division program. If Geneen wanted our hides, he had only to delve a little.

Rich Bennett introduced us with a quip about leaving the good golf weather in San Diego to tell them all about our Silver Strand Plot. We were launched. Slowly, deliberately, we presented the plan. Geneen said nothing, nodding on occasion in agreement with some statement. Bennett asked a few questions of the product line managers on the staff responsible for cable and communications areas. They gave quick answers, referring to the piles of papers scattered over the table in front of them. As the last slide passed, our brevet general manager sat down, looking exhausted. His voice had cracked several times in the presentation, and the controller's replies to financial questions had been halting. But it was over, and we waited for the decision. Thumbs up or down.

Geneen rose and said, "These gentlemen are taking on some big people. This is probably the largest investment we've made in facilities in a long time." He turned to us. "Just get the goddam plant built and start turning out cable." He motioned to the staff. "These people will take care of the rest. Any questions?"

There were no questions.

"Watch those bastards from Western Electric in Washington," Geneen said to me, "and don't even have a cup of coffee with them. Or the other competition. No matter how well you know them. There can't be any smell of collusion. We may have some problems. . . ." His voice trailed off. He waddled slowly across the expanse of carpet that separated the tables, followed by a gaggle of corporate vice presidents. He shook hands with the three of us in what we later learned was an unprecedented gesture of support. Soft-spoken and pleasant, he chatted for a few minutes while the assembled gathering sat in silence. He asked me about the markets, the prospects for government business, AT&T plans, and the program schedules.

"Good work," he said. "I'll be out to see that beachfront property sometime, too." Then he paraded out of the room, receiving nods and smiles as he trouped the line. The meeting was temporarily adjourned. Then tension lifted like a curtain. A few brave souls lit cigarettes on their way to the refreshment tables in the lounges.

"I feel as though I've just had a battlefield decoration pinned on," I said.

The controller looked at his hand. "I've been with this company twenty years, and this is the first time I've ever met with the president. And I just shook hands with him."

"Fred will never wash that hand again," a staff assistant said. "Congratulations. You just had holy water sprinkled over you, and you will shortly be inundated with more cooperation than you can use."

After basking in the reflected glory of Geneen's approval in the lounge, we packed our exhibits and headed back to the Barclay Hotel. In the Gold Room we began a half-hearted victory celebration, but the emotional drain had been too much, and the evening went flat after two drinks.

"What won Geneen over, do you suppose?" the general manager asked, now out of shock.

"We showed a lot of confidence. That's important. You can't come on tentative with Geneen. He wants a team that is all for hard charging," Binks said, now high on Scotch and blessed relief.

"What a relief to have the bloody thing over," said Moore. "Here's how."

And he drained the last drink of our one and only victory celebration ever.

Questions

1. What advantages did the conglomerate form offer Geneen?
2. At ITT, what are and are not a division general manager's prerogatives?
3. What is the typical relationship between line and staff? How is it different at ITT?
4. How does ITT treat organizational conflict?
5. Geneen's use of staff groups, annual "stress" presentations, and emphasis on goals and numbers proved highly successful in terms of ITT's growth in revenues and profits. Why do you think more organizations have not adopted his ideas?

GLOSSARY

Adhocracy. An organizational form characterized by high horizontal differentiation, low vertical differentiation, low formalization, and decentralization, which provides great flexibility and responsiveness.

Administrative component. All the personnel in an organization who engage in supportive activities.

Alienation. A feeling, held by employees, that their work is meaningless and that they are powerless to correct the situation.

Analyzers. Organizations whose strategy is to move into new products or new markets only after their viability has been proven.

Appeals system. A formal channel for grievances to be heard and acted upon.

Authority. The right to act, or command others to act, toward the attainment of organizational goals.

Autonomous work teams. Implementing job enrichment in a group of interdependent employees.

Autonomy. The degree to which a job provides substantial freedom, independence, and discretion to the individual in scheduling the work and in determining the procedures to be used in carrying it out.

Behavioral view of conflict. Conflict is a natural and inevitable outcome in any organization.

Boundary roles. Interfacing positions that reduce the threats of uncertainty posed by dependence.

Buffering. Protecting the operating core from environmental variations in supply and demand.

Bureaucracy. An organizational form characterized by division of labor, a well-defined authority hierarchy, high formalization, impersonality, employment decisions based on merit, career tracks for employees, and distinct separation of members' organizational and personal lives.

Bureaupathology. The use of rules and regulations by individuals to protect themselves from making errors.

Centralization. The degree to which formal authority to make discretionary choices is concentrated in an individual, unit, or level (usually high in the organization).

Chains of command. The superior-subordinate connections from the top to the bottom of the organization.

Change agent. The person or persons who initiate a change process.

Closed system. A self-contained system that ignores its environment.

Coalescing. The combining of an organization with one or more other organizations for the purpose of joint action.

Coalition. Two or more individuals or units who unite to protect or further a common interest.

Collegial structure. An egalitarian structure in which all members have an equal input into all important decisions.

Committee structure. Two or more individuals who come together, either temporarily or permanently, to bring heterogeneous inputs to a decision.

Competing-values approach. An organization's effectiveness depends on which individuals are doing the assessment and the interests they represent.

Complex environment. An environment made up of many diverse components.

Complexity. The degree of horizontal, vertical, and spatial differentiation in an organization.

Conflict. A process in which an effort is purposely made by one person or unit to block another that results in frustrating the attainment of the other's goals or the furthering of his or her interests.

Conglomerate structure. A structure made up of highly independent units that share a resource pool.

Control. The degree of influence that management has for directing the behavior of organization members.

Coopting. The absorbtion of those individuals or organizations in the environment that threaten a given organizations's stability or existence.

Coordination. The bringing together of diverse activities to ensure consistent movement toward the organization's goals.

Decentralization. Low centralization.

Defenders. Organizations whose strategy is to produce a limited set of products directed at a narrow segment of the total potential market.

Departmentation. Grouping like specialists together.

Differentiation. Task segmentation and attitudinal differences held by individuals in various departments.

Disturbed-reactive environment. An environment characterized by many competitors, one or more of which may be large enough to influence that environment.

Divisional structure. A structure characterized by self-contained, autonomous units, each unit overseen by a manager who is totally responsible for the unit's performance.

Domain. An organization's niche that it has staked out for itself with respect to products or services offered and markets served.

Dominant coalition. The most powerful coalition within an organization.

Dynamic environment. An environment in which the factors are changing over time.

Economies of scale. The economic efficiencies that result from larger size.

Efficiency. A ratio that reflects a comparison of some aspect of unit performance to the costs incurred for that performance.

Entropy. The propensity of a system to run down or disintegrate.

Environment. Those institutions or forces that affect the performance of the organization but over which the organization has little or no control.

Environmental uncertainty. The degree to which an environment is characterized by a large number of heterogeneous and rapidly changing factors.

Equifinality. A system that can reach the same final state from differing initial conditions and by a variety of paths.

Evolutionary mode. A strategy that evolves over time as a pattern in a stream of significant decisions.

Feedback. The degree to which carrying out the work activities required by a job results in the individual's obtaining direct and clear information about the effectiveness of his or her performance.

Flat structure. Low vertical differentiation.

Formalization. The degree to which jobs within the organization are standardized.

Functional structure. A structure characterized by similar and related occupational specialties being grouped together.

Goal-attainment approach. An organization's effectiveness as appraised in terms of the accomplishment of end goals.

Goal displacement. The displacement of organizational goals by subunit or personal goals.

Growth-need strength. An employee's desire for self-esteem and self-actualization.

Horizontal differentiation. The degree of differentiation among units based on the orientation of members, the nature of the tasks they perform, and their education and training.

Imperative. A variable that dictates structure.

Integrated work teams. Implementing job enlargement in a group of interdependent employees.

Integration. The quality of collaboration that exists among interdependent units.

Intensive technology. The utilization of a wide range of customized responses, depending on the nature and variety of the problems.

Interactionist view of conflict. The view that some conflict is absolutely necessary for an organization to perform effectively.

Job characteristics model. A model that identifies five job factors and their interrelationships and then demonstrates their effect on productivity, motivation, and job satisfaction.

Job design. The structure of job tasks, duties, and responsibilities assigned to an employee.

Job enlargement. Horizontal expansion of a job by adding related tasks.

Job enrichment. Vertical expansion of a job by adding planning, executing, and inspecting responsibilities.

Job rotation. Lateral transfers to increase skill variety.

Job satisfaction. The individual's satisfaction with the amount of various job outcomes that he or she is receiving.

Life cycle. The development of organizations through stages—from birth through maturity and decline.

Line authority. A superior's authority over all the activities of his or her subordinates.

Long-linked technology. Sequentially interdependent tasks.

Machine bureaucracy. A traditional bureaucracy characterized by highly routine operating tasks, very formalized rules and regulations, tasks that are grouped into functional departments, centralized authority, decision making that follows the formal chain of command, and an elaborate administrative structure with a sharp distinction between line and staff activities.

Management audit. A systems application that appraises organizational performance in ten key areas.

Management by objectives (MBO). A philosophy of management that assesses an organization and its members by how well they achieve the specific goals that have been jointly established previously.

Mass technology. Large batch or mass produced.

Matrix structure. A structure with a dual chain of command; combining functional departmentation with departmentation by product or project.

Mechanistic structure. A structure characterized by high complexity, high formalization, and centralization.

Mediating technology. The process of linking together different clients in need of each other's services.

Mutual task dependence. The extent to which two units in an organization depend upon each other for assistance, information, compliance, or other coordinative activities to complete their respective tasks.

One-way task dependence. The condition of one unit in an organization being unilaterally dependent upon another unit in the organization.

Open system. A dynamic system that interacts with and responds to its environment.

Operative. An employee who has no supervisory or managerial responsibilities.

Organic structure. Flexible and adaptive structures, with emphasis on lateral communication, nonauthority-based influence, and loosely defined responsibilities.

Organization. The planned coordination of the collective activities of two or more people who, functioning on a relatively continuous basis and through division of labor and a hierarchy of authority, seek to achieve a common goal or set of goals.

Organization design. The construction and change of an organization's structure.

Organization size. The total number of employees in the organization.

Organization structure. The degree of complexity, formalization, and centralization in an organization.

Organization theory. The discipline that studies the structure and design of organizations.

Organizational development. The study of individual and group change.

Organizational effectiveness. The degree to which an organization attains its short- and long-term goals, the selection of which reflects strategic constituencies, the self-interest of the evaluator, and the life stage of the organization.

Parkinson's law. The expansion of work so as to fill the time available for its completion.

Placid-clustered environment. An environment in which threats are clustered but changes take place slowly over time.

Placid-randomized environment. An environment in which demands are distributed randomly and changes take place slowly over time.

Planned organizational change. Any alteration in an organization's structure designed to help achieve organizational goals.

Planning mode. Strategy as an explicit and systematic set of guidelines developed in advance.

Policy. A statement that guides employees, providing discretion within limited boundaries.

Pooled interdependence. Two or more units that contribute separately to a larger unit.

Power. An individual's capacity to influence decisions.

Power-control. The view that an organization's structure is the result of a power struggle by internal constituencies who are seeking to further their interests.

Problem analyzability. The type of search procedures followed to find successful methods for adequately responding to task exceptions; from well defined and analyzable to ill defined and unanalyzable.

Procedure. A specific standardized sequence of steps that results in a uniform output.

Process technology. Highly controlled, standardized, and continuous processing.

Productivity. The quantity or volume of the major product or service that the organization provides.

Professional bureaucracy. An organizational form employed with highly skilled professionals and having high complexity, decentralization, and the use of internalized professional standards in place of external formalization.

Professionalization. The degree to which employees use a professional organization as a major reference, belief in service to the public, belief in self-regulation, dedication to one field, and autonomy.

Prospectors. Organizations whose strategy is to find and exploit new product and market opportunities.

Quality circles. A voluntary group of workers, with a shared area of responsibility, who meet regularly to discuss their quality problems, investigate causes, recommend solutions, and take corrective actions.

Quality of work life. A movement to improve the content of jobs.

Rationality. The belief that behavior is goal directed and consistent.

Rationing. The allocation of organizational products or services according to a priority system.

Reactors. A residual strategy that describes organizations that follow inconsistent and unstable patterns.

Reciprocal interdependence. The output of one unit that becomes the input for another unit.

Refreezing. Stabilizing a change by placing positive sanctions on changed patterns of behavior.

Ritual. A formalization process in which members prove their trustworthiness and loyalty to the organization.

Role. A set of expected behavior patterns attributed to someone occupying a given job in the organization.

Routineness. The degree to which an organization's technology is standardized, unvarying, and predictable.

Rule. An explicit statement that tells an employee what he or she ought or ought not to do.

Satisficing. Decision search characterized by seeking a solution that is both satisfactory and sufficient.

Sector structure. A structure characterized by grouping common divisions under a single executive, thus creating a more clearly defined industry identity.

Sequential interdependence. Procedures that are highly standardized and must be performed in a specified serial order.

Simple environment. The condition of few environmental factors needing to be considered when making a decision.

Simple structure. A structure that is low in complexity and low in formalization and where authority is centralized in a single person.

Skill variety. The degree to which a job requires a variety of different activities.

Smoothing. Leveling out the impact from fluctuations in the environment by offering incentives to environmental units to regularize their interactions with the organization.

Spatial dispersion. The degree to which the location of an organization's facilities and personnel are dispersed geographically.

Span of control. The number of subordinates that an individual manager can supervise effectively.

Specialization. The breaking up of the organization's activities so that employees' jobs are organized around narrow specialized skills.

Specific environment. That part of the environment that impinges directly on the organization's effectiveness.

Staff authority. The right to give advice and service.

Static environment. An environment in which its factors remain the same over time.

Strategic-choice. Decision makers' choice of strategic alternatives when they have considerable discretion.

Strategic-constituencies approach. An organization's effectiveness as determined by how successfully it satisfies the demands of those constituencies in its environment from which it requires support for its continued existence.

Strategy. The determination of the basic long-term goals of an organization and the adoption of courses of action and the allocation of resources necessary for carrying out these goals.

Superordinate goal. A common goal, held by two or more parties, which is compelling and highly appealing and cannot be attained by the resources of any single party separately.

System. A set of interrelated and interdependent parts arranged in a manner that produces a unified whole.

Systems approach. Evaluating an organization's effectiveness by its ability to acquire inputs, process the inputs, channel the outputs, and maintain stability and balance.

Tall structure. High vertical differentiation.

Task force. A temporary structure formed to accomplish a specific, well-defined, and complex task that involves a number of organizational subunits.

Task identity. The degree to which a job requires completion of a whole and identifiable piece of work.

Task significance. The degree to which a job has a substantial impact on the lives or work of other people.

Task variability. The number of exceptions encountered in one's work; from few to many.

Technology. The processes or methods that an organization uses to transform inputs into outputs.

Theory A organization. An organization designed to control employees through a tightly monitored structural system; the dominant North American model.

Theory X. The view that employees dislike work, are lazy, dislike responsibility, and must be coerced to perform.

Theory Y. The view that employees like work, are creative, seek responsibility, and can exercise self-direction.

Theory Z organization. An organization designed to control employees through socialization; used to describe certain highly successful American companies with characteristics that are also displayed by many Japanese companies.

Traditional view of conflict. The view that all conflicts are bad and must be avoided.

Turbulent-field environment. An environment in which change is ever present and elements in the environment are increasingly interrelated.

Unfreezing. The first stage in the change process which seeks to reduce entrenchment in the status quo.

Unit technology. Technology wherein units are custom made and work is nonroutine.

Unity of command. The view that every employee should have only one boss to whom he or she reports.

Vertical differentiation. The number of hierarchical levels between top management and operatives.

Work modules. A work form that breaks up jobs into two-hour time-task units.

NAME INDEX

A

Adams, J.S., 159
Aiken, M., 46, 55, 62, 86, 129, 138, 139, 280–82
Aldag, R.L., 151, 258
Aldrich, H.E., 86, 100, 110, 111, 295
Allen, S.A., 241
Allison, G.T., 83
Anderson, B., 3–6
Anderson, T., 108, 117
Argyris, C., 110, 111, 199, 223
Armenakis, A.A., 151
Athos, A.G., 325

B

Bacharach, S.B., 167
Bazerman, M., 278
Beams, L., 339
Bederian, A.G., 151
Bennis, W.G., 200–202, 210
Bergen, G.L., 293
Blake, R.R., 300
Blau, P.M., 108, 109, 110, 111, 112, 114
Bohlander, G.W., 262
Boland, M., 108, 117
Boland, W., 108, 117
Bonoma, T.V., 280–83
Boulding, E., 293
Brayfield, A.H., 248
Brief, A.P., 260
Brown, W.B., 247
Burck, C.G., 220
Burns, T., 145, 146, 148, 149, 154, 164

C

Cafferty, T.P., 300
Cameron, K., 36, 37
Campbell, J.P., 20, 22–23
Cannan, E., 48
Cass, E.L., 257
Chandler, A.D. Jr., 94, 96, 97, 99, 103–04, 105
Chandler, M.K., 146
Child, J., 86, 97, 99, 100, 104, 105, 109, 114, 115, 156, 166
Churchman, C.W., 143
Cole, R.E., 326
Coleman, H.J. Jr., 101, 103
Coleman, J.S., 303
Conaty, J., 112
Conlon, E., 278
Coppola, F.F., 210
Corwin, R.G., 298
Crockett, W.H., 248
Crozier, M., 180
Cummings, L.L., 159, 278

D

Dandridge, T.C., 119
Davis, L.E., 255
Davis, S.M., 216

Dearborn, D.C., 230
Delbecq, A.L., 130, 139
Deutsch, M., 288
Dewar, R., 55
Dill, W.R., 145
Donaldson, L., 86, 126
Donnelly, J.H., Jr., 52, 307
Doriean, P., 112
Dowling, J.B., 46
Downey, H.K., 144, 151
Drucker, P.F., 94
Duncan, R.B., 152, 153
Dunnette, M.D., 144, 288
Dutton, J.M., 294, 300

E

Emery, F.E., 145, 146–49, 154, 164
Etzioni, A., 20
Eubanks, S., 339
Evan, W.M., 28, 29

F

Feild, H.S., Jr., 151
Ford, J.D., 111, 166, 315, 316
Ford, R.N., 255
Frederick, R.R., 236
Freeman, J.H., 118, 316, 317, 320, 321
Frost, P.J., 134

G

Galbraith, J.K., 98, 214
Gardner, J., 320
Gerwin, D., 135, 137, 139
Gibson, J.L., 307
Gillespie, D.F., 112
Goggin, W.C., 218
Goodman, P.S., 19, 20, 22–23, 278
Gouldner, A.W., 197
Greiner, L.E., 279
Grinyer, P.H., 86
Gupta, N., 107

H

Haas, J.E., 56, 110, 112, 117
Hackman, J.R., 250–52, 260, 261–62
Hage, J., 46, 47, 55, 62, 72, 86, 87, 129, 138, 139, 280–82
Hall, R.H., 46, 54, 56, 110, 111, 112, 113, 114, 116, 117, 266
Haney, W.V., 293
Hannan, M.T., 118, 316, 317, 320, 321
Harvey, E., 126
Hatvany, N., 327, 328
Hawley, A., 108, 117
Hay, J., 192–93
Hedberg, B.L.T., 321
Hellriegel, D., 144
Hendershot, G.E., 118
Henderson, A.M., 46, 189
Herzberg, F., 255
Hickson, D.J., 62, 86, 107, 108, 110, 136, 138, 179
Hinings, C.R., 62, 86, 107, 136, 179
Hirsch, P., 98
Holley, W.H., Jr., 151
Hummon, N.P., 112
Hunt, R.G., 138

I

Iacocca, L., 319
Indik, B.P., 117
Inkson, J.H.K., 110
Ivancevich, J.M., 52, 307

J

Jacobs, D., 156
James, T.F., 110, 118
Janson, R., 252
Johnson, J.B., 333
Johnson, N.J., 56, 110, 112, 117

K

Kahn, R.L., 12, 253, 272, 293
Kaiser, H., 269
Katz, D., 12, 272
Kaufman, H., 20
Khandwalla, P.N., 114
Kimberly, J.R., 20, 107, 313
Klatzky, S.R., 118
Knight, K., 216, 217
Koenig, R., Jr., 139
Koontz, H., 51
Kotter, J.P., 275

L

Lawler, E.E., III, 52, 260
Lawler, E.J., 167

Lawrence, P.R., 46, 145, 149–51, 153, 155, 157, 216, 295
Leavitt, H.J., 300
Lee, C.A., 179
Levine, C.H., 315
Levinger, R.L., 110
Lewin, K., 274
Litterer, J.A., 113
Lorsch, J.W., 46, 145, 149–51, 153, 155, 157, 295
Louv, R., 338
Lucas, G., 209

M

Magnusen, K., 129
Mahoney, T.A., 134
Mannheim, B.F., 113
Mansfield, R., 109, 114
Martindell, J., 29
Maslow, A., 293
Mausner, B., 255
Mayhew, B.H., 110
McClelland, D., 223
McEwen, W.J., 163
McGregor, D., 70–71
McGuire, J., 93
McPherson, J.M., 110
Merton, R.K., 197, 198
Meyer, A.D., 101, 103
Meyer, M.W., 109, 111, 317
Miewald, R.D., 202–203
Miles, R.E., 101, 103
Miles, R.H., 143, 313
Mileti, D.S., 112
Miller, E.J., 299
Miller, G.A., 112, 199
Mills, D.L., 116
Mintzberg, H., 63, 83, 94, 113, 118, 146, 153, 157, 194, 195, 196, 222, 226, 227, 229, 236
Mitchell, T.R., 264
Moberg, D.J., 247
Mohr, L., 130
Molotch, H., 322
Montanari, J.R., 104, 112
Morgenthaler, E., 192
Morrison, A.M., 217
Mouton, J.S., 302

N

NaKane, C., 326
Negandhi, A.R., 157
Nixon, R., 95
Nystrom, P.C., 321

O

Oldham, G.R., 250, 252
Organ, D.W., 159
Ouchi, W.G., 46, 325, 333, 337

P

Parkinson, C.N., 114, 115, 116, 118
Parsons, T., 46, 189
Pascale, R.T., 325
Paterson, T.T., 82, 83
Pennings, J.M., 19, 20, 22–23, 62, 179
Perrow, C., 46, 65, 127–29, 130, 134, 135, 140, 191, 192, 204
Pfeffer, J., 20, 31, 134, 155, 170, 171, 172, 176, 180, 181, 283, 310, 312
Pheysey, D.C., 108, 136, 138
Pitts, R.A., 104
Pondy, L.R., 117, 300
Porter, L.W., 52
Price, R.L., 337
Pucik, V., 325, 327
Pugh, D.S., 62, 72, 86, 107, 108, 110, 136, 138, 166
Purdy, K., 252

Q

Quinn, R.E., 33, 36, 37
Quinn, R.P., 249

R

Reimann, B.C., 45, 46, 47, 157
Rico, L., 294
Robbins, S.P., 168, 266, 289, 294
Rohrbaugh, J., 33, 38
Rosenstein, E., 297
Ross, I., 318, 321
Rushing, W.A., 113, 118

S

Salancik, G.R., 31, 171, 312
Samuel, Y., 113
Sayles, L.R., 146, 181, 215
Schlesinger, L.A., 275

Schmidt, W.H., 288
Schneck, R.E., 179
Schoenherr, R.A., 108, 114
Schotters, F.J., 255
Scott, W.G., 312, 313, 314
Seashore, S.E., 27, 28
Seiler, J.A., 298
Selznick, P., 197
Shepard, H.A., 302
Sherif, M., 300, 301, 304
Short, L.E., 268, 273
Siegel, M., 192–93
Simon, H.A., 84, 97, 155–56, 168, 230
Sloan, A., 232
Slocum, J.W., Jr., 111, 144, 151, 166
Smith, A., 48, 247
Snow, C.C., 101, 103
Snyderman, B., 255
Spielberg, S., 209
Spray, S.L., 28, 29
Staines, G.L., 249
Stalker, G.M., 145, 146, 148, 149, 154, 164
Starbuck, W.H., 144, 321
Staw, B.M., 159, 171, 278
Stockman, D., 178–79
Storey, R.G., 151
Strauss, G., 297, 300
Suttle, J.L., 251

T

Taylor, F.W., 247
Terrien, F.W., 116
Teuter, K., 112
Thomas, K.W., 288
Thompson, J.D., 46, 130–34, 140, 144, 159, 163, 288, 310
Thompson, V., 198
Toffler, A., 224
Tosi, H.L., 94, 151
Trist, E.L., 145, 146–49, 154, 164
Tsouderos, J.E., 117
Turner, A., 339
Turner, C., 62, 86, 107, 136

U

Udy, S.H., Jr., 138

V

Van de Ven, A.H., 130, 139
Veiga, J.F., 321
Vroom, V.H., 248

W

Walton, E.J., 62
Walton, R.E., 257, 294, 300
Wanous, J.P., 260
Warkov, S., 108, 117
Warriner, C.K., 26
Weber, M., 46, 189–94, 202–4, 207
Weick, K.E., 26, 155
Whetton, D.A., 311, 313, 315, 322
White, S.E., 264
Whyte, W.F., 298
Woodward, J., 124–27, 130, 135, 136, 140, 153
Worthy, J.C., 52

Y

Yager, E., 259
Yanouzas, J.N., 321
Yasi-Ardekani, M., 86
Yuchtman, E., 27, 28

Z

Zald, M., 297
Zaltman, G., 280–83
Zimmer, F.G., 257
Zwerman, W.L., 126

SUBJECT INDEX

A

Adhocracy:
  definition, 210–11
  and power-control, 222–24
  strengths, 211–12
  weaknesses, 211–12
Administrative component, 45, 114–19, 316–17
Advertising, 163
Alienation, employee, 199
Analyzer strategy, 102–3
Appeals systems, 301–4
Aston group, 108–10
Authority, 5–6, 76–77, 79, 173–75, 304
Autonomous work teams, 257–58
Autonomy, 45, 250

B

Behavioral view of conflict, 290
Boundary roles, 159
Buffering, 159–60
Bureaucracy:
  definition, 189–94
  dominance of, 205–6
  dysfunctional consequences of, 196–200
  machine, 194–95
  and power-control, 206
  professional, 194–96

C

Centralization:
  and change, 282–83
  and complexity, 85–86
  definition, 46, 76–78
  and formalization, 85–87
  importance of, 84–85
  measuring, 87–88
Chain of command, 79–82
Change:
  agent, 272–73
  and decline, 320–22
  determinants of, 266–72
  interventions, 273–74
  managing, 265–68
  model, 268
  process, 274–78
  resistance to, 266–68
Client departmentation, 49–50
Closed system, 10–11
Coalescing, 162
Coalitions, 171–72
Collegial structure, 221
Committee structure, 220–21
Communication, 23, 36–37, 298–300, 306
Complexity:
  and change, 280–81
  definition, 6, 46, 47–54
  importance of, 54–55
  measuring, 55–59

Conflict:
and decline, 318
definition, 22, 288–89
resolution techniques, 300–306
sources of, 294–300
stimulation techniques, 306–7
views on, 289–91
Conglomerate structure, 241–44
Contracting, 162
Control, 22, 35–39
Coopting, 162
Coordination, 5
Craft technology, 128
Cycles:
life, 37–39
systems, in, 13

D

Decentralization (*See* Centralization)
Decision making, 82–83, 167–70
Decline, managing, 313–23
Defender strategy, 101, 103
Delegation of authority, 46
Departmentation, 48–50
Differentiation, 46, 149–50
Dissatisfaction, employee, 248–50
Divisional structure, 232–36
Division of labor (*See* Job specialization)
Domain, 144, 163–64

E

Effectiveness, organizational:
competing-values approach, 33–39
criteria, 22–23
definition, 20–24, 40
goal-attainment approach, 24–27
growth and, 311–12
importance of, 19
strategic-constituencies approach, 31–33
systems approach, 27–31
Efficiency, 22
Ends, 35–39
Entropy, negative, 13
Environment:
actual, 144–45
awareness, 12
and centralization, 157–58
complex, 152–53
and complexity, 157
definition, 142–45
disturbed-reactive, 147
dynamic, 152–53
and formalization, 157
general, 143–44
imperative, 154–56
managing the, 158–64
perceived, 144–45
placid-clustered, 147
placid-randomized, 147
simple, 152–53
specific, 143–44
static, 152–53
systems, role in, 10–12
turbulent-field, 147–48
uncertainty, 145
Equifinality, 14
Evolutionary mode, 95

F

Feedback, 250
Flat structures, 51–52
Flexibility, 22, 35–39
Forecasting, 161
Formalization:
and change, 282
and complexity, 72
definition, 6–7, 46, 61–63
importance of, 64
measuring, 72–74
techniques, 66–70
Functional:
departmentation, 49
structure, 229–31

G

Geographic departmentation, 50
Goals:
consensus, 23
displacement, 196–98
effectiveness criterion, 24–27
in organizations, 5
and rational behavior, 170–71
and strategy, 93–95
superordinate, 300–301
Growth:
as effectiveness criterion, 22
managing, 309–12
need strength, 251, 260

H

Horizontal differentiation, 47–50
Human relations model, 35–39

I

Information:
  control, 78, 176–79
  processing, 78
Integrated work teams, 257
Integration, 46, 149–50
Interactionist view of conflict, 290–91
Interdependence:
  pooled, 133
  reciprocal, 133
  sequential, 133
Internal process model, 35–39
Interorganizational strategies, 162–63
Intraorganizational strategies, 159–61

J

Japanese organizations:
  management system, 327–33
  success of, 326–27
Job:
  characteristics model, 250–52
  design, 247–62
  enlargement, 254
  enrichment, 255–57
  redesign, 247–62
  rotation, 252–53
  satisfaction, 22
  specialization, 5–6, 46, 48–49

M

Management audit, 29–30
Management by objectives (MBO), 24
Managerial interpersonal skills, 23
Matrix structure, 212–19
Means, 35–39
Mechanistic structures, 146, 182–83
Morale, 22, 36–37, 323
Motivation, 22, 323

O

Open system, 10–14
Open systems model, 35–39
Organic structures, 146
Organization:
  definition, 5–6
  design, 7
  effectiveness (*See* Effectiveness, organizational)
  structure, 6–7, 45–47
  theory, 7–8, 16

P

Parkinson's law, 114–19
Participation, 23, 297
People, 35–39
Planning, 22, 36, 37
Planning mode, 94–95
Policies, 67–68, 77
Power, 173–81, 199
Power-control:
  centralization and, 184
  and change, 283–85, 321–22
  complexity and, 183
  and decline, 317
  definition, 167
  environment and, 181–82
  formalization, 183–84
  model, 172
  technology and, 181–82
Problem analyzability, 127–29
Procedures, 67–68
Process departmentation, 50
Product departmentation, 49
Productivity, 22, 36, 37
Professionalization, 46
Professionals, 64–66
Profit, 22
Prospector strategy, 101–3

Q

Quality:
  circles, 258–59
  as effectiveness criterion, 22
  of work life (QWL), 248

R

Rational goal model, 35–39
Rationality, 170–71
Rationing, 161
Reactor strategy, 102–3
Readiness, 23
Resource acquisition, 36–37
Rituals, 69–70

Roles, 23, 67, 299
Route 1, 261–62
Route 2, 262
Rules, 67–68

S

Satisficing, 168
Sector structure, 236–39
Selection, 66–67
Simple structure, 226–29
Size, organization:
- and centralization, 114
- and complexity, 111–12
- definition, 107–8
- and formalization, 113–14
- imperative, 108–11

Skill variety, 250
Small business, 119–20
Smoothing, 160–61
Socialization, 65
Soliciting, third-party, 163
Span of control, 46, 51–52
Spatial dispersion, 52–53
Specialization (*See* Job specialization)
Stability, 23, 36–37, 182–83, 283–85
Standardization, 47, 61 (*See also* Formalization)
Strategic choice, 97–99
Strategy:
- definition, 94–95
- imperative, 96–101
- typologies, 101–3

Status incongruence, 298
Structure (*See* Organization structure)
Systematic study, 8–9
Systems:
- adaptation, 14
- approach to organizational effectiveness, 27–31
- characteristics, 12–14
- definition, 9
- growth, 13
- importance of, 14–15
- inputs, 12
- maintenance, 14
- outputs, 12
- transformation processes, 12
- types of, 10–12

T

Tall structures, 51–52
Task:
- force structure, 219–20
- identity, 250
- significance, 250
- variability, 127–29

Technology:
- and centralization, 139–40
- and complexity, 138–39
- craft, 128
- definition, 123–24
- engineering, 128
- and formalization, 139
- intensive, 131, 132–34
- job level, 136–37
- knowledge, 127–30
- long-linked, 131–34
- mass, 124–26
- mediating, 131–34
- nonroutine, 128
- organizational level, 136–37
- process, 124–26
- production, 124–26
- routine, 128, 135–36
- size and, 136
- uncertainty, 130–34
- unit, 124–26

Theory X, 70–71
Theory Y, 70–71
Theory Z organization, 333–40
Traditional view of conflict, 289
Training, 23, 69
Turnover, 22

U

Uncertainty (*See* Technology and Environment)

V

Values, conflict in, 33–39
Vertical differentiation, 47, 50–52

W

Work modules, 251–52